EDUCATIONAL PSYCHOLOGY

Allen J. Edwards, Series Editor
Department of Psychology
Southwest Missouri State University
Springfield, Missouri

Phillip S. Strain, Thomas P. Cooke, and Tony Apolloni. Teaching Exceptional Children: Assessing and Modifying Social Behavior
Donald E. P. Smith and others. A Technology of Reading and Writing (in four volumes).
    Vol. 1. Learning to Read and Write: A Task Analysis (by Donald E. P. Smith)
Joel R. Levin and Vernon L. Allen (eds.). Cognitive Learning in Children: Theories and Strategies
Vernon L. Allen (ed.). Children as Teachers: Theory and Research on Tutoring
Gilbert R. Austin. Early Childhood Education: An International Perspective
António Simões (ed.). The Bilingual Child: Research and Analysis of Existing Educational Themes

In preparation:

Erness Bright Brody and Nathan Brody. Intelligence: Nature, Determinants, and Consequences
Donald E. P. Smith and others. A Technology of Reading and Writing (in four volumes).
    Vol. 2. Criterion-Referenced Tests for Reading and Writing (by Judith M. Smith, Donald E. P. Smith, and James R. Brink)
    Vol. 3. The Adaptive Classroom (by Donald E. P. Smith)
    Vol. 4. Preparing Instructional Tasks (by Judith M. Smith)
Herbert J. Klausmeier, Richard A. Rossmiller, and Mary Saily (eds.). Individually Guided Elementary Education: Concepts and Practices
Samuel Ball (ed.). Motivation in Education

Early Childhood
Education
AN INTERNATIONAL PERSPECTIVE

Early Childhood Education

AN INTERNATIONAL PERSPECTIVE

Gilbert R. Austin

College of Education
University of Maryland
College Park, Maryland

ACADEMIC PRESS

NEW YORK   SAN FRANCISCO   LONDON   1976

A Subsidiary of Harcourt Brace Jovanovich, Publishers

ACADEMIC PRESS, INC.
111 Fifth Avenue, New York, New York 10003

United Kingdom Edition published by
ACADEMIC PRESS, INC. (LONDON) LTD.
24/28 Oval Road, London NW1

Library of Congress Cataloging in Publication Data

Austin, Gilbert R
    Early childhood education : an international
perspective.

    (Educational psychology series)
    Includes bibliographies.
    1.   Education, Preschool.   2.   Compensatory education.
I.   Title.
LB1140.2.A87   372.21   75-44761
ISBN 0-12-068550-7

To Sarah, Ethel, Catharine, and Eleanor

Contents

Preface

This book summarizes the results of a 5-year cross-cultural survey of early childhood education in the Western world. It provides insight into some of the issues of debate surrounding preschool education during the past decade. It approaches the discussion by focusing on the history of philosophical thought in early childhood education and provides information on the political and social—cultural changes that have stimulated interest in facilitating children's early learning experiences.

One of the main issues of debate reviewed concerns the recent and rapid growth in early childhood education programs. Are they a reflection of parents' and educators' beliefs that by stimulating cognitive gains in children during the critical period between 2 and 5 years of age, they will enhance life-long intellectual development of the child? Or is the proliferation of early education programs a result of very complex sociological, political, and economic changes in the relationships at all levels among institutions such as the family, school, church, and government? In an effort to present information on this question, a survey of each of the eight countries (Belgium, Canada, Federal Republic of Germany, France, England and Wales, Italy, The Netherlands, and Sweden) is presented. The final chapter presents some implications for American early childhood education.

This book is directed toward educators with teaching and research interests as well as toward students of the social sciences and education. While the book seeks to provide information from which the reader can compare and contrast preschools from an international perspective, it also urges those interested in research to extend their thinking about the impact of early childhood education to include bringing together the activities of welfare, health, and educational agencies to provide a comprehensive and supplementary support system to the family.

Inasmuch as these are the author's goals, the material in this book has been organized into three sections to facilitate these objectives: The first section includes three chapters: (1) an historical overview of early childhood education in the United States; (2) ideas and evidence showing the relevance of collaboration in international research; and (3) a summary of early childhood education in the eight countries surveyed.

The second section consists of eight chapters devoted to discussing the early childhood education programs in each of the eight countries surveyed. Each of these chapters includes a history of preschool education in the respective country, a report on the author's personal observational experiences, and a systematic presentation of information in such areas as organization and administration, pupil–teacher ratio, parent involvement, teacher training and education, cost and financial support, school size and facilities, and instructional methods and aids. Information is also presented on sociological variables such as reproduction rates, labor force changes, and preschool enrollments. Each chapter concludes by providing pertinent theoretical and research evidence.

The third section (Chapter 12) provides the necessary link with the overview presented in Chapter 1 and shows that growth in early childhood education in America has a parallel with that of Western Europe. The implications suggested are both social–cultural and political–economic and provide a base from which further international research may be initiated.

Acknowledgments

In addition to those educators listed in the acknowledgments at the ends of Chapters 4–11, I am indebted to many other people. I owe a special debt of gratitude to Dr. James Abert, a former Deputy Assistant Secretary in the office of the Secretary of HEW, who originally invited me to Washington, D.C. where this study began.

The opportunity to be head of a project on Early Childhood Education at the Center for Educational Research and Innovation, Organization for Economic Cooperation and Development, in Paris, and to work with members of its staff and with its director, Mr. J. Ronald Gass, was invaluable.

I am indebted to my research assistants at CERI, Karin Patzold-Lindhe, Dr. Antonio Benenati, and Asif Mirza.

I am grateful to Joanna Tyler, Joanne Calderone, Eleanore Lehr, and Dr. Laura Dittman, and to a number of faculty members at the University of Maryland, for their helpful comments on the book.

Many people have typed parts of the manuscript in its various stages, but special thanks go to my secretaries at the University of Maryland, Maizie DeLancey and Connie Morris.

This book would never have been completed without the continued support and encouragement of my wife, Eleanor, and the patience and forbearance of my children.

Early Childhood Education: The American Experience

Come, let us live with our children and learn from them [Froebel, cited in Ulich, 1950, p. 284].

Both types of data suggest that in terms of intelligence measured at age 17, about 50% of the development takes place between conception and age 4, about 30% between ages 4 and 8, and about 20% between the ages of 8 and 17 [Bloom, 1964, p. 88].

For many long years our society acted as if nothing happened "down there" in the years of childhood. Life—rightly spelled with a capital L—presumably began at some later time. This is no longer most people's understanding. Most know—an intellectual feat—that the childhood years are of great importance [Hymes, 1974, p. viii].

These quotations all reflect the importance of the period of life called "childhood." The concept of childhood is not very old. For most of man's existence on this planet, the only concept of a person was as an "adult." People did recognize that there were young, middle aged, and old adults, but nothing more.

In the last 200 years, two other important periods of life have been recognized: childhood and adolescence. In his book *Emile* (1762), Rousseau is credited with identifying the period of childhood as important. In it, and in other writings, Rousseau (cited in Ulich, 1950) indicates that a child is not just a small or young adult, but is in fact going through a unique period in his life—childhood—a time when, like a flower, the child is unfolding and growing. According to Rousseau, the care and nurture given to the child during this period of unfolding is of the greatest importance. Therefore, parents and society should provide the best possible growing conditions for the child during this period.

The concept of "adolescence" became accepted around 1800. Its recognition grew out of a variety of complex social changes, such as increased number of years of schooling covered by compulsory school attendance and the identification of this period of time being ideal for military conscription.

Before 1700 the care of children was almost totally a family responsibility, often including grandparents, aunts, and uncles. The society rarely intervened in the lives of children, and where it did it was to provide welfare aid to orphaned or abandoned children. In the 275 years since then, society has offered increasing assistance to children in need. This aid has evolved through three identifiable phases—welfare, health and, more recently, education.

The acceptance on the part of society that childhood is a unique period and that society has a responsibility to provide aid to children in need was a long time in coming. Even today it is the subject of important debate in all countries. In the United States, for instance, as recently as the early 1900s, children were still gainfully employed in an adult world of work. As early as age 8 or 10, they were expected to contribute either their labor on the farm or their small earnings from the factory or mine to increase the total family income. The laws on child labor and compulsory school attendance after age 6 may have defined the legal time frame of childhood, but their major effect was to put children older than 6 in the schools. They did nothing for the younger child. The welfare agencies, followed closely by the health professions, were the first to respond to the needs of young children. It was only after these services had provided minimal care that a concern for educating these children became an issue. Therefore, welfare and health concerns in the United States continued to dominate early child care for the poor.

Lazerson (1970), in a paper entitled "Social Reform and Early Childhood Education: Some Historical Perspectives," gives support to this notion. He says that although late nineteenth century preschools were begun as adjuncts to education for the well-to-do, they quickly became an institution for children of the poor. This movement was stimulated by the influx of immigration at the time. New immigrants typically lived in poverty, dwelling in the urban ghettos and settlement house facilities. Even when the preschool attained general acceptance in the larger community, it was still thought of as having a special purpose for serving the needs of poor children.

The focus of these early preschools remained on welfare and health needs of the poor child, as it was thought that poor children were unable to learn.

Stronger support of this idea grew out of the educational testing movement of the early 1900s. This attitude about the learning ability of poor children persisted through the progressive education era of the 1920s. During that time, "reading readiness" skills were important concerns only of middle-class family-oriented schools. For the most part, the educational needs of the poor child were ignored until the enactment of Head Start legislation in 1965.

The concept behind Head Start was based on a broad commitment to social reform. The thinking seemed to embody the idea that if the cognitive abilities of the poor child could be stimulated, then poverty might be eradicated from society. Most early Head Start programs used models of early childhood programs that had been created for middle-class children. However, the emphasis of these middle-class early childhood programs tended to stress growth in the social and emotional areas, and not in the cognitive area, where the disadvantaged children seem to need the most help. This emphasis is now changing, owing to a new concern for the total development of each individual. This concern, in turn, may be a consequence of a growing realization that education can significantly shape the very essence of our society. It is also acknowledged that programs for the young child must be comprehensive and include welfare, health, and education components.

During the last 30–35 years the importance of education has increased greatly. The annual expenditure of billions of dollars to support the educational effort in the United States is testimony to this fact. The percentage of the GNP spent on education has doubled or tripled over the last 30 years, depending on what one uses as the base. Part of this increased interest in education is a reflection of the greater concern for the potential contribution of education during the preschool years. This concern can be traced to a number of factors:

TABLE 1.1
Percent of GNP Spent on Education

School Year	
1939–40	3.5
1943–44	1.8 (low point)
1949–50	3.4
1959–60	5.1
1969–70	7.5
1974–75	7.7 (estimated)
1979–80	(7.5–8.0 (estimated)

Source: Office of Education, National Center for
Educational Statistics, 1974.

1. Increased concern for education followed from the considerable progress in providing adequate welfare and health care for all young children.
2. The writings of men such as Hunt (1961) and Bloom (1964) convinced many people that education offered before age 6 markedly affects later school performance, particularly as it concerns the children of the poor.
3. In the mid-1960s, the Federal Government was at last willing to become a partner with the state and local educational agencies in tackling the problem of education in general and early childhood education in particular.

In the decade of the 1960s the federal government for the first time joined with state and local educational agencies to work on the task of educating *all* the children in the United States. As the decade opened, the hopes for massive federal aid to education were badly damaged by brutal battles in the Congress over the church–state issue. With the defeat of federal aid to education through that program, most people predicted that involvement by the federal government in any important way in education was probably a long way off—certainly at least 10 years.

To understand better the problems that faced aid to education through the federal government, a brief review of the political process involved in the passage of a bill is presented. There are normally three groups involved: (*1*) the interest groups, i.e., the education lobbies; (*2*) the governmental agencies, i.e., the Office of Education; and (*3*) the president and his staff or Congress and its committees. This constellation of forces can be represented by the following diagram.

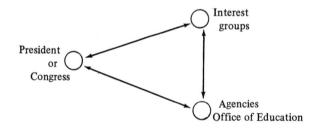

In the past, these three groups have never been able to agree on how the specifics of federal aid to education should work. They were split on such issues as church and state and civil rights. They were in agreement, however, on one important issue: Federal aid should be general aid. In addition, they did not want the federal government dictating to the states or local educational agencies on how the money should be spent. One of the major issues that had prevented agreement was resolved in 1964 with the passage of the Civil Rights Act.

With the election of Lyndon Johnson to the presidency, a substantial change seemed to take place. Three important pieces of legislation were passed which affected the lives of young children. In 1964 Johnson signed into law the Economic

Opportunity Act, which created the Office of Economic Opportunity (OEO). In November of the same year, under OEO, the first planning committee met and discussed the problems associated with launching the preschool program called Head Start. The program was officially announced in January, 1965, and Head Start was in operation on a nationwide basis by that summer.

A brief history of Project Head Start will serve to place the program in perspective. During the early 1960s, an increasing number of psychologists and educators, such as Bloom and Hunt, published books concerned with the effects of early experiences on human development. Much of their research suggested that preschool education might be an important step for disrupting the cycle of poverty experienced by large numbers of Americans. Head Start was in many ways a direct outgrowth of theirs and others' writings on the subject. Head Start was planned to be a comprehensive program, and therefore, was to be concerned with the welfare, health, and education problems faced by the children of the American poor. Its major objectives were the following:

> improving the child's health and physical abilities; fostering the emotional and social development of the child by encouraging self-confidence, spontaneity, curiosity and self-discipline;
>
> promoting the child's mental processes and skills with particular attention to conceptual and verbal skills;
>
> establishing patterns and expectations of success for the child in order to create a climate of confidence for his future learning efforts;
>
> increasing the child's capacity to relate positively to family members and others while at the same time strengthening the family's ability to relate positively to the child;
>
> developing in the child and his family a responsible attitude toward society and fostering constructive opportunities for society to work together with the poor in solving their problems;
>
> increasing the sense of dignity and self-worth within the child and his family. [Bissell, 1972, p. 2].

Most early Head Start centers were varied, hastily assembled adaptations of the child-centered nursery schools designed for attendance by middle-class American children. Few designed any special curricula to provide an enriching set of experiences for children of the poor. Since that early beginning, a number of preschool models for disadvantaged children based on different educational theories and methods have been developed.

After the enactment of the Head Start legislation in 1964 came the passage of the Elementary and Secondary Education Act (ESEA) in 1965. This represented another major breakthrough for the Johnson administration in the area of education. The ESEA was to be *the major* effort on the part of the federal government to help education and was to provide approximately $1–1.5 billion a year to the American school systems. Title I of the act provided aid to economically disadvantaged children in both primary and secondary schools. As part of Title I, early childhood education programs could be and were created in large numbers.

Endless words have been written about how ESEA was passed. Dr. Samuel Halperin, in a statement to the *Congressional Record* September 9, 1970, adequately summed it up when he said, "In 1965 the political imperative was to pass a bill. The first task of the administration's legislative team was to devise a bill which was politically viable." Politicians needed assurance that aid to education would not create another bruising battle over the church–state or civil rights issues.

Dr. Halperin further noted that there was a series of priorities in the passage of ESEA:

1. *Title I.* To provide aid for the disadvantaged in both big cities and rural slums.

2. To create some level of accountability, a concept first introduced by the late Senator Robert Kennedy. By this Kennedy meant that some method should be devised whereby the public could be informed of what the people in the educational establishment were doing with the large sums of federal money.

3. To bring about reform. It was hoped that the educational establishment would take itself in hand and look at some of its own problems, specifically the problems of teaching the disadvantaged. In effect, the federal government was attempting to buy educational reform.

4. *Title II.* To provide aid to obtain books for children both for classroom use and to increase library holdings. Various kinds of audio–visual material could also be purchased under this part of the act. It is important to note that these books and materials could be purchased by public schools and loaned to private schools. This was one way around the problem of providing aid to the private, primarily church-related, school sector.

5. *Title III.* To provide funds to obtain monies for school systems to try out new and innovative kinds of educational activity.

6. *Title IV.* To provide aid to educators involved in the difficult tasks of planning and evaluating the outcomes of these programs.

7. *Title V.* To provide aid to help state departments of education assume the increased burdens of operating these new federal programs.

It was also designed to strengthen the state department of education in providing leadership in education. This was badly needed at both the state and local level. It is important to remember that ESEA was meant to help state and local educational agencies, not to take over their functions. In accomplishing all of this, it should be noted that the original framers of the legislation felt that both time and money would be required to bring about educational reform.

It was stated earlier that normally three groups were involved in the passage of a law. In the case of Head Start and ESEA Title I this practice was not followed. The education lobbies and the Office of Education did not want aid to education passed in the form of categorical programs. They wanted federal aid with no strings attached. The primary motivating force for this program came from the president and his aides. The aides represented a collection of social and political scientists who wanted to bring about some changes in the area of education.

Additionally, it is important to note that a new group of people had been added to the three groups identified earlier. This group was made up of policy analysts. The concept of policy analysis had been introduced first in the Department of Defense when Robert McNamara was secretary. With policy analysis came the system of Program Planning and Budgeting Systems (PPBS). McNamara used system analysis to make explicit and systematic the decision-making process, to clarify objectives, and to state criteria. The system also called for the presentation of alternatives based on cost–benefit analysis. President Johnson indicated that PPBS was to be adopted by all federal agencies for their future planning. Therefore, the new education programs were to use PPBS. As indicated earlier, the late Senator Robert Kennedy had included in ESEA the stipulation that evaluations were to be mandatory. These two new ideas, PPBS and evaluations, are two of the most important outcomes in the War on Poverty as it affected education. The program Planning and Budgeting Systems enabled the secretaries of agencies such as the Department of Health, Education, and Welfare to ask many more penetrating questions than they had previously been able to ask.

In general, evaluations of Head Start and ESEA Title I show easily that children benefit when given medical care, good nutritional meals, and a warm supportive environment. What proved much more difficult to document was the ability of these early intervention programs to make a sustained difference in the area of cognitive (intellectual) development, primarily as measured by intelligence tests or achievement tests. One of the earliest evaluations of Head Start, conducted by the Westinghouse Learning Corporation, concluded that by the third grade it was very difficult to identify any children who still showed any benefit from the Head Start program. Similar findings were reported in the General Electric TEMPO study, which was the first major evaluation on ESEA Title I to look at the effectiveness of elementary and secondary programs as well as preschool programs.

After an extensive review of preschool programs, Bissell (1972) came to the following conclusions: Typically, studies of federal programs have shown increases on general ability and achievement tests immediately after participation in both summer and full-year preschool programs, with participants generally performing better than nonparticipants immediately after the program to a statistically significant degree.

Speaking on the same issue, Grotberg (1969) states:

> The increases were greatest when programs were of longest duration, when program objectives were well formulated and oriented towards the areas evaluated, and when the participating children's initial level of performance was low. In addition to reporting gains on measures of intellectual functioning, some evaluations also reported immediate positive effects on children's attitudes, motivation and social behavior as rated by teachers [p. 7].

Follow-up evaluations, however, indicated that the gains achieved by participant children generally lessened in the first or second year in public school. Apparently, increases in the rate of development promoted during the preschool experience in participant children on measures of ability and achievement are not sustained during the early elementary grades.

This phenomenon of "leveling off" in rate of development by participant children is usually explained as the inability of the public schools to support the development which Head Start and laboratory schools had produced. As Datta (1969) states:

> It may be naive to expect a child to continue to progress rapidly in a classroom where the teacher may be responsible for 30 or more children, may be primarily concerned with maintaining order and perhaps convinced that most of her students have little potential [p. 14].

The majority of Head Start and other compensatory preschool programs, although producing measurable immediate gains, seem not to have produced permanent increases in children's intellectual development.

Based on these and other disappointing results, the Congress passed the "Follow Through" legislation in 1967. This was the third program designed to aid young children from poor homes. Its main goal was concerned with educating young children and extending the benefits of Head Start into kindergarten and the early years of primary school. Its purpose was spelled out clearly in Section 222(a) of the Economic Opportunity Act, P.L. 90–22, which authorized

> A program to be known as "Follow Through" focused primarily upon children in kindergarten or elementary school who were previously enrolled in Head Start or similar programs and designed to provide comprehensive services and parent participation activities . . . which the Director finds will aid in the continued development of children to their full potential . . . .

Follow Through was to be a continuing program aimed at meeting the needs of the school-aged child who had attended a Head Start program.

A key provision in these school programs was that parents were to participate actively in both decision-making and day-to-day operations. This involved the creation of local programs to meet local needs. Follow Through was to be administered under a delegation of authority from the OEO to the United States Office of Education (USOE) at HEW.

Follow Through, as Head Start, was to be shaped by the program's focus on improving the child's "life chances," not simply his chances to succeed in school. Projects, therefore, emphasized several aspects of the child's development. This was accomplished through working with a range of institutions that influence the child, such as families, schools, community health services, welfare departments, and other social service agencies. The final evaluations of the Follow Through programs are not yet available. Some preliminary and tentative findings suggest that Follow Through programs do indeed sustain the initial gains made in Head Start through kindergarten and first grade. More time and study will be needed to see if these gains can be carried through the first three grades of elementary school.

The originators of the preschool programs just described hoped that early intervention, primarily academic intervention, would make a substantial difference in the child's later school performance. The results do not indicate that this goal has been achieved. Consequently, a number of people have begun to question the role of preschool education as it relates to early cognitive development. One critic is former Presidential Counselor Daniel P. Moynihan (1970), who observed that:

> By and large these programs have not achieved what was hoped for them. It is not to say they could not and that they don't achieve some things, but on balance, this subject has turned out to be more complicated than we had understood or thought, and there was no way to learn this except to try [p. H8494].

As just stated, the results of early intervention in the lives of young disadvantaged children as measured by later school performance have been inconclusive and disappointing. Some argue that we just do not know how to evaluate these programs and children. Others argue that we really have not tried; still others say failure is due to genetic differences that are not amenable to such preschool programs. The truth is probably a combination of these three factors.

A document that makes a comprehensive look at this complex social issue of fostering the maximum growth and development of young children was written by a Task Force assembled by President Johnson. Entitled *A Bill of Rights for Children* (1967), it set forth some basic ideas and proposed a path of action which should be helpful in moving toward the solution of this difficult problem. It states

> Our forefathers declared it to be self-evident that all men are created equal with inalienable rights to life, liberty and the pursuit of happiness. Even admitting unequal heredity, that equality of opportunity which they presumed to be an

inalienable right is a myth, for many infants and young children must develop in circumstances far less favorable than those of others [p. 1].

The authors go on to state that few children, even those of the wealthy, experience continuously ideal circumstances that would maximize their inherited potential for health, competence, and humanity. The dietary, health, and social circumstances of children born to the poor are typically far more harmful to optimal development than those for children born to the wealthy. Conditions encountered during the first 3 years of life are of great importance to mental development and competence. By the sixth year, unless life circumstances change radically, many children will be permanently damaged. Equality of opportunity to develop after birth, especially for children born to parents unable to provide adequate development-fostering circumstances, is dependent on society's efforts. Despite this, the attention paid by the government to the needs of children is low on the list of priorities. President Johnson's Task Force on The Rights of Young Children felt that existing programs not only were not doing enough, but also were not good enough. The Task Force stated that:

they fail because the services are themselves fragmented; . . . they fail because they are inadequate and . . . seldom provide a situation calculated to restore hope, confidence, and initiative in children's parents; . . . they fail from ineffective use of professional help; . . . they fail from attempting to intervene from the outside [p. 4].

The Task Force felt that more concern is needed for the conditions of early childhood, not merely more money or more manpower, to aid poor families. In addition, remedial programs to correct the damage that has already been done, preventive measures, new measures to foster intellectual and motivational development, and most importantly, fostering of a sense of family and community to help create a happy environment for the growth of children are needed. Although encouraged by what economic benefits, industrialization, and urbanization have brought to the United States, the Task Force felt that these forces have deprived children of some of their most important sources of strength and humanity, namely, the extended family.

Based on these considerations, the Task Force strongly recommended that the parents and other members of the extended family be encouraged to become actively involved in the proposed children's centers. Additionally, President Johnson's Task Force suggested the following measures to help correct deficiencies and encourage progress in caring for and developing the potential of the nation's young children.

The first recommendation was to establish a federal Office for Children under the auspices of HEW with an administrative head equal in rank to the other chief officers of HEW. This Office of Children would administer programs and federal grants to community-based Commissions for Children consisting of parents, professionals, and government or official personnel involved with the community's children. These commissions would plan and establish neighborhood Centers for Children and Parents. The centers would function to help consolidate community services and involve parents in planning and providing new day-care programs aimed at enhancing the development of competence in their children.

The Task Force recommended several things to aid poor children:

1. That federal funds be appropriated for disadvantaged schools and areas earmarked for Follow Through programs.

2. That federal grants be provided for the development of new curricula materials for homemaking and child-rearing in the public schools.

3. That federal awards be granted for development of effective innovations in programs for children aged 5–8 to facilitate cooperation between schools and Centers for Children and Parents.

Other suggestions for financial aid to communities and states included open-ended matching grants for encouraging experimentation, pilot studies of new types of programs, training programs, and expansion of Head Start. In addition, funds would be authorized for training professional and paraprofessional staff to meet future needs, especially in health, social work, and preschool education. The Office of Children would administer these and any other new programs. They would be responsible for maintaining the proper standards appropriate to such training.

The final recommendations of President Johnson's Task Force were to encourage research with special attention to the development of new kinds of experiences to help children achieve their full potential; to investigate new approaches to helping parents; to develop new curricula for preschool and primary school aged children; and to investigate the child-rearing practices of various social classes in the American society and in the various other cultures in the world.

While the Task Force recognized that the financial commitment of such broad programs would be huge, it recommended starting small, with pilot projects and the development of sound policy. The needs, it felt, are great, and any program must "be commensurate with the need."

> If we choose now not to mount the effort and meet the cost, we shall eventually pay a far higher price in human misery, and even a higher price in economic cost and loss. Nor can we refuse to mount the effort if we are true to our heritage, for we are confronted not merely with the needs of America's children, but with their inalienable rights [p. 16].

The Task Force felt that improving the quality of life for children would strengthen the nation and its prospects for the future. Through meeting the children's needs and developing their potential, there could be an increase in

American spirit and vitality fostered by cooperation and neighborly concern for the care of the children.

The sentiments of the Task Force, which led to their recommendations, were not different from prevailing concerns in the era of the "Great Society." While many agreed with them, only a small fraction of the recommendations were put into effect. Head Start and Follow Through are still in operation, but have not been expanded because appropriations have risen very slowly. There are many ECE programs funded under Title I or Title III, but few have experienced any great success.

There are no Centers for Parents and Children, no commissions for children, no Office of Children, and the massive funds for programs suggested by the Task Force have not materialized.

Although the federal government has not implemented the recommendations, the demand for early childhood education on the part of the public has increased dramatically. The following tables provide evidence of great growth in preschool enrollments.

Tables 1.2 and 1.3 deserve careful study. Table 1.2 shows that blacks have increased their percentage of attendance at the prekindergarten level more rapidly than the white population. It is also noteworthy that the greatest percentage difference occurred in the years in which Head Start and ECE programs under ESEA Title I were growing most rapidly. In the 1970s, as the funding increases slowed down, the white population began to close the gap. It appears that when opportunities for preschool are made available to the black

TABLE 1.2
Prekindergarten Enrollment, By Race: 1964-1972 (for 3- and 4-year-olds)

Year	Number enrolled (000's)			Percent enrolled		
	Total	White	Negro and other races	Total	White	Negro and other races
1964	439	374	65	5.2	5.3	5.1
1965	475	413	64	5.7	5.8	4.9
1966	627	513	114	7.6	7.4	8.7
1967	665	534	131	8.2	7.9	10.1
1968	738	604	134	9.4	9.3	10.4
1969	778	610	168	10.5	9.9	13.4
1970	1,003	824	180	14.1	13.9	14.8
1971	992	831	161	14.2	14.3	13.5
1972	1,213	1,015	197	17.9	17.8	18.4

Source: Statistical Policy Division, Office of Management and Budget, and the Social and Economic Statistics Administration, U.S. Department of Commerce. Social Indicators 1973. Washington, 1973.

TABLE 1.3

Prekindergarten Enrollment, By Family Income and Race: 3-year
Average, 1970-1972 (For 3- and 4-year-olds)

| | Number enrolled (000's) | | Percent enrolled | | |
Family Income	White	Negro and other races	White	Negro and other races	Difference
All incomes	1,250	281	21.5	24.3	2.8
Less than $3,000	50	55	15.3	20.2	4.9
$3,000 to $4,999	85	62	14.3	22.8	8.5
$5,000 to $7,499	148	56	13.5	25.7	12.2
$7,500 to $9,999	209	34	16.9	22.7	5.8
$10,000 and over	671	63	30.8	37.3	6.5
Income not reported	88	11	22.8	14.1	

Source: Statistical Policy Division, Office of Management and Budget,
and the Social and Economic Statistics Administration, U.S.
Department of Commerce. Social Indicators 1973. Washington,
1973.

population, they will use them. There is probably a greater need for preschool care for the black population, because the percentage of single-parent families is higher than for the white population. Between 1964 and 1972 the percentage of increase in use of prekindergarten by whites increased by 171%, while for blacks it increased by 203%.

Table 1.3 indicates that in 1970–1972 blacks earning between $3000 and $10,000 per year enrolled a higher percentage of their children in prekindergarten than did whites. It appears from these data that blacks value preschool education more than whites at all income levels. The percentage of difference favoring blacks increased as income increased. It is important to note, however, that for both blacks and whites the percentage of children in prekindergarten increased as family income increased. It appears that families whose income is higher value prekindergarten education more in both races.

Much of the War on Poverty that President Johnson launched with programs such as Head Start, ESEA Titles I and III, and Follow Through was based on the theory of cultural deprivation mentioned earlier. Cole and Bruner (1972) question a similar concept in their discussion of the "deficit hypothesis." They state that:

> Perhaps the most prevalent view of the source of ethnic and social class differences in intellectual performance is what might be summed up under the label "the deficit hypothesis." It can be stated briefly without risk of gross distortion. It rests on the

assumption that a community under conditions of poverty (for it is the poor who are the focus of attention, and a disproportionate number of the poor are members of minority ethnic groups) is a disorganized community, and this disorganization expresses itself in various forms of deficit. One widely agreed upon deficit is mothering; the child of poverty is assumed to lack adequate parental attention. Given the illegitimacy rate in the urban ghetto, the most conspicuous deficit is a missing father and consequently a missing father model. The mother is away at work or in any case less involved with raising her children than she should be by white middle-class standards.

. . . [This seems] to compel the conclusion that as a consequence of various factors arising from minority group status (factors affecting motivation, linguistic ability, goal orientation, hereditary proclivities to learn in certain ways—the particular mix of factors depends on the writer) minority group children suffer intellectual deficits when compared with their "more advantaged" peers [p. 162].

Cole and Bruner identify two long-standing precedents which they believe invalidate the deficit hypothesis: (*1*) ". . . the anthropological 'doctrine of psychic unity' which, on the basis of the 'run of total experience,' is said to warrant the assumption of intellectual equality as a sufficient approximation to the truth," and (*2*) ". . . the linguist's assertion that languages do not differ in their degree of development." Cole and Bruner go on to indicate that what are apparent differences are in fact the result of the inadequacy of present experiments and the idea of competence which is situational and context-loaded in favor of the white middle class. They argue we need to develop a comparative psychology of cognition.

While the Cole–Bruner argument is interesting, it does not change the everyday preschool situation with which young children, parents, and educators must deal. It is, however, something that should be investigated carefully. One aspect of the problem needing particular attention is identifying and studying the strengths in the daily experiences of the "disadvantaged" child. This would be a much more positive approach than continuing to use the concept of a deficit hypothesis as it functions in the Head Start, ESEA Title I and III, and Follow Through programs.

One example of building on the strengths of a poor preschooler's background would be to build on the child's strong relationship with the mother. This is one of the major reasons behind stressing parental involvement in ECE programs. It is hoped that, from this base, greater involvement of the father will take place. It is also hoped that as a result of greater involvement on the part of both parents that both the home life and the school life of the preschool child will be strengthened. The importance of a strong, stable home has been documented by Daniel Moynihan in his controversial study titled *The Negro Family: The Case for National Action* (1967). The use of men in the programs and the involvement of fathers were stressed by Moynihan as being particularly important.

Using a "positive approach" and building on the strong mother–child relationship to establish family involvement with ECE programs represents one way of designing educational programs that do not support the deficit hypothesis. Developing a stable relationship between family and community resources may be an initial step toward helping children to more fully develop their cognitive potential. In this way the whole child is considered. Fulfillment of social–emotional needs through better family and school life provides the foundation for development of full cognitive ability. Perhaps, in this way, long-range achievement potential can become a reality in future ECE programs created to benefit the poor child.

It is beyond the scope of this book to document all the issues that were part of the thinking that led to the creation of Head Start, ESEA Title I and III, and Follow Through. The reasons behind the American demand for early childhood education are many and diverse, but the major issues can be summarized as follows:

1. An increased awareness of general values of education and the need for it in an increasingly complex and changing society.
2. An increased desire to provide equality of educational opportunities for all, with particular attention being provided for the poor and children from minority groups.
3. An increased acceptance on the part of society of its responsibility to all children to assist their families in providing a rich and varied set of social experiences. This is particularly true for rurally isolated children and children in small families in high-rise apartments.

BIBLIOGRAPHY

Bissell, J. *Planned variation in Head Start and Follow Through* (mimeographed). US Department of Health, Education and Welfare. January 1972.
Bloom, B. *Stability and change in human characteristics.* New York: John Wiley & Sons, 1964.
Cole, M., & Bruner, J. Preliminary to a theory of cultural differences. In Ira J. Gordon (Ed.), *Early childhood education.* Part II of the 71st yearbook of the Society for the Study of Education. Chicago: University of Chicago Press, 1972.
Datta, L. *A report on evaluation studies of project Head Start.* Paper presented at American Psychological Association Convention, Washington, D.C., 1969. (Mimeographed)
Economic Opportunity Act, Public Law 90-22, Section 222(a), 1967.
Froebel, F. In Ulich, R. *History of educational thought.* New York: American Book Company, 1950.
Grotberg, E., *Review of research 1965–1969 on project Head Start.* Washington, D.C.: Department of Health, Education, and Welfare, Office of Child Development, 1969. (Mimeographed)
Halperin, S. *Congressional record,* September 9, 1970.
Hunt, J. *Intelligence and experience.* New York: Ronald Press, 1961.
Hymes, J. In foreword to *Childhood revisited.* J. Milgram and D. Sciarra (Eds.) New York: Macmillan Publishing Co., Inc. 1974.
Lazerson, M. Social reform and early childhood education: some historical perspectives. *Urban Education,* April 1970, *5*(1).

Moynihan, D. The Negro family: the case for national action. In L. Rainwater, and W. Yancy (Eds.), *The Moynihan report and the politics of controversy.* Cambridge, Mass.: The MIT Press, 1967.

Moynihan, D. in *Congressional Record–House.* Washington, D.C.: Government Printing Office. September 9, 1970.

Rousseau, J. In R. Ulich (Ed.), *History of educational thought.* New York: American Book Company, 1950.

Office of Education, National Center for Educational Statistics, 1974.

Office of Management and Budget, Statistical Policy Division. *Social indicators 1973.* Prepared for publication by the Social and Economic Statistics Administration, US Department of Commerce. 1973.

Presidential Task Force on Children. *A bill of rights for children.* 1967.

TEMPO, General Electric Co., Santa Barbara, Calif. *Survey and Analyses of Results from Title I Funding for Compensatory Education.* 1968.

Westinghouse Learning Corporation, Ohio University. *The Impact of Head Start: An Evaluation of the Effects of Head Start on Children's Cognition and Affective Development.* 1969.

The Potential of International
Research and Cooperation

One of the limiting factors in discussing early childhood education in the American experience is that most American preschool educators hold similar points of view about how and why young children should be educated. Their ideas were fostered by middle-class kindergarten training institutions in which the major curriculum concern and orientation was directed toward understanding middle-class children's social–emotional processes rather than their intellectual processes.

In an effort to more fully understand early childhood education, focus is now being directed toward international activities in the area of preschool education and the benefits that will accrue from cross-cultural cooperation and research. This query stems directly from the final recommendation of President Johnson's Task Force on ECE for investigations of the child-rearing practices in other cultures. It has direct bearing on the potential of American preschool education as well as development of international cooperation for early childhood education.

In other countries of the world early childhood education is now in public demand, receiving scholarly and governmental interest, and facing problems similar to those in the United States. The marked increase in ECE activity has led researchers in several nations to explore the possibilities of sharing their knowledge, information, methodology, and evaluations so that each may benefit from the others' experiences. Collaboration on an international level in educational research is one of the most promising vehicles for cooperative, qualitative approaches to research and practice.

The United States Government, through its different agencies, is deeply involved in international activities. Swift (1973), in a paper entitled "The International Dimension," used HEW as an example for indicating the diversity of American involvement in seeking international cooperation. The scope of HEW's international activity is almost as broad as its domestic charge. It includes research, planning of service systems, development of manpower resources, and surprisingly, some participation in the delivery of health care and other social service programs within the international context. An additional element is participation in the work of international organizations. The 10 examples that follow illustrate the diversity of this effort:

1. The US–USSR Cooperative Program in Medical Science and Public Health, through which the National Institute of Health and other branches of HEW's Health Division undertake collaborative programs with Russian health researchers.

2. A study of the Rehabilitation of Retarded Adolescents and Young Adults in Israel, conducted by an Israeli researcher with Social and Rehabilitation Service support.

3. A continuing analysis of the Social Security Programs of 125 countries by the Office of Research and Statistics, Social Security Administration.

4. A study of the General Provisions for Ambulatory Care in the British National Health Service by members of the staff of the Bureau of Health Services Research and Evaluation.

5. A study of child care in Denmark, conducted by an American researcher and supported by the Office of Child Development, Division of Human Development.

6. The Teacher Exchange Program of the Fulbright–Hayes Act, administered by the Office of Education, through which American teachers go abroad and foreign teachers come here.

7. The West African Regional Smallpox and Measles Program, conducted by the Center for Disease Control, which has eliminated smallpox and demonstrated control methods for measles in one of the world's last areas of endemicity for smallpox.

8. Inspection of drug manufacturing facilities outside the United States, when drugs made in such facilities are to be shipped to the United States, by the Food and Drug Administration.

9. Representation of the United States in the World Health Organization, with planning and review to identify and support American interests in WHO policies

and programs—a continuing function of the Office of International Health, OASH.

10. Participation of the educational policy-making and research of the Organization for Economic Cooperation and Development (OECD) by the Office of Education and the National Institute of Education.

The expenditures in these international efforts for HEW alone are estimated to be almost $100 million a year and growing. In documenting the reason behind this increase in international involvement, Swift (1973) makes the following points about "knowledge-gaining":

We've used a relatively new term, "knowledge-gaining," for the broad class of all processes through which new information of potential value can be acquired by the Department. It includes not only formal, scientific research and data collection but also examination of the workings of social and Governmental systems, the conduct of demonstration programs, consideration of dissemination methods for knowledge, and the enhancement of staff capability to acquire and use new information. An analysis shows that DHEW Administration and major offices are engaged in all these aspects of knowledge-gaining in international contexts.

International and domestic knowledge-gaining are not essentially different. But, a special attribute of international activities for DHEW is that they create an awareness, among administrators and professionals, that scientific and social problems exist in similar forms in many places in the world. This awareness can enlarge our capability to deal with domestic American problems. We can cite some special reasons which may make a foreign source of knowledge preferable, or absolutely necessary, for some kinds of knowledge-gaining.

1. The availability abroad of special research capabilities and facilities not readily available in the United States.
2. The existence abroad of "natural experiments" in health care, education or social services which have not been tried in the United States, to be studied for possible lessons from them.
3. The existence of information uniquely available abroad, as in studies of populations having characteristics in pure or accentuated forms which do not occur here.
4. Special sociopolitical circumstances which facilitate research programs not practicable in the United States, such as control groups for clinical research made available through centrally managed health care systems.
5. Cost savings through collaboration, in which two or more countries share the costs and labor of joint research of value to all.
6. Interaction with external ideas for enhancement of the capabilities of DHEW staff.
7. The availability of special funds, such as the U.S.-owned Special Foreign Currencies (e.g., PL-480 funds) which permit research abroad for which no funds can be allocated at home [pp. S-6, S-7].

Having identified some general areas of interest and collaboration as it involves international cooperation, let us turn our attention to the specific benefits and current problems in the area of cross-cultural research. The arguments in favor of international collaboration in research have been stated by many people. Eide (1971) states it as follows:

> International collaboration ranks among the most potent instruments of research policy in most fields, an instrument, however, which is frequently used far below its potential . . . .
>
> . . . The case for international research collaboration is easily stated. Most problems studied by research are common to most countries, though not necessarily equally relevant, and the findings should be valid far beyond the borders of any particular country . . . .
>
> . . . Furthermore, especially in the social sciences where controlled laboratory conditions are more difficult to state, the world at large constitutes a laboratory of social phenomena, offering a far wider factor set and more varying conditions than any national situation. Only against an international background can the dependence of research findings upon special national conditions be identified, and the validity of results be put to test [p. 66].

Eide points out, however, that a problem in international collaboration arises because of restricted access to findings classified as commercial and limited defense information. International collaboration also is discouraged by the mass of documents available, the difficulties of organization—and the lack of it—and the need for selection of relevant material from the total mass. This latter problem requires a great deal of additional resources and investigation.

Eide feels that the problems of international collaboration might be reduced if international research institutions changed their emphasis from in-house production to fostering contacts, communication, and on-going research. He continued by stating that by increasing attention to information selection and dissemination these institutions might be more effective aids to national research.

Eide said that the flow of information between researchers on the national level is the prime means of international collaboration. This, and effective utilization of the information, is far more important than the performance of research by international agencies. The aim of international institutions should be to stimulate national research. Any cooperative ventures must be evaluated in terms of their effect on stimulating research, not in their possibilities for saving national research efforts.

Usually, international organizations pretend that all countries are more or less devoted to the same value structure, while genuine conflicts are all but ignored. An open recognition of different political value structures and their effects on research and politics would probably benefit educational research. It might also lessen the tendency of the international agency to reflect the values of dominant nations.

Finally, Eide recommends that research be understood as a function of informative criticism and that this view govern the aim of collaboration as a different alternative for choice, not as a "product" to import without question. When international findings influence and widen traditional, nationally bound attitudes about what is feasible in education, the potentials of international collaboration will be realized. New alternatives based on such findings, which are critically appraised as to the effect of value structures on national priorities, may be a surprise in terms of the diversity and the extent of their contributions to practice.

Many of Eide's principles for international collaboration were embodied in the formation and operation of the Center for Educational Research and Innovation, of the Organization for Economic Cooperation and Development (CERI–OECD) based in Paris. The rising costs of education and the rising aspiration for expanded educational opportunity are among the matters of international concern that command the attention of OECD. The OECD originated in 1961 and currently has 23 member nations.

OECD is an example of an organization whose goal is to encourage international cooperation and on-going educational research. Initially, OECD's work in education was motivated by the shortage of scientific and technical personnel in many OECD countries. During the middle and late 1960s most OECD nations experienced a period of very rapid economic growth. This allowed governments at all levels to increase vastly their expenditures on education. During that same period, student confrontations increased in intensity and frequency and the cry for change and relevance in education was heard in many countries. Sensing the need for greater effort in education, CERI was created in 1968.

CERI began as a 3-year exploratory venture financed with a grant of $1 million from the Ford Foundation and $750,000 from the Royal Dutch Shell Group of Companies who set aside a further $264,000 in support of national projects that might contribute to the overall plan. Initial CERI objectives were to identify the major obstacles to long-term qualitative improvement in educational systems and practices and to promote research and experimentation in member countries to reveal and test practical ways around these obstacles. The center was conceived as a focal point both for cooperation between national activities and for making results of international efforts available to policy-makers, planners, administrators, and teachers in a form that would help them to solve their current problems.

CERI functions as a central intelligence, advisory, and management group whose primary task is to generate ideas and organizational frameworks to promote educational change in the OECD member countries. Much CERI work is done through joint project study groups. These experts develop position papers and then come together to "brainstorm" and confront each other's ideas, not just once but several times. These ideas can be discussed, argued, and perhaps tested in universities, school systems, training institutions, or ministries of education.

CERI tends to focus its efforts in four areas:

1. *Educational growth and educational opportunity:* This has been one of the core concerns of CERI since its creation. It focuses on the identification of existing successful programs for the socially disadvantaged and on alternative strategies to achieve equality of educational opportunity. Three current projects in this area are: (*1*) early childhood education, (*2*) recurrent education, and (*3*) new functions and structure of the school. The ECE project and the recurrent education project are direct outgrowths of CERI's work on equality of educational opportunity.
2. *Innovation and higher education:* Researchers are studying the problem of curriculum development in the universities.
3. *Curriculum development and educational technology:* The main concern in this area is to define existing trends.
4. *Innovation policies and structures:* This work has developed from a workshop held at St. John's College in Cambridge, England, during the summer of 1969.

These four areas of focus present a clear picture showing that the development of CERI's work in early childhood education has taken a number of directions. A strong area of concern is the possibility of work with underprivileged children.

In response to a CERI questionnaire on future programs, a considerable number of member countries expressed interest in the field of early childhood education. During 1969, CERI established a working group representing institutions in interested countries concerned with research and experimentation in primary school education. These efforts resulted in two publications: (*1*) *Evaluation Research and Action Programs Amongst the Educationally and Socially Disadvantaged,* by M. A. Brimer (1971), and (*2*) *Strategies of Compensation: A Review of Educational Projects for the Disadvantaged in the United States,* by A. Little and G. Smith (1971).

Generally speaking, these two evaluations, together with the other work carried on by the center, indicate that the attempts at intervention have been somewhat disappointing. The initial impact of these programs on children has been positive. Gains have consistently been noted immediately following exposure to preschool experiences. As the time between experiences and follow-up measures is extended, however, wide variations in the measured effectiveness of preschool experience begin to appear. Few studies show achievement differences between experimental and control groups 1 or 2 years following the intervention. It was concluded that research and evaluation efforts were very recent, and it is perhaps too early to expect major results in the effectiveness of preschool educational experiences.

It is clear that the potential of international research and cooperation is increasing. Interest from both American governmental agencies and CERI–

OECD is helping to provide vehicles for achieving ongoing cooperative research. Through international collaborative efforts, the limiting factors and barriers inherent in American and European ECE programs may be decreased. By gaining greater cross-cultural knowledge of ECE programs, new light may be shed on the problem of achieving qualitative approaches to educational research and practice. The study described in the following chapters was undertaken to increase this cross-cultural knowledge and understanding.

BIBLIOGRAPHY

Brimer, M. *Evaluation research and action programmes amongst the educationally and socially disadvantaged.* Technical Report, OECD/CERI, Paris, September 15, 1971.

Eide, Kjell. *Educational research policy.* Technical Report, OECD/CERI, Paris, September 30, 1971.

Little, A. and Smith, G. *Strategies of compensation: a review of educational projects for the disadvantaged in the United States.* OECD, Paris, 1971.

OECD. *History, aims and structure.* Information Service, OECD, Paris, 1971.

Presidential Task Force on Children. *A bill of rights for children.* 1967.

Swift, J., *The international dimension.* Final Report submitted to the Department of Health, Education and Welfare, Washington, D.C., Nov., 1973.

Early Childhood Education in Eight OECD Countries

This review will document what is happening in the area of early childhood education in eight countries: Belgium, Canada, France, Germany (FR), Italy, The Netherlands, Sweden, and England and Wales. It has three main purposes. First, it is an effort to relate what is known from research and development work to policy options. Second, there is a need to clarify the policy options and give the best possible indications of the costs and benefits of proceeding in the different directions. This confrontation of available research and development and policy options should indicate the most profitable line for cooperative research and development work. Third, there is a need, based on the final recommendation of President Johnson's Task Force, to investigate child-rearing practices in other cultures.

Accordingly, in order to gather the relevant information, a questionnaire was sent to the various ministries of education and numbers of preschools in these eight countries. These countries were chosen for the following three reasons:

1. They had developed reasonable educational statistics.
2. They were interested in the continued study of early childhood education.
3. They were judged to be representative of a wide cross section of opinion about, and practices in, early childhood education.

The evaluation evolved into three separate activities:

1. A set of standard tables based on the replies received from the eight nations was created.
2. Official documents, books, and articles by independent researchers about early childhood education were collected from each country and reviewed.
3. Separate country reports reflecting the work done under *1* and *2* were written. These reports were sent to experts in each country and to the appropriate ministers for review.

The general format of this review sought information in the following areas of concern:

1. Relationship between historical perspectives on preschool education and current ECE programs.
2. Knowledge about the increased demand for ECE:
   a. Size of household
   b. Reproduction rates
   c. Labor force changes
   d. Preschool enrollments
3. Information pertaining to the similarities and differences along the following variables:
   a. Organization and administration
   b. Physical facilities
   c. Pupil—teacher ratio
   d. Parent involvement
   e. Teacher training and education
   f. Cost and financial support
   g. School size and number of classrooms
   h. Instructional methods and aids
   i. Research in early childhood education
4. Review of recent research efforts.

HISTORICAL PERSPECTIVE OF EARLY CHILDHOOD EDUCATION

The first requirement of each report was to compile a brief history of ECE in that country for the purpose of putting present circumstances in perspective and understanding the roots of current practices.

Concern for ECE in the eight countries investigated dates back to the beginning of the eighteenth and nineteenth centuries with pioneering work conducted by Rousseau, Pestalozzi, and Froebel. These men recognized the necessity of providing education to help young children suffering severe deprivation due to war and/or slum conditions.

The major goal of these pioneers was to create educational centers in which they hoped to provide children with an environment that would compensate for their social, psychological, and intellectual deficits. As mentioned, Rousseau stated his philosophy of education and learning in *Emile*, and identified the period of childhood as special, not just an unimportant and wasteful stage through which the child must pass as quickly as possible on his way toward becoming an adult. Rousseau was most concerned with helping the child to develop naturally, to unfold and blossom to the greatest extent possible. His desire was to protect the child from the corrupting influence of the industrial society.

Pestalozzi and Froebel added to Rousseau's basic concepts the idea that ECE should be based on concrete experiences and sense impressions. Froebel is credited with identifying play as the real work of childhood and the best method by which children learn. Following these three early educational philosophers, a number of important scholars contributed to ECE knowledge. To name a few, there were, in England and Wales, Owens, McMillan, and Isaacs; in France, Oberlin and Kergomard; in Belgium, Decroly; in Italy, Aporti, Agazzi, and Montessori; and in The Netherlands, Langeveld.

Although created for the benefit of the poor, ECE programs in the eight countries, with the exception of France and Belgium, were adopted by the middle class, who could afford them, while provisions for the poor diminished. The historical curriculum offered in ECE centers was profoundly affected by this differing emphasis. Its early orientation changed from a concern for welfare, health, and education to one for social and emotional adjustment and creative expression based on the Froebelian idea of play. In recent years, interest in ECE for the poor has again gained importance. Programs similar to Head Start and Follow Through are now supported by government funds in England and Wales, The Netherlands, Germany (FR), Canada, Belgium and Italy.

Each of the countries studied was influenced in large part by the same people and factors, but the particular experience of each country brought about the creation of its own unique early childhood education programs, distinct in many respects from the programs of any other country.

Belgium

Private ECE centers (*salles d'asiles*) have existed in Belgium since 1825. As early as 1832 there were publicly funded *garderies*. However, *garderies* did not gain acceptance until around 1850, when Froebel's teaching became popular, and with it the idea that *garderies* should be more than just places where children were looked after. In 1879 Belgium passed a law empowering the state to require a community to annex a preprimary section to existing primary schools. Central government initiative in the ECE field ceased in 1884 when new school rules placed the responsibility for such activities in the hands of local authorities.

In 1921, a royal decree established preschools at Bruges, Laken, Brussels, and Liège. The 1920s were a period of profound development in psychology and pedagogy during which Froebel's methods were replaced by the work of Montessori. In June, 1927, a new program replaced early governmental directives. More recently, the preschools of Belgium (*écoles gardiennes* or *kleutershool*, depending on the language spoken) derive their methods from the work of Ovide Decroly. A Commission on Preschool Reform, appointed in 1970, is expected to report on ECE in the near future.

France

The influence of Rousseau was keenly felt in France in the last part of the eighteenth century. Preprimary education in France was started in 1779 by two different groups, one whose schools were called *écoles a tricoter* (knitting schools) and another, slightly later, whose schools were called *salles d'asile* (place of refuge).

The state absorbed these schools in 1833 under the name of *écoles maternelles* and they became a part of the national educational system supported by the French government. *Écoles maternelles* have always been concerned with providing health and welfare services to the poor. Their interests expanded to include educational concerns in 1886 and again in 1928, when sets of new guidelines were written for the schools. Nevertheless, the concerns of the *écoles maternelles* remained essentially protective and only secondarily educative until after World War II, when the central concern shifted to intellectual development of the child.

England and Wales

The history of ECE development in England is one of dramatic ups and downs. The concept originated with Robert Owen who established the first infant school in Scotland in 1816. Since the 1850s much of English preschool practice has been heavily influenced by the teachings of Froebel and the Froebel Society, whose leaders have been active in their field since 1875.

Enrollments in preschool included 24.2% of all 3–5-year-olds in 1870, and 43.1% by 1900. However, due to a series of reports claiming that preschool was at best not helpful to children and at worst actually detrimental to their development, enrollment declined to 22.7% in 1910 and dropped further to a low of 7.7% in 1955. Preschools were recommended only for those children who could not be cared for elsewhere.

The demand for ECE began to rise again in the 1950s and 1960s. By 1966 private organizations operated 600 play groups; the number grew to 7000 in 1971 with an enrollment of 170,000 children. Demand is still larger than the supply. One cause for the dramatic reversal was the Plowden report, *Children and Their Primary Schools* (1967), which directly countered the government's policy of opposition to the expansion of nursery schools. Its key recommendations included at least part-time nursery education for two-thirds of all 3- and 4-year-old children, with provision for about 15% full-time attendance. Also strongly recommended was the identification of educational priority areas where social and educational deprivation due to poor housing or high-rise isolation is the greatest. The Plowden report led to some expansion, doubling the places available in some centers.

Finally, in a 1972 White Paper, the government changed its policy from opposition to greatly increased support for the general expansion of ECE, particularly in deprived areas. It called on the nursery school to supplement the home, and concentrate on early identification of the needs of young children. It stated that the planning for expansion should be based on close cooperation of authorities with social groups, counting on the involvement of the parents.

Sweden

In Sweden, child-minding facilities opened in the 1830s and 1840s to care for children of working mothers. Compulsory education was introduced in 1842 for all children aged 7 and older, a comparatively late age to start. The growth of public nursery schools progressed slowly until the 1950s, largely because of the country's priority commitment to the primary and secondary schools. The main reason given for the disinterest in ECE programs was the lack of support from scientific research on the educational advantages of ECE. The social and emotional aspects of ECE were recognized, but were met in the Swedish system by other agencies. In 1968, the government created a preschool commission to take a deeper look at the objectives, organization, content and general quality of preschool education. Its report was submitted to the government in 1972.

Currently, care of preschool children aged 6 months to 7 years occurs outside the home in *lekskolor* (part-time) and *daghem* (full-time) nursery schools. The schools are run by local authorities. A few private centers also receive public support. Influenced greatly by declining birthrate, household size, and increasing numbers of working mothers, Swedish preschool enrollments increased by 167.3% in the 1960s.

Italy

The first infant school in Italy was established by a Roman Catholic priest, Abate Aporti, in 1828. In 1833, based on careful study of children and the conditions of their development, he wrote *The Manual of Education and Teaching for Infant Schools,* which stressed moral habits, intellectual stimulation, and physical activities. In 1894, the Agazzi sisters opened a home for preschool children which stressed training in sense perception and play.

Maria Montessori opened a school for retarded children in 1907. Her success in teaching retarded children led her to apply her methods to teaching normal children. In 1909, she published her first book, which was based on her work with slum children in Rome. In 1922, she was appointed government inspector of schools.

Most of the reforms of this early period were swept away by World War II, after which Italy adopted the English pattern of education starting at age 5. A preprimary state system was not established until 1968. Until then almost all preschool education took place in Roman Catholic organizations. The state is now aiming to provide preschool services, either state-run or private, to all parents desiring it. Nevertheless, Italy currently faces a shortage of space even in schools where education is compulsory.

Canada

Early childhood education in Canada started in the late nineteenth century, not for children of the poor, but for the educational emancipation of children of the wealthy who could afford to pay for careful individual attention to their needs. Shortly thereafter, ECE was adopted to help the poor as well. Concerned agencies sought to use kindergartens to supplement the care of children of immigrants and newly industrialized families.

Ontario provided free public preschool education as early as 1882. In 1885, noncompulsory kindergartens became part of its school system. Kindergartens are now standard in some of the provinces although they expanded very slowly until the 1950s and 1960s when enrollments grew dramatically in both the private and public sector.

Germany

As early as 1524, Martin Luther was urging the German people to send their children to school, particularly to receive a good religious education. This action helped foster the belief in the value of education among the German people.

In the beginning of the eighteenth century, Frederick William I ordered children to be sent to school and established schools where there were none. In 1736, the idea of compulsory school attendance was established by Frederick the Great. In the beginning of the nineteenth century, day care centers founded mainly by religious and philanthropic societies began to care for children of working women. Berlin mill owners established schools in the 1830s that were run by untrained teachers who believed in strong discipline for children.

In reaction to the deplorable conditions in these mill schools, Froebel opened his first kindergarten in 1837 with an emphasis on the importance of play. The kindergarten movement was adopted mainly by the middle class, ignoring the children of the poor. In 1851, kindergartens were proscribed by the Prussian government for "radical" teachings, and after 1860 they were run by private (religious) groups. Preschool education remains largely denominational in Germany to the present time.

Commissions to study the needs of preschool education were set up in 1953 and 1965. Both recommended the expansion of preschool education, but progress has been very slow. Discussions about the "if" and "how" to proceed with preprimary education are still going on in the German government.

The Netherlands

Freedom, a fundamental concept in ECE in The Netherlands, is embodied in the parents' right, guaranteed in 1815, to choose both the type of school and the type of instruction for their children. Therefore, early schools arose from the need for care of children of the poor during the work day and from the conviction that religious education was best begun early. Early child care centers, established in 1800, were designed to provide psychohygienic care and were used extensively by people of all economic classes who could afford the small fee. Unfortunately, official plans for teacher supervision of the untrained staff in the elementary schools were never practiced. Conditions deteriorated to such a degree that by the end of the nineteenth century physicians were alarmed and corrective legislation was introduced.

The ideas of Froebel and Montessori greatly influenced preprimary education in The Netherlands. A form of Froebel's kindergarten was popular until Montessori's ideas became widely known. Langeveld, a more contemporary influence, stressed the importance of the family unit receiving more attention. Current practice in today's kindergartens provides as much freedom as possible for individual development under the care of responsible adults.

Since 1860, preprimary enrollment has grown much more rapidly than the rate of population increase. Compulsory education at age 7 became law in 1900. In 1955, the law established a program for preprimary education.

Summary

In general, most of the countries initiated preschool education out of a need to provide health and welfare care for poor children. The noted exception is

Canada where ECE programs were originally developed to provide for the educational needs of wealthy children. Similar to the American experience, preschool education programs were influenced by the philosophical writings of early theorists such as Rousseau and Froebel. Also, there is a parallel between the American experience and the European experience in first providing for the health and welfare needs of poor children in the early preschool care programs.

This historical background provided information on the unique development of ECE in each of the eight countries. Against this framework, current government policies, educational practices, and research can be better understood.

EVIDENCE FOR CURRENT ECE DEMAND

The second issue focused on an explanation for the dramatic growth in public demand for ECE. The CERI questionnaire was designed to examine whether the demand reflected a concern for equal educational opportunity for all children, emphasizing cognitive inputs, or whether the demand was a response to other social phenomena. The statistical information which reflects long-term trends in the eight countries investigated provides some insight into this question.

Size of Household

The first set of facts concerns the size of households. The term "size of household" is a fairly ambiguous term which refers to all people residing together in one place. The household involves not only individuals and married couples but also children, the grandparents, and other relatives or associates living together as a unit. Table 3.1 and Figure 3.1 present the trends in household size for seven of the eight countries studied. Table 3.1 shows persistent and marked declines in average household size for periods of 50 years or more. This general trend may be considered parallel to a decline in birthrate and broadly associated with the global process of industrialization and urbanization. However, sudden or short-term fertility changes are not necessarily or immediately reflected in changes in household size.

The data indicate that the average household size declined in all countries over the period of time investigated. The most dramatic drop, from 5.92 to 3.86 persons, occurred in Canada. France experienced the smallest decline, reflecting a very stable household population. In 1965, the country with the smallest household size was Germany (FR), followed by Sweden. In 1970, over half of all families in Sweden had only one child.

Several patterns or trends emerge from the data on household size. Although irregularities and reverses are found in specific cases, the general trend of change in the size and structure of households and families is unmistakably linked to the long range process of demographic transition in the face of modernization,

TABLE 3.1
Trends of Average Household Size

Belgium		Canada		England and Wales		France	
Year	A.H.S.	Year	A.H.S.	Year	A.H.S.	Year	A.H.S.
1846	4.87	1871	5.92	1801	4.60	1881	3.70
1900	4.30	1901	5.07	1901	4.49	1901	3.60
1947	3.00	1951	4.11	1951	3.19	1940	3.80
1961	3.03	1966	3.86	1966	3.01	1962	3.20

Total Number of Years:

115	95	165	81

Decrease or Increase:

-1.84	-2.06	-1.59	-0.50

Germany(F.R.)		Italy		Netherlands		Sweden	
Year	A.H.S.	Year	A.H.S.	Year	A.H.S.	Year	A.H.S.
1871	4.63	N.A. [a]		1899	4.51	1860	4.28
1900	4.49	N.A.		1909	4.41	1900	3.72
1950	2.99	N.A.		1956	3.60	1950	2.90
1967	2.69	N.A.		1960	3.50	1965	2.80

Total Number of Years:

96	61	105

Decrease or Increase:

-1.94	-1.01	-1.48

Source: Analyses and Projections of Households and Families, prepared
         by the Population Division, Department of Economic and
         Social Affairs of the United Nations Secretariat. Document
         No. 71-16812.

[a] Not available.

industrialization, and urbanization. Such family changes could not have occurred
without the background of societal modernization.

Two major stages of demographic transition occur in sequential order for all
countries and may be distinguished for size of household. First, a country is
demographically represented by stage A, where a moderate or rapidly declining

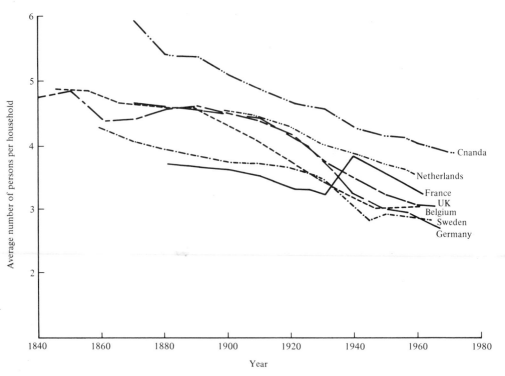

Figure 3.1. Trends in average household size. [From "Analyses and Projections of House-holds and Families" prepared by the Population Division, Department of Economic and social affairs of the United Nations. Document 71-16812, Table 3.]

mortality rate is combined with a relatively constant and very high birth rate. Second, stage B demographically represents a period where there is a substantial decline in birth rate combined with further slow declines in the mortality rate. For example, most developing countries of Africa, Asia, and Latin America are in stage A, while the developed countries of Western Europe are in stage B. The eight countries described in this status report are characterized by some distinct and sweeping tendencies: (*1*) a general decline in average size of household and family, (*2*) an increase in the proportion of small households and families and a decrease in large families, and (*3*) an increase in the proportion of nuclear families and single-person households and a decrease in the proportion of multigeneration extended families.

The stages A and B, identified above, have some important implications for the concept of childhood. In stage A, with its high birth rates and relatively high infant mortality rates, few parents can become as attached to young children as in stage B. The birth and/or death of a child apparently has to be a less traumatic event in the lives of parents simply because it is so common. The child is really not seen as an important person in his own right until he can begin to perform some useful work. Therefore, in stage A it would not be uncommon for parents to desert a child when they do not want it or cannot take care of it.

For instance, Gaston Mialaret, in his lecture presented at the annual meeting of the Association for Childhood Education International (1975), mentioned that in the seventeenth century the Brotherhood of Saint Vincent de Paul achieved their name by caring for foundlings. While life is not perceived as being less valuable when a country is in stage A, there does appear to be a different attitude toward children. Mialaret cited a quote by Montaigne, a Renaissance educator who reflected the opinion of his time when he said, "I lost two or three children in the cradle, not without regret, but without anguish."

The care of young children in stage A is commonly the responsibility of older siblings, since the mother has more important tasks to perform. In addition, in Western Europe, at least when it was in stage A, the child was further seen as unimportant because he had not reached the "age of reason." This was usually not attained until the child was about age 6 or 7. One of the natural outcomes of the lower birth rates and much lower infant mortality rates found in stage B is that the concept of childhood emerges as important in and of itself.

Reproduction Rates

The second piece of evidence that might shed some light on the issue of demand is reproduction rates. One might speculate that a negative correlation exists between education and number of children produced. The more education people have, it seems, the more they plan and control, rather dramatically, the number of children they have. Table 3.2 and Figure 3.2 indicate a pattern similar to Table 3.1 and Figure 3.1. The gross reproduction rates in all eight countries declined over the past 100 years. The reasons are not clear, but we may again speculate as we did for household size and suggest that the number of children in any single family is growing smaller. The gross reproduction rate does not, in itself, show that individual families are smaller, but rather that the nations are, on the whole, having fewer children. It might be concluded that this tendency is spread evenly across the population of a nation. The gross reproduction rate dropped most in England and Wales over the period of time considered. In the late 1960s Germany (FR) and Sweden had the lowest rate. France again presents the picture of a country with a very stable population.

Table 3.2 and Figure 3.2 warrant careful study, since they indicate that the decline in the gross reproduction rate is not smooth. Most countries investigated show a rise in gross reproduction during the period of time since the end of World War II.

To determine if this rising trend in gross reproduction is still occurring, additional information was collected on birth rates since 1965. Table 3.3 and

TABLE 3.2
Gross Reproduction Rates

Belgium		Canada		England and Wales			
Year	G.R.	Year	G.R.	Year	G.R.	Year	G.R.
N.A. [a]		N.A.		1851	2.3	1881	1.7
1900	1.9	1921	1.6	1901	1.7	1901	1.4
1947	1.2	1951	1.7	1951	1.0	1940	1.0
1961	1.3	1964	1.4	1966	1.3	1962	1.4

Total Number of Years:
    61   45   115   81

Decrease or Increase:
   -0.6   -0.2   -1.0   -0.3

Germany(F.R.)		Italy		Netherlands		Sweden	
Year	G.R.	Year	G.R.	Year	G.R.	Year	G.R.
N.A.		N.A.		1899	2.3	1860	2.2
N.A.		N.A.		1909	2.0	1900	1.9
1950	1.0	N.A.		1956	1.5	1950	1.1
1967	1.1	N.A.		1960	1.5	1965	1.2

Total Number of Years:
    17   61   105

Decrease or Increase:
   +0.1   0.8   -1.0

Source: Analyses and Projections of Households and Families, prepared
         by the Population Division, Department of Economic and
         Social Affairs of the United Nations Secretariat. Document
         No. 71-16812.

[a]Not available.

Figure 3.3 provide information on the number of births in each of the eight
countries from 1966–1970. In all cases, sharp decreases occurred over this
period of time. The decrease was greatest in Germany (FR) and Canada and least
in France and The Netherlands. Figures 3.1, 3.2, and 3.3 all indicate that the size
of households, gross reproduction rates, and birth rates in these eight countries

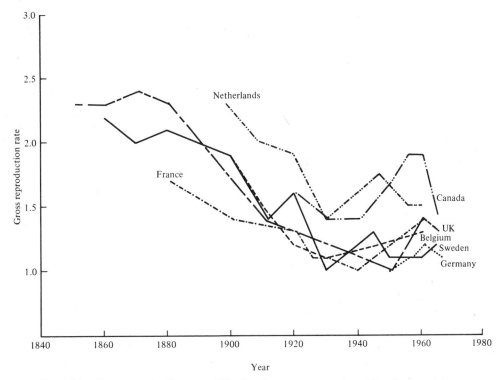

Figure 3.2. Gross reproduction rate, defined as "... average number of live daughters that would be born per woman, all of whom survive to the end of a potentially productive period of life [United Nations, *Demographic Yearbook, 1969.* New York: United Nations, 1970]." [From "Analyses and Projections of Households and Families" prepared by the Population Division, Department of Economic and Social Affairs of the United Nations. Document 71-16812, Table 3.]

have in the past, and continue today, to decline. By themselves the figures provide little information, but indicate a trend as well as a need for additional data.

Labor Force Changes

The labor force participation rates in Table 3.4 and Figure 3.4 offer a third piece of evidence about the causes of increased demand for ECE. In the period from 1960 to 1970, male participation rates in the labor force declined or remained unchanged in seven of the eight countries studied. Only in Sweden did they increase. The participation rates for females, however, increased in six of

TABLE 3.3
Births 1966–1970

	Births 1966	Rate per thousand of popu- lation	Births 1970	Rate per thousand of popu- lation	Difference in rate 1966–1970
Belgium	151,096	15.9	141,814	14.7	-1.2
Canada	387,710	19.3	369,647	17.5	-1.8
England & Wales	849,823	17.7	783,000	16.0	-1.7
France	863,527	17.6	848,300	16.7	-0.9
Germany	1,024,261	17.8	789,829	13.3	-4.5
Italy	979,940	18.9	900,870	16.8	-2.1
Nether- lands	239,611	19.2	239,015	18.4	-0.8
Sweden	123,354	15.8	109,825	13.6	-2.2

Source: United Nations Demographic Yearbook, 1970.

the eight countries. Only in Germany (FR) and Italy did they decline. The increase in female participation rates was highest in Canada and Sweden. In Table 3.4 and Figure 3.4, it is important to note the difference in percentages of women involved in the labor force. They are lowest in Italy and The Netherlands and highest in Sweden and the United Kingdom.

To summarize the evidence which might support the current increased demand for ECE, it seems reasonable to draw on the data showing changes in household size, reproduction rates, and labor force participation. It appears clear that the average household size has drastically declined in the last 100 years, and continues to do so. The extended family is no longer a common phenomenon in these countries. Women are also having fewer children and are choosing to participate in the labor force with far greater frequency than was true 10 years ago. These societal changes may have produced a number of changes in the demand for ECE. It might be speculated that smaller families could mean that mothers would request less care for their children since fewer children make it easier to keep the children at home. Then, too, if a mother is to have only one or two children, she may want to keep them at home as long as possible to enjoy the pleasure of seeing them grow up. What appears to be true, however, is the reverse.

Although there are no data to confirm this suspicion, I believe that if a mother has only one or two children, her desire for some kind of preschool or early child care for her children is high. If, however, a mother has four, five, or more

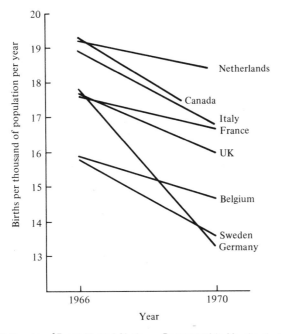

Figure 3.3. Birth rates. [From United Nations, *Demographic Yearbook, 1970.* New York: United Nations, 1971.]

children, then to have one or two of them in school or preschool does not really change her situation very much.

This complex phenomenon must not be viewed in isolation since it seems to be the result of a number of forces coming together. These are: (*1*) a greater economic demand in addition to desire on the part of women to actively participate outside the home; (*2*) the far wider use of birth control and family planning methods; (*3*) the better education of all people in these countries (more education seems to increase the demand for even more education); (*4*) the awareness that children from small families need to interact with other small children in social situations; and (*5*) little basis to suggest that harmful effects are incurred by young children in being separated from their mothers for a relatively short amount of time on a regular basis.

Preschool Enrollments

To help support the accuracy of these speculations, preschool enrollment data are presented as a fourth piece of evidence showing the increased demand for ECE programs. In Table 3.5 and Figure 3.5, preschool enrollments for the years

TABLE 3.4
Labor Force Participation Rates

	$\dfrac{\text{Total Labor Force}}{\text{Population from 15 to 64 years}}$ x 100		
	1960	1970	% of increase or decrease
Belgium			
Total	63.2	63.6	+0.4
Males	88.5	87.0	-1.5
Females	36.4	40.3	+3.9
Canada			
Total	62.3	64.0	+1.7
Males	91.9	86.9	-5.0
Females	32.0	40.8	+8.8
France			
Total	69.9	67.4	-2.5
Males	86.5	82.5	-4.0
Females	42.8	46.2	+3.4
Germany (F.R.)			
Total	70.5	70.9	+0.4
Males	94.9	94.9	0.0
Females	49.3	48.6	-0.7
Italy			
Total	64.1	55.7	-8.4
Males	93.3	83.6	-9.7
Females	36.7	29.1	-7.6
Netherlands			
Total	60.3	58.0	-2.3
Males	91.0	85.5	-5.5
Females	25.6	30.0	+4.4
Sweden			
Total	73.3	74.3	+1.0
Males	93.1	98.8	+5.7
Females	53.3	59.4	+6.1
United Kingdom			
Total	73.4	72.7	-0.7
Males	99.1	93.4	-5.7
Females	48.6	52.1	+3.5

Source: Labor Force Statistics 1959-1970, Organization for Economic
Cooperation and Development, Paris, 1972.

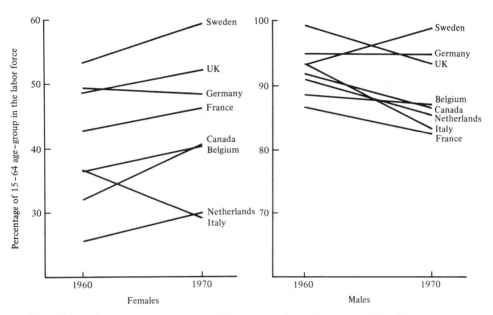

Figure 3.4. Labor force participation. [From *Labor Force Statistics, 1959–1970.* Paris: Organization for Economic Cooperation and Development, 1972.]

TABLE 3.5
Pre-School Enrollments 1960–1970

	1960	1970	(in 000's) % of increase
Belgium	405	458	13.1
Canada	146	413	182.9
England and Wales	150 (E)[a]	300 (E)	200.0 (E)
France	1,374	2,213	61.1
Germany (F.R.)	818	1,161	41.9
Italy	1,154	1,630	41.2
Netherlands	398	492	23.6
Sweden	49	112	167.3

Average Percent of Increase, 1960–1970: 50.8

[a]Estimated from available data.

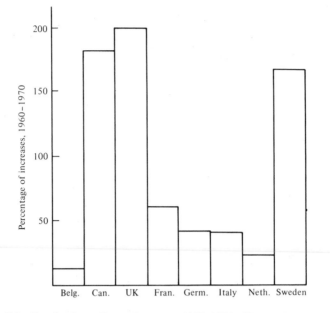

Figure 3.5. Preschool enrollment increases, 1960–1970. [From "Early Childhood Education in Eight OECD Countries." Organization for Economic Cooperation and Development, CERI/ECE/72.01, Parts I–X, April, 1972.]

1960 and 1970 are presented. Canada and Sweden experienced the largest growth and concurrently had the greatest proportional increases of women entering the labor force. The increase in preschool enrollments was much smaller in Belgium, which started with a large base in the 1960's. In Italy and France, where preschool education had even larger enrollments in 1960, there were moderate increases by 1970 of 41.2% and 61.1%, respectively.

Table 3.6 and Figure 3.6 show that the public sector was meeting more of the increased demand for preschool education: Public facilities grew 67% from 1960-1970, and private facilities only 31% for the same period. These figures give some indication that the private sector simply cannot absorb the increase in demand as rapidly and easily as the public sector. This is probably due in part to the rapidly increasing cost of providing early childhood education. The provision for public preschools in the 1960s in Italy is only a recent phenomenon. In 1970, they had only 134,000 children in public schools as compared to 1,496,000 enrolled in privately supported kindergartens. No breakdown of public and private schools could be made for England and Wales.

Table 3.7 and Figure 3.7 show the percentages of preschool pupils in attendance by single year of age and by age grouping. In Italy, about 1% of the 2-year-olds, 20% of the 3-year-olds, 60% of the 4-year-olds, 85% of the 5-year-olds, and 95% of the 6-year-olds attend school. In France and Belgium, 15% of

TABLE 3.6
Pre-School Enrollments, Private and Public

	1960		1970 (in 000's)	
	Private	Public	Private	Public
Belgium	265	140	270	188
Canada	7	138	64	349
England and Wales	24	209	31	319
France	196	1,178	323	1,891
Germany	165	652	234	927
Italy	1,154	0	1,496	134
Netherlands	314	84	369	123
Sweden	n.a.[a]	49	n.a.	131

Average Percent of Increase, 1960-1970: Private - 31.1
Public - 65.8

[a]Not available

the population is enrolled in a preschool at age 2, and in Belgium 90% of 3-year-olds are enrolled. In Sweden, even at age 6 only 70% of the children are in some form of preschool. Since Sweden has one of the highest percentage increases in the female labor force (6.1%), it is difficult to explain why only 70% of the children at age 6 are attending preschools. In England compulsory education begins at age 5, so 99% of this age group attend school. However, the percentage of children in school under age 5 is relatively low in England.

Table 3.8 and Figure 3.8 show enrollment percentages by age groups. The figures for ages 2-6 and 3-6 are perhaps the most dramatic and interesting. Again, they show that while preschool enrollments in Sweden and Canada have grown very rapidly, they are still below countries such as Belgium and France.

In all eight countries, the number of pupils enrolled in preschools indicates the number of spaces available and does not reflect the true demand. In all countries there are long waiting lists of children whose parents want them enrolled. Therefore, all enrollment figures are an understatement of the real demand. In countries such as Canada, Italy, Germany (FR), and England and Wales, perhaps half again as many 3- and 4-year-old children are seeking places as are available.

Summary

The second question regarding the demand for ECE programs is whether this demand reflects a concern for intellectual development and equal educational opportunity, or whether it reflects a response to other social phenomena.

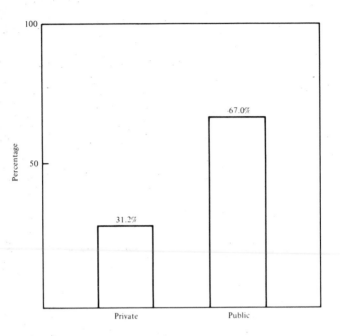

Figure 3.6. Percentage of increase in preschool enrollment, 1960–1970, private and public for eight countries.

TABLE 3.7
Percent of Pre-School Pupils in Attendance by Single Year of Age,
Ages 2 - 6, 1970-71

Country	Age				
	6	5	4	3	2
Belgium	99	99	95	90	15 (E)
Canada	99	85 (E)[a]	25 (E)	5 (E)	1 (E)
England and Wales	99	99	25	5 (E)	1 (E)
France	99	99	84	55	15
Germany (F.R.)	99	70 (E)	35 (E)	10 (E)	1 (E)
Italy	95	85 (E)	60 (E)	20 (E)	1 (E)
Netherlands	99	95	80 (E)	5 (E)	1 (E)
Sweden	70	25 (E)	10 (E)	2 (E)	1 (E)

[a]Estimated from available data

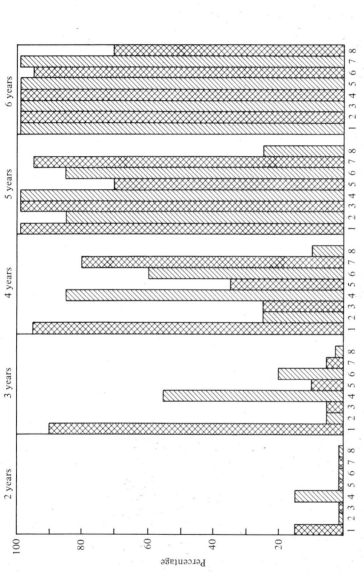

Figure 3.7. Percentage of preschool pupils in attendance by single year of age, 2–6, 1970–1971. 1 = Belgium; 2 = Canada; 3 = England and Wales; 4 = France; 5 = Germany (FR); 6 = Italy; 7 = The Netherlands; 8 = Sweden.

45

TABLE 3.8
Percent of Pre-School Pupils in Attendance by Age Groups, 1970-71

	Age Group			
	5 - 6	4 - 6	3 - 6	2 - 6
Belgium	99.0	99.0	95.8	79.6
Canada	92.0	69.7	53.5	43.0
England and Wales	99.0	73.7	56.5	45.4
France	99.0	94.0	84.3	70.4
Germany (F.R.)	84.5	68.0	53.3	43.0
Italy	90.0	80.0	65.0	52.2
Netherlands	97.0	91.3	69.6	56.0
Sweden	47.5	35.0	26.7	21.6

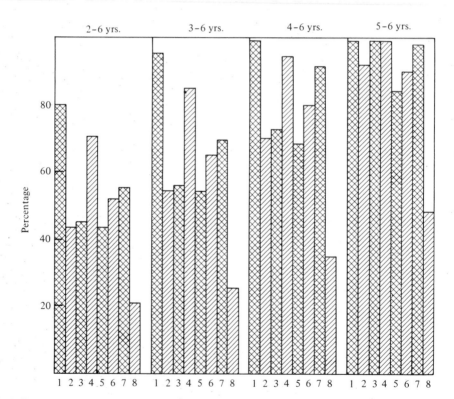

Figure 3.8. Percentage of preschool pupils in attendance, by age groups, 1970–1971. 1 = Belgium; 2 = Canada; 3 = England and Wales; 4 = France; 5 = Germany (FR); 6 = Italy; 7 = The Netherlands; 8 = Sweden.

The data seem to suggest that the demand for early childhood education reflects both factors. For example, changes in social phenomena, such as lower birth rates, smaller household size, and an increased participation of females in the labor force are coupled with a demand by women for greater equality of educational opportunity for their children.

France is a good case in point. While France has traditionally emphasized early learning, there is currently more pressure from the middle-class families for cognitive stimulation of all young children in preschools. Sweden approaches equal educational opportunity for all children by stressing cooperation in learning situations. While France and Sweden appear to value greater equality of education for all children, tending to steer away from labeling children as "disadvantaged," Germany, The Netherlands, Italy, and England and Wales tend to make special provisions for these groups of children.

That there has been a century-old tradition of emphasizing health and welfare needs of children in preschool is an important historical point. Only recently has the emphasis changed to stressing the educational needs of children.

The third issue focused on the similarities and differences between the eight countries on the following variables: (*1*) organization and administration, (*2*) physical facilities, (*3*) pupil-teacher ratio, (*4*) parent involvement, (*5*) teacher training and education, (*6*) cost and financial support, (*7*) school size and number of classrooms, (*8*) instructional methods, and (*9*) research in early childhood education.

ORGANIZATION AND ADMINISTRATION

The organization and administration patterns of ECE across the eight countries differ greatly. In Belgium and France, responsibility is highly centralized at the national level, whereas in the Netherlands the government does not directly control curriculum but maintains strong and effective control indirectly through the assumption of instructional costs. In Canada and Germany (FR), control of preschools rests with each regional government, which has its own guidelines for the organization and administration of ECE, although cooperation exists among the various regions within each country. In England and Wales, early childhood education is locally administered with help from nationally prepared guidelines and government inspectors. In Sweden and Italy, preschool is financed at the local level by parents or by the church. The real power, therefore, resides locally despite strong, central ministries of education in both countries.

There are also important differences among these eight countries as to what federal, regional (state), or local agency is given responsibility for preschool education or care. In France and Belgium, the control and responsibility is vested in the Ministry of Education at all levels. In Canada, the control also resides in the Ministry of Education, but is located at the provincial level.

Canada has no national control of education. In England and Wales, the responsibility is also located in an educational authority, but control is at local levels. The great number of playgroups are controlled at a local level, although they are administered by the Ministry of Health and Social Security. In Sweden, control rests with the Ministry of Social Affairs and the National Board of Health and Welfare. At the local levels, it rests with a Child Welfare Committee. In Germany, control is at the lander (regional) level, with organization given to welfare organizations, churches, and private societies, plus some public provision. For the public provision in towns, the burgomaster and town council are the regulating body. In Italy and the Netherlands, most provision for preschools is organized by church-related groups. Both countries provide very general guidelines, but real control rests with the church groups.

In most of the countries reported on, the job of supervision or inspection is a national one, with some of the work being done by regional or local inspectors. The major exceptions are Canada and Germany (FR), where supervision and inspection is provided at the regional or local level only. In all of the countries investigated, there seem to be two important changes taking place in the role of supervision and inspection. First, at all levels (national, regional, or local), supervision appears to be becoming a consulting and advising function rather than an "I will tell you how" function. Second, supervisors and inspectors are trying hard to be seen as resource people and providers of in-service training and workshops.

The whole question of who controls preschool education in each of these countries is an important issue of debate since the organization and administration, as well as the goals and objectives of preschool, are markedly affected by whether the controlling group has a background of concern in health, welfare, or education. The debate is made more difficult because of the rapid growth of preschool in terms of both enrollments and expenditures.

Private preschool education is extensive in seven of the eight countries; Sweden has almost none. Although subject to the rules and regulations of government in such areas as physical facilities and child safety, the private preschools are freer than the publicly controlled preschools to pursue the educational programs they and the parents desire.

Organizational differences are found in such characteristics as the permissible age of entry—2 in Belgium, France, Sweden, and Italy; 3 in England and Wales; 4 in Canada, Germany and Italy— and the age of leaving—5 in England and Wales and 6 everywhere else except Sweden and the Netherlands where it is age 7. In most countries, children are grouped by single year of age; some countries allow 2-year age groups such as 3- and 4-year-old children in the same class. Sweden, however, is experimenting with sibling groups which span the ages of 2½ to 7 years. The older children are taught responsibility for the younger ones.

In terms of their organization, preschools are usually separate from primary schools except in Belgium where they are commonly attached to the primary schools. The fact that most preschools are separate from primary schools may tend to reflect the belief that the two schools have different jobs to perform. As mentioned, a century-old tradition of preschool education has placed emphasis on health and welfare. Only recently have Belgium and France turned their attention to the educational needs of young children. With the new emphasis placed on developing intellectual growth in the young child, a major debate is now focused on how to bring these two school systems together.

There is growing consensus that the period of life from birth to age 9 or 12 should be viewed as a unity in the field of health, welfare, and education. There are many hurdles to achieving this unity. The Belgians are doing some particularly interesting work in which they are moving toward a "children's center" concept. The "child center" would combine the health and welfare concerns of preprimary and primary schools. The biggest obstacle seems to be getting the different agencies to cooperate. There appears to be a fear on the part of the agencies of losing some of their autonomy.

Physical Facilities

Physical facilities are similar in all countries. The furnishings consist of tables, movable chairs, and carpets for work or seating. Preschools usually have cubbyholes in which children store their materials and work. They also have large wall spaces for painting and displaying work. In addition, they may have climbing bars, water tables, sand boxes, plants, small pets, and toys.

What seems to be more important than the physical facilities is the way in which they are used and the manner in which the children and curriculum interact with them. In England and Wales, Sweden, The Netherlands, Germany (FR), and Canada, the children are free, in most cases, to explore life in a preschool. The children are rarely confined to their seats, and the teachers tend to work with the children where they are. In Sweden, the children are free to wander from class to class. In England and Wales, they may go outside to the playground at will. In these countries, there are few teacher-organized activities. The other countries, France, Belgium, and Italy, tend to have the children sit in their seats, either separately or around tables. The children tend to come to the teacher for instruction and are generally not free to get up and wander around. The difference in the children's use of the facilities may reflect the different pupil-teacher ratios found in the various countries.

Pupil-Teacher Ratio

Table 3.9 and Figure 3.9 show pupil-teacher ratios for the eight countries for both public and private preschools. Table 3.9 shows that England has the lowest ratio (19:1), and France the highest (43:1). It is important to note that all countries, over the 10-year period from 1960 to 1970, have reduced their

TABLE 3.9
Pupil:Teacher Ratio, 1960–1970

	1960			1970		
	Private	Public	Total	Private	Public	Total
Belgium	35:1	33:1	34:1	28:1	26:1	27:1
Canada	17:1	37:1	35:1	14:1	29:1	25:1
England and Wales	16:1	20:1	19:1	16:1	20:1	19:1
France	n.a.[a]	44:1	44:1	n.a.	43:1	43:1
Germany	23:1[b]	23:1	23:1	23:1	23:1	23:1
Italy	37:1	n.a.	37:1	38:1	24:1	37:1
Netherlands	34:1	35:1	35:1	31:1	31:1	31:1
Sweden	n.a.	40:1	40:1	n.a.	41:1	41:1

[a] Not available.

[b] Estimated.

pupil-teacher ratios. The single exception is Italy, where the ratio has risen by one child per teacher. This reflects a widely held belief that low pupil-teacher ratios should be better than higher ones. In general, the private sector tends to have lower pupil-teacher ratios; the difference is greatest in Canada. The exception is that the private sector ratios in Belgium and Italy are higher than the public sector ratios, and in The Netherlands they are the same. It appears, therefore, that parents are buying, in part, a lower pupil-teacher ratio when they choose to send their children to private preschools. This process may reflect both home and school sensitivity for the need to provide more individual help to each child. The range of pupil-teacher ratios raises an important question. Do these ratios make a difference, especially in preschool instruction?

It is important to note that Table 3.9 presents pupil-teacher ratios, not pupil-adult ratios. Pupil-adult ratios, where adults include paraprofessional or parent aides, would reduce Sweden's 41:1 ratio to 7:1. The England and Wales's ratio would be reduced from 19:1 to 10:1. Such adjustment would not change the ratio in France, where teachers have refused the help of paraprofessionals. The French preschools do have helpers to feed the children and to help dress and undress them, but their role is much more that of a domestic than a paraprofessional, since they do not teach.

In most of the countries reported on, some use is made of teacher aides, parent volunteers, and domestics. The reasons behind this are varied. Some educators feel that teachers' jobs have become unmanageable. They suggest that the use of aides can help. In other places, it is suggested that this is a good way to stimulate parental involvement and to increase school-community rapport. In still others,

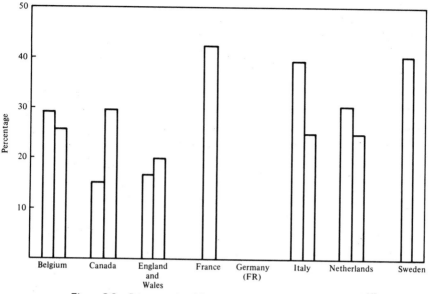

Figure 3.9. Private and public pupil per teacher enrollment, 1970.

the use of aides is seen as a way of helping disadvantaged adults get a start in a career development program; the aides may be promoted to assistant teacher and perhaps ultimately to head teacher. This last concept is only in its infancy in some of these countries. In places such as Sweden, and England and Wales, the use of aides is well advanced.

Table 3.10 and Figure 3.10 indicate that the number of teachers involved in preschool education has increased greatly over the 10-year period between 1960 and 1970. In all cases, increases reflect the expanding enrollments shown for the same time period in Table 3.5 and Figure 3.5. In six of the eight countries the percentage of increase in number of teachers is greater than the percentage of increase in enrollments, reflecting the declining pupil-teacher ratio documented in Table 3.9 and Figure 3.9.

There are two exceptions to this general trend. These are England and Wales, and Sweden, where greater use is made of teacher aides and paraprofessionals. In England and Wales, the greatest growth in preschool provision has taken place in play-groups, which depend heavily on the use of parent volunteers. The play-group movement is the middle-class answer to the problem of finding space for their young children when the public sector does not or cannot respond to the demand for early childhood education. This is not reflected in Table 3.10 or Figure 3.10. In Sweden, there is extensive use of teacher aides. If these factors are taken into account, then it can be stated that in all countries the pupil-adult ratio over the 10-year period has decreased.

TABLE 3.10
Number of Teachers

	1960	1970	% of increase
Belgium	11,890	16,992	42.9
Canada	4,170	16,580	297.6
England and Wales	1,432	1,506	5.2
France	26,646	43,500	63.3
Germany (F.R.)	35,000	50,000	42.8
Italy	31,441	44,413	41.3
Netherlands	11,537	15,954	38.3
Sweden	1,237	3,187	158.9

Average Percent of Increase: 55.8

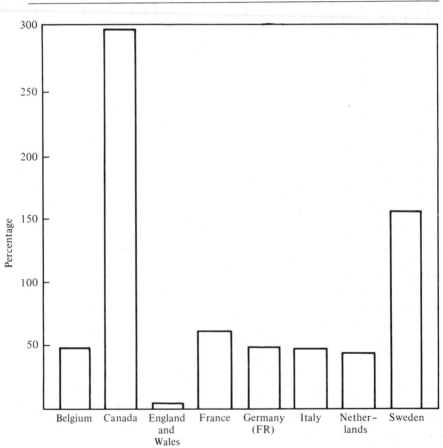

Figure 3.10. Percentage increase in number of teachers, 1960–1970.

Parent Involvement

In all the countries investigated, there is discussion and debate about the need to involve parents at all levels of schooling. In preschool, parental involvement has long been judged important. Mothers and preschool teachers in all countries commonly meet and discuss the child's needs and problems. There is a demand for even greater parental involvement on the part of some parents. They want to be involved in the choice of curriculum and the planning and organizing of the preschool. These trends are most evident in Sweden, England and Wales, and Germany (FR).

Teacher Training and Education

The course work taken by students preparing to be preschool teachers is quite similar in all eight nations. All include concern for the physical, intellectual, emotional, and social growth. The courses offered include the study of the psychology and development of young children, sociological history, philosophy, and theory and method of preschool education. In addition, such subjects as geography, mathematics, natural science, hygiene, the language of the country, music, art, home and family life, and a variety of similar subjects are part of the curriculum. Many countries are now including courses in ecology which cut across formerly separate subject areas. All countries have their students participate in student-teacher experiences of varying frequency and length of time. Many teachers (both those being trained and those doing the training) believe that student-teaching situations are potentially the most helpful. In all countries, in-service course work and graduate study are increasingly being offered by schools and colleges of education.

As Table 3.11 and Figure 3.11 indicate, teacher training starts at the youngest age in Italy, at 14, and lasts about 3 years. Canada and Germany have the lowest requirements for teacher training, as little as 1 year beyond the junior or senior year in a Canadian high school. German preschool training consists of a 2-year program in a technical school. The most stringent requirements are found in France, where there is a strong professional teachers' organization. France requires 4 years of training with a secondary school education, and 2 years with a baccalaureate, plus an examination. Most programs in the eight countries take place in teacher training colleges or colleges of education, except in Germany where prospective preschool teachers are trained in a special secondary technical school.

According to interviews and discussions the author had with various teachers and school administrators, there seems to be no feeling that important differences arise in the academic achievement of children in preschools as a result of

TABLE 3.11
Teacher Education

Country	Age of Admittance	Institute	Years of Study
Belgium	15	Teacher training college	4
Canada	17–18	Teacher training college	1–4
		(incorporated in the universities)	1–3
England and Wales	18	College of Education	3 + 1 opt. special studies
France	15	Teacher training college	4
	18	Teacher training college	2
	18	Practical training	2
Germany (F.R.)	16	Special Secondary Technical School	2
Italy	14	College of Education	3
Netherlands	15–16	Teacher training college	3
Sweden	19	College of Education	2

having teachers from a particular type of training program. This supports the thesis proposed by Coleman (1966), in his report entitled "Equality of Educational Opportunity," which stated that, in the early grades, teacher education or preparation does not seem to be an important variable. Some recent studies by International Educational Achievement (IEA) suggest that teacher preparation in the sciences and languages does affect student achievement in junior and senior high school. This difference seems to be a function of the number of courses taken in a subject area rather than in method courses on how to teach.

These are such paradoxical findings that they confound teacher training efforts. Long-held assumptions about what is important in terms of teacher training need much educational research in future years. Successful teachers seem to have, in general, three characteristics, at least as judged by principals, parents, children, and administrators with whom the author discussed the issue. It must be kept carefully in mind that these are subjective judgments and have no basis in empirical fact. Successful preschool teachers seem to have

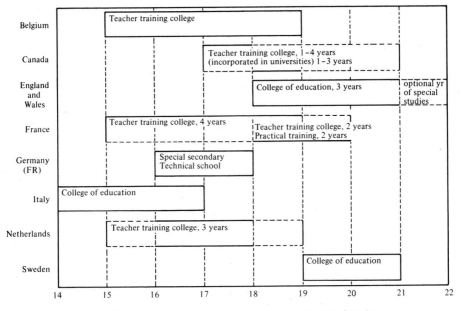

Figure 3.11. Teacher education: starting age, and length of study.

1. High verbal skills.
2. Knowledge of subject matter (in the case of preschool this means child growth and development).
3. A desire to be with children.

The listing is not meant to be a priority listing and another author might use different words or phrases, but in general, these are representative.

Cost and Financial Support

The cost of and government allocations for preschool education varies considerably among the countries and is reflected in Table 3:12 and Figure 3:12. In the school year 1970-1971, the per pupil cost of preschool education in these eight countries ranged from a high of 621 US dollars in Sweden to a low of 110 US dollars in France. Cost seems to be related, at least in part, to the pupil-teacher ratio, therefore, in Sweden the cost of the preschool program is substantially higher than in France as shown in Table 3.12. In Belgium, where the pupil-teacher ratio decreased by approximately 20% from a 34:1 ratio in 1960 to a 27:1 ratio in 1970, the cost of preschool education rose by 100%. In countries with constant ratios over the 10 years, such as France, and England and Wales, the cost rose only by 13.4% and 12%, respectively.

The source of financial support for preschool education in the eight countries

TABLE 3.12
Rate of Growth of Recurrent Per-Pupil Costs, 1965-1970[a]

	1965	1970	% of increase
Belgium	106	212	100.0
Canada	110	264	140.0
England and Wales	384[b]	430[b]	12.0
France	97	110	13.4
Germany (F.R.)	n.a.[c]	162[d]	
Italy	n.a.	104[d]	
Netherlands	125	144	15.2
Sweden	459	621	35.3

Average Percent of Increase, 1965-1970: 52.5

[a]Cost in U.S. dollars.

[b]Cost of nursery schools--no information is available on cost of nursery classes or playgroups.

[c]Not available.

[d]Estimated.

is closely related to the administrative responsibility for it. In Belgium, France, and The Netherlands, most of the money (90-95%) comes from the national government. In general, in these three countries, the local or regional authorities are responsible for the construction and maintenance of buildings. The national government reimburses them for a portion of these capital costs which range from 40% to 80%.

In Canada and Germany (FR), the national government makes little contribution to preschool education. Funds are raised at the regional level or paid by parents. In England and Wales, Sweden, and Italy, most of the money is raised at the local level.

The expenditures shown for preschools in Table 3.12 indicate a rather substantial difference across these eight countries. Table 3.13 provides data on the percentage of GNP each country allocates for all education. Canada and Sweden spend the largest percentage of their GNP on education; they are also third and first, respectively, in their expenditures on preschool. France, however, is next to last in percentage of GNP spent on education and eighth in amount of money spent on preschool education.

School Size and Number of Classrooms

Another factor concerning the similarities and differences of preschool programs is the size of the school and the number of classrooms. Across the eight nations, the average size of schools varies greatly. On the one hand, in Sweden

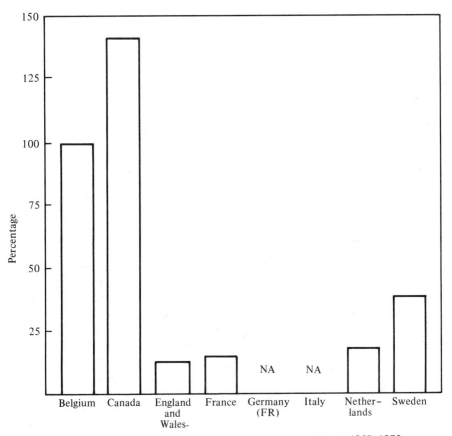

Figure 3.12. Percentage increase in recurrent per pupil cost, 1965–1970.

there are one-classroom schools of 40 children. On the other hand, in France there are eight-classroom schools with an approximate enrollment of 200 children. The average, however, is three-classroom schools with a total number of children varying from 60 to 90 and mixed in ages from 2 to 6. In this "average" situation, there are usually one school director and three professional teachers. Depending on the country, there might be additional teacher aides or parent volunteers.

Size of school is an interesting research variable. In terms of children's expected achievement gains as a result of a preschool experience, school size might be a more important variable than pupil-teacher ratio. This is especially true where one of the goals is to foster interpersonal growth. In the smaller preschool, there seems to be a greater sense of community. Larger preschools seem to take on a more businesslike way of doing things, which tends to decrease interaction and a feeling of caring.

TABLE 3.13
Percent of GNP Spent on Education by Each Country , 1969

	Percent of GNP
Belgium	4.97
Canada	8.35
France	4.75
Germany (F.R.)	3.08
Italy	5.80
Netherlands	6.86
Sweden	7.91
United Kingdom	4.97

Source: OECD Economic Surveys, 1973.

Instructional Methods and Aids

Instructional methods and approaches vary widely. Where the pupil-teacher ratio is high, as in France and Italy, structured, carefully planned programs are characteristic. In England and Wales, and Canada, where the ratio is comparatively low, the program is unstructured and child-oriented. This difference also reflects the varying traditions and orientations of early childhood education in the individual countries. For instance, in France the historical provision of child care for the poor evolved into the present system. However, provision in Canada came from middle-class families where social-emotional growth was of highest concern. Sweden exemplifies a country with a major instructional and curricular commitment to social and emotional development of children in preschools. The Swedes' most important educational concern is that people in their society learn to live in a cooperative manner. They also stress the development of a positive self-concept or self-image. A major difference between Sweden and the other countries is seen in its stress on total development as opposed to the emphasis on health or welfare or academic achievement.

The use of a variety of audio-visual material is widespread in all countries covered in this study. The use of films, film strips, and record players is extensive. The use of tape recorders is growing, particularly for use in dramatic play and in speech improvement. The use of educational television is an important issue of debate. In those countries where radio and television are state controlled, some attempts have been made. The adaptation of the American preschool program called Sesame Street has been tried in some countries. The results of this experiment have been mixed. The debate around this issue in England and Wales provides the reader with some insight into the discussion surrounding the uses of educational television.

The use of television as a medium for instructing young children has had a rather mixed reception in England. The *Times*, reporting on the results of a pilot study on Sesame Street in 1972, suggested that the receptivity of parents and children to Sesame Street was very high. Bogatz and Ball (1971), in reviewing the reception of Sesame Street in England, have the following to say:

> Perhaps the most publicized criticism of the show's style was made by Monica Simms of the British Broadcasting Corporation. In justifying the BBC's decision not to show *Sesame Street*, but to show *Huckleberry Hound* and *Yogi Bear*, she argued that *Sesame Street* had "authoritarian aims," evidenced in its intent to change children's behavior. (Apparently *Yogi Bear* is more democratic since it does not attempt to teach.) [p. 8].

In addition, they argued that Sesame Street used techniques normally used in television commercials. The *Times* article goes on to indicate as an alternative that the English children were in fact to be allowed to watch "Rainbow," "Inigo," "Pipkin," and "Mr. Thimble" in the fall of 1972. The *Times'* authors noted that they hoped that the producers would take advantage of both the experiences of Sesame Street and of the English reactions to it. It should be pointed out that in England the private television stations do show Sesame Street and it is rated as being heavily viewed.

Educational television in each country will have to be tailored to meet that individual nation's goals and objectives. All countries, however, feel it is a promising avenue to explore and will be looking at its potential carefully in the years ahead.

Research in Early Childhood Education

Research on preschool education in the eight countries investigated takes place under the auspices of both the individual governments in universities and research centers and in private organizations and foundations. Much of the work under way concerns cognitive development, particularly language skills, since it is the absence of these skills which seems to affect children from disadvantaged homes most adversely. Many researchers feel that more specificity is needed in developing instructional programs. This is based on findings that better results are obtained where programs are well-planned, with well-defined objectives and evaluation procedures. The application of various learning theories by a number of educational theorists such as Piaget, Wallon, Froebel, Decroly, Gesell, Langeveld, and Montessori represents a quest for a more valuable preschool experience for all children.

Summary

The question addressed in the third section was whether the similarities and differences between the countries have any real effect on children's academic achievement. This question is difficult to assess. A review of the eight countries has revealed some similarities and differences among such factors as organization and administration, physical facilities, pupil-teacher ratio, and teacher training and education, to mention a few. Perhaps of more interest is that despite the similarities and differences, few, if any, differences among children's academic achievement in the eight countries are apparent.

This statement is based on the author's recent observations and discussions with preschool educators, not hard empirical evidence. This leads the author to conclude that the manipulation of a single variable, such as age of entry, organization, curriculum, methods of instruction, or teacher training by itself is not important enough or strong enough to modify a pupil's performance in preschool. It might be productive, however, to manipulate a number of these variables in a planned way with constant evaluation for the achievement of a particular goal.

Earlier evaluation reports indicated that preschool programs that emphasized cognitive development tended to be successful for the poor, isolated, or recent immigrant children when structured and carefully planned. This suggests that a good deal more structure and careful planning than presently exists in most countries is needed in the preschool programs for the poor. This perception of the need for careful planning has received attention only recently and is currently one of the major subjects of on-going educational research.

In planning more structured preschool programs, the American experience with Head Start should be considered. As noted, Head Start evaluations indicated that most of the benefits of early school experience for the poor were apparently lost in primary school when no Follow Through programs were provided.

It is important to recall, therefore, that in almost all of the eight countries preschool programs were initiated in response to the health and welfare needs of poor children. Middle-class interest and involvement in ECE along with interest in children's cognitive development and achievement have been more recent concerns of preschool programs.

If intellectual achievement and equality of educational opportunity are to be realized goals, plans for them must take into consideration how children from different socioeconomic levels approach learning. Research seems to indicate that poor children attain greater achievement in structured, well planned, preschool programs, while middle-class children attain higher achievement in flexible preschool programs. When programs are not planned and administered to optimize benefits for the child, the child does not gain as much as he otherwise could. In addition, it must be remembered that ECE programs cannot be considered by themselves, but must be looked at within the context of the family and the situation in which the child is living.

REVIEW OF RECENT RESEARCH EFFORTS

The fourth issue of concern was directed toward obtaining information on preschool educational research efforts. In these eight countries, research with preschool education is still in its infancy. The following material presented is aimed toward giving the reader a feeling for the areas in which the different governments and university researchers are expending their money and effort. These efforts reflect different areas of emphasis and points of view.

England and Wales

In the last 15 years, some excellent research has been done on young children in England and Wales. There have been both cross-sectional and longitudinal studies. Four areas which need further work have been identified by Dr. W. D. Wall in a speech at OMEP in September, 1972.

1. The period of time between birth and age 5 is known to be extremely important in the development of a child. There is a great need to study the interaction of biological components, the environment, and early learning. There has not been much progress beyond Cyril Burt's in the 1920s, which documented the high correlation between social class and achievement.

2. There are three major domains of research concern: the cognitive, the affective, and the emotional. We need much more information on how environment, learning order, and feedback affect these domains. The work of the Newsons here is of particular importance.

3. Much more needs to be known about language usage and associated learning styles. Bernstein's writing and research should be pursued and extended.

4. Research is badly needed on the optimal conditions under which the first separation of parent and child should take place for any prolonged period of time, as in attending preschool. Clearly this will not be the same age for all children. The work of the Robertsons offers important information on this area of concern.

One of several researchers working in the area of preschool education is Dr. A. Halsey of Nuffield College, Oxford. He offers three general conclusions about preschool and child development, particularly as it concerns children from disadvantaged homes.

First, preschool is the most effective educational instrument for applying the principle of positive discrimination. This conviction rests partly on the theory that primary and secondary educational attainment has its social foundations in the child's experience in the preschool years, and partly on the evidence that positive discrimination at the preschool level can have a multiplying effect on the overwhelmingly important educative influences of the family and the peer group to which the child belongs.

Second, if properly understood, preschooling is a point at which the networks of family and formal education can most easily be linked.

Third, there is no unique blueprint of either organization or content which could be applied mechanically as national policy.

Some interesting research has been done in England that has ramifications for those educators involved in planning and evaluating preschool curricula. For example, Davie et al. (1972), in *From Birth to Seven*, make note of the effect that home environment has on children's development. A review of this book in *Education* (June 9, 1972) discusses home environment and concludes:

> ... the average gap in reading attainment between the children from unskilled families and those from professional families was found to be well over two years at the age of seven. However, disadvantage is cumulative, so that the gap between the least advantaged—those from large families, with an unskilled father, living in overcrowded homes and with poor amenities—and the most advantaged children was on average over four years [p. 545].

Crellin, Pringle, and West (1972), in *Born Illegitimate*, compare the school abilities of legitimate, adopted illegitimate, and illegitimate children, using the same data base and testing age as used in Davie's work. They found that quality of performance is strongly associated with whether the child is legitimate, adopted illegitimate, or illegitimate. In short, the legitimate child performs most ably and the nonadopted illegitimate child performs most poorly.

Psycholinguistics is another important area of research which has a direct bearing on preschool curriculum planning. The direct effects on language skills of some parent-child interactions have been reported by John and Elizabeth Newson (1968) in *Four Years Old in an Urban Community*. They found that differences in discipline methods had important implications for a child's later schooling. Middle-class mothers who discipline their children through verbal interaction instill important language skills. Working-class children do not develop these skills, since their mothers tend to discipline them by using nonverbal techniques.

The Plowden Survey (1967), one of the best known research studies in the area of early childhood education, showed that, taken together, the variables of parental attitudes and home circumstances account for the very substantial portion of the variance in performance, and that parental influence is important to children as students, especially to older children. One of the most heartening developments is increased parental involvement in the problems of preschool education. Parental involvement is seen as an important area of research activity in the future in England and Wales.

Belgium

As was noted in Table 3.8, the Belgians are already enrolling most young children in preschool, therefore, it is important to remember that the Belgians face problems of improving the overall quality of existing education rather than the creation of a whole new system. One must also keep in mind that there are *two* ministries of education, one for the Dutch-speaking portion of Belgium and one for the French-speaking, with research being coordinated between the ministries.

There are several main areas of research. First, there is the creation and evaluation of nursery school programs for children *less* than 3 years old and, as a result of this interest, the extending and restructuring of the programs in preschools. The following organization has been suggested by the commissions:

1. *Creches* from 0 to 18 or 24 months.
2. One prenursery class for the 2- to 3-year-olds.
3. Two classes for the 3- to 5-year-olds.
4. Two classes of transition for the 5- to 7-year-olds (the legal age for compulsory education would consequently become 5 instead of 6).

In this broader context, varied but related child-services such as family planning consultation, prenatal consultation, infant consultation, a mini-*creche* to receive children according to the parents' needs, and a nursery school with a center of leisure for young children, would all be offered at this one place, and parents would be involved in the organization and management of the center. Evaluation studies are now being done on the component services of these centers to see how the diversified agencies could work together.

The ministries of education commission also meets to discuss ways of adapting new research findings to preschool programs; it is especially interested in the psychological development of the child, and in applying new research findings and techniques in the areas of mathematics, language, music, and psychomotor education.

All of these proposed structural and program changes are a consequence of the general effort begun several years ago at the secondary level to renovate the entire educational system in Belgium. A number of the first recommendations addressed to the primary schools also apply to the preschools. Decroly's most important principle was "education for life by living." Some of his most important teachings are

1. Education should begin with the child and develop from there.
2. There should be less teaching for best teaching, that is, more of a "child discover for himself" teaching approach and less of a didactic one.

3. The teacher should seek to form more than inform.
4. There should be intensive practice of language and mathematics.

A second area of research interest is the development of tests and the testing of maturity and "school readiness" of children at the end of preschool; immaturity is believed to be one of the significant factors in the high repetition rate of first-year primary children, especially in French-speaking parts of the country. Suggestions that have come out of research in this area include a later school start, obligatory school readiness tests, and the creation of special schools for repeaters.

Another aspect of the study of maturity that has aroused special interest is an attempt to differentiate the early childhood education programs, adapting the curriculum to meet the special cognitive and psychomotor developmental problems of children who are mentally and physically handicapped. This includes research into socioeconomic and cultural variables which affect the school performance of these preschoolers. There are several organizations doing research in this area.

In Brussels, the *Service de Psychologie Genetique* in the Free University is doing fundamental work on the relationship between particular features in the environment and the degree of psychological development in children from birth to 7 years old. In Mons, three lines of inquiry are being pursued by the *Service des Sciences Psychopedagogiques*: (*1*) the progressive development of activities for the improvement of cognitive functions; (*2*) the improvement of material conditions and social relations at home and at school; and (*3*) the adaptation of practical educational means for use by parents with their own children. A number of projects are being conducted to try to improve the skills and aptitudes necessary for teaching preschool children. An intensive training project for children of 5 and 6 years of age has recently been started by the Educational Department in Antwerp on an experimental basis. The emphasis here is on activities that develop and train observational techniques, verbal expression, psychomotor development, and behavior of children in a group. An experimental program in mathematics for preschool children, introduced in September, 1972, gives a relatively detailed outline of how to teach mathematics. Its intention is not to teach the subject systematically, but to provoke the child's curiosity and intellectual activity. Other projects in Ghent and Liège are concerning themselves with aspects of (*1*) visual-motor education, the use of language, and concept formation, and (*2*) the diagnostic evaluation of sociocultural handicaps.

Although related in many ways to the work described above, the major research effort in Belgium is being directed toward the educational needs of disadvantaged children. Special attention is being given to psychological and social (cultural) as well as cognitive and physical development of disadvantaged children and ways to improve that development. An interuniversity project, started in 1969 and funded by the Van Leer Foundation, has been directed at compensations for sociocultural handicaps affecting children from birth to 7 years of age. Its stated objectives are: first, to determine the origin of affective and cognitive handicaps imputable to socioeconomic and cultural conditions and to identify the preschool programs that provide the prerequisite skills needed for primary schools and, second, to define the theoretical basis and optimal forms of a preschool education that will prevent the development of handicaps.

Germany

The Federal Republic of Germany clearly recognizes the potential value of research in the solving of many of its educational problems. The document "Educational Organization and Development in the Federal Republic of Germany 1970–71" emphasizes the need for a broadly based scientific research program embracing a large number of experiments.

Among the establishments now actively conducting research are

1. The German Institute for International Educational Research in Frankfurt whose interests include investigations of the sociology of the teacher, economic analyses of educational installations, and the development and trying out of curricula.

2. The Institute for Education Research in the Max Planck Society (Berlin), which is engaged, in particular, in basic research on factors that influence pupil performance, relations between education and behavior in the vocational world, and social processes in early childhood.

3. The University of Constance, which has several groups investigating, variously, educational planning, effects of the educational processes, and influences in teaching.

4. The Education Center in Berlin, which is primarily interested in curriculum development and providing academic advice for school experiments in science.

5. The State Institute for Educational Research and Planning in Munich, which provides academic advice for developments in the Bavarian school system and compiles data for regional educational planning.

Germany is now primarily interested in extending the school system downward to include 5-year-olds. It is hoped that the provision of preprimary education will eliminate some of the problems children from rural or low socioeconomic homes experience in primary school.

Preschool research efforts in The Federal Republic of Germany are oriented toward the compensation model. For example, there are a number of projects directed at the disadvantaged and the children of foreign workers. These pilot programs are located in Nord Rhine, Westphalia, Hesse, Hamburg, and Berlin.

Another research effort in creating a community kindergarten is being studied in Munich. Its orientation is to help the children, the school, and the community work more closely. It stresses the importance of helping the child understand some of the social problems the industrial society has created.

Sweden

In Sweden, an intensive educational research and curriculum development effort is underway. The aim of this effort is to identify beneficial kindergarten experiences for children. One important guiding principal, coming directly from the teaching of Arnold Gesell, is that the choice of experiences offered must always be made with due regard for the child's level of maturity.

What the educational researchers are seeking, as in Belgium, is a preschool program that meets the individual needs of young children. The driving force behind this effort is a concern that the *whole* child be seen as an entity to be developed, not just his mind. To this end, programs on different levels for different subjects may have to be planned for the same child. (Note that this is a different and more comprehensive concern than that specially aimed at "disadvantaged" children.)

A study conducted by Sverud and Stukat of existing preschool programs concluded that preschool achieves its most evident impact in areas where some kind of direct teaching takes place. They found this to be true in the area of social and emotional growth as well as cognitive growth. Stukat's results provided the main impetus for a new project aimed at the development of an experimental preschool program with the following main features:

1. The program is a supplement to the existing activities in preschool, planned to cover one-third of the preschool day.
2. The areas chosen for innovation are the same as those chosen by the Royal Preschool Commission (social training, communication skill, and concept formation).
3. The program is planned mainly for 6-year-olds.
4. The program will focus on making the preschool goals more concrete than usual. An attempt has been made to give the teachers examples of how concrete activities can be derived from general objectives.
5. The program has drawn upon ideas of Nomburger, Wrikson, Piaget, and Skinner.

In connection with the Stukat project, two special substudies are being conducted: (*1*) moral development in children from 4 to 8 years old viewed from multidimensional aspects, and (*2*) treatment of aggressive behavior in children in the preschool age groups.

Besides the evaluation of the preschools themselves, several studies are investigating the methodology and individually-adjusted teaching programs. Sandels, in Stockholm, is attempting to describe and measure the effects of learning in nursery school and to follow this up on the same children during their first term in the comprehensive school. The factors investigated were: general ability, reading and writing ability, maturity of behavior in traffic, color-form knowledge, musical knowledge, comprehension, social relationship, and creativity. The Linkoping preschool project concerned the effects of individually adjusted teaching in reading and writing for 6-year-olds in the preschool; these children will be followed through to grade 3 in the elementary school (see Sverud and Stukat).

Still other emotional and cultural variables affecting preschoolers are being studied by Kärrby and Sandels. (Kärrby's project on moral development of children concluded that the child's identification with parents and the emotional home climate are of chief importance in moral development. On the basis of his results, Kärrby has designed another project with the purpose of influencing certain aspects of social behavior, cooperation, and self-perception.)

Sandels's project directs itself to the emotionally disturbed children in preschool programs; the objectives are: (*1*) to construct and test methods to study the cognitive development of 5- and 6-year-olds; (*2*) to study the cognitive development of emotionally disturbed children in the preschool programs; (*3*) to describe the current working methods in preschools; and (*4*) to describe a way that a child-psychologist consultant could be used in the preschool programs.

The decision in Sweden to provide a more universal nursery schools organization (primarily for 5- and 6-year-olds) has initiated other research programs aimed at developing an optional organizational pattern for cooperation between nursery school and compulsory schools. The emphasis is not only on the organizational arrangements that would result from cooperation, but also on what consequences an easier and more natural transition to primary school might have on the compulsory school itself.

One project started in 1969-1970 in Malmo is described by Birgitta Gran (1972). She gives the main aims of the project:

1. To consider and compare objectives for teaching 6- and 7-year-old children, in which the target should be a direct adjustment between the activities of preschool and the teaching of primary school.
2. To invent, construct, test, and revise study materials and working methods that can be used in a modified preschool and comprehensive school system.
3. To investigate forms for cooperation between preschool and primary school, including a more intensive and immediate cooperation between teachers than exists at present.
4. To study possible ways of complementing family care, upbringing, teaching, and skill-training, paying particular attention to socially handicapped pupils.

5. To study and construct an upgraded school level encompassing both preschool and primary school.

This project is being conducted in three experimental areas: (*1*) methods and materials, (*2*) organization of collaboration, and (*3*) social psychology.

Another project, located at the Institute of Educational Research in Stockholm, is looking at methods of evaluating the effects of programs for young children. To acquire the data necessary for such evaluation, experiments are organized in three areas similar to the Gran project already described.

1. Method-materials with the purpose of giving the preschool new content.
2. Organization, with the purpose of constructing a nongraded school extending over 4 years.
3. Social psychology, with the purpose of making an inventory of the number of children with social handicaps and aiding them as effectively as possible with a supporting program.

The preschool commission also initiated a project to study (physically) handicapped children and ways to effectively integrate them into the (preschool) school system. The Swedes do not believe it is a good idea to have separate programs for handicapped children. They want to bring all children together in the same classroom as early as possible. They believe that it is important for normal children and handicapped to learn early how to live and play together. They believe this will be beneficial to both, since it will not foster the development of a variety of prejudices as isolation does.

The development of a universal preschool curriculum, with appropriate and beneficial experiences for kindergarten children (including some helping experiences for the disadvantaged) is the objective of the Swedish people. To this end the Swedish preschool educators want to develop individualized programs for each child, based not only on his cognitive development but on his unique level of maturity and his multidimensional functioning as a whole person. The preschool program will stress continuity between the preschool and primary school stages. For Swedish 5- and 6-year-olds, this will mean a concern for the total development of the child, not just preparation for the academic part of primary school.

France

The French are interested in the overall development of a comprehensive preschool program. Research is not being conducted in areas related to cultural disadvantage; Reuchlin (1971) examined the relationship between socioeconomic class and intelligence. He concluded that there are real differences across socioeconomic classes and that this observation is not the result of biased tests.

He believes that to explain these differences one should start from a cognitive theory such as Hebb's or Piaget's; Reuchlin argues that we need to take the factors of social environment into account when formulating a theory of development. The French wish to do research on learning theory which can be applied to all children, not just the disadvantaged.

In an experiment directed by Claud Saint Marc (1971) on individualized instruction, particular attention was paid to children who were commonly thought to have learning difficulties or were predicted to have learning difficulties when they reached primary school. These children came together in small groups twice a week and received structured language exercises which resulted in a considerable reduction in the number of repeaters.

Research under the leadership of Jean Vial aimed to create closer coordination between preprimary schools and the first class in compulsory school, and to evolve a pedagogical unity for the first three classes of primary school. The provision for a smooth transfer from preschool to primary school is a research topic of great interest to the French, and much research emphasis will be placed on it in the next few years. This research is being done under the direction of the *Inspectrices Générales.*

The two major research institutes concerned with research on young children are

1. The *Institut Pedagogique,* which is presently studying: identification of problems children have making a smooth transition from home to preschool, early diagnosis of deficiencies, development of spoken language, and the problems inherent in transition to a written language, motor development, and the development of the power of logical reasoning of young children.

2. The *Centre de Recherche de l'Education Specialisée et de l'Adaptation Scolaire,* which is studying the following group of topics: language and school problems, cognition and school problems; school and parent reaction to school failures, a sociological study of school failure, and a clinical study of school problems.

Also located in France are a number of other international institutions concerned with educational research on young children. The best known is perhaps the International Children's Center. The World Organization for Early Childhood Education, an international, nongovernmental group located in Paris, is fostering research on early childhood education.

Canada

In the last 10 years, much research has been done in Canada on the problems of educating young children. One of the major concerns is simply providing enough places for 3- to 5-year-olds in the preschool system. Although many agencies sponsor early childhood education programs as a way of equalizing educational opportunities, there are major differences in the educational content of these programs. Ryan (1971) questioned whether preschools have any lasting helping effects at all upon disadvantaged children. He recommended the following changes in the kindergarten program:

First, an increased emphasis upon the operational specificity of programs is needed. This was based on his observation that, with few exceptions, program goals are vaguely stated and adequate program descriptions are virtually nonexistent.

Second, in order to develop sophisticated intervention research strategies, a conceptual framework with goals, program features, and behaviors to be measured should be created.

Third, a set of guidelines were proposed for the evaluation of research. Especially it was proposed that evaluations be conducted at the intermediate stages of programs, a practice that might lead to alterations in program content. During the last few years, large amounts of time, talent, and money have been expended in an attempt to meet Ryan's three recommendations.

In the area of educational research competence, the creation of the Ontario Institute for Studies in Education has brought world acclaim to Canada for the excellence of its work. Evaluation studies by Bereiter, Fowler, and others have come to the following conclusions:

1. The Bereiter-Engelmann type program has clearly had more impact on IQ and achievement than the traditional, child-centered approach, but not necessarily more impact than other programs with a strong instructional emphasis.

2. The "traditional" nursery-school and kindergarten program is not a serious contender as an educational program. Not only has the "traditional" approach failed to achieve results comparable, in cognitive learning, to the more instructional approaches: It has failed to demonstrate any redeeming advantages.

3. The long-term effects of preschool instruction are about as good as can be expected; no preschool program shows any promise of making, by itself, any permanent difference in the scholastic success of poor children.

Evaluations of the Montessori methods of teaching preschool have been reviewed by Meizitis (1971). She found that a structured environment was more effective with disadvantaged children than unstructured programs, but that the same structured program was too restrictive for some middle-class children.

One study specifically aimed at preschool enrichment was done by Clark (1969), of Dalhousie University. His experimental group of children gained significantly in intelligence over the preschool year, but lost their advantage because the subsequent academic programs were not structured to support this cognitive growth. He also concluded that more *parental* education was needed to help children retain their gains from the enrichment program.

In other areas of interest, Fowler's (1971) research in teaching reading came to the conclusion that ". . . a mental age of 4 is close to the watershed of developmental readiness for reading . . . [p. 123]" and that ". . . Reading must logically wait upon the *consolidation* of the two-dimensional sequential coordinations of language prior to a child undertaking the more complex three-dimensional coordinations of reading [p. 123]." Therefore, reading readiness skills are more suitable instruction for children who have not attained a mental age of 4 than is formal reading instruction.

Two important policy questions raised are

1. If it is granted that education for poor children must be improved over the whole span of school years, then is it any longer necessary or practical to invest heavily in preschool education for such children?
2. Is there justification for heavy investment in a continued search for more effective methods of preschool education, or have the limits of effectiveness been reached?

The Netherlands

The Netherlands is just beginning to do empirical studies of education. Much time is now being spent on the development of instruments and techniques of doing research in the social sciences. To promote educational research, the Foundation for Educational Research was established by the Ministry of Education in December, 1965. The Foundation is responsible for the planning, coordination, and stimulation of educational research, and is the single sponsor of work that could be classified as basic research; the promotion of research takes the form of funding rather than the foundation itself doing the research. Most research is done in universities and university institutes. Several grants have been made to local school systems by the foundation. Grants are also made to the pedagogical centers founded by the national associations of nongovernmental schools. These pedagogical centers are deeply involved in curriculum research for the different school systems (primarily religious) which they represent.

The main area of practical interest for The Netherlands preschool researchers relates to the determination of how the home environment affects children's readiness for school; consequently much work is being done on compensatory and enrichment programs. These are attempting to identify areas of strength or weakness in present preschool programs and to find methods for improving them. A significant proportion of the research currently in progress is trying to evaluate the general benefits of previous preschool education for the older student. One special project in the northern part of The Netherlands, Project Friesland, is trying to determine the effects that bilingualism has on children attending monolingual schools.

Among several enrichment and compensatory studies is the University of Utrecht's project, funded by the Foundation for Educational Research, to help disadvantaged children. Disadvantaged children in The Netherlands would be identified as caravan or canal boat dwellers and inner-city slum residents. The following priority order has been set up to offer help to (*1*) the child, (*2*) the family, and (*3*) the community.

Three distinct research efforts were conceived at the Institute for Pedagogic Studies and the University of Utrecht—all with the same aim—to give the children of unskilled workers the best possible start in elementary school. The overall evaluation results are similar to those noted in the US Head Start programs, which indicate that improvement can be expected only in those areas of cognition or skill development that are specifically taught. Other projects focused on kindergarten and first-form elementary children are being conducted in Haarlem, Utrecht, and Enschede.

In another enrichment program, Dr. van Calcar trained teachers in remedial techniques and got parents actively interested in specific projects concerning their children; his results showed the remedial techniques and parental involvement to be successful. Dr. van Calcar is also directing a project investigating four specific aspects of intervention which involve: (*1*) educational help, that is, teacher in-service training, (*2*) building links between school and family, (*3*) building links between school and the community, and (*4*) provision of programs which foster social and emotional growth in children.

Preschool research efforts in The Netherlands reflect many points of view about where help is needed and who should provide it. The major effort at the moment seems to follow the American deficit model.

Italy

Preschool in Italy is clearly seen as a preparation for primary school entrance, and much research is directed at providing optimal preparation and compensation for culturally disadvantaged children. Studies are going on in several areas, including language competence, effects of various socioeconomic backgrounds, and parental involvement.

In the area of language ability, Parisi (1969) identified some aspects of language deficiencies of Italian children who were about to enter the first grade. Three substudies were undertaken, and it was found that socially disadvantaged children begin elementary school with serious deficiencies in many aspects of their language, but that preschool experience can be of real help in making up for that.

Interest in disadvantaged children is evidenced in several studies on the causes of various kinds of underachievement in culturally disadvantaged preschool children and kinds of preventive intervention that can be provided.

Andreani and Cavallini (1970) have conducted a 4-year study into causes of underachievement of disadvantaged children and pedagogical intervention to overcome such causes. Their areas of inquiry include study of the environmental factors (family, status) which affect the intelligence; study of environmental factors that have an influence on the formation of personality traits and the socialization process; the relationship between social class and language skill; the typical profile of the underachievers compared with the normal and overachievers; a definition of techniques of intervention to rehabilitate the underachievers; and experimentation with such techniques.

At the University of Pavia, researchers are trying to identify the factors that influence school achievement and maladjustment. They wish to try out intervention methods designed to prevent the effects of cultural deprivation in early childhood. The results obtained document the important influences of social and family conditions on the development of abilities and personality traits that underlie achievement in school. One solution suggested is that the teacher should seek to foster intellectual curiosity on the part of the child. Methods for doing this are now under study.

Research conducted by Rumi and Gualco (1970) is concerned with the smooth transfer of young children from home to school. Particular focus is on community environment, the role of parents, and the personality of the teacher.

The major research center for early childhood education is the *Centro Didattico Nazionale per la Scuola Materna,* in Brescia; its original charter assigned to it seven specific tasks:

1. To initiate pedagogical studies in preschool education.
2. To promote and guide experimental research that will help preschools prepare children for entry to the primary schools.
3. To study the present state of the art of preschool education in Italy and to make recommendations to the ministry for its improvement.
4. To keep parents, teachers, and educational administrators aware of the importance of preschool education.
5. To organize a center concerned primarily with preschool education and through this to provide courses for teachers and administrators to assist them in perfecting the methods they use.
6. To promote meetings between parents and preschool teachers to facilitate understanding of the child's problems on transition from home to school, and of the objectives of the preschool itself.
7. To create an understanding of the particular role of the preschool by publishing material relevant to teachers and to parents about the education of young children, both in Italy and elsewhere.

Much curriculum work on preschool education is being done in Italy, but as yet there are few major research efforts underway.

Summary

The concern of the preceding material has been to construct an overview of the research efforts in the eight countries. They represent widely divergent points of view on the importance of preschool education and the orientation which it should take. Yet, one clear finding seems to emerge from this effort. That is, whatever the goals of preschool education, the achievement of them will be more certain if the program reflects the following characteristics:

1. Its values and practices are in consonance with those of the parents, teachers, and community.
2. Its organizational characteristics reflect a high commitment to the project on the part of the preschool principal and other school administrators.
3. It provides staff training for teachers that is oriented toward the accomplishment of the program's goals.
4. It provides for parental involvement.
5. It reflects careful planning and frequent evaluation and modification of the program in light of what evaluation reveals about the successes and failures of the program.

The value of such a structured approach seems to be particularly important when helping disadvantaged children is the aim of the program.

The concern for the disadvantaged, which is so characteristic of the present thrust of early childhood educational research, seems to bring us full circle back to the original writings of Froebel. Froebel created the concept of kindergarten or early childhood education primarily to help poor children. It is important to note that while Froebel focused on the importance of play in a child's life, his approach to education through play was quite structured and goal-directed.

BIBLIOGRAPHY

Andreani & Cavallini. *Summary of the research and experimentation carried out in the primary school.* Associazone per la ricerca sperimentale sui problemi dei giovani. Milan, 1970.

Bogatz, G. & Ball, S. *The second year of sesame street: a continuing evaluation.* Princeton, N.J.: Educational Testing Service, November 1971.

van Calcar, C. *Development of compensatory early childhood education.* Amsterdam seminar on curriculum in compensatory early childhood education, Bernard van Leer Foundation, CurSem/PR/12, The Hague, 3 November, 1972.

Clark, B. *Progress report: April, 1968-April, 1969.* Dalhousie University, 1969.

Coleman, J. S. *Equality of educational opportunity.* Washington, D.C.: United States Government Printing Office, 1966.

Crellin, E., Pringle, M. L. K., & West, P. *Born illegitimate: social and educational implications* (a report by National Children's Bureau). London: John Gardner Ltd., 1971.

Davie, R., Butler, N., & Goldstein, H. *From birth to seven: a report of the National Child Development Study.* London: Clowes, 1972.

Ministère de l'education nationale et de la culture. *Hommage à Ouide, Decroly.* January, 1964.

Education, Volume 139, No. 23, June 9, 1972. *From birth to seven,* Councils and Education Press Ltd, p. 553.

Froebel, F. In R. Ulich. *History of educational thought.* New York: American Book Company, 1950.

Fowler, W. A developmental learning strategy for early reading in a laboratory nursery school. *Interchange,* 1971, *2*(2). The Ontario Institute for Studies in Education.

Gran, B. *Project Fol* (from Swedish "Forskola—lagstedium i samverkan"—preschool and primary school in cooperation), a research and development project. Department of Educational and Psychological Research, Malmö School of Education, Sweden, August 31, 1972.

Halsey, A. H. *Educational Priority: EPA problems and policies,* Vol. 1. London: HMSO, October 1972.

Husen, T. *International Project for the Evaluation of Educational Achievement.* International Study of Achievement in Mathematics: A Comparison of Twelve Countries. Vol. I and II. Stockholm: Almqvist and Wiksell, and New York: Wiley, 1967.

Kärrby, G. *Child rearing and development of moral structure.* Stockholm: Almqvist & Wiksell, 1971.

Mialaret, G. *I am somebody!* Washington, D.C.: ACEI Study Conference. April 14, 1974.

Miezitis, S. The Montessori method: some recent research. *Interchange,* 1971, *3*(2). The Ontario Institute for Studies in Education.

Newson, J. and E. *Four years old in an urban community.* London: Allen & Unwin, 1968.

Parisi, D. & Pizzamiglio, L. *Svilupp della comprensione sintattica dai 3 ai 6 anni in funzione del livello socioeconomico.* Instituto di psicologia del CNR, 1969.

Rumi, M. & Gualco, S. *Il banbino e la scuola materna*—Torino. SEI, 1970.

Ryan, T. Poverty and early education in Canada. Ottawa: Carleton University, 1971.

Saint Marc, C. *Travaux de Centre de Recherche de l'éducation spécialisée et de l'adaptation scolaire* (CRESAS). Numéro Special, 1971.

Sandels, S. *Investigation into nursery school methods.* School Research, National Board of Education Bureau, Sept. 14, 1969: 7, and 1970: 20.

Sandels, S. *Emotionally disturbed children in pre-school programmes.* Stencil. The Institute of Education, Stockholm School of Education, 1969.

Sverud, K. -A. & Stukat, K. -G. *Nursery school project.* The Institute of Educational Psychology, Gothenburg School of Education, 1971.

Wall, W. D. *The significance of recent research in early childhood in the U.K.* OMEP, World Council Seminar, London, September 1972.

Children and their primary schools (The Plowden Report) Central Advisory Council for Education, Vols. I and II. London: HMSO, 1967.

Presidential Task Force on Children. *A bill of rights for children.* 1967.

Secretary of State, Department of Education and Science. *Education, a framework for expansion* (White Paper). London: HMSO, 1972.

Most English parents in favor of "Sesame Street" and support for "Sesame Street." *The Times Educational Supplement.* July 14, 1972.

Early Childhood Education in England and Wales

INTRODUCTION

Interest in the education of young children in England and Wales can be traced to the work of Robert Owen, the socialist reformer. In 1816, he opened the first infant school, which he called his "institution for the formation of character," at the New Lanark Mills in Scotland. The passage of the Factory Act of 1819, which prohibited the employment of children under age 9 in factories, fostered a greater awareness of the problem of young children who could neither go to school nor be cared for at home because their parents went out to work.

The teachings of Froebel were brought to England and Wales by many people in the mid-1850s, where they gained ready acceptance. The Froebel society was founded in 1875 and through its leaders has had a strong influence ever since on the goals, organization and curriculum of nursery schools.

In 1870-1871, 24.2% of the 3- to 5-year-olds in England and Wales were in school; by 1900 this had risen to 43.1%, its high point; by 1910 it had declined to 22.7% (Blackstone, 1971). The decline can be attributed to documents such as the "Report on Children under Five Years of Age in Public Elementary Schools" by the Women Inspectors, published in 1905, which claimed that children were learning almost nothing in school and that in fact it might be having a detrimental effect on them. The report recommended that wealthy parents be discouraged from sending their children to school before the age of 5, while the poor should be encouraged to send theirs to nursery school rather than to schools of instruction. In 1907, a second study was authorized by the Board of Education. The consultative committee's report came to the same conclusions as did the earlier report. They recognized that some homes could not provide good care, and therefore, like the earlier committee, recommended the establishment of nursery schools for the poor.

The overall effect of these recommendations led to sharp declines in educational provisions for the 3- to 5-year-old age group. By 1919-1920 the percentage of this age group in school was 17.4; in 1920, 13.1; by 1955 it had dropped to 7.7, its lowest point (Blackstone, 1971).

In December, 1972, the Secretary of State for Education and Science issued a White Paper entitled "Education: A Framework for Expansion" that makes clear the government's policy to put an extensive effort into the area of preschool education over the next 10 years. The specific recommendations in this White Paper will be considered in their appropriate contexts in later sections of this report.

ENROLLMENTS, PRESCHOOL EDUCATION (1960-1970)

For the purpose of this study, nursery school education in England and Wales is defined in accordance with the "OECD Classification of Educational Systems," 1972, which gives it the following characteristics:

> Length of study in years equals up to three.
>
> Entrance requirement is to be two years old.
>
> Attendance is voluntary with fees in private sector and no fees in public sector. In the case of nursery classes attached to primary schools, admittance is at age 2. Provision of schools by local educational authorities is done on a voluntary basis [p. 10].

In evaluating participation in early childhood education in England and Wales, one must be fully clear at the outset on two particular points. The first is that this country is one of the very few places in the world where compulsory education starts at age 5. The first 2 years of this, therefore, contain an age group that elsewhere would be provided for by precompulsory classes or other facilities. The second point is the multiplicity of sponsorship or support in the preschool field. This makes assessment of total participation somewhat difficult.

Taking first the nursery schools and classes defined above, including the independent schools under the jurisdiction of the Department of Education and Science, enrollments over the 11 year period, 1960-1961 to 1971-1972, were as shown in Table 4.1. It should be noted that this discussion is about enrollments, not school places, which would be a smaller number as only one-half the part-time pupils would be counted. It would be seen that in the privately supported schools there has been a much slower growth in enrollments over this period as compared with the public sector, 29.1% and 69.9%, respectively. If we look at the period of time from 1965-1966 to 1971-1972, for which all figures

TABLE 4.1
Enrollments of 2 to 4-year-olds in All Schools in England and Wales

				(in 000's)
Year		Private	Public	Total
1960-61	FT[a]	24	203	227
	PT[b]	n.a.[c]	6	6 +
			(209)	(233)
1965-66	FT	20	218	238
	PT	12	20	32
		(32)	(238)	(270)
1966-67	FT	20	217	237
	PT	13	24	37
		(33)	(241)	(274)
1967-68	FT	18	229	247
	PT	15	30	45
		(33)	(259)	(292)
1968-69	FT	18	239	257
	PT	16	38	54
		(34)	(277)	(311)
1969-70	FT	18	246	264
	PT	14	46	61
		(32)	(292)	(325)
1970-71	FT	17	261	270
	PT	14	58	72
		(31)	(319)	(351)
1971-72	FT	17	282	299
	PT	14	73	87
		(31)	(355)	(386)
% of increase or decrease from 1960-61 to 1971-72		29.1	69.9	65.1
from 1965-66 to 1971-72		-03.2	49.2	43.0

Source: Department of Education and Science, London.

[a]Full-time   [b]Part-time   [c]Not available

are available, we see that there has been a decline of 3.2% in the private sector. In both the public and private sectors, part-time enrollments have risen more rapidly than full-time ones. The total change over the 11 years is 65.1%.

Table 4.2 presents population attendance rates for all children in preschool for England and Wales in the 11-year period from 1960-1972. The total age group in nursery school increased by 65.7% over the 11 years, but meanwhile the infant population had grown by 11.8%. Hence, there was an actual 47.7% increase in the percentage of the age group enrolled. All of the preschool provisions just mentioned come under the jurisdiction of the Ministry of Education and Science.

Enrollment data for nursery schools is presented in Table 4.3. It is only for these schools that complete data (financial, number of teachers, as well as enrollment) are available.

In addition to this preschool program, there are provisions offered under the auspices of the Department of Health and Social Security classified under three headings: day nurseries, registered premises, and registered persons. Table 4.4 gives what statistics are available for them for the years 1961-1971. It is clear from this table that the number of children cared for under the heading "registered premises" has increased more than elevenfold, or 1100%, from 1960-1961 to 1970-1971. This growth is accounted for in large part by the increase in play groups run on a cooperative basis by the parents.

The total number of children cared for in 1970 was 345,950. Counting children under both government departments (Tables 4.1 and 4.4) gives a total

TABLE 4.2

Population Attendance Rates in Pre-Schools in England and Wales from 1960-61 to 1970-71

			(in 000's)
	1960-61	1970-71	% of Change
Total age group 2 - 4 years in pre-school	233[a]	386	65.7
Infant population 2 - 4 years	2,108	2,356	11.8
% of age group enrolled	11.1	16.4	47.7

Source: Statistics of Education 1961, Part I, Table II.
        Statistics of Education 1972, Vol. I, Table V
        Department of Education and Science, London.

[a]Incomplete - part-time pupils in the private sector not known.

TABLE 4.3
Enrollments in Nursery Schools in England and Wales from 1960-61 to 1970-71

			(in 000's)
Year	Private	Public	Total
1960-61	6	24	30
1965-66	6	29	35
1966-67	5	29	34
1967-68	5	31	36
1968-69	5	32	37
1969-70	5	34	39
1970-71	5	36	41
% of increase or decrease from 1960-61 to 1970-71	-16.7	50.0	36.7

Source: Department of Education and Science, London.

of 403,000 in 1965 and 697,000 in 1970. The total increase over the 5-year period for all children is 73%. In the school year 1970-1971, approximately 29% of the children in England and Wales participated in some form of early childhood program. In the same year, the percentage of pupils in some form of preschool program in England and Wales by single year of age and by age group was:

	1970-1971			1970-1971	
Age	6	99%	Age	5-6	99%
	5	99		4-6	74
	4	25		3-6	57
	3	5		2-6	45
	2	1			

The aforementioned White Paper estimates that there are some 300,000 full-time places presently available in the nursery schools in England and it proposes a great expansion of this provision. Within 10 years, the government aims to meet the recommendation of the Plowden committee that 90% of the 4-year-olds and 50% of the 3-year-olds should be provided with nursery school experience. This would mean that approximately 750,000 4-year-olds and 375,000 3-year-olds would be attending nursery school by 1980. The vast majority of these children would be attending on a part-time (half-day) basis, whereas, for reasons of social necessity, 15% of the 3- and 4-year-olds would attend on a full-day basis. The White Paper further confirmed that the concept underlying the Educational Priority Area Act would be followed in meeting the

TABLE 4.4
Day Nurseries and Child Minders, England and Wales

Dec. of each year	Local authority ('maintained') day nurseries			Registered premises (private day nurseries and playgroups)		Registered persons (child minders)	
	No. of Nurseries	Approved Places	Children on Registers	Number	Children Permitted	Number	Children Permitted
1970	453	21,581	22,226	9,675	240,409	25,345	83,315
1969	444	21,142	22,030	8,159	196,100	17,957	69,055
1968	445	21,163	21,628	5,849	146,098	5,802	47,208
1967	444	21,169	21,598	4,382	109,141	5,039	42,696
1966	445	21,157	21,815	3,083	75,132	3,887	32,336
1965	448	21,396)		2,245	54,911	3,393)	
1964	455	31,532)	Not published	1,585	38,144	2,994)	Not published
1963	459	21,672)		1,243	31,045	2,597)	
1962	462	21,876)		932	22,591	2,202)	
1961	472	22,259)		747	17,618	1,780)	

Source: Annual Reports of the Department of Health and Social Security (formerly Ministry of Health)

demands for nursery school education; namely, that rural and urban disadvantaged children would be given first priority.

As far as trends in the future demand for places are concerned, three factors are of special relevance: birth rate, family size, and employment scale for married women. Statistics are available that enable extrapolations for all of these factors.

Trends of the average household size and gross reproduction rates in England and Wales can be derived from the result of a United Nations Study.[1] In 1801, the average household size in England was 4.6; in 1966 it was 3.01—a decline of 1.59 over the 65-year period. In 1851, the gross reproduction rate was 2.3%; in 1966 it had declined to 1.3%, a drop of 1%.

As to birth rates in England and Wales, we have the following information: In 1966 there were 17.7 live births per thousand population; in 1970 this had declined to 16—a drop of 1.7 per thousand over the 4-year period.[2] In short, the decline in the gross reproduction rate and in family size indicates a greater demand for places in early childhood education in England and Wales in the near future.

Table 4.5 offers the following information about participation rates in the labor force in the United Kingdom.

These statistics clearly show the marked increase of the participation rate of women over the 10-year period from 1960-1970. If this increase continues, we can expect a corresponding increase in demand for preschool education on social grounds.

ISSUES OF DEBATE

A detailed exposition of the changing social conditions in England and Wales that have led to the demand for more early childhood education is beyond the scope of this study. In any case, the topic is already well documented in Blackstone's *A Fair Start* (1971). It is relevant, however, to identify the principal reasons behind the demand at the present time.

For the past 15 years, national policy has been opposed to the expansion of nursery schools. In August, 1954, the Ministry of Education issued Circular 280 which stated that "the Ministry will expect the admission of children under five to be restricted or prohibited where their admission would stand in the way of a reduction in the size of over-large classes [p. 3]."

---

[1] *Analyses and projections of households and families.* Prepared by the Population Division, Department of Economic and Social Affairs of the United Nations Secretariat, 1971.

[2] The United Nations demographic yearbook. 1970.

TABLE 4.5
Labor Force Participation Rates - United Kingdom

	1960 %	1970 %
$\dfrac{\text{Total Labor Force}}{\text{Total Population}} \times 100$		
(a) Total	47.8	45.9
(b) Males	65.4	60.4
(c) Females	31.1	32.2
$\dfrac{\text{Total Labor Force}}{\substack{\text{Population from} \\ \text{15 to 64 years}}} \times 100$		
(a) Total	73.4	72.7
(b) Males	99.1	93.4
(c) Females	48.6	52.1

Source: Labor Force Statistics, 1959-70, O.E.C.D., Paris, 1972.

This position was reaffirmed in 1956 when the Central Government discouraged local authorities from expanding their nursery places so that the compulsory sector could take precedence. This policy was formalized and strengthened in Circular 8/60 issued in May, 1960, which imposed an almost total ban on the expansion of maintained or direct grant nursery education. This ban was relaxed slightly in 1964 and 1965 when permission was given to establish new nursery classes as long as they released a specified number of mothers to return to teaching. It remained in force until publication of the White Paper in December, 1972. Two reasons are commonly given by the department for its position:

1. The concentration of attention, money, and educational talent on extending the school leaving age from 15 to 16 years.
2. Until recently, a teacher shortage.

In opposition to the position taken by the government, there have been the proposals made in the Plowden Report, *Children and their Primary Schools* (1967). One of its key recommendations was a large expansion of nursery education for about two-thirds of all 3- and 4-year-olds, mainly on a part-time basis, but with provision for 15% to attend full-time. An equally strong proposal was that educational priority areas should be designated. These are areas of social and educational deprivation where green open spaces and play facilities are lacking, when housing conditions are poor, or where children are restricted by living in high flats. The actual wording of this report, under educational priority areas, reads:

> As a matter of national policy, 'positive discrimination' should favor schools in neighbourhoods where children are most severely handicapped by home conditions. The program should be phased to make schools in the most deprived areas as good as the best in the country. For this, it may be necessary that their greater claim on resources should be maintained [p. 66].

Some expansion of nursery schools took place following this report in 1967, but Circular 8/60 was still an obstacle. The first real signs of change in policy on the part of the government came with the launching of the Urban Aid Program in 1968. Since then there has indeed been an increase in nursery schools and classes in deprived areas. Nearly 18,000 additional full-time places have been approved in the last few years. In some cases, the number of places for the under-5-year-olds has been doubled. In Liverpool, Birmingham, and Leeds, numbers have risen by a third and in many other cities by over a quarter. In Inner London, more than 2000 new places were made available. More than 500 additional places have been created in Chester, where nursery education is provided for nearly 30% of the combined 3- and 4-year-olds. In Nottingham there were 400.

The pattern of expansion has been deliberately uneven because of the priority areas policy, because of the way urban programs operate, and because resources have been limited. For the time being, most new nursery places will have to be provided in densely populated urban areas where the children are probably the most acutely deprived. For example, districts that have a large recent immigrant population will undoubtedly receive high priority. The needs of these urban area and immigrant populations have been recognized for some time.

In 1954, the Save the Children Fund organized play-groups for supervised play activity of children between the ages of 2 and 5 years. In 1972, about 100 such groups existed in various types of premises in or near the main industrial centers where the need was greatest. Working within its limited charitable resources the SCF concentrates its efforts in areas that correspond generally to those identified in the Plowden Report as needing priority treatment.

In 1961, as a direct outgrowth of frustration over Circular 8/60, the Preschool Play-Group Association was formed. This association represents a chiefly middle-class response to the need for preschool experience among their own children; nevertheless, some progress has been made in setting up play-groups in working class districts such as Birmingham and Inner London.

The three major objectives of play-groups are

1. To provide places for children from 2 to 5 years.
2. To provide education by means of organized recreation.
3. To stimulate discussion on the above-mentioned objectives.

By 1966, 20,000 children between the ages of 3 and 4 years were enrolled in about 600 play-groups. The movement has continued to grow very rapidly, and by 1971 there were about 7000 play-groups for 170,000 children. Perhaps the greatest strength of the play-group lies in its strong emphasis on parental involvement. Its greatest weakness may be in the extent to which it relies on nonprofessionals as teachers. There is apparently a wide range of quality in the established programs.

In spite of all these recent efforts, the demand for places in nursery education is still far higher than the supply. According to a survey reported in the *Times Educational Supplement* (September 1, 1972), of 594 families in Sheffield, only 3% of the children under 5 were attending a nursery school or day nursery. The survey showed 43% of the parents would definitely want their children to attend, if facilities were only available. The problem would not be eased, however, by the provision of additional nursery school places alone; it would require a campaign of information on the availability of preschool opportunities to parents in redeveloped areas and to recent immigrants. More than half the parents interviewed were unaware of the facilities that exist already. The survey concluded with the observation that, as well as the lack of information, the long waiting lists probably discourage many parents from pursuing places actively.

Halsey (1972), writing in the *Guardian,* observes that "the pattern of pre-school provision so far is largely one of private suburban play-groups and publicly provided day nurseries, nursery schools and nursery classes. The statutory provision is inadequate and the private provision discriminates against those in greatest need [p. 32]." Dr. Halsey goes on to advocate ". . . a hybrid form of nursery center which is neither the expensive professional nursery school nor the amateur play-group [p. 32]." The idea is an interesting one, and Dr. Halsey expands on it in his book *Educational Priority* (1972).

In 1972, the Secretary of State for Education and Science asked local authorities for the first time to arrange their proposals for all services in an order of preference, indicating that from now on the number of nursery school places approved would partly depend on the priority they themselves attached to this sector of education.

Not everyone is in favor of expanding preschool programs. The reasons most commonly advanced against them are: high cost; exposure of young children to infectious diseases at an unnecessarily early and particularly susceptible age; and, doubts about the child's removal from parental care. Early removal may conflict with the child's need to have a one-to-one relationship with his mother. Robertson (1972), for example, maintains that the parent-child relationship is essential for both and that early separation (that is, before 3 years) should be undertaken only with great care and only on a part-time basis.

THE WHITE PAPER, DECEMBER 1972

It was only after this short review of early childhood education in England and Wales was near completion that the government White Paper, "Education: A Framework for Expansion," was published and the author has been glad to amend his text in the light of it. So far as concerns nursery schools and the like, its policies have been widely acclaimed in the country. A number of the issues of debate have now been stilled. It is proper, therefore, that the last word in this section should go to the White Paper.

It states clearly that the new expansion of nursery school education will seriously take into account the concept of positive discrimination. This will be a particular priority for the years 1974-1976. It sees nursery school education as a supplement to the home, not as an attempt by the state to supplant it. A major benefit of the expanded scheme lies in the early identification of needs of young children, predominantly in the social, psychological and medical areas. The White Paper goes on to recommend that local authorities planning for this expansion should cooperate closely with relevant social groups in the community (particularly with the existing play-group movements) and build on their strengths and assets. It anticipates that there may be a wide diversity of response from local communities to the new initiative. The participation of parents in a variety of ways is to be encouraged as something beneficial both to the parents and to the school system. For parents in particularly disadvantaged areas, it stresses the importance of building a bridge of understanding between the home and the nursery school, and subsequently (with the help of teachers too) between the nursery school and the infant school where the children will go afterwards.

The major issues of debate concerning the provision of preschool education in England and Wales seem, therefore, to be the following:

1. Call for equality of educational opportunity for all.
2. Increased numbers of mothers working.
3. Weakening of role obligations within the family.
4. Isolation of young families in new communities outside the extended family group.
5. Living conditions, such as crowded accommodation in old houses and high block flats.
6. Poor provision of playing space in urban areas and lack of companions in rural areas.

THE AIMS AND OBJECTIVES OF EARLY CHILDHOOD EDUCATION

In reviewing the literature on early childhood education in England and Wales, it has proven to be quite difficult to find a specifically stated set of objectives. All the people involved doubtless have a general set of feelings about what they wish to do for the children, but very few have propounded it in an analytical way. Blackstone, writing for the Fabian Society in 1972, offers the following as a set of aims of nursery education. She states

Let us begin by considering the traditional aims of nursery education in this country. These are to provide for the child one or two years of regular attendance, not necessarily full time, at an educational institution before he starts compulsory school. In this setting he will be given the opportunity of meeting other children and will be encouraged to learn to cooperate with them and to accept requirements of being one of a large number. He will be given more specific training in tasks like dressing himself and eating in socially accepted ways. His emotional development is encouraged by improving his self-confidence, enhancing his independence, teaching him to curb his aggressive impulses and so on. His intellectual development will be stimulated too by the provision of equipment and materials designed to promote motor and perceptual skills and by music, poetry, stories and games, which directly or indirectly are designed to improve the linguistic ability and develop imagination and creativity. Outdoor equipment is used to help consolidate the home in all these aspects, not to replace it [p. 5].

The Workers' Educational Association (1971) offers the following reasons for preschool education:

(a) Attendance at a nursery school provides children with a *stimulating environment* where they can mix with other children and adults, enjoy space and play equipment and have the professional care and educating influence of skilled people . . .

(b) Children need opportunities to get to know people outside their own family circle and to *form some relationships* which are less close and emotionally charged.

(c) They benefit from the physical and medical *care of professionally trained workers.*

(d) There are children with *special needs,* for which nursery education can compensate, e.g. (1) children living in isolation in tall buildings, (2) children of working mothers, (3) culturally deprived children, (4) children from overcrowded homes, (5) children from poor environments, (6) mentally or physically handicapped children, (7) children from immigrant families [p. 2].

As we have seen, early childhood education in England and Wales (as in many other countries) was started by people who were primarily concerned about the plight of the poor, the deprived and handicapped children. In England and Wales these early leaders were most concerned with getting large numbers of children in the industrial slums of the 1900s off the streets and into a safe place.

Parry and Archer (1972) point out the following changes in the principal concerns of the preschool movement in England and Wales:

1918: Nurture, nutrition, and care.
1939: Emotions and creativity.
1969: Intellectual development.

As is true in many other countries, as the years passed it was the middle class who saw the benefits of placing their children in early childhood educational settings and who had the money to pay for them. Hence, although set up for the poor, early childhood educational programs were adopted by the preschool play-group associations movement, due to the very slow growth in terms of grants paid out of public funds for the less advantaged children in the population. Indeed, it is only recently that educators, and particularly social scientists of the world, have rediscovered the importance of early childhood education for deprived children.

In further explanation of the evolution of the emphasis in early childhood education, it is relevant that governments have come to make increasingly more adequate provision in the original two basic areas of concern (health and nutrition) through other channels. This has made it possible to pay more attention to the educational aspects of early childhood education, particularly as they may be a remedy to the great disparity in subsequent scholastic achievement between children with a middle-class background and those who come from underprivileged homes.

One of the traditional strengths of the early childhood educational programs is parental involvement. There have always been debates as to whether the programs offered should be an upward extension of the home or a downward extension of the school. Despite this, parents have far more commonly been involved in early childhood educational programs than in what goes on later at school. Much of the current emphasis in England and Wales on greater parental involvement in their children's schools is based on the success of preschools. A number of writers (Bernstein, Blackstone, and the Newsons, in particular) have stressed the importance of parents' feelings of control over their children's situations; Coleman (1966) referred to it as a "control of destiny." It is widely believed that extending parental involvement at the preschool to the lower social classes is a way of beginning to encourage them to participate more actively in their children's subsequent development at school.

Parental involvement is seen as one of the major strengths of play-group associations, which, as Table 4.4 indicates, have grown extremely rapidly in the last 10 years. The White Paper stressed the importance of these groups and the parents involved. One question it raised, however, was the quality of these parents' educational training. It advocated that more help in the form of trained early childhood educators should be made available to the play-groups. A great deal of the present pressure for increased provision of preschool has come from the parents involved in the play-group movement. Their major motivation seems to be a basic concern with the social and emotional growth of young children and the feeling that a preschool experience can help provide for that growth.

ORGANIZATION AND CONTROL

For the stranger to understand the working of the nursery schools in England and Wales, it is necessary first to know the essentials of the English school system.[3] Its first distinctive feature is the degree to which it is decentralized, while a balance of power is held between three forces: the Department of Education and Science (DES), which represents government; the local education authorities; and the teachers (particularly the headmasters or headmistresses of the schools). The curriculum is the responsibility of the headmaster (or headmistress), aided by the senior teachers. The responsibility of the DES is to obtain three-quarters of the costs of education from public funds and to ensure compliance with legislation vis-à-vis education. To this end, there is the corps of Her Majesty's Inspectors, some 300 of whom are concerned with primary schools and the maintained nursery schools. The DES also sets standards for teacher training (both preservice and postservice) and for education itself. It decides on the broad outlines of the school and establishes norms for the minimum requirements. It also has consultative and negotiative functions.

The local educational authorities (LEAs), who are autonomous, have responsibility for educating the children. They obtain the first quarter of the costs of education from local sources: the central government, as we have seen, provides the final three-quarters. The LEAs construct schools and colleges, appoint and discharge teachers, and supply all material and equipment needed. The heads of the schools are in charge of setting up the programs for the maintained nursery schools.

There are three different authorities that may approve sponsorship of early childhood educational programs. These authorities and their programs are as follows:

1. Department of Education and Science.
   a. Maintained nursery schools
   b. Maintained nursery classes attached to primary school
   c. Independent nursery schools
      i. Recognized as efficient
      ii. Other

[3] Burrows, L. J. Speech at United Kingdom OMEP seminar. September 1972.

2. Department of Health and Social Security—Day Nurseries.
3. Local Health Authorities.
   a. Registered premises for the day care of children, that is, independent nurseries and play-groups not designated as schools
   b. Registered child minders caring for eight or more children, that is, independent nurseries and play-groups not designated as schools, and not coming into the "registered premises" classification

Attendance at all types of nursery schools may be full or part time, that is, 5 full days from 9:00 A.M. until 3:30 P.M., 5 mornings, or 5 afternoons.

The play-groups supported by the Save the Children Fund are really nursery schools run by professionals but organized by a voluntary society. A large number belong to the Preschool Play-Groups Association (PPA) catering to some 170,000 children and advised by 7000 voluntary area organizers. The PPA is very concerned with educational standards and does all it can to raise them by training, advising and appointing local organizers. By the Act of 1970 the play-groups are responsible to the Social Services Division. Some local educational authorities have taken existing play-groups under their wings, both financially and educationally. Kent, for instance, has appointed a joint infant play-group adviser; Bristol links all its play-groups with maintained nurseries or day nurseries; play-groups in Devon receive direct financial assistance, advice, and guidance from the school authorities, with help from the Social Service Division.

Separate from the schools, and with a different type of staff, are day nurseries for children from 6 weeks to 5 years who, from a health point of view or because of deprived or inadequate backgrounds, have special needs that cannot otherwise be met. These are the responsibility of the Department of Health and Social Security.

Every maintained or grant aided nursery school must be supervised by a qualified teacher who may be assisted by nonqualified staff. The nursery classes must have a qualified teacher. An experienced nurse may be in general charge of the children, but she is responsible to the head teacher. Play-groups are usually staffed and run by the mothers themselves, some of whom may be qualified teachers or nurses, although trained staff may be hired. The day nurseries employ nurses and nursery assistants rather than teachers. There are also some play-groups organized on a commercial basis by people who have had no recognized training. They are, however, subject to the scrutiny of the Department of Health.

The headmaster makes the decision as to what and how the schools should teach. The head teacher decides how the school should be organized, what books and equipment should be used, and what should be the relationship with parents. The headmaster has wide areas of discretion, but he is also subject to a number of restraints, such as parental interference.

At its best, the teacher's use of freedom is reflected in the astonishing degree of change that is seen in the British infant school movement, for which the teachers are largely responsible. The teachers' training colleges, as centers for the diffusion of ideas, are another important element in the cycle of innovation.

One should note here the immense influence exerted by the London Institute under the leadership of Susan Isaacs and Dorothy Gardner. The work of the Department of Child Development at Birmingham, particularly since World War II, has contributed significantly to the changes in the infant school movement, as have the Froebel Institute and its college at Roehampton. These institutions trained many pioneers of innovation, who carried their ideas to other colleges and into local school systems. They also helped disseminate these new ideas through in-service courses offered to experienced teachers.

PHYSICAL SETTING: A VISIT TO A LONDON NURSERY SCHOOL

The school visited was located in one of the older parts of London in a neighborhood of flats and small shops. It was built after the war and was perhaps 15-20 years old.

It consisted of two very large rooms (approximately 15 X 10 meters each) separated by a glass and wooden partition. Both rooms opened onto a large asphalt area (50 X 40 meters). There were also two lavatories and a couple of small rooms for work and storage. The headmistress had a private office and a secretary.

There were 110 children attending the school—30 full-time (14 in each class) and 80 part-time, morning or afternoon (20 in each class). There were one teacher and two assistants for each group, giving a ratio of approximately one adult to each eleven children. Additionally there was one domestic employee.

The children were 3 or 4 years of age, approximately 90 4-year-olds and 20 3-year-olds. They were mixed in the two classes. The teachers and their assistants were very friendly, and the children seemed to be really enjoying themselves. The headmistress explained that planning was done only in the most general sense and that most of the time the teachers tried to extend and broaden what interested the child at the time. She called it "watching for teachable moments."

The nursery school was light and airy and the walls were covered with many samples of the children's work. In each room there was a large collection of toys and games, as well as a few books, but most story books were kept in the headmistress's office from which teachers got them. The corners were set up variously as a home, a block, or a doll's house. There were a few desks and chairs in groups around the room, but most were empty as the children were generally free to come and go as they wished. In the hallway between the rooms there was a water table where a number of children were happily playing with small plastic containers, boats, and other things. In one of the rooms there was a small stage set up, with a piano nearby and a number of other musical instruments in a box. There was also a play telephone booth. The playground had a swing, a set of seesaws, some climbing equipment, and an old van in which the children might play.

The school day lasted from 9:00 A.M. until approximately 3:30 P.M. The children in the morning came from 9:00 A.M. to 11:30 A.M.; those in the afternoon from 1:00 P.M. to 3:30 P.M. Of the 40 full-timers, 30 stayed for lunch; 5 of them had it free because of family need.

There was no formal parent group, and the headmistress did not want one established. She felt she knew her parents, and said that parents often stayed and watched in the morning or talked with the teachers or their assistants about their children's problems when they came to pick them up. There seemed to be an easy relationship between the parents and the staff personnel. The headmistress added that most of the teachers live outside that part of London and it would be very hard for them to come back in the evening for parent-teacher meetings.

Most of the children come from lower middle-class or upper lower-class homes. There was no contact with the infant school that they would be attending later. It was the headmistress's feeling that something should be done by the staff, both of the nursery school and the infant school, to work out transition problems, but she had been headmistress for 10 years and in fact had had very few complaints about how well her children have adapted to the infant school.

There was a long waiting list for the few available spaces: some 50 names. Normally, children were taken in turn as they applied, but exceptions were often made when there was a real need, for example, on account of sick parents or a one-parent family. This practice of giving first priority to those most in need is a recommendation from the Department of Education and Science. The headmistress expressed a concern for more nursery schools. She said she could easily fill another the size of hers in the same neighborhood.

Daily Program in a Nursery School in London

9:15-9:45	Children arrive.
9:15-11:00	Free play. Choice of sand, water, clay, paint, bricks, cooking, cottage, woodwork, constructional toys, dressing-up, house-play, table toys, outdoor, tricycles, scooters, gardening, books, stories, experimenting with musical instruments, etc.
11:00	Music for those who want it (15 minutes or so).
11:30	Group story.
11:45	Morning group leave.
11:55	Children prepare for dinner.
12:00	Dinner (children from both classes in one room, with four adults).
12:35	Quiet plays, books in room and rest beds for those who want them.
1:15	Afternoon children arrive. Free play as in the morning.

3:00   Music.
3:15 (from)   Full day children leave (very gradually).
3:30   Group story.
3:45   All children go home.

TEACHERS AND THEIR TRAINING

One of the earliest teachers' training institutions was the Home and Colonial Infant School Society founded in 1838, by Rev. Charles Mayo and his sister Elizabeth Mayo, to establish infant schools and to train teachers for them. Its aims were to provide a place where children could be cared for while their mothers were working and to teach the elements of reading, writing, and arithmetic.

Certified teachers in England and Wales receive a 3-year training course in a recognized training college after having obtained a General Certificate of Education, Ordinary Level, obtained generally at or before 18 years of age.[4] The colleges of education are the principal sources of teachers for the maintained schools. Qualified teachers are required to serve a probationary period normally of 1 year. There are over 150 colleges of education in England and Wales as well as departments of education in some polytechnic colleges and in universities. At the regional level, the organization of teacher training is based upon the universities, all of which have institutes of education with which the surrounding teacher training institutes are affiliated. Also affiliated to the institutes are the local education authorities and the practicing teachers. The institutes and their affiliated bodies form area-training organizations which approve the syllabuses and courses proposed by their constituent colleges, conduct examinations recognized by the department for the teachers' professional qualifications, arrange refresher and other courses, and foster educational research. They have no responsibility for the financial or administrative control of the individual colleges.

Training colleges are provided either by local educational authorities or by voluntary bodies, many of which are religious denominations. The colleges provided by local education authorities are maintained by them out of pooled funds to which all local authorities subscribe, in proportion to the number of children on the registers in their area.

Of the 150 teacher training colleges mentioned above, 43 have programs for the training of preprimary teachers. They produce about 1800 nursery school teachers each year.

So far as concerns the training and professional situation of preschool teachers, a UNESCO publication of 1965 gives the following information:

[4] OECD. *Classification of educational systems.* 1972.

Its objective is to prepare the students for working with children aged two to seven.

(a) The student follows a three year professional pedagogical course including the psychology and development of young children, sociology, history, philosophy, and theory and methods of education.

(b) The student also elects a major course in one field study for his personal and intellectual development during three years (e.g. English literature, history, religion, biology, geography, mathematics, physical education).

(c) The student may also take a minor course which is of a shorter duration.

(d) The student must follow some obligatory courses (e.g. English, mathematics, religion, physical education).

(e) The students will also do practical work during the three year course. The practice comprises child observation, child-minding, supervised teaching practice at school [p. 162].

A recent innovation in preschool teacher training is the introduction of degree courses usually involving 1 year tacked on to the other 3 in some specialized teaching subject (for example, an advanced training course on the problems of teaching young children).

Qualified teachers in nursery schools may also have assistants. These have received 2 years of training (over the age of 18), part of which is practical. They are paid a lower salary than the teacher. Older women who have had appropriate experience with children other than those in their own families may become assistants after a single year's course.

Because of the shortage of teachers, it has been suggested that nursery assistants should be used much more widely. However, the number of teachers available depends on the local authorities, decision about levels of expenditure, and the priority they give to teacher supply.

Most preschool teachers in England and Wales belong to one or more of the established teachers' associations. The aims of these are partly educational, but they are mostly concerned with advancing the professional status of their members. Many of the early curriculum development funds were secured by the teachers' groups. Teachers form the majority of members of the Schools' Council for Curriculum and Examinations, an independent body advisory to government and to an action research agency. When any consultative or advisory committee is being established locally or nationally, it almost always includes representatives from the teachers' associations.

The preschool teachers in England and Wales have a great deal of freedom on professional matters, such as curriculum and instructional methods. They have in general used this wisely, and many of the recent innovations in preschool and infant school have resulted from it.

Table 4.6 contains information on the numbers of teachers in maintained nursery schools and those in the private sector. The pattern is much the same as for the enrollment data set out in Table 4.1, where, over the last 10 years, there

TABLE 4.6
Staff in Nursery Schools – Full-time Teachers and Full-time Equivalent
of Part-time Teachers

	Private sector			Public sector		
	FT	FTE	Total	FT	FTE	Total
1960–61	395	75[a]	470[a]	1,070	1	1,071
1965–66	308	59	367	1,073	14	1,087
1966–67	236	49	285	1,078	18	1,096
1967–68	236	53	289	1,181	23	1,204
1968–69	273	85	358	1,223	30	1,253
1969–70	227	70	297	1,279	28	1,307
1970–71	206	69	275	1,330	26	1,356
1971–72	229	90	319	1,423	28	1,451
% of increase from 1960–61 to 1970–71			−32.1			35.5

[a]Estimated

has been a marked decline in the private sector and a sharp increase in the public
sector. The total number of teachers increased by 29.6%, which corresponds
with the 36.6% increase in enrollments. It must be recalled, however, that many
more teachers are employed in the nursery classes than in maintained nursery
schools. The best estimate of the number of adults involved in preschool
programs in England and Wales is approximately 18,000.

Using the enrollments in nursery school (Table 4.2) and the number of
teachers (Table 4.6) it is possible to calculate the pupil-teacher ratio. This is
given in Table 4.7, which shows that there has been a change over the 10-year
period from 20:1 to 18:1. It is important to note that the pupil-adult ratio is
much lower, approximately 10:1, since most teachers are supplied with an
assistant. Again, it is important to note that we are speaking here of maintained
nursery schools.

In the primary schools in England and Wales in 1960, the pupil-teacher ratio
was, in the public sector, 30:1; in 1970 this had dropped to 29:1. In the private
sector in 1960, the ratio was 11:1, and in 1970, 29:1. These figures show clearly
that one of the things parents are supporting in England and Wales at both the
preprimary and primary levels in private school education is a very low pupil-
teacher ratio.

It can be estimated for the data given above that the pupil-teacher ratio in
nursery classes attached to primary schools in 1960 was 30:1, and in 1970, 29:1.
Both are substantially higher than those found in nursery schools. This fact
accounts in part for a rather considerable difference in cost between the two.

The government White Paper, in announcing provisions for the very marked

TABLE 4.7
Pupil:Teacher Ratio in Nursery Schools

	Private	Public	Total
1960–61	16:1	21:1	20:1
1965–66	13:1	22:1	20:1
1970–71	12:1	19:1	18:1
1971–72	12:1	19:1	18:1

expansion of nursery schools in England and Wales, recommended a pupil-teacher ratio of approximately 13:1. There are approximately 10,000 qualified teachers in nursery schools at the moment in England and Wales. Within the next 10 years it is expected that this figure will rise to some 25,000 as a result of the government's new initiative in this area.

FINANCING EARLY CHILDHOOD EDUCATION

Information on expenditures for preschool is available only for children who attend publicly maintained nursery schools. The total number of children attending nursery schools in 1965-1966 was 29,000; in 1970-1971 it had risen to 36,000. This means we have expenditure data on approximately one-tenth of the children identified in Table 4.1. We do, however, have an estimate on the rest.

Maintained nursery schools are financed out of the block grants paid by the central government to local authorities, and this covers slightly more than 75% of their operational cost. No fees are charged, and places are normally allocated according to the length of time on waiting lists. However, many of the places are assigned on a priority basis to children of working or unmarried mothers, families where there is long-term illness, or large, disorganized, low income families where the mother cannot cope with all her children.

Information on expenditure is readily available only for the public sector of maintained nursery schools. Table 4.8 shows the capital, current, and total expenditure in this sector for the years 1965-1966 to 1970-1971. It is interesting to observe that over this 6-year period there has been an 81.7% increase in total expenditure in pounds, while enrollments for the same period only rose by 24.1%. The difference in percentage of increase between pounds and dollars is accounted for by devaluation of the British pound. Expenditure for classes for 2- to 4-year-olds in public sector primary schools are not available.

The total expenditure for the years 1965-1966 to 1970-1971 has been converted to United States dollars for comparisons later in this study. It will be seen that over this 5-year period the total increase in maintained nursery school expenditure equals 56.1%.

Table 4.9 represents information on per pupil costs in public nursery schools

TABLE 4.8

Public Nursery School Expenditure in England and Wales from 1965-66 to 1969-70

Year	Capital	Current	£'000 Total Capital Current	$'000 Total Capital Current
1965-66	136	3,273	3,409	9,507[a]
1966-67	241	3,476	3,717	
1967-68	161	3,698	3,859	
1968-69	114	4,006	4,120	
1969-70	319	4,487	4,806	
1970-71	934	5,260	6,194	14,844
% of increase from 1965-66 to 1970-71	586.8	60.7	81.7	56.1

Source: Department of Education and Science, London

[a]Official Exchange Rates, O.E.C.D.

for the years 1965-1966 to 1970-1971. One can see that costs have risen by $32 over the 5-year period. Since the rate of inflation for education in the country is unknown, it would probably be safe to conclude that only a small part of this $32 was, in fact, available for additional expenditure per child. The annual per capita gross national product in Britain is $2170. In 1969, the average per capita expenditure on education was $4.97.[5]

It is interesting to compare nursery school costs with those for primary and secondary schools in England and Wales. In 1965, the average cost per child in nursery school was $318; in primary school it was $192. In 1970 the figures were: nursery school $350, primary school $202, secondary school $478. Hence it costs 1.5 times as much to educate a nursery school child as one in a primary school and approximately the same for a nursery child as for a secondary school student.

The figures given above also provide us with an estimate of the cost of educating preschool children in nursery classes. These are preschools that are attached to primary schools and that account for a much larger proportion of the 2- to 4-year-old group attending preschool than do nursery schools that are independent of the primary schools. We can estimate that the cost per child in nursery classes in 1965 was $192, and in 1970, $202. In nursery school, the cost in 1965 was $318; in 1970, $350. These figures indicate that it cost approxi-

[5] OECD. *Economic surveys.* 1972.

TABLE 4.9
Public Nursery School Per Pupil Costs in England and Wales in U.S.
Dollars from 1965-66 to 1969-70

Year	Current Expenditure	(in 000's) Number of Children	$'000 Per Pupil Cost
1965-66	9,227	29	318
1970-71	12,602	36	350
Total Increase			32

mately 1.5 times as much to educate a child in a nursery school as one in a nursery class.

Independent preschool programs such as those run by the PPA are financed by private bodies and organizations. A small grant of £3000 was first given in 1967 by the central government to the association (and this has now been raised to £7000 per annum). A few local authorities are also subsidizing play-groups. In 1969, the Department of Health and Social Security announced a capital grant of £9000 and a recurring grant of £45,000 to the PPA, to be paid in 1972. There are other play-group organizations providing care for young children, mostly in large cities where masses of working-class people live. One of the most important of these is the Save the Children Fund Play-Group, which is financed out of its own charitable resources.

In May, 1972, the Secretary of State for Education stated that the total annual expenditure on preschool education was about £12.5 million, excluding any contributions to the play-group associations, and that, based on present policies, this would rise to about £15 million per year in the mid-1970s. This is about 2.5 times larger than the expenditure reported in this study for maintained nursery schools (6.1 million), which shows how small this segment of the early childhood education program is.

As to the future, the White Paper anticipates a special building program that will cost approximately £15 million a year for the years 1974-1976. It also expects that annual government expenditure on education for children under 5 (approximately £42 million in 1971-1972) will rise to £65 million in 1976-1977.

INSTRUCTIONAL METHODS

The general philosophy underlying instructional methodology in nursery schools in England is a direct outgrowth of the teachings of Froebel. It is well summarized in a statement by Cusden (1938):

> The nursery school is first and foremost an educational institution which takes the whole child for its provision. . . . It is equally concerned with the physical, mental, and emotional phase of the child's development and is specifically designed to provide conditions which will contribute to the natural and progressive growth of the child's faculties, the development of robust physique, the formation of desirable habits, the stimulation of healthy mental and spiritual reactions to social environment [p. 51].

Thus, the nursery school methods tend to be child-centered, and no formal lessons are given. The children occupy themselves in indoor and outdoor play; they draw, paint, model, listen to stories, sing and dance to music, play shop, and practice domestic duties.

In recent years, the methods have used and stressed the developmental approach, which draws heavily upon the writings both of Gessell and of Dewey. Their pragmatic approach was that the young child should be free to create his own educational and learning environment and that the teacher's main function is to assist him in that task. This philosophy stresses the concept of readiness; that is, the teacher is to wait until the child has demonstrated a readiness to master a concept before she attempts to teach it to him. It was the hope of the leaders of the nursery school, and the progressive movement of the 1930s, that these methods would help to initiate reforms at higher levels in the educational system. Apparently, this hoped-for outcome has occurred, at least to some degree, as one can see by the healthy and vigorous growth of the British infant school, which seems to be much more concerned with the development of the whole child than with specific academic achievements. However, one must not express this opinion too strongly, because some believe that much of the British infant school instructional methodology grew out of the teachings of Montessori, who was never particularly welcome in the nursery school movement in England.

One of the areas of chief concern in the debate over early childhood education in England turns on the concept of readiness, particularly as it affects children from economically-deprived homes. Blackstone (1972), discussing the possible benefits of a more structured language curriculum, states

> Many teachers fear such an innovation, because they are committed, quite rightly, to the principle of informal education and learning and teaching, arising from the children's interests and environment. It is necessary to convince them that the preliminaries to the basic skills, or what used to be called the three R's, may be more effectively accomplished by drawing out of the situation, more opportunities for structured teaching. The latter has the advantage that it concentrates the teacher on the achievement of certain goals and provides her with a specific route to attain these [p. 18].

Halsey (1972) supports this point of view as follows:

> Preschools must be for learning and therefore need professional guidance, a carefully worked out curriculum, and organized links to the infant school, but at the same time there is the need for parental cooperation and local community involvement [p. 27].

RESEARCH ON EARLY CHILDHOOD EDUCATION

In the last 15 years, some very good research has been done on young children in England and Wales. There have been both cross-sectional and longitudinal studies. Four major pieces of research will be reported here.

In a recent speech on the significance of research in early childhood education in the United Kingdom, Dr. W. T. Wall (1972) made the following points:

1. Ages 1 to 5 are known to be extremely important in the development of a child. There is a great need to study the interaction of biological components, the environment, and early learning. There has not been much progress beyond Cyril Burt's in the 1920s, which documented the high correlation between social class and achievement, particularly the mother's style of learning. Current research is increasingly regarded as highly crucial.

2. There are three major domains of research concern: the cognitive, the affective, and the emotional. We need much more information on how environment, learning order, and feedback affect these domains. The work of the Newsons and Burton White should particularly be studied.

3. Research is badly needed on the optimal conditions under which the first separation of parent and child should take place for any prolonged period of time, as in attending preschool. Clearly this will not be the same age for all children. The work of James Robertson was reviewed in this context.

4. Much more needs to be known about language usage and associated learning styles. Bernstein's work was cited as an example of research that should be pursued and extended.

Research has advanced so rapidly in England in the past 15 years that only now are the benefits beginning to show. Teachers, too, are becoming much more involved, particularly in action research. For example, the Schools Council Research Organization is controlled by teachers, which gives hope that its results will have real implications for the classroom. Two of the more interesting preschool studies under the auspices of this organization are the identification of good practices in preschool, and the preschool language project.

The best known research study on early childhood education in England is "Children and Their Primary Schools" (Plowden Report, 1967). Its main purposes were to study the interaction between the home and school as it affects the performance of children in the primary schools and to reform the primary schools accordingly. Three major areas were studied: parental attitudes, home circumstances, and the state of the school. A series of questionnaires were sent to parents, teachers, and interested lay people. Of the parents approached, 95% cooperated in interviews.

The relevant results of the Plowden survey are summarized in Table 4.10. This shows that, taken together, the variables of parental attitudes and home circumstances account for a very substantial portion of the variance in performance,

TABLE 4.10

Percentage Contribution of Parental Attitudes, Home Circumstances and State of School to Variation in Education Performance

	Infants	Between Schools		All Pupils
		Lower Juniors	Top Juniors	
Parental Attitudes	24	20	39	28
Home Circumstances	16	25	17	20
State of School	20	22	12	17
Unexplained[a]	40	33	32	35
	100	100	100	100

	Infants	Within Schools		All Pupils
		Lower Juniors	Top Juniors	
Parental Attitudes	16	15	29	20
Home Circumstances	9	9	7	9
State of School	14	15	22	17
Unexplained	61	61	42	54
	100	100	100	100

Source: "Children and Their Primary Schools" (The Plowden Report), Central Advisory Council for Education. H.M.S.O. 1967, Vol. I and II.

[a] The unexplained variation is due to differences between children which have not been covered by our variables, and also to errors in measurement. That so much variation has been explained – the amount in the between-schools analysis is remarkable for an inquiry of this kind – is due in part to the comparatively simple nature of the criterion variable, a reading comprehension test.

much more than variables in the school. This finding is very much in line with the results of the Coleman (1966) study of equality of educational opportunity in the United States.

It is of particular interest that the influence of parental attitudes tends to be greater on older than on younger children. In discussing the variable "state of the school", the Plowden Committee (1967) says:

> Our findings can give hope to the school, to interested parents, and to those responsible for educational policy. Parental attitudes appear as a separate influence because they are not monopolized by any one class. Many manual workers and their wives already encourage and support their children's efforts to learn. If there are many now, there can be even more later. Schools can exercise their influence not only directly upon children but also indirectly through their relationships with parents [p. 36]. Some readers may be surprised at what they suppose to be the comparatively small influence of the school. To feel thus is to misunderstand the table. What emerged as important about the schools was the experience and competence of teachers. . . . The parents have usually had their children in their care for their whole lives, whereas most of the class teachers . . . had been with the children only for the best part of one school year [p. 35].

As a direct outgrowth of the Plowden Report, a number of educational priority area projects were established, as already mentioned. The results of 3 years of action research in the four districts involved have been extensively reported in "Educational Priority: EPA Problems and Policies" (1972) by A. Halsey of Nuffield College, Oxford. Dr. Halsey lists three general conclusions of considerable interest in our present context.

> The first is that preschooling is the most effective educational instrument for applying the principle of positive discrimination and this conviction rests partly on the theory that primary and secondary educational attainment has its social foundations in the child's experience in the preschool years and partly on the evidence that positive discrimination at the preschool level can have a multiplying effect on the overwhelmingly important educative influences of the family and the peer group to which the child belongs.
>
> Second, preschooling is a point of entry into the development of the community school. It is the point at which, properly understood, the networks of family and formal education can most easily be linked. It is, by the same token, the point at which innovated intervention can begin in order to break the barrier which, especially in Educational Priority Areas, separates the influence of school and community; the point where the vested interests of organization and custom are most amenable to change.
>
> Third, there is no unique blue-print of either organization or content which could be applied mechanically as national policy. On the contrary, the essential prerequisite is correct diagnosis of the needs of individual children and of particular E.P.A. conditions (which it cannot be too often repeated vary enormously) with all that this implies for a flexible provision of nursery education for the under-fives in the Educational Priority Areas . . . [p. 27].

For early childhood education, perhaps the most important comment is

> Children who commence full-time schooling before the age of five are, as they approach the transfer to junior schools or classes some two years later, more advanced educationally and better adjusted in school than those who commence school after the age of five, irrespective of the socio-economic status of their families [p. 24].

It must be kept in mind, however, that only 15% of the entire population studied had attended any form of precompulsory education. We would expect this to bias the findings, because they would not be based upon a random sample of the population. On the other hand, in England and Wales there are priority assignments for the limited number of places in preschool, and these favor those from the most needy homes. The finding is, therefore, more representative than it would be otherwise. *From Birth to Seven* (Davie *et al.*, 1972) analyzes the effects of the following variables: bad housing, family size, working mothers, social class and height, smoking in pregnancy, ability and attainment, the need for special education, sex differences, class size, behavior, and adjustment. A review of Davie *et al.*, in *Education* (1972) comes to the general conclusion that:

> ... the average gap in reading attainment between the children from unskilled families and those from professional families was found to be well over two years at the age of seven. However, disadvantage is cumulative, so that the gap between the least advantaged—those from large families, with an unskilled father, living in overcrowded homes and with poor amenities—and the most advantaged children was *on average* over four years [p. 545].

Another study using the same data base and testing age, *Born Illegitimate* (Crellin, Pringle, and West, 1971), compares the school abilities of three groups of children: legitimate, adopted illegitimate, and illegitimate children not adopted. Six comparisons are offered: general knowledge, oral language ability, creativity, Draw-a-Man test, reading, and arithmetic (Table 4.11). The findings were based upon a battery of tests, and teachers' perceptions of the children are very consistent over the six areas measured. Quality of performance is found to be strongly associated with whether or not the child is legitimate, adopted illegitimate, or illegitimate and not adopted. In short, the legitimate child performs most ably and the nonadopted illegitimate child most poorly.

A significant study of urban child-rearing practices, *Four Years Old in an Urban Community* (Child Development Research Unit, University of Nottingham, 1968), was prepared by John and Elizabeth Newson. The urban community was Nottingham in the English Midlands. The sample of children involved was 700. The method employed was extensive taped interviews with the parents. The authors found that there are important differences in the discipline methods

TABLE 4.11
Per Cent Below Average

	Legitimate	Adopted Illegitimate	Illegitimate
General Knowledge	28	16	45
Oral Ability	21	14	32
Creativity	33	33	44
Draw-a-Man Test	28	26	40
Reading Ability	28	18	49
Arithmetic		31	38

used by middle-class and working-class parents. Those of the middle class discipline with words, working-class parents by nonverbal means. In situations such as childrens' quarrels, middle-class mothers interfere; they want to introduce a feeling of justice both to their child and the child he is quarrelling with. They do this through the intervention of words. Working-class parents, on the other hand, are inclined to let the children settle their own quarrels. One of the obvious results of the oral intervention is that the middle-class parent spends more time interacting with his child than does the working-class parent, and thus reinforces the importance of language. In disputes with his mother, the middle-class child is rewarded when, by his reasoning ability and his success in communication, he can convince her that he is right. This creates in him a feeling of equality and a recognition that democratic principles are being applied to him. Working-class mothers tend not to encourage their children to argue or dispute points with them. This is not to say, however, that the working-class mother cannot talk if she wishes; it was found that she would do so at great length with the interviewer. It is more that she chooses not to talk with her child. Her methods of interacting with him are nonverbal. The Newsons believe that such differences in child-rearing practices between the social classes have important implications for the child's later schooling. These findings coincide with the conclusion of Basil Bernstein (1971), who has written extensively on the importance of different language backgrounds among young children of different classes.

Four major conclusions emerge from a consideration of the current research on preschool education in England and Wales.

1. Home circumstances account for a very substantial portion of variation in student performance. For one example, middle-class children perform better than lower-class; for another, legitimate children perform better than illegitimate.

2. Parental attitudes have a direct effect on children as students, especially older children. One of the most heartening developments is increased parental involvement in problems of preschool education.

3. Children who commence full-time schooling before the age of 5 later show themselves much more advanced educationally and better adjusted in school than those who commence later, irrespective of familial socioeconomic differences.

4. Television is a great potential tool for preschool education. Research in this area, however, is embryonic and inconclusive.

ACKNOWLEDGMENTS

The author wishes to acknowledge the contributions of the many people who have made this report possible: Mr. W. D. Wall, Dean, Institute of Education, London, who reviewed and commented on the manuscript; Mr. L. Burrows, Her Majesty's Chief Inspector of Primary Education; Miss E. McDougall, Her Majesty's Inspector, Department of Education and Science; Mr. G. Goatman and Miss E. Smith, Statistics Branch, Department of Education and Science; Miss Blackstone, London School of Economics; Miss Magraw, Head, Rachel Keeling Nursery School; and Miss Roberts and Mrs. Harvey, of the *Organization Mondiale pour l'Education Pré scolaire,* United Kingdom.

BIBLIOGRAPHY

Austin, G., & Antonsen, D. *A review of preschool educational efforts in five countries.* OECD, 1971. Mimeographed.

Bernstein, Basil. *Class, codes and control,* (Vol. 1). London: Routledge & Kegan Paul, 1971.

Blackstone, T. *Preschool education in Europe, Studies on permanent education* Strasbourg: Council of Europe (No. 13/1970).

Blackstone, T. *A fair start—the provision of preschool education.* London: Allen Lane The Penguin Press, 1971.

Blackstone, T. *First schools of the future.* Fabian research series No. 304, July 1972.

Blackwell, F. National Council for Educational Technology—*The primary extension programme, England.* Paper presented at Seminar on Curriculum in Compensatory ECE, Jerusalem, November 1972.

Burrows, L. J. Speech at United Kingdom Organisation Mondiale pour l'Education Préscolaire seminar. September 1972.

Coleman, J. S. *Equality of educational opportunity.* Washington, D.C.: United States Government Printing Office, 1966.

Connor, E. *The Journal of the Liverpool Educational Priority Area Project,* No. 3, Summer 1970.

Crellin, E., Pringle, M. L. K., & West, P. *Born illegitimate: social and educational implications* (a report by National Children's Bureau). London: John Gardner Ltd., 1972.

Cusden, P. *The English nursery school.* London: Kegan Paul, 1938.

Davie, R., Butler, N., & Goldstein, H. *From birth to seven: a report of the National Child Development Study.* London: Clowes, 1972.

Halsey, A. H. *Educational Priority: EPA problems and policies* (Vol. 1). London: HMSO, October 1972.

Halsey, A. H. Schools are for learning in. *The Guardian,* June 28, 1972.

Jones, J. *Priority area play-groups and day care centers, Birmingham, England.* Presented at Seminar on curriculum in Compensatory ECE, Jerusalem, November 1972.

Lovett, T. *The role of school managers in educational priority areas.* The Liverpool Educational Priority Area Project, Occasional papers No. 3., 1970.

Midwinter, E. *Educational priority areas: the philosophic question.* The Liverpool Educational Priority Area Project, Occasional Papers No. 1., 1970.

Midwinter, E. *Home and school relations in educational priority areas.* The Liverpool Educational Priority Area Project, Occasional papers No. 3., 1970.

Morell, D. *Education and change.* Joseph Payne Memorial Lectures to the College of Preceptors, 1966.

Newson, J. and E. *Four years old in an urban community.* London: Allen and Unwin Ltd. 1968.

Palmer, R. *Starting school: A study in policies.* ULP, 1971.

Parry, E. M., & Archer, H. *The significance of recent research in early childhood in the U.K.* OMEP, World Council Seminar. September, 1972.

Pulman, K. *The Liverpool EPA: A description.* The Liverpool Educational Priority Area Project, Occasional Papers No. 2., 1970.

Robertson, J., *Young Children in Hospitals.* New York: Basic Books, 1959.

Schultze, W. *Schools in Europe* (Vol. 2, Part A.). Weinheim: Beltz Verlag, 1968.

Taylor, P., Exon, G., & Holley, B. *A study of nursery education* School Council working paper 41, Evans-Melhuen. Education. 1972.

Trouillet, B. *Die Vorschulerziehung in neun Europäischen Ländern.* Weinheim: Beltz Verlag, 1968.

Waddington, M. *The years from 5 to 7 in comparative education* (Vol. 1). Nr. October 1, 1964.

Wall, W. D. *The significance of recent research in early childhood in the U.K.* OMEP, World Council Seminar, September 1972.

Board of Education, United Kingdom, *Report of the women inspectors on children under five years of age in public elementary schools, 1905.*

United Kingdom, *Report of the consultative committees upon the school attendance of children below the age of five, 1908.*

Children and their primary schools (The Plowden Report) Central Advisory Council for Education. HMSO 1967, Vol. 1 and II.

Council of Europe: August 3, 1971. Committee for general and technical education, symposium on preschool education, aims, methods and problems.

Council for cultural cooperation. *School systems–a guide.* Education in Europe, Council of Europe, Strasbourg, 1970.

Education, Volume 140, Number 2, July 14, 1972. Lady Plowden addresses SEO at the annual summer meeting, 31-32. Councils and Education Press Ltd.

Education, Volume 139, No. 23, June 9, 1972. *From Birth to Seven,* p. 553. Councils and Education Press Ltd.

Education, Volume 139, No. 26, June 30, 1972 Nursery Schools, Play-groups, p. 646. Councils and Educaton Press Ltd.

Ministry of Education, United Kingdom, Circular 280, 1954.

Ministry of Education, United Kingdom. Circular 8/60, May, 1960.

National Bureau for Cooperation in Child Care, Play-Group Project, Southwark, London.

OECD. *Classification of educational systems, United Kingdom.* Paris, 1972.

OECD. *Economic surveys.* Paris, 1972.

OECD. *Labor force statistics, 1959-1970.* Paris, 1972.

OECD/CERI. *Innovation in education—England.* Technical report, Corbett, A., 1971.

Reports on education, December, 1968, No. 51.

Reports on education, January, 1969, No. 52.

Secretary of State, Department of Education and Science. *Education, a framework for expansion* (White Paper). HMSO, 1972.

Mrs. Thatcher shares aims of all involved in nursery campaign. *The Times Educational Supplement,* May 19, 1972.

Most English parents in favor of "Sesame Street" and support for "Sesame Street." *The Times Educational Supplement,* July 14, 1972.

Working class are always disappointed. *The Times Educational Supplement,* September 1, 1972.

Innovators should go beyond the curriculum. *The Times Educational Supplement,* September 1, 1972.

United Nations demographic yearbook, 1970.

United Nations. *Analyses and projections of households and families.* 1971.

UNESCO. *La formation et la situation professionnelle des enseignants préscolaires.* decembre 1965.

Worker's Educational Association. *Service center for social studies.* Background notes on social studies, No. 2, 1971.

Early Childhood Education in Canada

INTRODUCTION

In late nineteenth century Canada, early childhood education began as a privilege for wealthy children. The initial organizers of kindergarten viewed childhood as a special time for the growing and unfolding of children's talents, and the preschool was seen as the place to foster this growth and development. Thus, in this setting, the children's natural tendencies toward spontaneity and individuality were to be channeled into social adjustment and cooperation. All of this was strikingly asocial; kindergarten teachers talked about the child, not classes of children; they discussed individual needs and projects to meet these needs. All this was possible because the program addressed only the needs of the wealthy.

If kindergarten began as an idea for the educational emancipation of the children of the wealthy, it was soon adopted to help the poor as well. It was stimulated by a concern over immigrant life and early industrial poverty. Settlement house workers, philanthropists, and educators sought, then as now, to make the kindergartens into a supplement for the children of the poor. The rationale for this commitment quickly became familiar. Parents who worked, were poor, spoke a foreign language, and had problems adjusting to the urban environment could help their children adjust to their new environment by sending them to kindergarten.

One of the first provinces to provide free public preschool education was Ontario, in 1882. Kindergartens became part of the elementary school system in Ontario by permissive, not mandatory, legislation passed in 1885. School boards in other provinces have added them by gradual stages until they have become standard in some provinces. By and large, however, kindergarten education in Canada spread very slowly until the end of World War II. As in many other nations, it has only been in the last 20 years that the Canadians have turned again to early childhood education as a possible way of solving some of the problems faced by educators in trying to provide a more adequate educational preparation for children who come from poor home backgrounds.

This review will describe developments in early childhood education in Canada from 1960 to the present.

ENROLLMENTS, PRESCHOOL EDUCATION (1960-1970)

The OECD "Classification of Educational Systems" (1972) gives the following characteristics for nursery schools and kindergartens in Canada:

Nursery schools
1. Length of study in years equals up to three years.
2. Entrance requirement is to be three years or over.
3. The majority of these schools are private. In some provinces they require the approval of provincial authority. These schools are generally included in statistical reports on education. Quebec, Ontario, and Manitoba are gradually bringing children of this level into the public school system.

Kindergartens
1. Length of study equals generally one year.
2. Entrance requirement is to be 5 years old.
3. In the public sector, these schools are attached to primary schools and are included in their overall statistical reports. There are private kindergarten schools and also classes which are attached to private elementary schools [p. 1].

Table 5.1 presents enrollments for private and public kindergartens and nursery schools, and therefore includes children aged 3 to 5, inclusively. The substantial growth of 814.3% shown for the private sector over the past 10 years is, however, open to question because the 1960-1961 enrollment figure is an estimate. If the 5-year period 1965-1970 alone is taken, the growth would be no more than 33.3%. In the public sector there has been an increase of 152.9% over the 10-year period.

The total column in Table 5.1, using the estimate based on a very high figure for the private sector, shows that there has been an overall increase of 182.9% over the 10 years. If, however, the 5 years between 1965 and 1970, for which

TABLE 5.1
Enrollments in Kindergartens in Canada from 1960-61 to 1970-71

| | | | (in 000's) |
Year	Private	Public	Total
1960-61	7[a]	138	146
1965-66	48	219	268
1966-67	50	245	295
1967-68	53	275	328
1968-69	58	316	374
1969-70	61	346	407
1970-71	64	349	413
% of increase from 1960-61 to 1970-71	814.3	152.9	182.9
% of increase from 1965-66 to 1970-71	33.3	59.4	54.1

Source: Statistics Canada, Educational Division, Projections
          Section, Ottawa.
[a]Estimate (survey on private sector started only with 1965-66 year).

we have better statistics, were taken, the private sector would be seen to have grown by 33.3%, the public sector by 59.4%, and the total by 54.1%. The ratio of children attending kindergartens in the private sector as compared with the public sector shows an interesting fluctuation. In 1960-1961, 4.7% of all children attending a kindergarten were estimated to be going to a private one. In 1965-1966, this figure had grown to 17.9%, but in 1970-1971 it dropped to 15.5%. Of the children attending kindergarten in 1970-1971, 84.5% went to a public school. The increased enrollment of preprimary children (aged 3-5 years) in public school is partly attributable to the rising attendance of the junior kindergartens, which are oriented to serving the 4-year-old.

The total increase of 182.9% in kindergarten enrollment can be compared with a 13.3% increase for primary schools over the same 10-year period. This clearly shows where the major expansion has taken place.

Table 5.2 gives population attendance rates for kindergartens for the 10-year period from 1960-1961 to 1970-1971. It shows that in 1960-1961 the percentage of the total population of children 3 to 5 years of age in school was 11.4, and that by 1970-1971 this had grown to 34.2. Since the vast majority of kindergarten children are actually 5-year-olds, it is perhaps more revealing to look at statistics on that age group, or as near to it as possible. In 1960-1961, 33.5% of the "5-year-olds" were in kindergarten, and for 1970-1971 the figure appears to be 110.4%. The reason for the excess above can be explained by the

TABLE 5.2

Population Attendance Rates in Kindergartens in Canada from 1960–61
to 1970–71

	1960–61	1970–71	(in 000's) % of Change
Total age group 3 - 5 years in kindergartens	146	413	182.9
Infant population 3 - 5 years	1,278	1,206	-5.6
% of age group enrolled	11.4	34.2	200.0

Source: United Nations Demographic Yearbook, 1970.

relatively small number of 3- and 4-year-olds contained in the school enrollment
figures. Table 5.2 also clearly illustrates the statistic that there has been a 5.6%
decline in the infant population (3- to 5-year-olds) during the last 10 years. This
gives an overall change of 200% in the enrollments from the last age group over
the same period.

The 5.6% decline in the 3- to 5-year-old group, noted above, has further
importance when we note that in the year 1968-1969 the primary school
population also began to decrease. This has created both problems and possibilities in Canada. It has meant empty primary classrooms that could be filled by
preprimary classes; but, by the same token, it has meant retraining primary
teachers for preprimary jobs. Too often, it seems, primary teachers have brought
primary school practices with them to the kindergartens. This has produced
some friction between the regular preprimary teachers and those who have been
retrained into the methods of instruction and the basic objectives of this level of
instruction.

In the school year 1971-1972, the following percentages of children were
involved in some form of preschool program. The information is given both by
single year and multiple year age groupings.

6	99%	5-6	92%
5	85	4-6	70
4	25	3-6	54
3	5	2-6	43
2	1		

So far, we have been considering statistics from a national viewpoint. There is,
however, considerable variation in enrollments between provinces, and these are

TABLE 5.3
Enrollment Ratios by Province: 1951-52, 1967-68, 1980-81, As
Proportion of Five-Year-Olds

	1951-52	1967-68	1980-81 (projected)
Newfoundland	–	71	86
Prince Edward Island	3	2	80
Nova Scotia	103	104	105
New Brunswick	–	1	72
Quebec	6	63	125
Ontario	64	91	154
Manitoba	28	52	85
Saskatchewan	14	20	60
Alberta	1	2	9
British Columbia	7	42	82

Source: Zsigmond and Wenaas (1970).

demonstrated in Table 5.3. It is worth noting that, in Nova Scotia, kindergartens are part of the regular school, so that almost all 5-year-olds attend, while the growth of kindergartens in Quebec from 1951-1967 was the largest for any province during that 16-year period. The percentages sometimes exceed 100% because the enrollment statistics include, once again, 2-, 4-, and 5-year-olds, while the population statistics are for 5-year-olds alone (Zsigmond and Wenaas, 1970).

As to future demands for places in kindergartens and nursery schools, the most cogent factors are probably the birthrate, family size, and proportion of women working outside their homes. Taking the birthrate first, in 1966 in Canada there were 19.3 live births per 1000 of the population. By 1970 this had dropped to 17.5, a decline of 1.8 live births per thousand, or 9.3%, over the 4-year period.[1] Table 5.2 has already taken this into account.

Household size in Canada has also decreased. In 1871, the average number of persons per household was 5.92; in 1900 it was 5.07; in 1951 it was 4.11; and in 1966 it had dropped to 3.80. In short, over 95 years the average household in Canada had decreased by 2.06 children.[2] The same set of statistics gives the gross reproduction rate in 1921 as 1.6; in 1961 it had risen to 1.9; but by 1966 it had declined sharply to 1.4. So over this 45-year period, the gross reproduction rate had dropped by .2%.

It is observable that parents with smaller families especially desire their children to mix with others outside the home, even at very early ages, and that

[1] *United Nations demographic yearbook.* 1970.
[2] *Analysis and projections of households and families.* Population Division, Dept. of Economic and Social Affairs, The United Nations Secretariat.

kindergartens seem to be the right place for this. It can be expected, therefore, that with the current decrease in family size in Canada, there will be a corresponding increase in demand for places in the kindergartens.

Statistics for women doing daily work away from their homes in Canada are given in Table 5.4. It will be clear from these that, while the labor participation rates of males over the period 1960-1970 have either remained the same or have decreased slightly, the participation rate of females has increased. Unfortunately, only one statistic on the participation rate of married females is available, but this indicates that the number of married females working in the total population is higher than the statistic just for females working in the total labor force. Since another reason for children attending kindergarten is that many mothers work, these figures assure a continuing demand for places.

ISSUES OF DEBATE

The issues of debate in Canada on early childhood education are particularly varied, a reflection of Canadian society itself. The Royal Commission on Education in Ontario (1945-1950) made the following recommendations as to public responsibility for preschool education:

(a) That, conditional upon maintenance of a required minimum standard of education in grades I to VI inclusive, as determined by the Minister, local educational authorities be permitted to establish nursery schools and classes for 3-year-old and 4-year-old children.

(b) That attendance at such schools or classes be voluntary and on a half-day basis.

(c) That the full cost of the establishment and operation of such schools or classes be the responsibility of the local educational authority.

(d) That, for pupils attending such classes, local educational authorities be authorised to charge such fees as they may deem necessary. [In Fleming, 1971b, p. 41, Vol. III.]

From this, it is apparent that the Royal Commission's first concern was for primary education and that preprimary came second. Clause 4, authorizing local authorities to charge as necessary for preprimary programs, often favored the children of wealthier parents.

In 1957 the Economic Council of Canada stressed the relationship between education and economic progress, pointing out that increasing the investment in human capital is probably the best single way of moving a society forward. In its view, an important development was increased concern for poor or otherwise disadvantaged Canadian children. This, of course, raised the crucial question of how to create better educational opportunities for them. Reid (1968) is more specific about the relationship between early childhood education and economic

TABLE 5.4
Labor Force Participation Rates – Canada

	1960 %	1970 %
$\dfrac{\text{Total Labor Force}}{\text{Total Population}}$ x 100		
(a) Total	36.5	39.6
(b) Males	53.9	53.9
(c) Females	18.8	25.2
$\dfrac{\text{Total Labor Force}}{\begin{array}{l}\text{Population from}\\ \text{15 to 64 years}\end{array}}$ x 100		
(a) Total	62.3	64.0
(b) Males	91.9	86.9
(c) Females	32.0	40.8

Source: Labor Force Statistics, 1959–70, O.E.C.D., Paris, 1972.

development. He observes that:

> On the one hand there is the question of preparing individuals for the world-of-work and of maximising their contribution to economic growth in this era of permanent scientific and technological revolution (popularly called the "age of automation"). For this goal an additional $1 million invested today in pre-primary school education could reduce by at least several million dollars the expenditures that will be necessary to train and retrain many of today's four- and five-year-olds fifteen years from now for the radically changed world-of-work of 1983. If, in other words, the approach to preparing individuals for the world-of-work had a deeper and a longer-run perspective in decision-making than it has at present, Canada would have a much more rational and efficient allocation of funds today [p. 334].

The size of the problem of providing educational opportunity for the disadvantaged children of Canada is thoroughly documented in the Education Report of the Special Senate Committee on Poverty published in 1971. The following passages are especially relevant in the context of the present survey:

> Little can be done to change the socio-economic mix of young Canadians reaching the final years of high school by a continuation of massive infusion of public funds into universities, community colleges or indeed into the high schools themselves. Some semblance of equity in that mix in the final years of high school depends

primarily on such equity in grade 8 which in turn depends on preferential educational programmes for the children of the working poor and public assistance recipients when they are three, four, and five years old.

The 530,000 poverty children under the age of six are, of course, found in every region and every province in Canada. . . . That a wide variety of programmes must be made available to reach these young children of the poor is made clear by the following facts concerning where the children live.

Across Canada as a whole, over 50 per cent of these children live in rural areas. . . . Whereas about 57 per cent of these children in male headed families live in rural areas of Canada, only 16 per cent of the children in female headed families live in rural areas. (The children in female headed families make up about 10 per cent of the total). . . .

The poverty children of Quebec make up about 35 per cent of the Canadian total. This is followed by Ontario with about 21 per cent, then the four Atlantic provinces with about 20 per cent, then the three Prairie provinces with about 18 per cent and finally B.C. with about 6 per cent. . . .

The implications for learning programmes of the geographical distribution of Canada's poverty children under 6 years of age are numerous. For one thing there is no single panacea educational programme which could possibly be devised to meet both the needs of the poverty children in rural New Brunswick and the inner city slum areas of Vancouver and Toronto. . . .

Somewhere between 10 and 15 per cent of Canada's poverty children under 6 years of age are "non-white," that is, they are Negro (Black), Indian, Metis, or Eskimo [p. 11].

The Canadian Teachers' Federation, testifying before this Senate Committee, elaborated on this last point by saying that:

. . . Particular emphasis is placed on the severe educational problems of the Indians, Eskimos, Metis and Negroes of Canada. While they often suffer the general problems associated with poverty, they have additional problems resulting from cultural differences . . . the native peoples, urban or rural, and the Negroes, (constitute) the most intractable problem [p. 13].

Complicating the whole issue are problems posed by recent immigrant arrivals in Canada. In 1966 the numbers were these:

Birthplace	Number	Percent of total
English-speaking countries	95,000	49
French-speaking countries	9,000	5
Others	91,000	47
Total	195,000	101

The educational implications of such statistics are illustrated, for example, by the situation in the Borough of Scarborough, Ontario. ". . . in the spring of 1970, five elementary schools in areas described as heavily new Canadian or low-income failed more than 20 per cent of their grade eight students, and almost all of these children went to specialised vocational schools." The borough-wide failure average was only 8%, and in some schools no one failed. This should not have come as a surprise to the members of the Scarborough School Board, however, because in 1967 a study (attitudes and perceptions of grade 9 secondary school students) showed that a vastly disproportionate number of children in families where Italian was the language usually spoken at home were in the truncated, dead-end, 2-years stream in their secondary schools. Returning to the words of Senate Committee on Poverty's report:

> There are in Canada today over 530,000 children under six years of age belonging to over 300,000 families living below the poverty line. At the most, 50,000 of these children are today receiving some kind of learning help from resources other than those internal to their families. Most of these children who *are* receiving outside learning help are five years old. The one, two, three and four year old poverty children desperately need learning help; they are not getting it. What is needed above all is a commitment by the people of Canada that these children must and shall receive learning help (if only on the hard-headed economic grounds that a dollar spent on their learning to use "words" at the age of two will save ten dollars spent on largely ineffective remedial English or French language training in the elementary school) [p. 20].

It then makes the following specific recommendations:

1. The establishment of a Canada child development center.
2. Home tutoring programs for children 1 year to 3 years of age.
3. Home educational television (ETV) for children 1 year to 4 years of age.
4. In-school programs for children beginning at the age of 3.

The report concludes with the statement:

> The basic sad facts remain: there are between 85,000 to 100,000 poverty children in Canada who are four years of age and only 10 per cent at the very most are in some sort of pre-kindergarten training situation either public or private. . . . Add to these 75,000 excluded poverty four-year-olds, about 90,000 excluded poverty three-year-olds and at least 50,000 excluded poverty five-year-olds, and the magnitude of Canada's public policy failure during the 1950s and 1960s at the pre-kindergarten and kindergarten level becomes starkly apparent. . . . There is so much money being wasted today in Canada in education at the university, community college and secondary school levels that a conserted, successful drive to eliminate costly duplication of facilities and programmes and to weed out "feather-bedding" would release more than sufficient funds to employ skilled resources to ensure that at least every poverty five and four-year-old received school-sponsored, high-quality, compensatory education programmes [p. 29].

T. Reid (1972), writing a year after this was published, is even more insistent:

> The implementation of first-rate education programmes for all three-, four- and five-year-old children born into poverty in Canada would enable the vast majority of them to be out of the cycle of poverty within 15 years. In order to achieve this

objective, the government sector of Canada must first decide that in our society the children of the poor are going to be educated. There has never been such a commitment by the government sector. There is not today such a commitment. It does not appear that in the near future the government sector intends to make such a commitment [p. 104].

The Federal Department of Regional Economic Expansion, for example, had already started a major project called "New Start" in selected areas in six of the provinces. This was designed to increase the level of educational achievement, particularly for young children; and, as already pointed out, there have been very substantial increases in the number attending kindergarten over the last 10 years. There have also been the beginnings of growth in the junior kindergarten movement. Where such facilities have been made available, they have been restricted to children who were most in need of them. But it must be said that, for the most part, local school systems have made no substantial effort to provide for the prekindergarten age group, despite the mounting evidence of the importance of an adequate emotional, social, and intellectual environment for such young children. Where prekindergartens are provided, it is usually on a private or voluntary basis, which tends to discriminate against the disadvantaged parent. McPhee (1973) pointed out the isolation of young families in rural communities, the disappearance of the extended family, the increase of families with young children living in high rise apartments and the inadequate provision of playing areas in urban and suburban neighborhoods are major contributions to the increased discussion about the need for education of the young in this country.

One of the more interesting and provocative documents on early childhood education from the private sector was prepared jointly by the Canadian Mental Health Association in Ontario and by the Junior League of Toronto in 1971. It seeks to bring an awareness of the young and their problems into the curriculum of secondary schools and certain instructional programs for adults. The main recommendations are

That school curriculum should include a year of study of the human infant and child, to be available to both males and females before they reach school-leaving age and to include experience in caring for infants and preschool aged children in day care centers, located in schools or by means of field trips to day care centers. That prenatal instruction should emphasize the emotional and intellectual needs of infants and the period when mother and new born are in maternity wards and hospitals should be used for such instruction, if possible by means of special closed-circuit television programs [p. 31].

The status of women in Canada, particularly as it concerns young children and the perceptions of a woman's identity, is an issue of considerable importance. In 1970 a report issued by the Royal Commission on the Status of Women in

Canada had the following to say:

> As we pointed out in chapter I, society moulds children's perceptions of the world and of themselves. Boys are expected to be interested in sports, girls in cooking and babies, and so dishes and a doll-carriage are given to the little girl and a base-ball glove to the little boy. Inevitably a nurse's outfit is given to the girl and a doctor's case to the boy. . . .
>
> In the *Young Canada Reading Series,* used in Ontario and Alberta, the more versatile characters are almost invariably males. Pirates, Eskimos, Bible figures—interesting individuals in general—are seldom women. Boys in the stories are typically active and adventurous but girls are not. In another series, the *Language Patterns Program,* used in Ontario, the father is often shown as an understanding and kind person who takes his children on interesting expeditions. The mother, on the other hand, stays at home to prepare the meals and to tell the children what is best for them. . . . The Commission deplores the use of text books that provide so little recognition of the capabilities of women. Therefore, we recommend that the provinces and the territories adopt text books that portray women, as well as men, in diversified roles and occupations [p. 173-175].

In summary, the major issues of debate, as they concern the education of young children in Canada, appear at present to be threefold:

1. The need to develop education for the young child with due consideration for his individual and social needs.
2. The demand for equality of educational opportunities, beginning with first-rate programs for 3- to 5-year-olds from poor, deprived or newly-immigrant families.
3. The recognition of the increased importance of education in relation to the social and economic problems and challenges in Canadian society.

THE AIMS AND OBJECTIVES OF EARLY CHILDHOOD EDUCATION

The aims and objectives for preschool education in Canada vary in each one of the provinces. Fleming (1971b), writing about education in general, observes that:

> There are two opposing propositions which broadly categorise educational thinkers:
>
> (i) that the child can best attain self-realisation as an individual and a social being if he is shaped by experiences selected and organized by competent members of adult society;
>
> (ii) that he has within himself the urge toward growth, of which learning is a natural part, and that this impulse, if properly nourished, will carry him to the realisation of his full potentialities for individual and social development [Vol. III, p. 1].

In the area of preschool education, Canadians, for the most part, have chosen the second of these two options. Their preschools, in their aims, tend to stress that the child has within himself the urge toward growth and that he, better than anyone else, knows what his needs are. This is reflected in the objectives recommended for young children's education by the Royal Commission on Education in the province of Quebec (1964) namely:

1. To satisfy actual needs.
2. To develop the child's personality.
3. To give the child the possibility of occupying himself in accordance with his interests and particular aptitudes.

In an attempt to be specific about the aims of Ontario, Fleming (1971b) proposed the following eight objectives for nursery schools and kindergartens:

(1) To assist in the development of fundamental habits of living through the acquisition of proper health habits associated with rest, play and exercise, eating, and toilet practices.

(2) To develop and improve the use of language through listening to stories told by the teacher, relating personal experiences, looking at and discussing pictures, and communicating with fellow-pupils in play and other school situations; and gradually to develop "reading readiness" through these and similar exercises and experiences.

(3) To assist informally in the growth of the number sense through games and special activities appropriate to particular times of the day and season.

(4) To introduce aesthetic training by learning and appreciating simple tunes and rhythms; and, in art, by enlarging the appreciation and thoughtful use of different kinds of materials.

(5) To assist moral and spiritual development through morning prayer, sacred songs, verse speaking, and Bible stories.

(6) To provide an environment in which the child may develop a feeling of security and gain a sense of "belonging" so that he becomes less and less dependent on the teacher.

(7) To develop in the child a feeling of adequacy in meeting ordinary situations appropriate to his age by mastering the use of, and gaining confidence in his ability to handle, selected play equipment.

(8) To teach the child to work and play with others of his own age in an acceptable manner; to respect the rights of others and to await his turn; to select materials for games and activities, to use them, and then to replace them in their storage places [Vol. III, p. 132].

In the province of Alberta the Commission on Educational Planning (1972) offered the following:

For education in Alberta to become a life-long process, schooling should begin at the earliest age at which a child may derive benefit. All young children are endowed with greater potential for imagination, creativity, innovation, reasoning and understanding than was previously supposed. Few children have this potential developed to its fullest extent, either in their homes or in other parts of their environment.

From the earliest age this potential must be realised, rather than neglected or smothered. Once young children are ready to reap rewards and satisfaction from planned learning experiences, they should not be kept waiting too long for the opportunity. The principle of public responsibility for free education, which is accepted for older children, should apply to younger children as well. It is deserving of particular attention in the decades ahead.

Early education before the age of six should have three major functions . . . :

Stimulation: Opportunities should be offered for learning a variety of attitudes, skills and behaviours which will promote aesthetic, emotional, intellectual and physical development. This does not mean a downward extension of conventional schooling; rather, it means approaching each child on his terms—his language, his previous experiences, his likes and dislikes, his strengths and weaknesses, his family. In short, expression should be given to the principles of context, diversity, equity and personalization by fostering such growth. . . .

Identification: The identification function is concerned with the child's development of an appropriate self-image which helps him discern who he is. . . .

Socialisation: The young child can, of course, become too self-centered. He should also become aware of and sensitive to others; to learn that what others think or feel is important. At the same time, socially acceptable ways of behaving must be acquired. Thus, early education should also focus on helping children to learn to live with others [p. 51].

According to these statements, instruction in the three R's has no priority place in kindergarten education in Canada, nor is there any stress on cognition or early educationally oriented learning. The kindergarten and junior kindergartens seem more to be outward extensions of the home, filling complementary roles with the family in the process of bringing up the very young. From this it follows that parental education and involvement in the work of the kindergartens are areas of high concern for the average Canadian, at least in the provinces we have been considering.

ORGANIZATION AND CONTROL

The British North American Act of 1867, which united the Canadian provinces under a federal form of government, provided in subsection 93 for provincial autonomy in education, but it protected the rights of religious minorities in a clause that said that no provincial law should prejudicially affect any rights or privileges with respect to denominational schools which existed by the law at the time each province became part of the dominion.

As a result of this law, Canada has 10 provincial educational organizations, and in each of the provinces there is a ministry of education. In the Yukon and North West territories, the Canadian government itself has responsibility for educating school-aged children.

It is difficult to pick a particular date or province for the organization of the first preschool or kindergarten in Canada. In Ontario, which has usually been the leader in education, kindergartens were first organized in 1882 and made part of the elementary school system by legislation passed in 1885. School boards have added them by gradual stages until they come closer to being universal in the provinces (Fleming, 1971, Vol. III, p. 40).

In the predominantly French speaking province of Quebec, preschool education grew in response to a demand for providing a safe place for poor children to go during the day while their parents worked. The influence of the French *école maternelle* is apparent here, as are the teachings of Oberlin, Montessori, Kergomard, and Pape-Carpentier.

In the other nine provinces, the organization of kindergartens derives more from the ideas of Froebel, Owen, Buchanan, McMillan, Peabody, and Dewey. It had a strong social motivation in that:

1. It was hoped it would lead to social reform.
2. It was based on a recognition of the uniqueness of early childhood.
3. It was seen as a way of modifying the primary and secondary schools which followed it.

This use of kindergartens as a socializing more than an educational instrument is most noticeable, as in the United States, among the more affluent communities.

Despite variations in the educational system in the different provinces there is, nevertheless, a common pattern of organization and administration across the country. In general, responsibility for education is decentralized, a great deal of it resting with the local authorities. However, each of these authorities is ultimately responsible to a provincial Minister for Education. As already noted, there has been a tendency in recent years for the provincial level to become much more directly involved—not least because an increasingly high share of the cost is being financed by provincial funds.

Although in almost all provinces there are both private and public preschools, there are some exceptions. In Prince Edward Island, preprimary education is conducted in private kindergartens only. However, it is planned that provincial policy decisions will encourage public kindergarten enrollment and provide for 1700 places, starting in 1976.

In Nova Scotia, preprimary education for children age 4 and younger is organized by the Public Health and Welfare. Kindergarten, for children of age 5, is a part of the school system and comes under the Department of Education. Compulsory education starts at age 7.

In Alberta, most kindergartens are run independently of the public school system. The majority of private schools are church schools and most of them are Roman Catholic. The curriculum in private preschools parallels that of the public preschool very closely, for two major reasons: first, the ideas of both groups are similar; and second, the private schools commonly receive substantial subvention aid from the provincial government and therefore are subject to provincial legislation governing preschool education.

There are three main types of Canadian institutions providing care for children under the age of 6. They are day nursery, nursery school, and kindergarten. The day nursery (*garderie*) is designed primarily for the care of children of working parents, who leave them there for the full day. Children as young as 1.5 years are admitted. The nursery school is generally a private institution that may be operated as a cooperative venture or for profit. Most nursery school children are 3 or 4 years old and attend the school for half a day. The kindergarten is found in the public schools in most of the large cities, and there are private kindergartens too. Most kindergartens accept only 5-year-olds, but increasing numbers of 4-year-olds have recently been attending junior kindergartens. Over the last years, Quebec, Alberta, and Ontario followed the example of Ottawa and Toronto and began to establish junior kindergartens with an emphasis on providing an "uninterrupted first school [McPhee, 1973, P. 6]." As McPhee has pointed out, while the main idea for the junior kindergarten was first to support disadvantaged children, this emphasis has changed over time to include all children of 4 years of age, and to extend the range of the programs into the first 3 years of studies in primary school. This provides the child with an ungraded school experience between the ages of 4 and 8.

PHYSICAL SETTING: A VISIT TO A TORONTO KINDERGARTEN

The school observed was fairly typical of public schools in the center of Toronto. A large building, 70 years old, and a somewhat newer and smaller 40-year-old building housed 600 children from junior kindergarten to the sixth grade. There was not enough space for all the children, and three portable classrooms had been added in the schoolyard to accommodate the overflow. The whole school will be rebuilt within the next 2 years.

The school drew its children from an ethnically mixed area in the city. While the majority were "Anglo-Saxon" (mostly middle-class) at least 40% of the children came from Italian, Chinese, West Indian, and other backgrounds. For many, English was their second language.

The principal was an energetic young man who had a close working relationship with his teachers and maintained close community ties. There were frequent evening meetings between the school personnel and parents.

The school maintained four half-day kindergarten classes for 5-year-olds and two junior kindergarten classes for 4-year-olds. Kindergarten children attended school either for 3 hours in the morning class or for 2 hours in the afternoon. The kindergarten class observed on this visit was a morning one, held in a typically large, bright, and airy room. Large, colorful children's paintings on the walls added a feeling of warmth and cheerfulness. The room was divided into activity areas: a carpeted area around the piano where the children sat; a cluster of tables to work on; a phonograph area where children could sit by themselves or in small groups to listen to music or story-telling; and an art area, with some easels placed together near two sinks.

There were 22 children in this classroom, and 2 teachers. Officially, one of the teachers was an assistant, but in practice the teaching and the chores were shared, with the main teacher still assuming responsibility for parental reports and the overall direction of the class. The teacher was an enthusiastic young woman with 5 years of teaching experience. She seemed to enjoy her job and was very much concerned with her children as individuals. She tried to maintain contact with the parents of the children and encouraged parental participation in the classroom. Two parents came in each week to help in the class.

While the Board of Education in the city provides the general outline of a curriculum for the kindergartens, the actual method and plan of instruction is left to the school and, ultimately, to the teacher. The teacher of this classroom did not adhere to a strict daily plan. She believed in letting the tempo and interests of the children lead her lessons. She used indirect teaching for the greater part of the time, making the most of the spontaneity of the "right teaching moment." For example, during a music time, while the children were singing an Indian song that mentioned the name of a lake, she took time out to have a short discussion with the children about lakes.

Instead of a general plan of the day, the teacher had a reservoir of possible activities in her mind so that if the children did not pick any for themselves, she was ready with ideas. An attempt was made to alternate quiet sitting times with some kind of physical activity. Usually the second part of the morning was set aside for activities of the children's own choice and, of course, what went on in the different parts of the room changed with the children's interests. For example, there was some quite advanced spontaneous map-making by boys interested in racing their cars.

The teacher described her method of instruction as that of "exposure and experience." There was little formal teaching as such. Instead, the teaching was incorporated into the play and activities of the day. When the school's budget allowed, the children were taken on trips into the community. Again, the emphasis was on the children enjoying themselves and learning from their own experiences. Thus, they might go to a farm where they could play with the animals and have a picnic afteward. This was a new experience for these city children.

For materials, the teacher relied upon standard equipment such as large building blocks, a doll's house, "dressing-up" clothes, paints, sand and paste. Audiovisual media were also used extensively—films, phonograph, radio, tapes, and cameras. This teacher had a special interest in music, and she used records, songs, and the piano extensively in her teaching. The games and play in general were rich in learning experiences.

The teacher believed her main purpose was to prepare these children for life, and she helped them to set and achieve their own little objectives. She was concerned also that they should be adequately prepared to enter the first grade; hence, her program included mastery of number concepts, the alphabet, fluency in language, and a readiness to cooperate in social groups. The main provisions for reading readiness were activities involving concentration and listening. Piagetian tasks such as sorting and classification were taught through the use of card games.

Daily Program in a Kindergarten in Canada
(Followed very flexibly)

9:00	Entry.
9:05	Attendance.
9:05-9:30	Conversation, Story, Show and Tell, Music.
9:30-10:30	Activity Time.
10:30-10:45	Tidy Up.
10:45-11:00	Juice and Cookies.
11:00-11:15	Rest (Music Appreciation).
11:15-12:00	Outdoor Play.
12:00	Dismissal.

TEACHERS AND THEIR TRAINING

Admission requirements to teacher training colleges vary somewhat from province to province. They generally require graduation from high school—in some provinces at the junior matriculation level (that is, after 12 years of compulsory education), in others at the senior level (that is, after 13 years at school). The usual age of admission to a teacher training college or a university with a school of education is 18 or 19. In general, teachers have a 1- to 2-year training period before they take up paid teaching duties.

According to OECD "Classification of Educational Systems" (1972), kindergarten teachers are included with primary trainees. Primary school teachers, as a general rule, are trained either in teacher training colleges or in faculties or departments of education, and secondary school teachers are trained only in the latter.

Teacher training colleges exist only in four provinces: Nova Scotia, New Brunswick, Quebec, and Ontario. In the other six, both primary and secondary teacher training takes place in the faculties or colleges of education. In the future, most teachers' colleges will be incorporated in the universities. In Nova Scotia, however, there is no plan to integrate them. In New Brunswick, all teacher training will take place in universities by 1972-1973. The emerging pattern in Quebec is for students to first complete the 2-year academic program in a *college d'enseignement général et professionnel* (CEGEP) and then to go to a university for teacher training. In Ontario, teachers' colleges are rapidly being integrated with the university system. Only six now remain independent. Admission requirements have recently been raised from grade 13 to completion of first year of university. It should be noted that since 1973-1974, only persons with a university degree can be accepted for teacher training in Ontario.

UNESCO's *"La formation et la situation professionnelle des enseignants préscolaires"* (1965), in the Canadian section, suggests the following as important areas of concern for training preschool teachers. The programs for pre-teacher training (subjects differ from school to school) generally consist of the following:

1. *Science and humanities:* literature, maternal language, history, geography, mathematics, psychology, mental hygiene, biology, chemistry, philosophy, religion (Roman Catholic or Protestant), sociology, zoology, art, and music.

2. *Theoretic courses:* educational philosophy, child psychology, pedagogy, tests and measurements, child hygiene, development of programs, family-school relations, parental education, social science, special preparation to educate handicapped children.

3. *Methods:* Most of the aforementioned subjects are taught with the preparation of the students for educating small children in mind, for example, preparation of children's literature and arithmetic, and the use of audiovisual materials.

4. *Practical work:* The amount of practical work demanded or given as a part of the college training varies from a couple of weeks to about half a year. It consists of observations and practical work in preschools attached to the college.

The training of elementary teachers varies widely from that of secondary teachers. Tables 5.5 and 5.6 illustrate this variation as well as further variations from province to province. Similar statistics for preprimary teachers are unavailable, but in all likelihood their training period is less than that of the primary teachers.

Uneasiness about teacher training caused the Ontario government to institute an enquiry, the results of which (the Hall-Dennis report) were published in 1968. The implications of this were expressed with more force by Mr. W. Pitman, a member of the Ontario legislature, speaking in the legislature shortly afterwards:

> To be quite honest, we really cannot make very great strides in either elementary or secondary schools until we have done something pretty significant about teacher education. I think it became quite evident after the publication of the Hall-Dennis report [that] teacher education did not prepare people really for the kind of curriculum building which is necessary for a modern teacher. Teacher education did not provide *sensitivity* which would allow teachers to relate not only to students but

TABLE 5.5

Percentage of Elementary and Secondary School Teachers with
University Degrees, By Province

	1966-67	
	Elementary	Secondary
Newfoundland	6	46
Prince Edward Island	3	47
Nova Scotia	17	65
New Brunswick	8	50
Quebec	6	41
Ontario	11	75
Manitoba	9	70
Saskatchewan	9	64
Alberta	22	68
British Columbia	25	75
Canada	11	61

Source: Based on data from provincial Departments of Education and
Dominion Bureau of Statistics.

also obviously to parents and others in the community. Teacher education certainly
did not prepare young people for what one might call social activism as it relates to
education. . . . [p. 3925]

One of the great problems that we find is that so far the teacher education
candidates come out and they find either one of two things. They are not capable of
coping with the new development of open schools, or they are well equipped to deal
with the new developments, but they cannot fit into what could be called the old
bottles, the old system which may be the one followed by the school and the
particular board for which they are hired. . . . The faculty of education must have a
planned programme to involve itself with local school systems, with curriculum workers, with principals and teachers, with administration, with school boards, with
parent-groups, and with different levels of government. These relationships must not
be considered as a conglomeration of nuisances, but rather as essential sources of
much that will influence what they are doing [p. 3931].

Since Mr. Pitman's address, a number of important changes have been made in
the teacher training system in Ontario. Those especially relevant to primary and
preprimary teachers have already been specified.

Table 5.7 gives the numbers of teachers involved in kindergarten education in
Canada over the 10-year period from 1960-1970 and shows increases of 985.4%
in the private sector and no more than 222.6% in the public sector. The growth
in the private sector, however, is based upon an estimate only of the number of
teachers involved in 1960, all the other figures being factual. If a comparison is
made between 1965 and 1970, where the figures are known, growth in the

TABLE 5.6
Average Years of Professional Training After Matriculation, Elementary
and Secondary School Teachers, by Province

	1960–61		1966–67	
	Elementary	Secondary	Elementary	Secondary
Newfoundland	0.9	2.6	1.3	3.3
Prince Edward Island	0.9	2.4	1.4	3.4
Nova Scotia	2.0	4.2	2.5	4.4
New Brunswick	1.3	3.2	1.7	3.3
Quebec	1.5	2.5	1.9	2.3
Ontario	1.9	4.4	2.1	4.2
Manitoba	2.0	3.5	2.0	3.8
Saskatchewan	2.4	4.1	2.8	4.2
Alberta	2.2	3.3	2.6	3.5
British Columbia	2.6	4.7	2.9	4.6
Canada	1.8	3.7	2.1	3.5

NOTE: These data are based on certificate levels. But, on this basis,
the averages for Manitoba, Saskatchewan and Alberta are actually
understated. For these provinces, the average number of years of
teacher education after junior matriculation in 1966–67 was estimated
as follows: elementary – Manitoba 2.4, Saskatchewan 3.0 and Alberta
3.2; secondary – Manitoba 4.6, Saskatchewan 4.7 and Alberta 4.7.
There are indications that the comparable average years of education
would also be somewhat higher in Quebec than the indicated levels
in the table.
Source: Based on data from Dominion Bureau of Statistics and
         estimates by Economic Council of Canada.

private sector comes out at 61.2% over the 5 years. For the same 5-year period,
the change in the public sector was 115.5% and the total change 97.6%.

Pupil-teacher ratios in kindergartens from 1960-1961 to 1970-1971 are offered
in Table 5.8. In both sectors, there were declines in the number of students for
each teacher. This was especially the case in the public schools, where there was
a drop of eight children per teacher over the 10-year period. Yet it is perhaps
significant that during the three periods of comparison, the private schools had
only about half the number of children per teacher as the public schools. So,
what parents were getting in 1970-1971 in private preschool education was a
much lower pupil-teacher ratio than in public school.

FINANCING EARLY CHILDHOOD EDUCATION

The British North American Act of 1867 gave responsibility for education to
the provinces. The provinces delegate executive authority to the local municipal-

TABLE 5.7
Kindergarten Teachers in Canada from 1960-61 to 1970-71

Year	Private	Public	Total
1960-61	410[a]	3,760	4,170
1965-66	2,760	5,630	8,390
1966-67	2,800	6,640	8,440
1967-68	2,940	7,900	10,840
1968-69	3,310	9,660	12,970
1969-70	4,070	11,280	15,350
1970-71	4,450	12,130	16,580
% of increase from 1960-61 to 1970-71	985.4	222.6	297.6

Source: Statistics Canada, Education Division, Projections Section.

[a]Estimate (survey on private sector started only with 1965-66 year)

ities. Educational revenue comes, then, from two major sources: provincial taxation and local taxation. The exact share varies with the ability of the local community to raise tax revenues, and ranges all the way from 95% to 35% being paid by the provincial government. Looking at Canada as a whole, however, it can be said that about 57% of all educational funds come from the province, 30% from local taxation, and 12% from federal contributions. Other sources account for about 1%. Most of the federal contributions go to universities, as operating grants, building funds, student loans and research grants, and to postsecondary institutes, colleges, and other adult education courses. In the private sector, the contribution from provincial government would be substantially higher than it would be in the public sector, because private schools do not have any local tax base upon which to draw (Whitworth, 1969). In 1968, the per capita gross national product of Canada was $3550. Annual per capita expenditure on education was $8.35.

The matter of control of education, whether local, provincial, or federal, has for some time been an important issue in Canada. As things are, control

TABLE 5.8
Pupil:Teacher Ratio in Kindergartens from 1960-61 to 1970-71

Year	Private	Public	Total
1960-61	17:1	37:1	35:1
1965-66	17:1	39:1	32:1
1970-71	14:1	29:1	25:1

appears to be moving toward the provincial legislatures. Lind (1971) traces this trend toward centralization. Taking Ontario as an example, his conclusion is as follows:

> Our schools are part of a much larger social system, and the people who run that system need schools to continue what they are doing. And that basically is to keep the next generation in line and to prepare it for post-industrial capitalistic social order. The forms of control and conditioning may change as capitalistic society develops, but unless the society is fundamentally changed both in purpose and structure the schools will remain the institutions they are [p. 104].

A statement by Les Vipond (1972) is relevant at this point:

> In Canada, for example, the income spread between the poorest and richest income categories may very well have widened during the past two decades by at least 30 per cent in real (constant) dollars. . . . There is little doubt that the 1971 Census will show a further widening of this gap. . . . Canadian income distribution data shows virtually no change in the last 20 years. The wealthiest 20 per cent received 41.1 per cent of the total in 1951, 38.4 per cent in 1961 and 38.7 per cent in 1969; whereas the share of the poorest 20 per cent was 6.1 per cent in 1951, 6.6 per cent in 1961 and 6.9 per cent in 1969 [p. 21].

It is awareness of statistics like these that has caused the dramatic shift of the past few years to greater centralization of control at provincial level; for here only is it possible to bring about greater equity of financial opportunity.

Table 5.9 presents kindergarten expenditures in Canada for 1965 through 1970 for both private and public sectors. In both categories the rate of expansion has been considerable, with the exception of capital expenditures in the private sector, which grew 9.1% in the 5-year period.

The 285.1% increase in current expenditures in the public sector is the largest for any country included in this series of reviews. The reason for the different percentages of increase in the two total columns (252.9% and 263.8%) is accounted for by the differential rates of exchange in Canadian and United States dollars. Canada is one of the few countries whose money increased in value by comparison with the United States dollar during this 5-year period.

Table 5.10 gives private, public, and total per pupil costs in United States dollars for the years 1965-1970. It will be seen that the cost of public kindergarten education has risen almost 50% more rapidly than in the private sector. The $154 total increase in cost per pupil represents a 140% increase over the 5-year period. When this is compared with the 123% increase in the primary school during the same period, it is clear where the greater effort is being directed. This no doubt is the result of the sharp rise in kindergarten enrollment and decline in the demand for primary places (Table 5.2). The comparable cost per pupil figures are: kindergarten: 1965–$110, 1970–$264; primary: 1965–$231, 1970–$500.

TABLE 5.9

Kindergarten Expenditure in Canada from 1965-66 to 1970-71

Year	Private		Public		C$000's Total Capital Current	$000's Total Capital Current
	Capital	Current	Capital	Current		
1965-66	110	5,960	1,540	25,720	33,330	30,911[a]
1966-67	100	6,600	1,720	33,070	41,490	
1967-68	120	7,630	2,200	45,060	55,010	
1968-69	170	9,320	2,530	61,170	73,190	
1969-70	150	12,820	3,110	80,800	96,880	
1970-71	120	14,950	3,490	99,060	117,620	112,469
% of increase from 1965-66 to 1970-71	09.1	150.8	126.6	285.1	252.9	263.8

Source: Statistics Canada, Education Division, Projections Section.

[a]Official exchange rates, O.E.C.D.

INSTRUCTIONAL METHODS

The instructional methods used in the Canadian kindergartens reflect to a large degree the two traditional linguistic cultures of Canada.

Throughout Quebec, and in many of the Roman Catholic preschools in other provinces, the model of the French *école maternelle* is followed. In these preschools, there is an emphasis on planned sensorimotor and manipulative experiences. The Royal Commission on Education, Quebec, 1964, gives a clear indication of the approach

Based on pedagogical and psychological observations children can benefit from sensory, motor, affective, and mental education starting from age four. The average child by age four has developed biologically enough to make it interesting and challenging for him to be involved in some such motor activities as singing, dancing and playing, as part of an organised group. His ability to benefit from the use of communication skills is well developed. The child's intellect has developed enough so that he can begin to think before he acts (prelogical thinking) and is less controlled by his emotions. At age five and a half the child is building his analytical and verbal abilities based primarily upon concrete experiences. The child's natural curiosity is growing rapidly and he asks why about many things that he does not understand. He has a great need to feel accepted and loved and the school must provide this kind of an atmosphere.

In the English-speaking provinces of Canada, the teaching method follows the ideas of Froebel, McMillan, Dewey, and the progressive school of the 1930s and 1940s of the United States. The Report of the Commission on Educational

TABLE 5.10
Kindergarten Per-Pupil Costs in U.S. Dollars from 1965–66 to 1970–71

Year	Private			Public			Total		
	Current Expend. 000's	No. of Children 000's	Per Pupil Cost	Current Expend. 000's	No. of Children 000's	Per Pupil Cost	Current Expend. 000's	No. of Children 000's	Per Pupil Cost
1965–66	5,527	48	115	23,853	219	109	29,381	268	110
1970–71	14,295	64	223	94,722	349	271	109,018	413	264
Total Increase			108			162			154

Planning, Alberta, 1972, offers a quotation that exemplifies this:

> The basic methods credo of the future must be that the learner learns by doing. The strategies and tactics of the teacher are, then, to develop learning environments in which the learner has the fullest opportunity to explore—intellectually, culturally, socially and physically; to seek orderly explanations—conceptualizing the events and objects in his environment as it is, and as it ought to be; and to test his explanations—both in real and vicarious ways.
>
> To explore, to seek, to test are the essential ingredients of method and the learning transaction. But it is the learner who is to explore, to seek, to test; and it is the teacher whose methods must be formed by these objectives. The teacher must coordinate the effects of various learning environments upon particular learners or types of learners. The issue in method is not which environment is best, but rather which environment is best for a particular person in order to produce a desired change [p. 198].

With the younger age levels, aged 2 or 3, there is concern that schooling of any sort might be harmful because of disruption of the mother-child bond. This is an area, however, where a good deal more research needs to be done.

In discussing the question of instructional methodology as it is used in Canadian kindergartens, Bereiter (1972) observes that the recent debate in Canada, as in many other countries, turns on the use of definite instructional objectives as against child-centeredness. This is a matter that most affects the children from poor homes.

RESEARCH ON EARLY CHILDHOOD EDUCATION

In the last 10 years, much research has been done in Canada on the problems of educating young children. One of the best and most comprehensive reviews of the subject is Ryan's (1971) "Poverty and Early Education in Canada." The following excerpts from this report are self-explanatory:

> Educators are well aware of the fact that children from economically and socially disadvantaged environments enter school minimally capable of coping with the demands to be made upon them. Early problems in adapting to the school situation lead to experiences of failure, frustration, and punishment. The cumulative effect of such experiences eventually results in removing one's self from a noxious situation through absenteeism, failure, or dropping out of school. A clear example of the latter is seen in the case of the Canadian Indian, whose attrition rate between Grades 1 and 12 is about 94 per cent as compared with a 12 per cent national dropout rate ... [p. 1].

On the provision of junior kindergartens and the question of who benefits from them, Ryan offers the following comments:

Actually, four-year-old kindergarten enrichment classes originated in Ottawa in 1940 and shortly after spread to Toronto. Only recently have these junior kindergartens begun to appear with any regularity in the inner-city locations; however, the absolute number across the country is still insufficient in order for those children mostly in need to gain the presumed benefits. Although it is commonly stated that one goal of the junior kindergarten is to promote the development of language skills for children from the more depressed areas of cities, there is no information available on the comparability of the actual programs in terms of curriculum as well as the quantity and quality of teacher-child interactions. Furthermore, despite the fact that junior kindergartens have existed for 30 years, with one exception, there have been no adequate evaluations made of the effects of such programs. . . .

An assessment of the cultural, socioeconomic, and familial characteristics of the families using the junior kindergartens showed that, although the kindergartens were located in the inner city areas, children from middle-class English-speaking homes were more likely to take advantage of the facility than were their counterparts from lower socioeconomic, non-English-speaking homes. The junior kindergarten experience did lead to gains in intelligence and school achievement for some of the children but these beneficial effects diminished over the successive four years . . . [p. 4].

As a result of his review, Ryan offers the following three recommendations for change in kindergarten programs:

First, an increased emphasis upon the operational specificity of programs is needed. With few exceptions, program goals are vaguely stated and adequate program descriptions are virtually nonexistent. . . .

A second guideline for developing sophisticated intervention research stems from the fact that interventionists have largely failed to adopt a conceptual framework from which not only goals but program features and behaviors to be measured could be derived. . . .

A third set of guidelines pertains to evaluative research. This writer is convinced of the obligation to conduct evaluative investigations of intervention programs in view of our limited knowledge of program benefits, especially after a few years have passed. In Canada, there is a need to conduct evaluations at the intermediate stages of programs, which might lead to alterations in program content [p. 8].

In Canada, during the last 10 years, large amounts of time, talent, and money have been spent in an attempt to meet Ryan's three recommendations. In the area of educational research competence, the efforts of Ontario have probably been most successful. The creation of the Ontario Institute for Studies in Education (OISE) has brought world acclaim to Canada for the excellence of its work. The following excerpts are taken from three researchers working at OISE. The first is from Bereiter (1972), who draws these three conclusions from a series of evaluation studies conducted by himself and others.

1. The Bereiter-Engelmann program has clearly had more impact on IQ and achievement than the traditional, child-centered approach, but not necessarily more impact than other programs with a strong instructional emphasis [p. 5].

2. The "traditional" nursery-school and kindergarten program is not a serious contender as an educational program. Not only has the "traditional" approach failed to achieve as good results in cognitive learning as the more instructional approaches, it has failed to demonstrate any redeeming advantages [p. 9].

3. The long-term effects of preschool instruction are about as good as can be expected. However impressive the immediate results of preschool compensatory instruction may be, and however much encouragement may be drawn from follow-up achievement data, the fact remains that no preschool program shows any promise of making, by itself, any permanent difference in the scholastic success of poor children [p. 12].

In discussing these findings, Bereiter raises two important policy questions and proposes some answers and recommendations.

(a) If it is granted that education for poor children must be improved over the whole span of school years, then is it any longer necessary or practical to invest heavily in preschool education for such children? In other words, is preschool education anything more than the stone in the stone soup?

(b) Is there justification for heavy investment in a continued search for more effective methods of preschool education, or have the limits of effectiveness largely been reached? . . .

The wise strategy for the present would seem to be to look for elementary school programs that are more successful than the present ones at washing out the effects of differences in earlier school experience. This strategy does not, however, preclude the continued search for more effective methods of preschool education. On this matter we have to ask ourselves what increased effects we would want or have any reason to expect were possible. . . .

I think, therefore, that we are at a point where development of preschool programs, if it is to proceed any further, has to be joined to elementary school curriculum design. The two questions: "What does a child need to know in order to be ready for first grade?" and "What does a child need to know in order to get the most out of being four years old?" have about yielded their all. . . .

Only by joining preschool education with elementary school curriculum can we begin plausibly asking the potentially much more productive question: "What things can we teach a child of four and five that can then be built upon in the first grade and after [p. 16]?"

Bereiter's question, "What can we teach at four and five that will be helpful later?" is a fundamental one. The most carefully developed work on this, previous to Bereiter's own, is probably Montessori's, which was done between 1900 and 1940. Montessori's methods have been adopted in many countries of the world for use with many different types of children.

Miezitis (1971), reviewing research on the Montessori method, reaches the following conclusions:

A well structured environment, precisely what a majority of lower-class children lack at home, allows the child to learn the cultural expectations and rules. . . . It is not surprising then that permissive, unstructured preschool programs that feature a higher degree of autonomy with numerous alternatives and low normative pressures are particularly unsuitable (super-optimal) for disadvantaged children, and even for many middle-class children. . . .

The Montessori method presents an intermediate degree of structure, encouraging independence within a structured environment. This method is more successful with disadvantaged children than are unstructured early-childhood-oriented programs. . . .

With middle-class children the problems are different. According to Hunt and Dopyera (1966) the typical middle-class child . . . is concerned with rules, being right, and complying with authority . . . the Montessori environment may be too restrictive in terms of experience to challenge the child to experiment beyond concrete rules and conformity and hence may prevent children . . . from moving on to the next level. The nondifferential results from comparative studies with middle-class children (McMorrow, 1970; Miezitis, 1971; and Rudominer, 1970) raise the question to what extent the middle-class school environment duplicates the typical middle-class home environment in terms of attitudes, values, motivational orientation and feedback system, and degree of cognitive stimulation in terms of materials content, and method of instruction. It is only when highly specific content not normally taught in the middle-class home is introduced, as in the case of the Bereiter (1967) study, that differences in program effects emerge. In order to produce an educational impact with middle-class children, it may be necessary to experiment with different kinds of educational approaches [p. 57].

The mastery of reading skills is of fundamental importance to success in primary school. Probably more research has been done on reading than on any other skill subject, yet we still know little about how to teach it successfully to a child who comes from a deprived home or has a learning deficiency of some kind. Some have attempted to help children learn to read by starting to teach them when they are 2, 3, or 4 years of age. Fowler in *Interchange* (1971), discussing the results of his research, comes to the following two conclusions on this subject:

That a mental age of four is close to the watershed of developmental readiness for reading. . . .

Reading must logically wait upon the *consolidation* of the two-dimensional, sequential coordinations of language prior to a child undertaking the more complex three-dimensional coordinations of reading. And, presumably, the child must have mastered, have become reasonably well controlled and fluent in language operations and coordinations to have a reasonable probability of progressing in reading. Fluency in language would fall at about the age of four, sometimes three, and, occasionally, two (Fowler 1962a, 1962b) for brighter children whose proportionately accelerated language competence is reflected in the heavy verbal component of general ability measures by this age (Meyers and Dingman, 1960) [p. 122].

Clark (1969), of Dalhousie University, has reported on a preschool enrichment program in Nova Scotia.

Brunswick-Cornwallis Preschool was originated in 1963 with two major purposes: (1) to provide planned experiences to prevent the academic retardation characteristic of culturally disadvantaged children, and (2) to provide interracial experiences to reduce prejudice amongst Negro and white children. . . . children who had attended the preschool had a mean gain of 11.0 points in intelligence, whereas a control group showed an average loss of 0.4 IQ points over the preschool year. Unfortunately, two years later the gains attained by the preschool group were no longer evident, while the control group continued its downward movement . . . both groups performed below average on an achievement test. . . . The gains shown by preschool children in terms of intellectual development are lost by Grade 2. . . . It must be emphasized that the quality of the academic programs that children enter following preschool enrichment must be modified if improvements in cognitive development are to be sustained; furthermore, an active program of parent education would increase the likelihood of more durable gains [p. 29].

The previous four writers have taken a rather behavioristic approach to teaching young children, stressing the importance of cognition and achievement skills. Mialaret (1971), of the University of Quebec, however, suggests that we should take a much broader view of the child and the aims of early childhood education:

It goes against nature to study the child by arbitrarily establishing different ages or different stages. The child is a human being, who has a longitudinal unity. At the present time, genetic psychology allows us to have a scientific conception of the child. This scientific conception defines and specifies a contemporary conception of education. At the base of this conception that we call education is confidence in the future of man and in the powers of education. This would not be sufficient if we did not also have certain ideas on the role of the child and of man in society. If we wish to prepare a child to become a citizen who is capable of fulfilling his role in contemporary society, we must start at the earliest age to prepare him for this task. That is why we think it is true to say that the child is the father of the man [p. 23].

Piwowar (1969) gives some comparative information on the performance of kindergarten and nonkindergarten children in prereading tests. Kindergarten-educated children significantly surpassed nonkindergarten-educated children on measures of visual and auditory discrimination, but not on measures of letter name knowledge or ability to copy letters. He suggests that failure to obtain differences on these educationally significant abilities reflects "restrictions on the kinds of activities that may be included in kindergarten programs set by the manual currently authorized for use in Alberta kindergartens [p. 30]." Although this study offers no assurance that the two groups of children were initially comparable in aptitude, the fact that differences showed up in areas where teaching is authorized, and not in other (possibly more significant) areas where teaching is prohibited, may indicate something about the influence of provincially determined policies.

King (1967) describes an attempt to develop a research-based kindergarten reading program. This study compared kindergarten children in Calgary, who received an experimental reading program, with children in the regular kindergarten program, which, as noted above, did not include alphabet or reading instruction. On the Murphy-Durrell test of reading readiness, the following distribution was obtained of children in the lower and upper halves according to test norms:

	Experimental	Regular
Above norm	71	26
Below norm	32	80

This was obviously a highly significant difference in favor of the experimental group, although statistical tests were not reported.

From this brief review of research, three points in particular stand out:

1. That the number of places provided by the educational agencies in Canada for 3-, 4-, 5-year-olds is inadequate.
2. Early childhood education programs are sponsored by many agencies as a way of equalizing educational opportunities for children of the poor, recent immigrants, and Canadian Indians and Eskimos.
3. There are major differences of opinion as to what this educational content should be during these preschool years.

ACKNOWLEDGMENTS

The author wishes to express his gratitude for the cooperation of the many people who made this study possible, in particular Messrs. M. Wisenthal and Z. Zsigmund, who supplied him with statistical data; Mr. T. Reid of the Ontario Legislature; Messrs. C. Bereiter and M. Kornberg of the Ontario Institute of Studies in Education; and Messrs. J. Bishop and L. Everett of the University of Alberta.

BIBLIOGRAPHY

Bereiter, C. An academic preschool for disadvantaged children: conclusion from evaluation studies. In J. C. Stanley (Ed.), *Preschool programs for the disadvantaged: five experimental approaches to early childhood education.* Baltimore: Johns Hopkins University Press, 1972.

Clark, B. The Brunswick-Cornwallis Pre-school: A program for disadvantaged white and Negro children. *Child Study,* 1967, p. 29; 17-27.

Clark, B. *Progress report: April, 1968–April, 1969.* Dalhousie University, 1969.

Fleming, W. G. *The expansion of the educational system.* Ontario's educative society/I. Toronto: University of Toronto Press, 1971a.

Fleming, W. G. *Schools, pupils and teachers.* Ontario's educative society/III. University of Toronto Press, 1971b.

Fowler, W. A developmental learning strategy for early reading in a laboratory nursery school. *Interchange,* 1971, *2*(2). The Ontario Institute for Studies in Education.

Fowler, W. On the value of both play and structure in early education. *Young Children,* October 1971, pp. 25-36.

Fowler, W. Development learning approach. *The Merrill Palmer Quarterly of Behavior and Development,* April 1972, *18*(2).

Fowler, W. Research and development: longitudinal investigation of children in attendance at the Woodbine Day Care Center. *Interim Progress Report,* December 1972.

Fowler, W., *The development of a prototype infant and child day care center in metropolitan Toronto, year II progress report.* Ontario Institute for Studies in Education, October 1973.

Greenfield, T. B., House, J. H., Hickcox, E. S. & Buchanan, B. H. *Developing School Systems: Planning, Organization, and Personnel.* The Ontario Institute for Studies in Education, 1969.

Hall-Dennis Report. *Living and learning.* Ontario Institute for Studies in Education, 1969.

King, E. M. Innovations in beginning reading instruction. *Early Childhood Education,* Summer 1967, *1,* 26-41.

Lind, L. The rise of bureaucracy in Ontario schools. *This Magazine is About Schools.* Bryant Press, 1971.

McPhee, S. Canada: basic issues identified. *Developments in Early Childhood Education.* OECD, 1973.

Mialaret, G. Le rôle de l'éducation préscolaire dans l'éducation permanente. *Interchange,* 1971, *2*(2). The Ontario Institute for Studies in Education.

Miezitis, S. The Montessori method: some recent research. *Interchange,* 1971, *2*(2). The Ontario Institute for Studies in Education.

Piwowar, D. G. Performance on pre-reading tests (M. Ed. thesis, University of Calgary, 1969).

Reid, T. Priorities in educational expenditure: the essential basis. *The Dalhousie Review,* Autumn 1968, *48*(3).

Reid, T. E. Education as social intervention in the cycle of Canadian poverty. *The best of times/the worst of times, contemporary issues in Canadian education.* Stevenson, H. A., Stamp, R. M., & Wilson, J. D. (Eds.) Toronto: Holt, Rinehart and Winston of Canada, 1972.

Ryan, T. *Poverty and early education in Canada.* In press, Ottowa: Carleton University, 1971.

Vipond, L., *Developing social policy in conditions of dynamic change.* Report on the Canadian Committee to the XVI International Conference on Social Welfare, 1972.

Whitworth, F. E. *Canada 1970. The official handbook of present conditions and recent progress.* Ottawa: Queen's Printer for Canada, 1969.

Zsigmond, Z. E., & Wenaas, C. J. *Enrollment in educational institutions by province, 1951-52 to 1980-81.* Prepared for the Economic Council of Canada. Ottawa: Queen's Printer for Canada, 1970.

Education Division, Projection Section. *Advance statistics of education, 1971-1972.* Statistics Canada, Ottawa.

Canada, The Council of Ministers of Education. *Ontario: Organisation of education in 1970-71.*

Report of the Canadian Committee of the International Conference on Social Welfare. *Developing social policy in conditions of dynamic change.* June 1972.

Legislature of Ontario debates, official report—daily edition, third session of the twenty-eighth Legislature, June 11, 1970. Toronto: The Queen's Printer, 1970.

Les amis de Sèvres, No. 2, 1971: Aspects de l'école Québécoise.

OECD *Classification of educational systems, Canada.* Paris, 1972.

OECD *Labour force statistics 1959-1970*. Paris, 1972.

Report of the Royal Commission on Education in Ontario, 1945-1950.

Rapport de la Commission Royale d'enquête sur l'enseignement, dans la province de Quebec 1964. Première et Deuxième Parties.

Report of the Commission on Educational Planning. *A future of choices.* Queen's Printer for the Province of Alberta, 1972.

Report of the Royal Commission on the Status of Women in Canada, September 28, 1970.

Report of the Special Senate Committee on Poverty. *Poverty in Canada.* Ottawa, 1971.

The Junior League of Toronto, The Canadian Mental Health Association in Ontario. *The troubled child—project report . . . a beginning.* May 1971.

UNESCO. *World survey of education II, primary education.* 1958.

UNESCO. *La formation et la situation professionnelle des enseignants préscolaires.* Décembre 1965.

United Nations demographic yearbook. 1970.

United Nations. *Analyses and projections of households and families.* 1971.

Early Childhood Education
in Sweden

INTRODUCTION

The modern Swedish kindergarten developed out of a variety of child-minding facilities that came into existence in the nineteenth century. These first institutions were created in several of the larger cities, between 1830 and 1840. Growing industrialization, and the particular need for working mothers led to their appearance. Their primary aim, therefore, was child-minding or care giving.

Compulsory school attendance for all children 7 years of age was introduced in 1842. The reason for the choice of age 7 for the beginning of compulsory education is unclear. It is apparently associated with the problems of getting small children from rather isolated rural villages to school. One must keep in mind that Sweden is a large but sparsely populated country.

From the early 1900s to the 1950s, the number of children in public kindergartens grew very slowly. The reasons behind this slow growth are numerous. The major reason, however, is an overriding commitment on the part of the Swedish educational authorities to the formation of the 9-year comprehensive primary and secondary school. This decision, taken on political and social grounds, was directed at creating greater social equality and providing education for all. This commitment to educational reform must also be seen within the much larger commitment to social, economic, and welfare reform that has taken place in Sweden in the last 30 to 40 years. Broad social reform is a part of the present Swedish way of life. It is no longer a matter of heated debate, but a part of the political climate.

A commitment to preschool has not been a high priority in either social or educational reform. Besides, the question of providing a nursery school education for all children has not been looked upon with favor by the Parliament until recently. The main reason given has been that scientific research on the psychological development of children under age 7 has not conclusively indicated any important educational advantages resulting from it. There is little debate over its social and emotional benefits, but these needs have been met in other ways to some extent. Recently, however, the question of preschool provision has again been raised.

Educational reform in Sweden has customarily taken place through the work of royal commissions. A Preschool Commission was created in 1968. Its purpose was to take a deeper look at the objectives, the content, the organization of preschool education, and to comment on general concerns for quality and quantity of preschool education. The purpose of preschool is seen, not as a preparation for primary education, but as a method for the development of the whole personality of the child. Particular emphasis is placed on developmental psychology, rather than learning psychology.

ENROLLMENTS, PRESCHOOL EDUCATION (1960-1970)

The OECD "Classification of Educational Systems" (1972) gives the following characteristics of play schools (*lekskola*) and day nurseries (*daghem*) in Sweden.

> Length of study equals up to five years. Entrance requirement is to be six months of age. A nursery school can be either a *lekskola* (part-time) or a *daghem* (full-time). In the *daghem*, the children aged 6 months to 7 years are divided into 3-4 groups according to age. Most of the nursery schools are run by the local authorities. The very few private ones usually receive financial support. A board of enquiry was appointed by the Government in 1968 (Barnstugentiedningen) to carry out research concerning the provision of centres for children prior to and during the first years at school. The board of enquiry was to take into account the suggestion that nursery schools should be made available for all children prior to compulsory school [p. 42].

In the present survey, the term kindergarten will be used to include both the *lekskola* and the *daghem*. Table 6.1 gives the number of children enrolled for the years 1960-1961 to 1970-1971. It will be seen at once that there has been a very rapid growth in the kindergartens over these 10 years. The actual percentage increase is 167.3%. Information is not available on the number of children

TABLE 6.1
Enrollments in Kindergartens in Sweden from 1960-61 to 1970-71

			(in 000's)
Year	Private	Public	Total
1960-61	n.a.[a]	49	49
1965-66	n.a.	64	64
1966-67	n.a.	70	70
1967-68	n.a.	85	85
1968-69	n.a.	98	98
1969-70	n.a.	112	112
1970-71	n.a.	131	131
% of increase from 1960-61 to 1970-71		167.3	167.3

Source: National Central Bureau of Statistics, Sweden.

[a]Not available.

enrolled in private kindergartens in Sweden. It is judged, however, to be very small.

Table 6.2 shows population attendance rates in kindergartens for the same 10-year period, during which there has been a 16.9% increase in the population of children between the ages of 2 and 6. In relation to Table 6.2, two points should be noted: first, that population statistics are given for children from 2 to 6 years of age, not 6 months to 6 years, the range given in the OECD statement

TABLE 6.2
Population Attendance Rates in Kindergartens in Sweden from 1960-61 to 1970-71

			(in 000's)
	1960-61	1970-71	% of Change
Total age group 2 - 6 years in kindergartens	49	131	167.3
Infant population aged 2 - 6 years	515	602	16.9
% of age group enrolled	9.5	21.8	129.5

Source: United Nations Demographic Yearbook, 1970.

(the 5-year period is much more realistic because there are very few children in kindergartens between the ages of 6 months and 2 years); and second, that the 16.9% population growth for this age group exceeds by almost 7% the figure anticipated for 1970-1975 by the OECD in its educational policy and planning (1967) document. The United Nation's population figures were checked against the OECD demographic trends in member countries (1971). The OECD population figure is a 16% increase for the 10-year period. If these population statistics are correct, and we believe they are, then a substantial revision in planning on the part of the Swedes is called for to take care of a very substantial increase in children in the primary schools in the years to come.

The overall percentage of increase for children enrolled in kindergartens for the 10-year period 1960-1970 was 129.5%, again an impressive growth. But in 1970-1971, only 21.8% of the population between ages 2 and 6 was enrolled. During the same 10-year period there was a 3.6% increase in enrollments in the first grade of the comprehensive school.

The percentage of children attending preschool in Sweden by single year of age and by age group in the school year 1970-1971 was as follows:

6	70%	5-6	48%
5	25%	4-6	35%
4	10%	3-6	27%
3	2%	2-6	22%
2	1%		

The principal factors affecting future demand for places in kindergartens are birthrate, family size, and the numbers of mothers working outside the home. As for the birthrate, in 1966 there were 15.8 live births per thousand people in the Swedish population. By 1970 this had fallen to 13.6, a decline of 2.2 live births per thousand (or 11.4%) over a 4-year period (United Nations Demographic Yearbook, 1970).

Trends in average household size and gross reproduction rates in Sweden are as follows: In 1860, the average household size was 4.28; in 1900 it was 3.72; in 1950, 2.9; and in 1965, 2.8.[1] Thus, over the 105-year period, the average household size in Sweden has declined by 1.48. During the same 105 years, the gross reproduction rate in Sweden fell from 2.2 to 1.2. Family size in Sweden, therefore, is smaller these days, and fewer children are being born.

Labor-force participation of men and women in Sweden is shown in Table 6.3. It can be seen that, over the last 8 years, the participation rate of women has risen sharply. This points to an increasing need for child-minding facilities for the very young in Sweden.

[1] *Analyses and projections of households and families.* Population Division, Department of Economic and Social Affairs, of the United Nations Secretariat, 1971.

TABLE 6.3
Labor Force Participation Rates - Sweden

	1960 %	1970 %
Total Labor Force $\times$ 100 **Total Population**		
(a) Total	48.6	48.7
(b) Males	62.2	58.9
(c) Females	35.1	38.4
Total Labor Force $\times$ 100 **Population from 15** **to 64 years**		
(a) Total	73.3	74.3
(b) Males	93.1	88.8
(c) Females	53.3	59.4

Source: Labor Force Statistics, 1959-70, O.E.C.D., Paris, 1972.

ISSUES OF DEBATE

The major issue of debate concerning Swedish preschool education is the question of its role in the creation of a better society. A better society is defined as one in which man has a real regard for other men. Fors (1972) says it this way:

> The trend in Sweden has been towards a steadily increasing responsibility on the part of the community for the social security of its citizens, and for the provision of increased social services [p. 9].

Thus it has become the responsibility of the national, regional, and local governments to insure, through their social policies, that everyone is given the maximum amount of freedom to develop himself to his fullest potential and thereby benefit society. In education, this has meant rethinking and restructuring the entire school system. Maclure (1971) describes the process:

> But what stands out as abundantly clear is that the reform has its origin in bold decisions taken on political and social grounds and that the commitment to social equality and mass education which these decisions entailed has now become part of the Swedish way of life—no longer a matter of acrimonious debate, but rather part

of the political climate. The reforms emanate from a Royal Commission set up in 1946. . . . The 1946 Commission, in which the politicians were strongly represented, cut through the pedagogic controversies and demanded a policy squarely based on social and political premises. In effect, they asserted that education was too important to be left to the educational experts. Instead of allowing pedagogic considerations to determine educational organisation, the Commission insisted that the educational system, a potent agent for social control, should be subordinated to basic social policies, and in particular to ideals of social equality and co-operation on the one hand, and the development of individual talent on the other [p. 9].

As observed earlier, most of the reforms relating to education and social policy in Sweden have resulted from the appointment of royal commissions. In the directive to the Child Centres Committee of 1968 we find the following:

The responsibility for the upbringing, supervision and care of children rests chiefly with the home. The community has, however, to a great extent undertaken a responsibility within this field, among other ways through the provision of child centres by local authorities. Changes in the family structure and living conditions have brought a greatly increased demand for public measures to assist parents with the care of their children. In increasing numbers of families both parents go out to work. For unmarried and divorced parents organized child care is a condition for their ability to support the family by paid work. Child centres also fulfill an important educational function in teaching children group activities under pedagogical guidance [p. 1].

The same document gave these objectives to the child center committee:

All child centre activities are based on the same fundamental pedagogical principles. Their goal—in cooperation with the home—is to promote the all-round, harmonious development of children emotionally, socially and intellectually, and to help in their positive adaptation to society . . .

The aim in the pedagogical work is to stimulate the children's social development . . . . Children from a nonstimulating environment are often handicapped in comparison with children who have grown up in an emotionally and culturally more stimulating environment. . . . Organized group activities are also of great significance for children who have no brothers or sisters. . . .

The aim in the entire school system in the last decades has been to create equal opportunities for all children to receive good schooling irrespective of their place of domicile, parents' economy, and other home conditions [p. 2].

From this document follow eight tasks to which the committee was to address itself:

1. The first task of the committee should be to investigate the internal activities at nursery schools and day nurseries, particularly for children aged 5 and 6. . . .
2. The drawing up of a strict curriculum for preschool activities can hardly be considered. On the other hand, recommendations for organization of the work and

.for the form of different activities should be of great value. After defining and formulating the goal for what may be said to be preschool pedagogics in a wide sense, therefore, the committee should draw up recommendations concerning the content and form for the activities. . . . The committee should examine this question, taking into account also the consequences it may have on compulsory school. In this connection I would emphazise that the committee should base its proposals on unchanged conditions in respect of the start of compulsory schooling. . . .

3. The committee should discuss how a more universal nursery school organization, primarily for 5- and 6-year-olds, should be coordinated with other child centre activities. . . .

4. The introduction of a more universal nursery school organization would involve a number of practical problems in sparsely populated areas. . . .

5. The committee should examine what measures can be taken to bring about increased organized leisure-time activities for children of school age. . . .

6. Not only must the local authorities—which have the chief responsibility—be stimulated to extend leisure-time facilities, but these must be made attractive for the children; it is also necessary to win the interest of parents in the idea of organized leisure-time activities and supervision of their children, even of school age.

7. The committee should consider the question of the age groups to which traditional leisure-time activities should be directed. One possibility is that the day centres for school children should accept children up to 9 years of age—i.e. the lower primary school level—and that separate forms of activity be arranged for older children. Special attention should be paid to the possibility of the joint use of premises with schools, youth centres, etc.

8. The committee should devote attention to the special questions associated with the possibility for handicapped children and youth to participate in child centre and leisure-time activities for older school children [p. 3-5].

It is clear from this whole directive that the government saw the importance of preschool education in many contexts, not just in caring for children, large or small, for 5 or 6 hours a day. It reflects the way education has been viewed in Sweden as an integral part of the whole scheme of social development. The ultimate aim of the commission was that by 1975 all children whose parents so desire will be attending a child center at age 5 or 6.

One of the matters that has particularly excited the commission is the role of parental involvement in preschool activities. In addition to this, they are considering whether to pay the husband or wife who stays home with the child. The place of men in bringing up their children, and the part they should play in educating them, is being discussed at great length. There seems to be no clear consensus on this point, nor much research. Also involved in this is the issue of greater community living, which is being advocated by some young adults in Sweden.

It is already clear that the preschool is seen as an upward extension of the home, not a downward extension of the school. One of the main reasons for this is the great need in Sweden for socioemotional contact between small children, since over 40% of families in Sweden are one-child families.

The results of research have provoked discussion of the place of planned instruction in the Swedish kindergartens, a matter of particular importance concerning children from deprived or recently immigrant homes. The research also stresses the preparatory role of kindergartens in getting children ready for their comprehensive school. This in turn has led to the question of who should be responsible for preschool education, the National Board of Health and Welfare, or the National Board of Education. The outstanding issue, however, will be how to finance the Royal Preschool Commission's recommendations. The cost of the proposed program will be very high, and the Swedish Parliament will undoubtedly have to decide upon priorities within the whole sociological area of which the preschool is only a part.

In summary, the following are the main areas of concern in Sweden regarding the matter of preschool education:

1. Changes in the family structure and living conditions that necessitate the intervention of the state to assist parents with the care of their children.
2. The participation in group activity as a means to promote the socio-emotional development of young children.
3. The provision of facilities to give real freedom for women to choose between working at home and outside the home, and to make life possible for single men or women who have children in their care and who must, at the same time, earn a living.
4. Society's need to recruit into the labor force women who, in the absence of such facilities, are obliged to stay at home.
5. The necessity of preschool education and care for children from all backgrounds, but especially those who are handicapped or come from remote or deprived homes or from recently immigrant families.

THE AIMS AND OBJECTIVES OF EARLY CHILDHOOD EDUCATION

To be properly understood, the principles behind the Swedish preschools and their designed function must be considered in relation to Swedish societal objectives as they concern education as a whole and the general policy for schools. These are described in "Educational Policy and Planning—Sweden," (1967) as follows:

> The precise statement of over-all objectives is not a primary concern of Swedish educational planners. The plans are drawn up on a rather pragmatic basis and do not always fit neatly into any general ideology. The objectives of Swedish educational policy, and some of the subsidiary aims deriving from them, can, therefore, be defined only in very general terms. . . . Underlying Swedish educational policy is what may be called a democratic value premise. This implies that privileges in any field that cannot be justified on "rational" grounds should not be allowed to continue. "Social democracy," to quote the government party programme of 1959, "is against income differences arising from social and economic privileges and power positions, but

accepts those attributable to differences in achievement through work or in skill, responsibility or initiative [p. 46]."

The following are the general objectives:

Objective 1: All Swedes of school age should enjoy an equal right to public education, without regard to income, social origin, sex or place of residence ...

Objective 2: The school should aim at safeguarding and strengthening the democratic system.... It follows from Objective 2 that:

there should be a considerable common core of learning, particularly in the comprehensive, but also in the upper secondary schools;

provision should be made for frequent group work and discussion in order to strengthen co-operativeness and tolerance among the pupils;

particular attention should be given to fostering an understanding of the functioning of the Swedish and other social systems;

critical and independent thinking should be encouraged, and excessive stress on absorption of factual data should be avoided.

Objective 3: Educational policy should contribute to general economic development, e.g., by producing the required types and amounts of qualified manpower. However, this goal is often subordinate to the first two.... Objective 3 is often thought of as being in harmony with the first two objectives, in view, e.g., of the interdependence of the supply and demand of HQM and the considerable external economies implicit in the second objective.

Objective 4: "The educational system should be made more flexible [to fit] the shifting talents, interests and plans of the pupils ... as well as a continuously changing labour market...." This objective, which can be seen to constitute a prerequisite for the attainment of the first three general goals, requires flexibility in administrative procedure and in planning ("rolling planning") as well as a continuous, or "rolling," reform throughout the educational system. Such flexibility is necessary in order to enable the system:

to change itself in response to the changing structure of demand for education by the individual members of the society as well as the equally dynamic requirements of the economy;

to provide sufficient breadth in the content or educational offering and to allow for changes in student school careers. It should be possible for individuals to alter their educational decisions either during the normal school career or later (adult education), thus eliminating "dead ends" in the system.

Objective 5: The educational system should make efficient use of limited human and real resources. This objective is not of the same type as the four previous goals but rather constitutes a fundamental condition for their implementation [pp. 45-49].

Returning now to nursery schools, the official objectives set for them (SOU 1951-15) state that acting in cooperation with the home, they should develop children physically, intellectually, emotionally, and socially, helping their positive adaptation to society by:

1. Stimulating a comprehensive development.
2. Laying the basis for habits such as order and cleanliness.

3. Assisting in the creation of a fundamental conception of right and wrong.
4. Teaching them respect and responsibility for common property.
5. Evoking the feelings of the importance of helping others.
6. Teaching respect of others and their different points of view.
7. Providing knowledge of the surrounding environment and society.
8. Supporting the development of greater independence.

The preschool goals are broad in scope, directed toward the whole personality development rather than toward narrow functions. Stukát (1966), with regard to official statements, summarized them as follows:

> *Physical*—health, hygienic habits;
> *Motor*—body control, manual ability, rhythm;
> *Social and emotional*—routine habits, social adjustment (respect for rules, consideration for other people's interests, trustful attitude to other children and to adults, independence), emotional adjustment (confidence, frankness, frustration tolerance, absence of nervous disturbances such as anxiety, inhibitions, psychosomatics, lack of concentration);
> *Intellectual*—constructive, creative, and aesthetic interests, general knowledge, language expression, vocabulary, moral concepts, aesthetic ability, school readiness [p. 27].

Stukát (1966) also conducted a survey among preschool teachers and those responsible for their training to ascertain their views of what a child should gain from preschool. The consensus was that the child should:

1. Learn to work in a group.
2. Learn to act spontaneously—to overcome shyness and suppress nervous behavior.
3. Learn good habits—to be tidy, punctual, and polite.
4. Learn self-help skills such as how to dress and undress.
5. Learn respect for rules and prohibitions.
6. Learn to sit still and listen, and develop concentration abilities.
7. Develop manual dexterity and skill in the use of tools.
8. Improve his speaking ability and overcome speech defects.
9. Develop curiosity and stimulate aesthetic interest.
10. Learn motoric control over one's body.
11. Become accustomed to good hygiene habits.
12. Learn something about nature, social environment, and the community.
13. Prepare himself for school.

Considering the relationship between the preschool and the home, Mueller (1971) says

> Swedish nursery schools are seen as a supplement to the often small Swedish nuclear family and day nurseries and free time centers are seen as a substitute for care in the

home. The Board of Education now emphasizes in its recommendations that buildings and room arrangements should be "homelike." Thus they are to function as an extension of the home rather than the school. The Board of Education intends that "Children should learn to function together in a group and [they] should jointly obtain certain knowledge of conditions outside the home, for instance by excursions or field trips. . . ." This is a reflection of the philosophy of early childhood education in Swedish pre-schools which do not at present attempt any direct preparation for primary school and provide very little in the way of actual instruction. They are intended, instead, to provide an extension of upbringing in the home, and to offer children contacts with other kinds of environments in order to prepare for later social demands of school life [p. 8].

Mueller continues to indicate ways in which the generally agreed aims of the Swedish child care centers should be implemented:

(1) physical-sensory stimulation—there should be time and opportunity to cuddle, pat, and fuss over the child.
(2) stimulation of motor activity—children have lots of room and freedom to move about.
(3) social stimulation—children have lots of attention from both adults and older children.
(4) cognitive stimulation—children are talked with and given opportunities for speech development.
(5) perceptual stimulation—there are materials and opportunities for many different sensory impressions.
(6) emotional stimulation—the children know that care-taking people are fond of them [p. 8].

The Royal Preschool Commission's report gives the following as proper objectives for nursery school education:

The main objective for early childhood education, according to the commission should be to give each child the best possible conditions with the cooperation of the parents to develop and exploit their emotional and cognitive resources. It would then be the basis for the development of the child as an open and considerate human being, able to pose his own solutions to problems and come to his own conclusions with or without the aid of others. It ought to stimulate children to search for knowledge in a creative way and use it not only to improve their own life but also the life conditions of others. The main content of early childhood education programs should aim at:
(a) helping the child develop and stabilise an image of himself as an individual;
(b) providing for the continual development of the communication skills, and ability of the child in cooperation with the environment;
(c) providing the development of concept learning in order to help the preschool child understand the fundamental concepts and simple relationships between concepts before they start school [p. 17].

Using the findings of most recent research into the process of children's learning, the commission proceeded to outline the different developmental stages in early education and their practical implications. It does not see the teaching of specific content of knowledge as one of its aims; the emphasis should be on learning how to learn. The program should include an introduction to natural science, linguistic training, and training in numerical concepts, but the actual instruction in these areas should be in line with the child's natural cognitive development and maturation; the development must not be forced or hindered. In the preschool some elements of the theatre, cinema, art, music, and natural science should be introduced into the children's games to encourage their familiarity with these aspects of culture.

Another responsibility of preschool education in Sweden is to introduce the children favorably to the school environment, so that they have a positive attitude toward it. Visits to primary schools are to be organized for nursery children. Meetings of preprimary and primary school teachers will also help their transition to compulsory education when the time comes. Cooperation with parents is regarded as very important. They are introduced to the purpose of the preschool when their children are first enrolled. Meetings should be held to enlist subsequent participation of parents, and they should be encouraged to attend the school whenever possible.

The pattern for the preschool envisaged by the Royal Commission is more a confirmation of what presently exists than something radically new. It continues to draw heavily on the teachings of Arnold Gesell, Jean Piaget, and Erik Erikson, all of whom stress the concept of "readiness" and development of the whole child for learning, not just his mind.

ORGANIZATION AND CONTROL

Education in Sweden is strongly centralized. Paradoxically this centralization is used to maximize the freedom of regional and local school authorities, as well as the individual discretion of administrators, teachers, and students. Maclure (1971) puts it this way:

> Instead of allowing pedagogic considerations to determine educational organisation, the commission insisted that the education system, a potent agent for social control, should be subordinated to basic social policies, . . . cooperation on the one hand, and the development of individual talent on the other [p. 9].

The commission Maclure refers to is the Royal Commission set up in 1946. Its recommendations came out in 1948 and resulted, in the early 1950s, in the organization on an experimental basis of what is known as the comprehensive school. For all practical purposes, this is an unstreamed primary and secondary school that encompasses 9 years of education. The general aim of the comprehensive school is to give every child the maximum amount of education from which he specifically can benefit. By 1956 the system had been adopted by over

95% of the schools in the country. By now, there can be only a few Swedish children who do not attend a comprehensive school.

Maclure (1971), commenting on the central administration, says

> If the clarity with which social and political goals have been articulated is the first key to an understanding of Swedish educational reform, the second concerns the system of educational administration. Swedish education is tightly controlled and directed by the central government, through the Ministry of Education and its twin administrative agencies, the National Board of Education and the Office of Chancellor of the Universities. School reform and innovation is, therefore, directed from the centre. The initiative is handed down through Parliament to the National Board of Education, which in turn must organise change and create the circumstances in which the innovation takes place. The strong central control extends not only to matters of organisation and of "quantitative" planning, but also to the "qualitative" planning of the school curriculum. The syllabus and study plan for each type of school is the direct responsibility of the central government. Commissions set up to carry through major changes in organisation have been expected to plan the whole programme of studies as well as the administrative changes which a new system of organisation might entail [p. 10-11].

The Ministry of Education has prime responsibility to formulate legislation for Parliament. This proposed legislation is almost always the result of a study by an appointed royal commission. The day-to-day work of implementing the recommendations of the Ministry of Education with the aid of royal commissions falls to the National Board of Education, which has the task of implementing the decisions taken by Parliament. Below the National Board of Education are approximately 24 administrative units called county school boards, which are regional governmental bodies. The County School Board has its own staff members whose functions include inspection of schools, future school planning, and further implementation of existing plans at a county level. Below the county school boards are approximately 464 local authorities, ranging in size from those that can be run by a local head teacher to those requiring a director of education supported by strong professional staff, such as the city of Stockholm (population 800,000).

Comprehensive schooling lasts for 9 years in Sweden. Children normally start in the autumn term of the year in which they reach the age of 7. If, however, a child is either particularly mature or particularly immature, it is possible to advance or to retard his entry by 1 year. For the first 6 years, the number of hours per week spent in school are as follows:

Grade 1	20
Grade 2	24
Grade 3	30
Grade 4	38
Grade 5	40
Grade 6	39

This organized pattern of time allocation illustrates the high regard the Swedes have for introducing children to school slowly. It also reflects a respect for developmental psychology teachings, in that the children in grade 1 only spend one-half as much time in school as those in Grade 6.

Swedish preschool education does not come under the Ministry of Education, but the Ministry of Social Affairs. Below that, the National Board of Health and Welfare, the county administrations, and the Child Welfare Committee have the responsibility for supervision. They give grants for the establishment and operational costs of the child centers. Local authorities are responsible for the establishment and running of 90% of the child centers and their staffs. The remaining centers are run by organizations outside the control of the Ministry of Social Affairs or by private individuals.

Preschool and free time centers have developed in Sweden as an integral part of the child welfare system. These facilities are provided on the initiative of the local authorities and are encouraged by the state, if they are set up as child centers. If not, they take the form of nursery schools.

Anyone wishing to set up a day nursery or a child center can obtain a state starting grant to cover most of the initial costs and additional funds, if necessary. To qualify for state reimbursements, the organizers of child centers must take all places available for activities lasting at least 5 hours per day. This means that there must be facilities for rest and sleep, and for serving food. If the nursery school is in a residential area eligible for state loans, a housing loan can be obtained for the building. New centers can be organized under varying auspices: public, private, or combinations of public and private groups or individuals.

To begin a child center, the local community must first prepare an estimate of the day-care needs for the municipal 5-year construction plan. The survey on which this estimate is based is the responsibility of the local child welfare committee. It is carried out under their direction by the day care unit in the social bureau.

There are basically three kinds of preschool institutions in Sweden, for which the Swedish National Board of Health and Welfare (1971) give the following particulars:

> (1) Day nurseries (*daghem*). The day nursery receives children age six months to seven years, during the hours when parents are at work away from home. Normally, therefore, they are open from Monday to Friday from 6:30 A.M. to 7 P.M. and on Saturday from 6:30 A.M. to 2 P.M. The children are looked after in groups of up to 15 for five and six years old, 12 for three and four years old. For the youngest there must be one nurse for every four babies. The day nurseries are closed on Sundays, and also during the summer and on Christmas holidays.
>
> (2) Leisure homes or day care centers (*fritidshem*). Leisure homes are intended for children in the lower department of the comprehensive school (seven to twelve years old). They care for children of working parents during the free hours of the

school day, up to five hours, and during holidays. They are open Monday to Friday from 7 A.M. to 6 P.M. and on Saturdays from 7 A.M. to 2 P.M.

(3) Kindergartens (*lekskola*). Kindergartens provide for only three hours daily attendance and accept children between four and seven years of age. The hours of attendance are from 9 A.M. to 12 noon or from 12 noon to 4 P.M.–five days a week. They are closed, as are regular schools, during the holidays. Kindergartens are normally located near centers of population of young children, such as housing estates or apartment complexes. They are usually housed in separate single-story buildings, specifically designed for their use. The maximum size of the groups in which the children are looked after is dependent on the ages; for five and six years old there may be 20 children to one-teacher, for three and four years old there may be only 15 children to one-teacher, but many kindergartens are just one teacher institutions [p. 1].

The Royal Preschool Commission has proposed two independent changes in the organization of preschools: first, that day nurseries and kindergartens should be called preschools (*forskola*); second, that these preschools may be organized either as full-time institutions with a minimum of 5 hours attendance, or as part-time institutions with a minimum of 3 hours attendance. It recommends that provision of preschool education for all children of 6 years of age should be accomplished by 1975, but that it should not be made compulsory. Children who have special needs for preschool should be given first priority (that is, children with physical, mental, social, or linguistic handicaps). The commission advocates that towns begin planning for preschools now, so that they may be included in the towns' next building programs. Apartment complexes which exceed 200 units must provide for preschool facilities when the plans are initiated.

The commission's recommendation means that the organization of the preschools should in fact not be based on a horizontal division by age, but on vertical groupings whereby, for instance, children of 6 months and those of 2.5 years should be together with a maximum group size of about 12. It proposes the formation of sibling groups for children between the ages of 2.5 and 7.5 years, with a maximum of 20 children in each group. Among the advantages of this kind of vertical grouping is that older children will learn to cooperate with and help the younger. This concept is based on the assumption that many Swedish children are raised in "nuclear" families with one child. This arrangement provides few opportunities for contact with older or younger children.

There are two further proposals of sociological significance. The first is that preferential treatment should be given to handicapped children and to those of recent immigrants. Once this principle is accepted, considerations about special material and instructional methodologies required will need to be carefully worked out. The second sociological proposal endorses an existing premise of the Swedish preschool system. That is, it should be an upward extension of the home, rather than a downward extension of the comprehensive school. Parental involvement is, therefore, an important and necessary component of the new organizational pattern.

PHYSICAL SETTING: A VISIT TO A KUNGSBACKA[2] KINDERGARTEN

The preschool was on the ground floor of a standard type, three-story, red brick apartment building about 5 years old. It looked well kept. Outside there was a fenced playground (8 × 40 meters), a lawn, and a sand pit.

There were two teachers. Each had two groups, one from 9:00-12:00 A.M. and the other from 1:00-4:00 P.M. There were about 20 children in each group, most of them 6-year-olds. The two groups had a common entrance and hallway. The children who belonged to the "Bluebell" group went to the left, while those who belonged to the "Sunrose" went to the right.

The "Bluebell" accommodation consisted of two fairly large rooms, one about 6.5 × 9 meters and the other one about 6.5 × 10 meters. The smaller room had wall-to-wall carpeting, the other a linoleum floor. In the smaller room, there was a shelf on the windowsill with all kinds of wooden toys, and under it there were bigger wooden boards and small benches. Along the other wall there were cushions of various kinds and sizes, pillows, and a big mattress. There was also a piano. In one corner there was a carpenter's bench. The bigger room had, on one side, a little kitchen department with a refrigerator, two sinks, a stove, and a number of cupboards. There were also three tables, each seating about seven children. There were shelves on the walls, where paintings, games, and smaller toys were kept. In one corner, there was also a big chest of drawers in which each child had his own drawer. Near one of the sinks was a special table used for painting.

When the school was visited, the "Bluebell" teacher had "fruit" as a theme for the week. There were pictures of various kinds of fruit on the walls, and a huge inflated red apple hung from the ceiling. She said she would finish this theme by the following day and would then go over to something else though she had not decided exactly what. Her intention on the visitation day was "to talk about vitamins, different kinds of fruit, health, and so on." The rest of the time that day was to be devoted to free play or activities that the children chose themselves.

This teacher had two student teachers to help her. Most teachers only have one. The morning's program was as follows:

9.00 The children were admitted by one of the student teachers, and some were helped to undo difficult buttons and coats. As they walked in, they shook hands with the teacher and said "How do you do." Then they placed their fruit in their drawers and then went back and sat down on the floor.

[2] Kungsbacka, a town located near Gothenburg, Sweden.

9.05 The teacher called out the names to see if anybody was missing and each child replied with the name of the fruit that he had brought that day. Then, one of the children pulled yesterday's sheet off the wall calender and they said in chorus the date, name of the day, the month, and year.

9.15 There was a big picture on the wall full of different kinds of fruit, and the teacher asked the children if they could recognize any of them.

Most of the children could name the kinds they were used to, such as apples, pears, tomatoes, peaches, cherries, bananas, but with the more exotic types, identification became more difficult. One little girl recognized pineapple, and everyone was properly impressed. The teacher asked if all these different kinds could be bought now, and the children were doubtful. The teacher asked why we eat fruit, and the children offered different suggestions: healthy, good for the teeth, cheap. The question came up regarding health, and the teacher talked about different kinds of vitamins. One little boy said he had eaten the round, red kind of vitamins. The discussion moved into origin of the fruit. Most of the children knew that oranges were imported but some kinds of fruit were grown in Sweden.

9.25 The teacher took the children into the other room to watch slides about a class in an elementary school that started to swap fruit instead of pictures of movie stars or hockey players.

9.40 The class finished with slides, and a discussion started as to who should be at the carpenter's bench. The children could not come to an agreement themselves so the teacher appointed two girls. Three or four boys started building a house from boards. Two other boys began painting, and were reminded by the teacher not to forget to put on aprons. Two others started to play with an electric train. Most of the girls stayed in the bigger room and started sewing tablecloths or making necklaces. The teacher told them to watch out so they would not spill the beads all over the floor. The house-building activity grew to include five or six boys. Lively discussions ensued, but no conflicts.

One of the student teachers was at the girls' table and helped out when the sewing became too difficult. The other one was sitting and just looking at the children while the teacher put away the projector.

The two girls at the carpenter's bench were hammering away, while at the house-construction small conflicts started and two boys walked away. The others seemed to have lost interest in it and started instead to jump on the cushions. This became wilder and wilder but gradually turned into the game "ship-wrecked."

The teacher supervised all these activities, and after a while she went over to the boys who were painting and commented on their work. After a while they stopped. The "ship-wrecked" boys had now started to play war and aimed at each other with sticks going "bang, bang." This upset the teacher who reprimanded them and forbade them to play anything that had to do with war.

10.00 Everybody finally became involved in "approved" activities. The girls at the sewing table were talking about how much money would buy how much goods. The "shooting" boys had stopped and were lying on the cushions telling stories. One of the student teachers went over to the carpenter's bench to help the children find nails and sandpaper. The other one was still helping the girls with their sewing. A boy went over to the story-telling boys and wanted to join them, but was rejected. The teacher came and tried to settle the issue, and eventually an agreement was reached on a compromise basis.

The girls at the carpenter's bench went to the teacher and asked to paint the things they had made. They were told they must sand-paper them a little more; after about 5 minutes they returned, and the teacher said they could start painting.

10.20 The sewing stopped and instead, the girls, one boy and one of the student teachers were playing a game. In the other room, the boys were again working on their house. After a while they got tired and started to tear it down. This was done so loudly that the teacher came and said they must be careful not to hurt themselves with the boards. When the house was down, they started to reconstruct it.

The other children were still playing with the student teacher or painting. Two girls stopped playing and went over to the carpenter's bench; the other two girls were still painting the things they did before.

10.40 The housebuilding finally stopped and the boys made collisions with cars.

The girls stopped playing their game with the student teacher and started sewing again or making things on which to put hot saucepans. After a while, the teacher rang the bell and told all the children to start to tidy up. Nobody complained; everybody helped. The teacher and the student teachers supervised all this.

Then the children got ready to eat. They went to their places at the tables and when everybody was seated, the children at one table were told to go and pick up their fruit. Then the children at the other table went. Nobody started eating until everybody had his fruit. The teacher put on a record and everybody started to eat.

11.15 The teacher gave the children drawing books in which they were to draw fruit, the week's theme. At the end of the term, when the books become full of drawings, the children take them home to the parents.

11.40 The children all went into the other room and say down on the floor. The children wanted to sing different songs, and a vote was taken. The teacher explained how voting works, and that the minority accepts the majority. Afterwards, the minority sang their song, too. There were some individual contributions to the singing, and soon it was time to go and put on coats. Many of the children needed help to tie shoelaces or do up difficult buttons. When they were ready, they went home.

TEACHERS AND THEIR TRAINING

The OECD report, "Educational Policy and Planning—Sweden" (1967) offers the following observations about teachers and teacher training in Sweden:

> The teacher issue may of course turn out to be the most crucial hindrance to meeting the new school's objectives, particularly the first one ("all-round development of talents"). Individualised education within the framework of the class . . . presupposes, among other things, a training of the teacher directed towards this aim. Many of the present-day teachers have not had such training [p. 100].

This statement reflects a truism, that is, that teachers teach as they were taught, not as they were taught to teach. It is the breaking down of this built-in resistance to new teaching methods to which Sweden has particularly addressed itself.

The OECD "Classification of Educational Systems" gives the following information about the training of nursery school teachers in Sweden:

Place of training: nursery schools, Teachers' Training Colleges.

Length of study: 2 years.

Exhibit A
One Week's Program in a Swedish Preschool
Theme: Different Kinds of Household Work

	Monday	Tuesday	Wednesday	Thursday	Friday
Common get-together	Talk about different kinds of work in preschools and home	Talks on how to wash up the dolls' clothes	Talks on baking	Talks on how to take care of clothes and shoes	Puppet-show in connection to earlier talks
Fairy-tales	"At my place" (by I and L Sandberg)	The rest of "At my place"	Tale about traffic and play	Flannel-board talks in connection to the talk	Same as
Occupations	Different kinds of tidying-up jobs	Washing up dolls' clothes, creative occupations	Baking of muffins	Brushing of shoes	Dolls' party
Rhythmics	The children's ideas of the prepositions "on, of, under, in, in front of, and behind" are practiced	Pea-bags: The children move about in different ways in the room	Physical education, stretching and bowing movement, jumping	Competition play	Competition play
Outdoor play	Preschool playground	Preschool playground	Preschool playground	Walk to the park to feed birds	Preschool playground

Source: Persson, Kerry: Förskola (Pre-school), LT's Förlag. Stockholm 1970.

Applicants must have completed the *Grundskola* (9-year comprehensive school) and have six months practical experience.

Age: 19 years.

The leaving certificate and three years of practical experience give admission to *Lärarhögskola* for a 1-year course for teaching handicapped children [p. 80].

Mueller (1971) provides some additional information on the requirements for acceptance into the nursery school teacher training colleges. She indicates that the applicants must have satisfactory final marks from the 9-year course in a comprehensive school or the equivalent. They must have previous experience in the care of infants (less than 7 years old) in the form of 16 weeks training or practical work. In addition, they must have completed 16 weeks of practice teaching with a qualified nursery school teacher in a group care facility.

The practical experience must follow the curriculum laid down by the National Board of Education, which includes a rather precise set of aims for the instruction in each subject. It includes instructions and helpful comments in the form of guidelines that cover the proper rate and sequence of instruction to optimize individual learning and help the student to see the relationship between what he is doing as a teacher and what he is learning about himself and his capabilities as a teacher. It is hoped that, as a result of this experience, the student will integrate into his developing style an interest in his pupils and the material being taught as well as his ability to teach it.

The training in the teachers' college stresses a study of developmental and child psychology and their applications to pedagogy. Approximately 45% of the course is devoted to these subjects. Other study includes civics, child psychiatry, health, ethics, Swedish, music, rhythm, painting, modelling, art, and handicrafts.

By an order of the Swedish government, instruction at all levels in its school system must be as individualized as possible. This applies also to the training of nursery school teachers. The planning of studies and the shaping of the individual curriculum are done cooperatively by the college professor and the student concerned. The independence of students is stimulated by their being given ample opportunity to express their individual opinions and to assume responsibility for realizing their own educational goals. Participation of several students in a group project is encouraged, for example, in some aspect of child psychology or pedagogics. This practice makes possible deeper and more comprehensive studies than are within the reach of students working singly. Such groups, however, are very loosely formed and last only for the period of a particular project. During the training of teachers there is continuous monitoring of their work, again on a cooperative student-teacher basis. In the course of this, the student's strengths and weaknesses are identified with two purposes in mind: first, to aid the student; and second, to improve the quality of the teacher training. Grades, insofar as possible, are kept in the background; but final marks are assigned on performance both in the formed courses and in practice training.

In the spring of 1970, there were 5268 applicants competing for 1710 places in 14 nursery school teacher training colleges. This competitive entrance factor commonly results in acceptance going to those applicants who already have up to 2.5 years of practical work to their credit.

The Swedish government gives positive encouragement to men entering the preschool teaching profession. Since the autumn of 1971, they have been able to enter nursery school teacher training colleges on a "free quota" (15% of available spaces if their credentials are acceptable, even if not fully comparable to the best of the female candidates). In 1971, 62 men (of 225 male applicants) were accepted.

The Royal Preschool Commission gives very high priority to teacher training and in-service training. It believes that traditional instructional methods should be developed. More use must be made, for example, of new techniques such as videotaping and microteaching. It is also concerned that a course in adult psychology should be added to the professional educational curriculum so that the preschool teachers can be more aware of the process of adult socialization in their work with parents. Another recommendation is that teacher training should include a course in ecology and physical planning, to equip the teacher to deal with her children in matters relating to the environment. The commission also feels that teachers work too much in isolation. It therefore recommends that teachers, architects, psychologists, sociologists, and physicians be brought together to cooperate in the training of preschool teachers.

Integration of the training of preprimary school teachers with that of primary school teachers, so that each will have a better understanding of what the other is doing, is another strong point in the commission's report. In compulsory education, it is very common in Sweden for a teacher to be promoted with her class for several years. Whether this practice will be extended to bridge the preschool and the primary school, however, is not yet clear. In the area of in-service training, the commission recommended a deeper and more profound education in psychology and sociology, particularly through the use of observational methods. It also recommended that increased attention be given during in-service training courses to the problems of educating handicapped children. It is desired that they should be considered as regular members of their class wherever this is possible.

Table 6.4 presents information on the number of kindergarten teachers in Sweden and shows that there has been a 158.9% increase in them over the 10-year period. This coincides very closely with the 167.3% increase in enroll-

TABLE 6.4
Kindergarten Teachers in Sweden from 1960-61 to 1970-71

Year	Private	Public	Total
1960-61	n.a.[a]	1,231	1,231+
1965-66	n.a.	1,685	1,685+
1966-67	n.a.	1,874	1,874+
1967-68	n.a.	2,216	2,216+
1968-69	n.a.	2,497	2,497+
1969-70	n.a.	2,853	2,853+
1970-71	n.a.	3,187	3,187+
% of increase from 1960-61 to 1970-71		158.9	158.9+

Source: National Central Bureau of Statistics, Sweden.
[a]Not available.

ments in kindergartens over the same time-period. Thus, the pupil-teacher ratio has not changed much. As Table 6.5 indicates, it has increased by only one student. The pupil-teacher ratio in 1970 was 41:1.

It is important to note that we have been considering qualified teachers only. The numerous assistants of a wide variety that are found in Swedish preschools are not included in the statistical tables. However, they play an important part as described in *Child Centres Activities in Sweden* (1971):

> At the Day Nurseries and the Nursery Schools, Pre-School Teachers and Children's Nurses are employed. The Pre-School Teachers have been educated for two years at a Pre-School teacher-training College and the Children's Nurses have attended shorter courses of one term or 34 weeks. At the Free time Centres, Free time Leaders are employed, often assisted by Children's Nurses. Free time Leaders have a two years education at a Vocational School comparable with the Pre-School Teachers' education. In addition to the Staff working directly with the children, cleaners and kitchen personnel are also employed at the Child Centres [p. 2].

The standard set by the National Board for the number of children per staff in preschools is recorded by Mueller (1971) as follows:

Child centre	Age	Maximum No.
Day nurseries	6 mo.-1 year	8
(*Daghem*)	2 years	10
	3 & 4 years	12
	5 & 6 years	15
Nursery school	3 & 4 years	15
(*Lekskola*)	5 & 6 years	20
Fritidshem	7 to 11 years	15

In this same context, the Royal Preschool Commission has recommended that the adult to child ratio be 1:4 in the infant and toddler group and 1:5 in the group of children between 2.5 and 7 years old.

In 1965, the pupil-teacher ratio in comprehensive schools was 16.7:1 in the lower department, 17.9:1 in the middle department, and 13.7:1 in the upper

TABLE 6.5
Pupil:Teacher Ratio in Kindergarten from 1960–61 to 1970–71

Year	Private	Public	Total
1960–61	n.a.[a]	40:1	40:1
1965–66	n.a.	38:1	38:1
1970–71	n.a.	41:1	41:1

[a]Not available.

department. The major reason for these class sizes is found in the new principle of individualized instruction that was introduced at the time of reform (1968)— the fewer the pupils per teacher, the greater the chances for the success of this method.

FINANCING EARLY CHILDHOOD EDUCATION

Starting at the compulsory school attendance age of 7, education in Sweden is free. Its cost is shared between the State and the municipalities, 60% and 40%, respectively. At the precompulsory level, however, there are different arrangements, depending upon the kind of school. Since 1966, the Swedish government has encouraged the formation of early childhood education enterprises called "child centers." A child center is defined by Mueller (1971) as a:

> ... voluntary effort on the part of local authorities, strongly encouraged by the state. The term "Child Center" is used to cover day nurseries, nursery schools and free time centers for children 7 to 11 years old. ... Although 85% of the child centers are under the jurisdiction of municipal authorities, 15% are sponsored by associations, industry, and county councils. Anyone setting up a day nursery which meets the standards can obtain a state starting grant to cover most initial costs and additional funds, if necessary, are available as loans. State support to nursery schools was abolished in February 1966-67 to encourage greater allocation of resources to full day care so that more mothers could participate in the work force. ... To qualify for state reimbursement the organizers of a child center must make all places available for activities lasting for at least 5 hours per day. This means that there must be facilities for rest and sleep and the serving of cooked food. If the nursery school is in a residential area which is eligible for state loans, a housing loan can be obtained for the building. ... If voluntary agencies request no public subsidy, they are not obliged to adhere to state standards [p. 10].

The Swedish National Board of Health and Welfare publication "Child Centres Activities in Sweden" gives the following information on costs in 1971:

> About 90% of all child centers are under local authorities' auspices. About 10% are managed by associations, organizations, companies, the Church and private people. The building costs vary but the average is between 11,000 S.Kr. ($2126) and 15,000 S.Kr. ($2900) per child for a child center in a separate building. The running costs are at present estimated at an average of 8500 S.Kr. ($1643) per child and year in a day nursery, 6500 S.Kr. ($1256) per child and year in free-time center, and 1500 S.Kr. ($290) per child and year in a nursery school. For a family day nursery the expenses per child and year are estimated at about 6000 S.Kr. ($1160). Government grants are given for the establishment of a child center by 5000 S.Kr. ($967) per child to be admitted. In addition, a loan of 4000 S.Kr. ($773) per child can be obtained. Grants from the General Inheritance Fund, limited to 50% of the purchase costs, are received for furniture and other equipment. Government subsidies are given to the running costs of day nurseries with 2800 S.Kr. ($541) per child and year, and to free time centers with 1500 S.Kr. ($290) per child and year. In certain

cases government subsidies are also given to local authorities for the administration of family day nurseries with 35% of the expenses for the salary of the day care-taker. The nursery school receives subsidy from the General Inheritance Fund for the building costs and the equipment covering, however, at the most, 50% of the expenses. Aid for the running costs is not available. The parents' fee depends on the income of the family, its number of children, and how many of them visit the child center, and how many days of the week the child is at the center. Because of this, the fee varies between 1 to 34 S.Kr. ($.20 to $6) per child and day. On an average, the parents' fee is about 7 S.Kr. ($1.25) a day at a day nursery, and 100-125 S.Kr. ($19-24) per term at the nursery school [p. 3].

The Swedish per capita gross national product is $3840. The per capita expenditure on education is $7.91.[3] Table 6.6, which gives data on kindergarten expenditures in Sweden from 1965-1966 to 1969-1970, shows that capital expenditure has been increased almost twice as fast as current expenditure. The total increase over the 5-year period was 153.2%. This is a very high rate when compared with the OECD figure of 73%, or about 3.3% per year for the 15 years between 1950-1965.[4] If we were to project that percentage of increase for the same 5-year period 1965-1970, it would equal approximately a 16.5% increase at the compulsory school level as against the 153.2% increase for the kindergartens. It must be pointed out, however, that the OECD figures take inflation into account, while this has not been attempted in this study. Where the Sw. crowns have been changed to US dollars, the 153.2% increase remains valid because their was no change in the relative value of the two currencies during the 5-year period.

Table 6.7 shows that per pupil expenditures in kindergartens have increased by the equivalent of $162 over the 5 years between 1965-1966, 1969-1970. Compulsory school expenditures in Sweden for 1965-1966 were $707 per child. Using an estimated increase of 16.5% over the 5-year period, the 1970-1971 per pupil expenditure in compulsory school should be $823, which would give an increase of $116 over the 5-year period. In short, in 1965 the ratio of kindergarten to compulsory school expenditure was 3:5; by 1970, it had changed to 4:5, a clear indication of the increased effort put into preschool education during those 5 years.

As to the financing of early childhood education in the future, the Preschool Commission recommends that the cost of operating the children's centers should be borne by local governments, but state aid should be forthcoming for construction charges.

The present plan calls for only part-day (3 hours) attendance, and this should be provided free to all children whose parents want it. To implement the idea of positive discrimination, all children would be examined at 6 months, 1.5 years,

[3] OECD. *Economic surveys.* 1972.
[4] OECD. *Educational policy and planning, Sweden.* Paris, 1967.

TABLE 6.6
Public Kindergarten Expenditure in Sweden from 1965–66 to 1969–70

Year	Capital	Current	SK '000 Total Capital Current	$ '000 Total Capital Current
1965–66	19,611	151,814	171,425	33,136[a]
1966–67	29,481	193,963	223,444	
1967–68	42,152	237,859	280,011	
1968–69	63,792	265,503	329,295	
1969–70	74,543	359,587	434,130	83,917
% of increase from 1965–66 to 1969–70	280.1	136.9	153.2	153.2

Source: National Central Bureau of Statistics, Sweden

[a]Official Exchange rates, O.E.C.D.

and at 4 years, so that those with special needs could be identified early and given priority admission. Through these centers, preschool education should be available (although not compulsory) to a much larger proportion of 6-year-olds than is now the case. Indeed, the commission hoped to offer education to all 6-year-olds by 1975, and later to the 5-year-old and younger groups.

INSTRUCTIONAL METHODS

The instructional program of the Swedish preschool is influenced by the ideas of Froebel, Montessori, and Decroly. The Swedish believe that developmental and child psychology, not learning psychology, should be the basis for instruction. Concretely, this means that spontaneous activity, social activities, and interest centers are characteristic features.

Sandels (1969a) says that the instructional methodology in nursery schools up to and including the 1940s and 1950s used the "interest center" method, which aimed at stimulating the child's development intellectually, socially, emotionally, and physically. The teacher planned the "interest center" for a certain period, varying from 1 or 2 weeks to a month, prepared common experiences, talks, occupations, and so forth, in connection with the center, and then carried out the project with great flexibility. Since the end of the 1950s, however, the "interest centre" method has played a smaller role in nursery schools. The emphasis has changed to free play and spontaneous free creativity.

TABLE 6.7

Public Kindergarten Per Pupil Cost in U.S. Dollars from 1965–66 to 1969–70

Year	$ '000 Current	'000 No. of Children	Per Pupil Cost
1965–66	29,346	64	459
1969–70	69,508	112	621
Total Increase	40,162	48	162

Mueller (1971) makes clear that the three major frameworks that support the Swedish philosophy on early childhood instruction are those of Arnold Gesell, Jean Piaget, and Erik H. Erikson. She specifically notes that "... until recently Arnold Gesell's work has been the major guide for nursery school teachers who viewed children as being endowed with an innate epigenetic mechanism which guides the proper rate as well as the proper sequence of development. Teachers, therefore, awaited cues from the child concerning his social and psychological and physical maturation [p. 4]."

Most new kindergarten teachers use a pedagogical approach similar to that of the English infant schools, "the discovery method." They offer the child a physically and socially stimulating environment so that he may learn in a relaxed and informal way what he is ready to discover in his world. The teachers offer guidance, but do not impose structure; they teach children the rules of the appropriate social behavior for participation in small groups with their peers and with adults who are not in their family.

The instructional methods are extremely informal and programs in day nurseries and kindergartens are only loosely planned as follows: free play, with materials available, and getting together for music, songs, conversation, storytelling, rhythmic exercises, dancing, gymnastics, and so forth. Individual or group work is supported by the teacher, but the initiative is left to the children. Much emphasis is placed on giving the youngest children opportunities to participate in games that promote their development and using materials particularly suitable for them.

Instructional plans are normally made out for a week at a time, but they are often modified because of some current event. Special plans are made for the big occasions of the year such as Christmas and Easter and for the spring, summer, autumn, and winter vacations.

Some kindergartens in Sweden are using an adaptation of the Montessori system to introduce the children to prereading and prewriting if they are ready. In fact, readiness is central to the discussion of the aims and objectives of early childhood education in Sweden. During the 1960s, there was a demand for more intellectual stimulus in nursery schools. However, teachers who believed they would be doing the child harm if they tried to teach him to read and write before he was ready saw this as a threat to the special aims of the nursery school and its instructional methods. By and large, the Swedish preschool teacher still waits for cues from the child as to his social, physical, and physiological maturation. Only after these are clearly visible does the teacher attempt to guide the child to the next higher stage. In the face of this, however, pressure is being exerted to offer 5- and 6-year-olds more specified experiences in preschool than they presently receive, particularly in relation to their cognitive and social development.

The Preschool Commission's discussion of instructional methods was centered around three models, the learning or transmission model (mainly identical with behavior modification principles), the developmental psychology model (mainly a Gesell model), and the integration model (based on cognitive and psychodynamic theory) of Erikson. The one finally chosen for preschool education, as well as for guidelines for cooperation between individuals in preschools, was the "integration model." The commission further recommended that this model provide for instruction in preprimary school that can result in some children learning to read, write, and count, while others who are not ready to develop these skills can do so later. The commission recommends that research be intensified on the best ways to integrate the efforts of preschool and compulsory school education. It believes that the instructional methods of a preschool character should, if necessary, be continued on into primary school according to the needs and development level of each child.

RESEARCH ON EARLY CHILDHOOD EDUCATION

In discussing the role of educational research in Sweden it is important to place it in its proper context. Maclure (1971) states:

> The interplay between the politicians and social scientists has amounted to a dialogue inside and outside the several Royal Commissions. Much of the dialogue is inconclusive: policy in the end has had to be based on judgement, aided but not determined, by research. Professor Husen's comment . . . is still to the point: the research findings' "first and foremost importance lay in the fact that they have contributed to removing a host of prejudices and showing that what was involved in the debate were value judgements rather than facts. The school reform is, after all, a political question [p. 10]."

Husen's statement is important since it expressed well the proper role of educational research in aiding policy-making.

Maclure also identifies five basic strategies of Swedish educational innovation:

(1) Clear political decisions on the goals of the educational system and the objectives to be achieved in each type of school. These major political decisions have, on the whole, been taken on the advice of Royal Commissions on the basis of which the Minister of Education formulates legislation for Parliament.
(2) The refinement of these general goals and objectives into a working curriculum and study plan for each type of school.
(3) A programme of in-service training for teachers to assist the introduction of new curricula and teaching methods.
(4) A programme of Research and Development to support the policies of reform and innovation.
(5) A system of continual revision by which the curriculum and study plan for each type of school is constantly assessed in terms of its own objectives [p. 15].

In Sweden, an intensive educational research and curriculum development effort is underway. The aim of this effort is to identify appropriate and beneficial kinds of kindergarten experience for children. One important guiding principle is that the choice of experiences offered must always be made with due regard for the child's level of maturity. This principle comes directly from the teachings of Arnold Gesell whose work is highly regarded in Sweden.

What the educational researchers then are seeking is a preschool program that meets the individual needs of young children. The driving force behind this effort is a concern that the whole child be seen as the entity to be educated, not just his mind. To this end, programs on different levels for different subjects may have to be planned for the same child.

Stukát (1966) conducted a study which had as its purpose the evaluation of existing preschool programs. This involved comparing 130 preschool children with 130 home-educated children on a number of variables related to preschool objectives. The evaluation was carried out when the children were in grade 1, and a follow-up with a more limited number of variables was undertaken in grade 3. The results indicated that positive effects appeared in those areas to which special attention was given, for example, general knowledge, vocabulary, verbal expression, daily life routines, painting, and manual-constructive tasks. Areas with more intangible objectives, such as social-emotional adjustment and mental health, did not show corresponding effects. There seems to be no general transfer of achievement to elementary school subjects. The conclusion, therefore, is that preschool achieves its most evident impact in areas where some kind of direct teaching takes place.

The results of Stukát's evaluation study provided the main impetus for a new project aimed at the development of an experimental preschool program based on the experience gained. In the words of Stukát and Sverud (1971), the main features of this project were

(1) The program is a supplement to the existing activities in preschool. It has been planned to cover one-third of the preschool day.

(2) The areas chosen for innovation are the same as those chosen by the Royal Preschool Commission, which are social training, communication skill, and concept formation.

(3) The program is planned mainly for 6 year olds, although it can be used in nongraded settings with children at varying ages.

(4) More attention is given to making the preschool goals more concrete than is usual. An attempt has been made to give the teachers examples of how concrete activities can be derived from general objectives. The aim has been to suggest a way of thinking, a way of relating lofty goals to the manifold and dynamic daily school life.

(5) The program has been drawn upon ideas of Nomburger, Wrikson, Piaget, and Skinner. The teachers are given rather detailed methodological suggestions related to the different objectives, and a variety of material has been developed. In addition to activities aimed at goals in one area, an attempt has been made experimentally to integrate activities which aim at different objectives, e.g., concept training using family or society situations, and using the opportunity for language training situations [p. 3-4].

The evaluation of the project has been performed by comparing 500 children who followed the experimental program and 500 control children. At present the results of the field phase are being analyzed.

In connection with this same project two special substudies are being conducted:

1. Moral development in children 4 to 8 years old viewed from multidimensional aspects. This study will include 500 children. Instruments, interviews, child play, and projective tests will be used.

2. Treatment of aggressive behavior in children in the preschool age-group. The purpose here is to work out a treatment for aggressive behavior on 6-year-olds based on Bandura-Walters theory of learning social behavior. The study will include 15 children in an experimental group and an equal number of children in a control group. The treatment is accomplished by using structured child play and evaluated by observations in unstructured play situations.

The discussion in Sweden about providing a more universal nursery schools organization primarily for 5- and 6-year-olds has initiated research programs to develop an optimal organizational pattern for cooperation between nursery schools and compulsory schools. The emphasis is not only on the organizational arrangements that cooperation would present, but also on what consequences an easier and more natural transition to primary school may have on the compulsory school itself. To this end, experiments with sister and brother groups, in which children of 5 to 6 years old are integrated in preparatory classes in elementary school under the supervision of specialized assistants, are taking place in Malmö, Västerås, and in Ströms municipality in Jämtland. After the results of these and perhaps other studies have been evaluated, more general forms of cooperation between preprimary and primary schools can be decided.

Birgitta Gran (1972) describes the main aims of the FÖL project (preschool and primary school in cooperation) which started in 1969-1970 in Malmö:

> (1) To consider and compare other forms of objective for the teaching of children between the ages of 6 and 7, in which the target should be a direct adjustment between the activities of the preschool and the teaching of the primary school.
> (2) To invent, construct, test, and revise study materials and working methods that can be used in a modified preschool and comprehensive school system.
> (3) To investigate forms for cooperation between preschool and primary school, including a more intensive and immediate cooperation between teachers than exists at present.
> (4) To study possible ways of complementing family care, upbringing, teaching and skill-training, paying particular attention to socially handicapped pupils.
> (5) To study and construct an upgraded school level encompassing both preschool and primary school [p. 1].

The project is being conducted in three experimental areas: methods and material, organization of collaboration, and sociopsychology.

In the methods and material experimental area, a partly new and more structured content for the preschool is being worked out. This is based on suggestions from working groups composed of subject experts, preschool teachers, and primary school teachers, for specific activities that would encourage developments in mathematics, childrens' knowledge of social surroundings, linguistics, and esthetic subjects. The educational program of the Preschool Commission has served as a general guide so far as the content of activities is concerned. The commission's "corner-stones" for educational activity in the nursery schools have also been kept in mind, so that the preschool and the parents should jointly create such conditions that:

> (1) the child develops and stabilises a conception of himself as an individual. This is the basis for the child later being able to collaborate with others;
> (2) the child develops communication skill in his interaction with the environment. Gradually, the child ought to recognise his innate means of expression, and to make use of them in words, sound, movement, and pictures;
> (3) an appropriate concept formation develops in the child, so that he understands basic concepts and simple system relations before his entrance into school. This does not mean that the child first of all obtains knowledge, but that he learns how to learn . . . [p. 2].

The work of construction was started in the spring term of 1971 and about 200 descriptions were worked out.

The Västerås school project was started in 1971. It was planned in the following way: Children from preschools and primary schools would be brought together so that they could share materials and space. The children could change between the preschool "class" and the primary "class" to meet their different needs, for example, preschool children who are mature enough to learn reading can join the primary class for this subject, while primary school children who have a great desire for movement can share preprimary school activities for some of the day. The teachers cooperate in teams and have one conference a week. They have evaluated the project as successful, and it is being continued.

In Ströms municipality, which is in a rural district, preschool children of 5 and 6 years in three primary schools are being integrated on a trial basis. In each school, the number of preschool children varies between three and six, and primary school children between six and ten. The preschool children have their own room, but experience a certain degree of cooperation with those in the primary school. The preschool activity goes on 2 days a week. The primary school teacher and one assistant are responsible for the integrative part. A preschool teacher works as a consultant for the preschool activity in the different schools.

Following on the Preschool Commission's proposal for a new program in the preschools, a number of studies of methodology are being made in Stockholm, Umå, and Linköping. One of these, located at the Institute of Educational Research in Stockholm, is looking at methods of evaluating the effects of programs for young children. To acquire the data necessary for such evaluation, experiments are planned in three areas:

1. Method-materials with the purpose of giving the preschool a new content.
2. Organization, with the purpose of constructing a nongraded school extending over 4 years.
3. Social psychology, with the purpose of making an inventory of the number of children with social handicaps to aiding them as effectively as possible with a supporting program.

During 1971-1972 an elementary school organization was worked out in accordance with the following nongraded model:

Teacher	Primary group	Corresponds to
D	9-year-olds	grade 3
C	8-year-olds	grade 2
B	7-year-olds	grade 1
A	6-year-olds	preschool

Cooperation between groups is intended to take place during certain periods when there are common items in the curriculum. Cooperation between teachers will be effected by exchanging classes and teamwork. The children will work on individual levels and pass through the gradeless elementary school in 4 years, during which time constructions, evaluations, and measurements will be made of their progress.

Another project in Stockholm was "investigations on the subject of nursery school methodology [Sandels, 1969a]." This aimed to describe and measure the effects of work in one nursery school, and to follow this up on the same children during their first term in the comprehensive school. The factors investigated were: general ability, reading and writing ability, maturity of behavior in traffic, color-form knowledge, musical knowledge, comprehension, social relationship, and creativity.

The project started in 1968 with a total number of 13 children, seven boys and six girls of 6 years of age (one boy was 5 years old). During the spring term of 1971, a comparison was made of the results of the nursery school and comprehensive school investigations. Hypotheses were then created which could provide the basis for a system of coordination between the two types of school.

The Linköping project was concerned with investigating the effects of systematic individually-adjusted training in reading and writing for 6-year-olds in the preschool, traced through to grade 3 in the elementary school. Three groups were compared: an experimental group *E,* a preschool control group *C,* and another control group C_2 consisting of children from grade 1 in elementary school. The experiment started during the autumn of 1971 and ended in spring 1972.

The national principle already referred to, that handicapped preschool children should be educated in regular classes whenever possible, is itself based on research results that concluded two things: first, that handicapped children seem to learn best in a normal class where they do not feel isolated and different, and second, healthy children form better ideas about handicapped children when they have associated with them. It is particularly important that this association take place at an early age.

In this context, the Preschool Commission initiated a project to study handicapped children who have been integrated with normal children, and identify any problems that arise from their participating in child center and leisure-time activities. This project is directed by Professor I. Johannesson at the University of Lund, and its precise aims are to study attitudes and value systems of and toward handicapped children in preschool; to explore methods for influencing these attitudes; to describe and evaluate models for integrating handicapped children in preschools; and to construct methods and materials for promoting cooperation and integration between handicapped and nonhandicapped children.

This investigation includes immigrant children with linguistic problems as well as Swedish children with motor, auditory, and intellectual defects.

A second project at the Stockholm Institute of Education (The Sandels project) is concerned with emotionally disturbed children in preschool programs. Its objects are:

1. To construct and test methods to study the cognitive development of 5- to 6-year-olds.
2. To study the cognitive development of emotionally disturbed children in preschool programs (5- to 6-year-olds).
3. To describe the current working methods in preschool programs.
4. To describe one way that a child-psychologist consultant could be used in the preschool programs.

The group under observation consisted of 34 children who were diagnosed as emotionally disturbed; the control group was 37 normal children, matched with respect to sex, age, and the preschool they attended. Data for these 34 pairs of 5- to 6-year-olds were collected during the school year 1970-1971. The instruments for showing the cognitive processes were divided into elements that describe cognitive activity, cognitive ability, and cognitive products (retained knowledge of 5- to 6-year-olds at preschool). Data relating to environment, the way of working, and the reactions of the children at the preschool were obtained by interviews in which parents were included, and direct observation. The results of this project were to be reported during the school year 1971-1972.

Kärrby (1971) has made a thorough analysis of children's self-corrective responses to control of behavior by the parents. His conclusion is that moral development is a function of different processes. The child's identification with parents and the emotional home climate are of chief importance. Other moral characteristics, such as self-critical ability, have apparently stronger relation to cognitive and verbal learning processes. On the basis of the results and conclusions, Kärrby has designed a more applied project, with the purpose of influencing certain aspects of social behavior, cooperation, and self-perception.

In summary, the principal motivations for research in the preschool area in Sweden at the present time appear to be these:

1. A concern for sibling grouping of children of 5 to 8 years of age.
2. The development of team teaching.
3. A concern for early intervention, especially for children with difficult social backgrounds or language problems.
4. The development of flexible school buildings to accommodate different preschool programs, to facilitate new organizational arrangements, and to allow for attendance of handicapped children.

5. Parental involvement, in that preschool is seen as an outward extension of the home as distinct from a downward extension of the compulsory school.

ACKNOWLEDGMENTS

The author wishes to acknowledge the valuable help received from: Mr. S. Winberg, of the National Board of Education; Mrs. D. Edmar of the Ministry of Education; Mesdames B. Ronnbled, S. Henriksson, and G. Schyl-Bjurman, of the Ministry of Social Affairs; Messrs. L. Liefgren and F. Bergman, of the National Central Bureau of Statistics; Miss B. Gran, of the Malmö School of Education, and Mr. K. G. Stukat, of the Gothenburg School of Education.

BIBLIOGRAPHY

Austin, G., & Antonsen, K. *A review of pre-school educational efforts in five countries.* Stencil. OECD, 1971.

Blackstone, T. *Pre-school education in Europe.* Stencil. Council of Europe, 1970.

Dahllöf, U. *Svensk skolreform under 25 år. Huvuddrag: Utvecklingen, 1940-1970.* Pedagogiska Institutionen, Göteborgs, Universitet.

Fors, A. *Social policy and how it works.* Kugelbergs Boktryckeri AB Stockholm, 1972.

Gran, B. *Project Fol* (From Swedish "Forskola–lagstedium i samverkan"–preschool and primary school in cooperation), a research and development project. Department of Educational and Psychological Research, Malmö School of Education, Sweden, August 31, 1972.

Henrysson, S. *Elementary instruction in orientation.* Method System developments, L.H.V.M. Institute, 1971.

Johannesson, I. The Lund pre-school project. In K. G. Stukat, & K. A. Sverud (Eds.), *A survey of current pre-school research projects in Sweden.* Stencil.

Körrby, G. *Child rearing and development of moral structure.* Stockholm: Almqvist and Wiksell, 1972.

Maclure, S. *Innovation in Education, Sweden.* Paris: OECD/CERI, June, 1971.

Mueller, J. *Pre-school education and day care for Swedish children.* Stencil, September, 1971.

Persson, K. [Pre-school.] *Förskola.* Stockholm: LT's Förlag, 1970.

Salzer, M. *L'éducation en Suède–No. 17.* Ministère Royal des Affaires Etrangères, October 1971.

Sandels, S. *Investigation into nursery school methods.* School Research, National Board of Education Bureau, Sept. 14, 1969: 7, and 1970:20(a).

Sandels, S. *Emotionally disturbed children in pre-school programmes.* Stencil. The Institute of Education, Stockholm School of Education, 1969b.

Schyl-Bjurman, G. *Målet för förskolan barnets fostran.* Stencil. Bidrag: Intellektualisering Socialisering-Stockholm, September, 1971.

Sjølund, A. *The effect of day-care institutions on children's development: An analysis of international research.* Stencil. 1971.

Stukàt, K. G. *Förskolan och skolstarten.* Stencil. 1971.

Stukàt, K. G. *Lekskolans inverkan på barns utveckling.* Stockholm: Almqvist and Wiksell, 1966.

Sverud, K.-A. & Stukat, K.-G. *Nursery school project.* The Institute of Educational Psychology, Gothenburg School of Education, 1971.

Trouillet, B. *Die vorschulerziehung in neun europäischen* Weinheim: Ländernj Beltz Verlag, Band 8, 1969.

William-Olsson J. *Förskolebarnets situation i dagens samhälle–sociliserings–processen,* 1971.

Council of Europe: *Research into preschool education symposium, 1971.* Strasbourg 1972.

Extract from the government directives to the Child Centres Committee. Stencil. April 28, 1968.

Innehåll och Metoder i Förskoleverksamhetan: Diskussions–PM Fran 1968 års Barnstugeutredning. Göteborg Offsettryckeri AB, 1971, 71.6499.

Lärarhögskolan i Linköping: Plan för Skolforsknings projekt Läs och Skriv: Förskola 70. Stencil.

National Board of Education, Informationssektionen 10.6. 1971(4). *The training of nursery school teachers in Sweden.*

OECD. *Educational policy and planning, Sweden.* Paris, 1967.

OECD. *Reviews of national policies for education, Sweden.* Paris, 1969.

OECD. *Labour force statistics 1959-1970.* Paris, 1972.

OECD. *Demographic trends in member countries.* Paris, 1971.

OECD. *Classification of educational systems.* Paris, 1972.

Pressmeddelande budgeten: Utbildhing och forskning 11.1. 1972, Stencil.

School Research in the Swedish National Board of Education Budget Requests for 1971-72 in School Research, National Board of Education, Bureau 14, 1970:26.

SOU 1951:15: Betänkande avgivit av 1946 års kommittee för den halvöppna barnavården.

SOU 1967:8: Barnstugor, barnavårdsmanna skap och barnölylycksfall.

SOU 1972:26: Forskolan Del I och Del II Forskolan Betankande

SOU 1972:27: avgivit av 1968 ars barnstugeutredning.

The Swedish National Board of Health and Welfare. *Child centres activities in Sweden.* 1971.

United Nations demographic yearbook, 1970.

United Nations. *Analysis and projections of households and families.* 1971.

Early Childhood Education
in France

INTRODUCTION

The French concern for educating young children can be traced to the writings of Jean-Jacques Rousseau. His books *Emile* (1762), *La Nouvelle Héloïse* (1764), and *The Social Contract* (1767) called attention to the importance of the concept of childhood. *Emile* has often been called the charter of childhood, for it laid down a plan for education to make an ordinary child morally responsible and intellectually capable. Rousseau felt that childhood was a unique time and that a child during this period of time should not be considered just a small adult. He was one of the first philosophers to point out the relationship between society, the home, and the problems of education.

Preprimary education in France actually started in 1779, when a group of schools called *écoles à tricoter* (knitting schools) was formed. At about the same time, another group called *salles d'aile* (a place of refuge) was created. The state took over the support of these schools in 1833, when they were absorbed into the national educational system and changed their name to *écoles maternelles*. The *école maternelle* has, since its creation, been very concerned with providing care and health services to the young children of the poor. This orientation was expanded to include educational concerns when, in 1886 and again in 1928, a set of guidelines for the *écoles maternelles* were drawn up.

From the 1920s until after the Second World War the *écoles maternelles* did not change much. Their function was primarily protective, secondarily educative, and they continued to fill important social needs, especially for the poor. In the 1950s and 1960s, the emphasis changed from protection to education, with particular concern being given to intellectual development of the child.

This review will describe developments in early childhood education in France from 1960 to the present.

ENROLLMENTS, PRESCHOOL EDUCATION (1960-1970)

For the purpose of this study, early childhood education is defined in accordance with the OECD's "Classification of Educational Systems—France" (1972), which gives the following characteristics for the *école maternelle:*

(a) Length of study in years equals up to 4 years.
(b) Entrance requirement is to be 2 years old.
(c) For children between 2 and 6, State or private schools; instruction of this kind is also given in nursery classes attached to primary schools [p. 10].

Table 7.1 presents public and private *école maternelle* enrollments for 1960-1961 through 1970-1971. It will be seen that, over the 10-year period, a very substantial increase has taken place in both the public and the private sectors. The private sector has expanded slightly faster, but the difference is very small. It should be kept in mind, however, that the private sector contains far fewer children—only 15% as many as those attending *écoles maternelles.* The total increase in enrollments for the 10 years is 61.1%. This substantial growth

TABLE 7.1
Enrollments in Ecoles Maternelles in France from 1960–61 to 1970–71

Year	Private	Public	(in 000's) Total
1960–61	196	1,178	1,374
1965–66	271	1,507	1,778
1966–67	285	1,600	1,884
1967–68	301	1,688	1,990
1968–69	313	1,727	2,040
1969–70	322	1,794	2,116
1970–71	323	1,891	2,213
% of increase from 1960-61 to 1970-71	64.8	60.5	61.1

Source: Ministère de l'Education Nationale, Direction chargée
des Affaires Budgétaires et Financières.

TABLE 7.2
Population Attendance Rates in Ecoles Maternelles in France from
1960-61 to 1970-71

			(in 000's)
	1960-61	1970-71	% of Change
Total age group 2 - 5 years in ecoles maternelles	1,374	2,213	61.1
Infant population 2 - 5 years	3,199	3,397	6.3
% of age group enrolled	42.6	65.1	52.8

Source: United Nations Demographic Yearbook, 1970.

can be compared with a decline of 15.1% in primary schools enrollments for the same period of time.

Table 7.2 presents population attendance rates in *écoles maternelles* for 1960-1961 through 1970-1971, and shows also that there was a 6.3% increase in the infant population over this period of years. This fact, taken together with the 61.1% increase in the age group attenting *écoles maternelles,* indicates that overall there was a 52.8% increase in the number of children attending.

The number of children attending preschool varies in different parts of the country: There is a greater rate of attendance in the south compared to the north of France, and in urban areas compared to rural ones. The VIth Government Plan projects that the percentage of children in *ècoles maternelles* should be:

	VIth Plan	
	1969-1970	*1976*
5 years	100	100
4 years	83	90
3 years	55	62
2 years	14	16

In 1971-1972, the percentage of children attending the *école maternelle* by single year and by multiple year age groupings was:

6	99%	5-6	99%
5	99	4-6	94
4	84	3-6	84
3	55	2-6	70
2	15		

From this information, it is clear that the government is making good progress in attaining its projected attendance goals for 1976.

The United Nations Demographic Yearbook (1970) offers us the following information about live birth rates in the French population. In 1966, there were 17.6 children born per thousand in the population; in 1970, this had declined to 16.7, indicating a .9 drop in the number of live births per thousand over this four year period, or a decline of 5.1%.

Trends of average household size and gross reproduction rates in France can be derived from "Analyses and Projections of Households and Families," prepared by the Population Division, Department of Economic and Social Affairs of the United Nations Secretariat. According to this source, in 1881 the average household size in France was 3.7; in 1962 it decreased to 3.2, a decline of .5 over 81 years. During this same period the gross reproduction rate had dropped from 1.7 to 1.4, a fall of .3. Thus the average household size in France has clearly been declining, and this may well occasion an increased demand for early childhood education in the coming years.

Participation rates in the labor force in France are shown in Table 7.3.

The 1970 percentage of 46.2%, for women between 15 and 64 years of age who

TABLE 7.3
Labor Force Participation Rates - France

	1960 %	1970 %
$\dfrac{\text{Total Labor Force}}{\text{Total Population}} \times 100$		
(a) Total	43.3	42.0
(b) Males	n.a.	55.9
(c) Females	n.a.	28.7
$\dfrac{\text{Total Labor Force}}{\begin{array}{l}\text{Population from}\\ \text{15 to 64 years}\end{array}} \times 100$		
(a) Total	69.9	67.4
(b) Males	86.5	82.5
(c) Females	42.8	46.2

Source: Labor Force Statistics, 1959-70, O.E.C.D., Paris, 1972.

[a] Not available.

work outside the home, is 3.4% higher than it was in 1960. During the same period of time, the total force participation rate dropped by 2.5%, and the male participation rate declined by 4%.

Demand for early childhood education in France is, then, to be based on the following facts: (*1*) a long tradition of sending children to school early, (*2*) an increased belief in benefits of preschool education, (*3*) decreasing family size, and (*4*) increasing number of working mothers.

ISSUES OF DEBATE

The debate in France about education in general, and the *école maternelle* in particular, turns on the question of democratization (equality of educational opportunity). The O.E.C.D. *"Reviews of National Policies for Education: France [1971]"* summed up the thoughts of M. Guichard, the French Minister of Education, as follows:

> Instead of the term "democratization," . . . . [He] preferred "collective betterment" (*promotion collective*), insofar as the concept of betterment could not basically disregard the quality of the education provided [p. 115] . . . . Social advancement affects those being taught. Democratization concerns the system. Social advancement demands the essential. Democratization can be satisfied with formal results: in the extreme, it may sacrifice the quality of education in favour of reflecting, in schools and university statistics, the relative importance of social classes in the working population [p. 148].

The quality of improvement by definition, M. Guichard concluded, implies an actual advance.

This statement is particularly interesting in relation to the *école maternelle,* because what seems to have emerged as an issue is not the number of poor children who are enrolled, but the quality of the education offered. This can be considered in three parts: (*1*) quality of the transfer from home to preschool, (*2*) quality of the preschool program itself, and (*3*) quality of the preparation for entry into primary school. The evidence, in general, is that French parents like the *école maternelle* and that the transition from home to preschool is smooth. The youngest (2- or 3-year-olds) first attend only half a day. Parent-teacher interaction is encouraged. The quality of the preschool program itself is very high; indeed, most French people think the *école maternelle* is the best of all their schools.

Most preschools are interesting and stimulating places to visit. They have lots of plants, birds, and animals to observe, a reasonable supply of things for the children to play with, to construct and to draw on. The major problem seems to be the high pupil-teacher ratio (43:1) which makes it almost impossible to give much individual attention, particularly in the area of language development. This has given rise to the question of whether the quality of education in the *école maternelle* could not be improved, particularly in ways that would affect performance in primary school. At present, many children experience difficulty when entering primary education, and the rate of repeating is, by consequence, high. It is understood that the French authorities are currently studying ways and means of creating a better relationship between these two levels of schooling. It is perhaps relevant here to recall that the general guidelines for the curriculum content of an *école maternelle* were originally developed in 1881, and are badly in need of revision. They should place much more stress on the world in which the children presently live.

The French, then, like many other countries, are tending toward a change in the *école maternelle*. It would shift from a kind of child-minding institution particularly concerned with social and physical development to one that adds an intellectual component to these objectives. This is not to imply that the French *école maternelle* has previously neglected the intellectual aspects of growth, but in the future it will almost certainly put greater emphasis on the intellectual aspects, particularly for children who come from poor homes.

There may yet be another reason for this change in emphasis. In an article on the influence of social factors on growth and development of the child, Marcel Graffar (1971) draws attention to two of the conclusions of longitudinal studies that have been made simultaneously in Brussels, London, Paris, Stockholm, and Zürich: (*1*) Differences in weight and height among children belonging to different social classes that were significant at the turn of the century are no longer statistically evident; and (*2*) mental development remains strongly linked to the socioeconomic conditions in which a child is brought up. The first of these findings might well be seen in France as confirmation that the first objectives of the *école maternelle* (physical care and health) have been fulfilled, leaving the way open for an additional purpose. The second supports the present attitude that emphasis should now be placed on intellectual aspects of growth, which can serve as a first step toward providing greater equality of opportunity in the educational field, independent of the social background of the child.

Attendant on the achievement of equality of educational opportunity in the *maternelles* are notable problems presented by children who come from poverty-stricken homes, from disorganized or recently immigrant families, or from homes with working mothers. Here the major concerns are for both care-giving and education. The answer in the *école maternelle* has traditionally been to treat all children as if they come from the same background and, therefore, to offer them a single program. The concept of positive discrimination in education seems rather foreign to the French educator, and he does not have much faith in the compensatory programs that have been carried out elsewhere. What concerns the research bureau more at the moment is development of Piagetian learning theory that would be basically applicable to all children, and yet perhaps particularly helpful to those who come from homes with special problems.

The debate concerning the *maternelles* also introduces problems of regional distribution. There is a great need for more of them in rural areas in France, but because of geographical and population problems they have been hard to establish. Nevertheless the French government is actively engaged in dealing with the problem. The most likely solution appears to lie in bringing children from several communities together until there are enough of them to make an *école maternelle* economically feasible.

In 1970, an association [*Groupe d'Etude pour la Défense et la Renovation Permanente de l'École Maternelle* (GEDREM)] was created with the aim of defending the interests of young children and seeing that the education they received met their needs. The object of the group is to provide a permanent forum where issues of debate may be discussed with a view to recommendations being sent to the ministry. The group has already identified the following as matters of particular concern in the area of early childhood education.

Quantitative problems
1. The tendency for parents to leave their children for longer periods of time in school (from 6:45 to 17:30).
2. The tendency of parents to enroll their children at an early age (starting with 2-year-olds).
3. Large classes (pupil-teacher ratio 43:1, 1970-1971).
4. Classes in rural areas, often with long distances for small children to travel in order to attend.

Qualitative aspects or problems
1. The importance of maximizing the equality of educational opportunity to compensate for social inequalities.
2. The ECE's contribution in preparing 5-year-old children for school (that is, learning reading, writing, and arithmetic), emphasis on a step-by-step method based on latest thinking in the field.
3. The need for better teacher training—the experiments being carried out in Dijon with introduction of staff assistants less qualified than present teachers (teachers' union opposed this concept).
4. The relationship between preprimary and primary school especially for those in *classe d'attente* (waiting classes). (It is essential for the efficacy of *école maternelle* that a link or a continuity is assured between the preprimary and primary school).
5. The emerging need and demand for smaller classes where the pupils are guided and taught by well-qualified staff.

In summary, it seems fair to express the conditions of the *école maternelle* in these changing times in words written in 1971 about French education as a whole:

The advent of mass education thus implies emergence of a new relationship between the school and the community. The school can no longer be perceived as an institution planted in the community by an external authority which has its own purpose for doing so, and can effectively set its own standards of performance for the school. It is instead a social service, whose shape has been at least in part influenced by popular demand, and whose functioning cannot be controlled by the exercise of governmental authority alone. The school has become a place where contesting social demands must be negotiated and resolved, not simply an instrument of State decisions imposed from above.[1]

This review of the issues concerned with the *école maternelle* in France leads us to suggest the following five major areas of debate:

1. Equality of educational opportunity independent of socioeconomic or geographical origin.
2. The increased numbers of working mothers.
3. The problems associated with internal and external immigration, and more adequately meeting the needs of children who come from poor and disorganized families.
4. The problem of the transition between the *école maternelle* and the primary school.
5. The problem of providing individual help with the present student-teacher ratio (43:1).

THE AIMS AND OBJECTIVES OF THE *ECOLE MATERNELLE*

We have seen that the *école maternelle* started with the intentions of giving protection, improving health and nutrition, and providing opportunity for social interaction for young children. The educational component was small, if it existed at all. From 1879, however, they began to assume a much more reasoned purposefulness, the principles of which continued to be active until the 1950s. This development and its consolidation was largely due to a remarkable woman, Pauline Kergomard, who was *inspectrice générale* from 1879-1917. To her, the most important things for children of nursery school age were freedom and activity, especially through play, which she saw as their essential and natural right. She opposed keeping the very young seated and allowed the teaching of readiness skills in reading, writing, simple arithmetic, and natural science, but only after the age of 6. She disliked the use of the term "school" for the *école maternelle,* because of its formal implications, and insisted that the sexes should be mixed. In most other schools in nineteenth century France, they were separated.

The *école maternelle,* under Pauline Kergomard's leadership, aimed to provide a real life situation for the child that was favorable for the harmonious and

[1] OECD. *Review of national policies for education, France.* Paris, 1971, p. 30.

diverse developments of the child's character and social relations. Considerable attention was given for maturational problems and physical development. The teacher was expected to foster the child's natural curiosity by supplying many different things for him to manipulate or play with, seeing that he was fed properly, and that he had a place to rest when he was tired. Such were the objectives that lasted until after the end of World War II.

Today, the aim of the preprimary education is overtly twofold: social and educational. The *école maternelle* provides a comprehensive training covering many different aspects organized in a somewhat structured way. The areas of emphasis are: physical education, initially concentrating on rhythmic movements; sensory education, stressing sensory experiences; manual education, motivating, and reinforcing the child by a wide variety of sensory and motoric exercises; social education and moral training, teaching the child a certain basic set of ethical notions; and aesthetics, concentrating mainly on music and drawing. As to intellectual training, the nursery school plays a purely preparatory role. Recitation, writing, prearithmetic and prereading are taught in a concrete way.[2] The main changes in objectives over the last 20 years are the provision of a wider variety of social and physical activities for the child, and an increasing concern with education in its stricter sense.

The reasons for education assuming a more important role in the curriculum of the *école maternelle* are threefold. The first is, as we have seen, the increasing demand for greater equality of educational opportunity and the belief that this can be assisted by intervention in the child's intellectual life at a younger age than formerly thought. A child is no longer sent to an *école maternelle* just for its social and physical well-being; he goes there for intellectual and cognitive benefits as well.

The second major reason for this change is connected with the first; it is pressure from parents to get their children better prepared for the exactions of the primary school. The repeating rate in a French primary school is very high (Blot, 1969, p. 687):

	1960	1966
Grade 1	24.0%	22.5%
Grade 2	18.5%	19.6%
Grade 3	18.5%	19.0%
Grade 4	20.0%	19.9%
Grade 5	19.0%	19.0%

In the first five grades of primary school approximately one child out of two, or 50%, repeat one grade. These repetition rates are not found randomly across

[2] OECD. *A Review of National Policies in Education: France.* Paris, 1971.

the different social groups. As in most other countries, they are markedly higher for children from poor socioeconomic backgrounds than among those from middle- or upper-class homes. There is, however, another body of opinion that opposes the *maternelles* specifically preparing children for the primary school, the main argument being that it would impose on the *maternelles* the same rigidity from which the primary schools suffer. They would prefer reducing the failure rate by changes in the primary schools. More specifically, it has been suggested that the objective of primary education, and consequently its content and methods, should be modified by grafting onto it some of the qualities of the nursery school. They would thereby become less exacting in certain fields, such as the acquisition of a mass of precise knowledge within a fixed time limit, and more exacting in others, for example, the development and formation of the child's personality. It would also help if pupils were under the same master for two consecutive years, say the last year of nursery school and the first year of primary school.[3]

Reacting to pressure from parents and educators to modify the rigidity of the primary school, the French Ministry of Education announced a sweeping change in December, 1972. The heart of the reform, according to Education Minister Joseph Fontanel, is "a new balance between theory and practice (with the accent on practice), between children's spontaneity and formal pedagogy. In the past, we have been overly suspicious of their spontaneity."[4]

The third major reason for recent changes in the curriculum of the *école maternelle* may be the increasing numbers of middle-class children attending these schools. Middle-class people tend to know how to control or manipulate systems much more adequately than those from less advantaged backgrounds. As the number of parents in this group grows, it will be interesting to see the impact on the development of the *maternelles* in the next few years.

ORGANIZATION AND CONTROL

The organization of education in France is very highly centralized. As a former French Minister of Education said of his department, "it is the largest administration in the world except for the Red Army. Its structure was so conceived that the smallest decision taken, the most anodine circular, decided the function of the whole machinery down to its most elementary units. In such circumstances, the temptation was to try to regulate activities rather than to get things going, to offer suggestions, or to give direction [OECD, 1971, p. 152]."

So far as concerns the *écoles maternelles,* the organizational pattern within the system is as follows:

[3] OECD. *Reviews of national policies for education: France.* Paris, 1971.
[4] *L'Éducation.* No. 158. 14 décembre 1972.

At the head, of course, is the minister, who is responsible for determining the important lines of educational development and policy. Below him are five *inspectrices générales*, who have the responsibility of overall inspection of the *école maternelles* on a national basis. Their principal function is to advise the minister on matters of a pedagogical nature.

Directly responsible to the minister is a set of 23 *recteurs*, each of whom is responsible for one of the 23 *rectorates* (educational regions) into which the country is divided. Below each *recteur* are a number of *inspecteurs d'académie*, who take the important day-to-day decisions for the *écoles maternelles* in their own particular areas. Reporting to the *inspecteurs d'académie* are 150 *inspecteurs départementaux*, responsible between them for covering the 95 school districts into which France is divided. Their task is to go to the individual *école maternelle*, talk with the *directrice* and the teachers and perform the normal duties of an inspector of schools. The best of these *inspecteurs départementaux* are moving away from the concept of inspection to one of cooperative counselling with the *directrice* and teachers.

In actual charge of the *école maternelle* is the *directrice*, if it is large enough, or a head teacher, if there are no more than 5 classes. The regulations indicate that for a single building with 300 children, the *directrice* should teach part-time: In a school with over 400 children the *directrice* should not teach. A *directrice* of an *école maternelle* is nominated by a *recteur*, who works in close consultation with other *recteurs* and *inspecteurs des écoles maternelles*. To be nominated as a *directrice*, a teacher must pass an examination and have her name put on a list (*liste d'aptitude*) by a commission. She must also have taught for at least 8 years and be more than 30 years of age.

Responsibility for what goes on in the classroom is primarily that of the teacher and the *directrice* in charge of the school. Great variety is found here, dependent in most cases on the talents and interests of the teacher. The large number of children is a very real problem.

The *directrice* of the *école maternelle* normally has a private apartment for herself and her family in the school, the hope being that by living on the spot, she can become more easily involved with the local community. Sometimes teachers also live in school, although this practice has become less common recently. They still, however, receive a rent subsidy if they live out.

All teachers and officials in the *école maternelle* organization are subject to the normal French evaluation system: a 20-point scale on which people at all levels are evaluated by those immediately above them. Thus, the teacher and the *director* are evaluated by the *inspecteur*, and the *inspecteur* by the *inspecteur d'academie* and by an *inspectrice générale* in the pedagogical field. This rating system, with its somewhat rigid guidelines, is often cited as the chief reason why there has been relatively little innovation in French schools. In the main, however, this is not true for the *maternelle;* one can often see and hear people talking about changes that are being fostered there. But at any level in the French school system, the real key to innovation seems to be in the hands of the *inspecteur.*

The working day at an *école maternelle* is a long one. The school may open as early as 7:00 in the morning, for children whose mothers are going to work early. They are then supervised at play by two or three assistants until formal educational activities start at 8:30 or 9:00. These continue until 11:30 or 12:00, with perhaps a half-hour break for playing out in the fresh air. Between 12:00 and 1:30, most of the children go home for lunch. Those who stay for lunch are taken care of by assistants. The youngest children, aged two or three, have an hour's rest. Formal school opens again at 1:30 or 2:00 P.M. and continues until 4:30 or 5:00 P.M. Again there is a half-hour break, for play outside or in the gymnasium, during the afternoon. Although the school closes formally at 4:30 or 5:00 P.M., some children will stay until 6:00 or 7:00. During this time they are looked after by the teacher's assistants. The schools are open on Saturday, both in the morning and in the afternoon. At a minimum, then, the school day lasts 8 hours, which, by most countries' standards, is a very long day for young children. It is seen to be a necessity, however, more because so many mothers work than for educational reasons.

"Waiting classes" are special classes within the organization of *écoles maternelles* for children too immature to start primary schooling. A few special classes have been set up in some Parisian nursery schools to observe children with signs of disabilities so that remedial intervention may be undertaken early enough to avoid their joining waiting classes. Handicapped children are generally integrated with those who are normal in preprimary school. In urban areas of 50,000 inhabitants, those who cannot follow the ordinary preschool activities have the option of attending special classes with only 8 to 15 pupils. The number of pupils in each class depends on the handicap (visual, auditory, motor, behavioral, linguistic, intellectual, or emotional). The aim of these classes is to educate the children so that they can continue directly either into specialized primary classes or into normal classes in primary school.

PHYSICAL SETTING: A VISIT TO A PARISIAN KINDERGARTEN

The school visited was located in a working-class district of Paris. The building was constructed in 1935 as a primary school. Since then, a part of it had been taken over by the *école maternelle,* which had its own entrance and fenced play area and occupied two floors. On the first floor, there was one classroom, a gymnasium, a dining room, and a small room where the younger children could sleep. A part of the classroom was also used as a bedroom during rest time. The second floor contained six other classrooms.

The classrooms were approximately 10 X 8 meters and were furnished with small groups of desks and tables, a desk for the teacher, and a blackboard. One wall was covered with white paper for painting. In different corners, tables had been put together in such a way as to make them similar to parts of the children's homes (for example, a bedroom corner and a kitchen corner). The walls in the classroom, in the corridors, and in the entrance hall were covered with children's paintings. Boxes, which could be found in almost all the classrooms, were filled with different materials for painting, decorating, and construction. Each class had its own flowers and goldfish, which the children tended. The gymnasium was a large room (approximately 13 X 16 meters) with doors opening onto an asphalt playground.

There were 336 children enrolled in the school, with 48 in each class; normally, however, the class attendance was no more than 25-35 per day. The children were apportioned to classes according to age:

1 class for children born 1968-1969, aged 3 and 4
1 class for children born 1968, aged 3
2 classes for children born 1967, aged 4
1 class for children born November-December, 1966, and January-March, 1967, aged 4 and 5
2 classes for children born January-October, 1966, aged 5 and 6

The school day started at 8:30 A.M. and ended at 4:30 P.M., but those children whose parents wanted them to stay on could do so. The youngest children slept between 1 and 3 hours a day. Ninety of the children stayed for lunch (between 11:30 A.M. and 1:30 P.M.), after which they were looked after by three assistants who returned in the afternoon for those children who stayed after 4:30 (approximately 50). These assistants also cared for the children during holidays and on the nursery school teachers' free day (once a week).

The children had medical and dental check-ups regularly. If the teachers discovered physical defects, the children were sent at once to a doctor. For these checkups there was a bus that took the children and returned them to school.

Handicapped children were integrated with those who were normal. It is not until they reach primary school that the decision is made as to where and how they should be specifically educated. The school had a headmaster and preschool teachers, of whom one was male. It was visited periodically by an *inspectrice.*

Curriculum

The educational guidelines for the school were provided by the *inspectrice,* but she was known to be very open to teachers' initiatives for change. This particular school was trying modest variations in order to give each child the maximum possibility to use and develop his imagination, invention, and creative ability. The general approach used by the teacher stressed the development of harmonious relations between herself and the child, as well as between the child and other children. The activities chosen were the basis for the development of each child's aptitudes and abilities, and should help each child learn about and understand society.

The children were not taught to write but were introduced to writing by graphic and painting exercises. In the course of these, they learned to make different shapes (circles, lines, etc.), and these signs later would be used to symbolize an object which had a name and which the child could then repeat and reproduce.

Learning the language was based on face-to-face intercommunication. Themes were chosen relevant to the activities of the children (for example, an event, a painting, or a story) and these were described, discussed, and criticized by the class. Each child was encouraged to ask questions and to express himself in a correct way.

Learning to count was a natural part of the daily activities. While playing, the children discovered elementary mathematics: big, much bigger, small, equal, etc. There was also a balance for the older children to play with.

The activities during the day were quite varied. The children did gymnastics, danced, sang, painted, and played with dolls or built with blocks. They also played in the corner of the room set up as a kitchen. Some activities involved the whole class (gymnastics, singing, storytelling, etc.), while others were decided by the individual children from among proposals made by the teacher.

The school had a great variety of instructional materials for the children to use. Plastic toys, beads, beans, coffee beans, macaroni, clay, and so on are provided. These items obviously appealed to the creative and imaginative ability of the children, for they had produced a large number of original things from them. Others talked about, discussed, and painted a visit they had made to another preschool. In another class, they had been talking about castles, and had built one out of cartons and paper. Such activities varied, of course, in simplicity and complexity according to the understanding and maturity level of the different age groups. The children in each class were assigned to one of several groups, each of which had its own easily recognized emblem, such as a flower or a picture of the sun. This introduces the child to the notion of belonging to a community and, additionally, tells him where to look for his overcoat and other personal possessions. These groups had different tasks during the week, which not only helped the working arrangements of each class but gave substance to the feeling of group spirit and loyalty.

The educational program of this school was based on spontaneous interest and activity on the part of the children. The role of the teacher was to be observant and sensitive to their needs. It is clear, however, that a novice teacher could sometimes have a hard time taking care of a group of 30-40 active children. Much of her time might well be spent in trying to stop them from quarrelling, yelling, or all rushing around at the same time. Even the best educational guidelines are of little help in these circumstances. The teacher is permitted to correct a disobedient child by punishing him in front of all the others or by not letting him join the others during a free play period, but she may not strike him.

Even though this school was housed in the same building as a primary school, there was no cooperation between them. It seemed that primary school teachers considered they had so little in common that any kind of collaboration with their colleagues in the *maternelles* would be pointless.

TEACHERS AND THEIR TRAINING

A former *inspectrice générale,* writing about the training of staff for preschool education, states her view of the basic requirements in these words:

> Parents are the first educators of children, but they need to be helped. On the one hand they need to be prepared for their role, and on the other there must be institutions which can not only look after their children but also educate them.

> The personnel of these establishments should be trained for a dual role—social and educative. From the *crèche* to the kindergarten the infant should be taken in hand by personnel well-informed in everything touching not only upon health and psychology but also upon the training of sensorial and motor activities of the young child. This personnel should receive training based upon a general culture equal, at least, to that required for teaching in primary schools. It is desirable, moreover, that this training should be common to preschool personnel, primary school teachers, and social workers who are in contact with the young child and his family in order to favor constructive collaboration later between these different people [Herbinière-Lebert, 1970, p. 5].

It is believed that few would disagree with these objectives. The present official position, however, is this: Certified teachers receive a course ranging from 2 to 5 years, depending upon whether they have earned a *baccalauréat.* Entrance in either case is by competitive examination. Those with the *baccalauréat* will be admitted to training at about 18.

There is, in fact, no special course for nursery school teachers. However, the student teachers in these colleges generally complete a period of training in a nursery school. In addition to this, the written part of the primary teacher's proficiency examination (CPA) includes as an option "nursery schools." This examination is taken mainly by supply primary teachers.[5]

Under the heading of primary teaching training, the O.E.C.D. document says

[5] OECD. *Classification of educational systems: France.* Paris, 1972.

(1) Preparation for *"baccalauréat"* in 2-3 years, depending on whether candidate begins in 2nd or 1st year.

(2) A professional training proper of two years, open to the above mentioned candidates after pass in *"baccalauréat"* and to holders of *"baccalauréat"* who have passed the competitive entrance exam to third year. Course ends with award of CFEN. However, in order to become certified, probationary primary teachers must sit the practical examination of the CAP (certificate of teaching proficiency). Certificates awarded entitle students to teach in primary education [p. 19].

During training, nursery school teachers study psychology, pedagogy, social anthropology, cultural aesthetics, history, regional geography, mathematics, chemistry, biology with practical experience, language, music, gymnastics, and drawing. The first years are mainly devoted to studying problems of development and pedagogy as it concerns young children. During the second year there are practical experiences in nursery schools, under the supervision of a teacher. The emphasis in the training of teachers is placed on active teaching methods, with particular attention given to small group instruction. The areas of emphasis are: teaching language, reading preparation, writing, and early number work; approximately 75% of the teachers' training is devoted to theoretical subjects and 25% to practical experience in a nursery school.[6]

In recent years there has been some concern about the training of students for nursery school who feel that they have not had enough pedagogic training or practical work in an *école maternelle.* Many of the students find the aims and objectives of their training, as well as the purpose of the course material being given, to be unclear.

Écoles maternelles are organized in three sections on the basis of the children's age; namely, 2-4, 4-5, and 5-6. The training of teachers attempts to coincide with the declared level of interest on the part of the trainee. This is particularly true as it concerns the practical experience part of the course.

In the self-selection process that largely determines the type of appointment on leaving college, important differences are revealed between those who choose to teach in the *école maternelle* and those who prefer the primary school. Student teachers who want flexibility and freedom to try out their own ideas tend to choose the *maternelle,* because the primary school is so rigid in its structure. It would seem, therefore, that the *maternelle* gets the better and more able of the teacher college graduates. It is interesting in this connection that, after appointment, few nursery school teachers transfer to a primary school, but many primary teachers transfer to the *école maternelle.*

Table 7.4 gives the numbers of teachers in *écoles maternelles* between 1960-1970. It shows that there has been an overall increase of 63.3%. This coincides very closely with the total increase in enrollments of 61.1% shown in Table 7.1.

---

[6] UNESCO. *The training and professional situation of pre-school teaching.* 1965.

TABLE 7.4
Ecole Maternelle Teachers in France from 1960-61 to 1970-71

Year	Private	Public	Total
1960-61	n.a.[a]	26,646	26,646
1965-66	n.a.	33,099	33,099
1966-67	n.a.	34,906	34,906
1967-68	n.a.	36,331	36,331
1968-69	n.a.	39,512	39,512
1969-70	n.a.	41,304	41,304
1970-71	n.a.	43,500	43,500
% of increase from 1960-61 to 1970-71		63.3	

Source: Ministère de l'Education Nationale, Direction Chargée des Affaires Budgétaires et Financières.

[a]Not available.

The total number of teachers added in the 10-year period is 16,854, which means that, on the average, 1685 classes were added per year.

Table 7.5 gives the pupil-teacher ratio for *écoles maternelles* for 1960-1961 to 1970-1971, and it will be seen that the average has declined very little. The ratio of 43 children to 1 teacher is very high. In fact, it is the highest in any country in this study, which explains why, among other reasons, the French can afford to have such a large number of children in preprimary school. It should be pointed out, however, that this number represents the children registered in a class and not the daily attendance, which is considerably lower. Based on personal communications with Madame M. Abbadie, a reasonable estimate of the actual number of children in a class in a day, as distinct from those registered, is understood to be: age 2-4, average daily attendance 20, registered 35; age 4-5, average daily attendance 35, registered 45; age 5-6, average daily attendance 35, registered 45. The size of class in the *écoles maternelles* is currently a matter of

TABLE 7.5
Pupil:Teacher Ratio in Ecole Maternelle from 1960-61 to 1970-71

Year	Private	Public	Total
1960-61	n.a.[a]	44:1	44:1
1965-66	n.a.	46:1	46:1
1970-71	n.a.	43:1	43:1

[a]Not available.

major concern to the people working in them and to the Ministry of Education. In the present economic climate, however, it is very difficult to see how class numbers can be reduced, especially in face of the large enrollment increases already documented in this report.

The general feeling among staff in the *école maternelles* is that the ideal number of children per teacher is somewhere between 20 and 25. They do not consider that a lower ratio (for example, 1:5 or 1:10) would be particularly beneficial, since this would allow the adults to interfere too much in the daily lives of the children, leaving them less free to interact among themselves.

By way of comparison, in 1960 the French primary school pupil-teacher ratio was 34:1; in 1970 it had dropped to 27:1, a decrease of seven children. This implies that the French have been putting a good deal more effort and money into the primary school than the *écoles maternelles*. However, it also reflects a 10.6% drop in enrollments in the primary school between 1965 and 1970, which was caused by a population decline and not any dramatic change in the primary school itself.

In the nursery schools in France, the domestic staff helps the young children at meal times, rest times, and when dressing to go home. They do not assist the teacher in the classroom. The only times they may be in the classroom are before school starts, during lunch time, and after school.

FINANCING EARLY CHILDHOOD EDUCATION

As a result of the leadership of Jules Ferry, in 1881 a law was passed which abolished fees in all preprimary and primary schools. (Fees at the secondary level were not abolished until 1936). Therefore, attendance at an *école maternelle* is free of cost to any French child.

The evolution of the state's role in financing education is well summarized in "Reviews of National Policies for Education: France" previously cited:

> It should be noted that, more than in other spheres, the part played by the state has been of prime importance in the development of education. In contrast to the present situation, the educational demand of households at the end of the 18th century was negligible (usually for economic reasons) and training on the job was sufficient to meet industry's needs where skills were concerned. From this period onwards, the state therefore provided incentives, not only on humanitarian grounds but, more particularly, for political reasons, namely, a desire to achieve national unity through culture and language, to set up a enlightened democracy by means of education, and, at a later stage, the desire felt in some quarters to create a new ruling class. . . . However, the part played by the state, while not very significant at the beginning, assumed increasing importance throughout the 19th and 20th centuries . . . . According to the Constitution of 1946, the state has a duty to organize "state-provided, free, secular education at all levels [p. 27]."

In 1970, the French education budget was a little over F 26 *milliard*, which represents 17% of the total national budget, as against F 4.5 *milliard* in 1958, or 9.4%. This is a 7.6% increase over the 12-year period. The French per capita gross national product in 1969 was $2920. The per capita expenditure on education stood at $4.75.[7]

The central government pays between 65% and 80% of the total cost of educating children in the *école maternelle.* This covers both capital and current expenditures. The percentage of aid is dependent on the regional zones within which the school is located. The state pays 100% of the teachers' salaries from the current expenditures budget. The commune contributes approximately 20% of the cost of operating the school and buying supplies and equipment. Providing maintenance is totally the responsibility of the local authorities. The commune must also supply domestic help to care for the children before and after the formal school day, as well as taking care of the children during meal times. It is important to note that a town could, if it chose, supplement the supplies and equipment budget quite substantially. Hence, one can find some schools that are much better off materially than others. But this is about the limit of freedom that the local authorities have. They cannot, for instance, hire additional teachers to reduce the pupil-teacher ratio. Teachers are employed by the state, and the number of teachers assigned to a particular school is specifically controlled.

A nursery school may be established by ministerial decision at the request of the municipal council of any commune of over 2000 inhabitants. The school building is financed jointly by the state and the local community—with the state assuming the greater part—while as previously stated, the commune undertakes to cover operating costs for a period of not less than 10 years. The school must enjoy full autonomy in primary education as regards organization. It provides for children from 2 to 6 years old in three different sections. (The ages of children in these sections are 2-4, 4-5, and 5-6).

Private (primarily Roman Catholic) *écoles maternelles* come within the law of December 31, 1959, which settled the relations between the state and private education and continued their eligibility for financial assistance. They may either request complete integration with the public system or keep their own identity, contracts being signed to regularize their position. The private school that accepts assistance is obliged to submit to pedagogical control as well as to financial control by the appropriate administration. For this reason, the private schools tend to be very similar to the public schools. There are a very small number of nonreligious private schools, generally for the children of the wealthy, which receive a subvention from the state.

[7]OECD. *Economic surveys.* 1973.

Table 7.6 shows capital and current expenditures in both the private and public sectors for the years 1965-1966 and 1970-1971. The capital expenditures apply only to the public sector. The substantial rise in current expenditures in both public and private sectors is almost identical over the 5-year period, an increase of between 61% and 62%. The total capital and current expenditures over the 5 years increased by 64.4%. For purposes of comparison, Table 7.6 additionally gives the expenditures in US dollars for the year 1965-1966 and for 1970-1971. In these terms, the percentage increase is only 44.3%. The reason for the discrepancy between the 44.3% and 64.4% figures is that the dollar figure is expressed at official exchange rates and so reflects the fluctuation of the French franc. By presenting the material in this manner, account can be taken of the inflation that has occurred over the 5-year period.

Table 7.7 presents per pupil expenditures for both private and public *écoles maternelles*. Here again we can see that the two systems spend approximately the same amount of money per year educating the child. Under the total column "per-pupil cost," we see that the average cost for educating the child in either public or private school in France 1970-1971 was $110, an increase of $13 per child over the 5-year period.

Comparable figures are available for primary school expenditures for 1965-1966 and for 1970-1971 in France. For 1965-1966, they are: primary, $149; *école maternelle*, $97; difference, $52. For 1970-1971 they are: primary, $196; *école maternelle*, $110; difference, $86. Hence, over the 5-year period, the differential expenditure rate has increased and continues substantially to benefit the child in primary school.

One of the major problems involved in financing the education of young children in France is the regional distribution of wealth. Many of the rural and agricultural communities cannot afford the expenditures that local and economic conditions impose upon them. For this reason, since 1964, the Government has adopted a sliding scale of support for education depending upon the ability of the local community to meet the actual costs.

INSTRUCTIONAL METHODS

The instructional methodology used in the *école maternelle* is very eclectic. It draws heavily on the teachings of Kergomard, Decroly, Montessori, Binet, Wallon, and Merleau-Ponty. In their systems of instruction, the teacher was seen as the originator and organizer of the learning situation and the child as the receiver of knowledge rather than as the creator of his own. They also believed that instruction should proceed from the concrete to the abstract. These ideas conflict sharply with those of Froebel and Dewey, for instance. Nevertheless, they are well-suited for use with large groups of children.

TABLE 7.6
Ecole Maternelle Expenditure in France from 1965-66 to 1970-71

Year	Private		Public		FF000's Total Capital Current	$000's Total Capital Current
	Capital	Current	Capital	Current		
1965-66	n.a.ᵃ	134,043	82,000	700,082	916,125	188,749
1966-67	n.a.	152,484	92,000	731,209	976,693	
1967-68	n.a.	163,497	108,000	810,433	1,081,930	
1968-69	n.a.	197,878	125,000	887,771	1,210,649	
1969-70	n.a.	215,963	150,000	1,078,742	1,444,705	
1970-71	n.a.	217,038	158,741	1,130,183	1,505,962	272,353
% of increase from 1965-66 to 1970-71		61.9	93.5	61.4	64.4	44.3

Source: Ministère de l'Education Nationale, Direction Chargée des Affaires Budgetaires et Financières.

ᵃNot available.
ᵇOfficial exchange rates, O.E.C.D.

197

TABLE 7.7
Ecole Maternelle Per-Pupil Costs in U.S. Dollars from 1965-66 to 1970-71

Year	Private			Public			Total		
	Current Expend. 000's	No. of Children 000's	Per Pupil Cost	Current Expend. 000's	No. of Children 000's	Per Pupil Cost	Current Expend. 000's	No. of Children 000's	Per Pupil Cost
1965-66	27,617	271	101	144,238	1,507	96	171,855	1,778	97
1970-71	39,251	323	122	204,395	1,891	108	243,645	2,213	110
Total Increase			21			12			13

It is in the area of instructional methods that the five *inspectrices générales* can make their greatest contributions. Their major responsibility is pedagogical, and their functions should be instructional. They do, in fact, interact constantly with the 150 preschool *inspecteurs, directrice,* and teachers on matters of instructional methods, and they spend much time on in-service training for both new and experienced teachers. The ministry also issues *Bulletin de l'education nationale* which discusses matters of instructional methodology. Conferences are also organised on an annual and semiannual basis. One of the most important of these is named after Pauline Kergomard.

As already observed, the *école maternelle* is divided into three sections, based on age. The following description of the instructional methods employed at these different levels is taken from the OECD's "Review of National Policies of Education," France, 1969:

> Considerable importance is attached to the progressive nature of the training given in nursery schools. During the four years' nursery schooling the child's psychological development is appreciable, although the rate of progress varies ... teaching within each section must be as closely adapted to the individual as possible.
>
> *Junior section: two to four years old.* At this age a child is still absorbed in the relationships between himself and the surrounding world and takes little interest in the activities of others. There are many sensorimotor activities (water, sand, filling-up, building, household activities, the use of bolts, screws, and nuts, etc.), and children try to imitate the actions of others. Accuracy of gesture, dexterity, and a sense of balance are sought in manual activities. Esthetics training mainly takes the form of listening to stories, singing, and music. Intellectually, the children discover notions of order and practice classification exercises. Finally, mastery of the language essential to expression is basic to this training.
>
> *Intermediate section: four to five years old.* At this age, imitation becomes more systematic and varied, and creative activities are introduced which provide the opportunity to exercise memory and power of concentration. The child's esthetic sense grows richer, and more elaborate activities are proposed: rhythmic dances, drawing, and poems. On the intellectual level, attention is still focused on language.
>
> *Senior section: five to six years old.* Here the child is beginning to be aware of those around him. The training is concentrated on accustoming him to strange surroundings, developing his esthetic sense, and getting him to control his impulses. The first principles of right behavior are then introduced. Esthetic activities are more varied: modelling, drawing, dancing, singing, music, and poetry. Manual activities are organized around specific subjects and motivated by direct contact with reality. They help to sharpen observation and develop the ability to concentrate. Finally, the basic techniques of understanding, beginning with the acquisition of a written vocabulary, are introduced in this fourth year.
>
> It has in fact now been established that learning to write and to express oneself in writing come before the ability to read [p. 43].

In practice, the high registration rate of 43 pupils per class makes it very difficult to accomplish all this, particularly with children who come from the lower socioeconomic class. There is a natural tendency on the part of teachers to gravitate, for example, toward those children who are beginning to show particular facility with language, since it is most important. This very commonly works to the disadvantage of children who come from the poorer homes where the development of a facility in language is little considered.

This points up one of the instructional problems the teacher has to face, but, in general, it is very difficult, if not impossible, for her to interact on an individual basis with all 43 children. Nor, indeed, were those instructional methods designed for education in the sense of getting the children ready for primary school. As we have seen, however, pressures are building that may in the long run bring about changes in this direction and in the teacher-pupil ratio.

Parental involvement is not seen officially as part of the instructional system for the young children we are considering. In the ministerial law for preschool education, participation by parents is neither recommended nor authorized. Nevertheless, parents from middle-class (*bourgeoisie*) districts bring their children to school and talk to the teachers, and most of them take an active interest in what is being done. The teachers are told to encourage this. Parents in poor districts, on the other hand, seldom come to school or talk to the preprimary school teachers about their children.

It may be concluded that parental participation in the work of the *écoles maternelles* is not high. It depends on the initiative of the parents, who almost certainly will be members of the middle class.

RESEARCH ON EARLY CHILDHOOD EDUCATION

Probably the best known educational researcher in France is Alfred Binet (1857-1911), who was Director of the Psychological Laboratory at the Sorbonne. His area of interest was higher mental processes, particularly as they are demonstrated in everyday life. In 1895, he opened a laboratory in Paris for child study and experimental teaching. He was impressed with Francis Galton's work in science and set out to develop a system of measurement along similar lines for psychology, to assess both personality and intelligence. The most outstanding result of this was the Binet Intelligence Scales which he worked out between 1905 and 1911. The production of such scales had been requested by the Paris educational authorities to help them identify children with special educational problems and needs.

Binet also made a great contribution in revealing the proper choice of the materials to use in the testing situation. These were everyday things, all easily obtainable. This gave the scales great surface validity, and subsequent statistical analysis confirmed an equal validity in research. It also enabled the scales to be easily administered by people with a modest amount of training. The greatest testimony to Binet's achievement is the fact that his scales have stood the test of time so well. They are still used in most countries in the world as the basis for all intelligence testing.

In a paper entitled "*Les Facteurs Socio-Economiques du Développement Cognitif*," Reuchlin (1971) examines the relationship between socioeconomic class and intelligence as measured by tests. He concludes that there are real differences across social class and that this observation is not the result of biased tests. He believes that to explain differences of intellectual level among children of different socioeconomic classes, one should start from a cognitive theory such as Hebb's or Piaget's.

Reuchlin argues that to help children from the lower socioeconomic class make greater progress in school, we need to develop a theory of development that takes the factor of social environment into account. This theory should be developed, he argues, in the "natural environment," not in a laboratory. Thus Reuchlin's work carries Binet's beyond the laboratory into the "milieu of life," the actual environment of the child.

Research on a national scale into problems of educating the very young comes under the aegis of the *Institut National de Recherche et Documentation Pédagogique*, formerly the *Institut Pédagogique*, which is a division of the Ministry of Education. It has two units studying the problems of educating young children: the *Institut Pédagogique* and the *Centre de Recherche Specialisée et de l'Adaptation Scolaire*.

The *Institut Pédagogique* is presently concerned with: preventive education (identifying and researching the problems of making a smooth transition from the home to the preschool); early diagnosis of deficiencies; the development of spoken language and the problems inherent in transition to a written language; motor development; and the development of the powers of logical reasoning in young children, particularly in relation to prearithmetic skills.

The *Centre de Recherche de l'Education Specialisée et de l'Adaptation Scolaire*, set up in 1968, is pursuing the following group of topics: language and school problems; cognition and school problems; psychomotor function and school problems; school and parent reaction to school failures; sociological study of school failures; and clinical study of school problems.

In addition to the work being done by these two institutes, further research is being carried out under the direction of the *inspectrices générales*. They are primarily concerned with improving the relationship between the *école maternelle* and the *école élémentaire*, employing developmental psychology, with particular emphasis on the interactions of genetics and the developmental process. The aim is ultimately to ensure that experience in the *école maternelle* in no way hinders the child's development.

There are a number of other important institutions, albeit international ones, located in France and concerned with educational research on young children.

The best known perhaps is the International Children's Center, which was established jointly by UNICEF and the French Government in 1950 and directed by Dr. Nathalie P. Masse. Its major interest is health and nutritional education, particularly in developing countries. Another branch of UNICEF located in Paris is concerned with early childhood education particularly in the developing countries of North Africa.

Also located in Paris is, of course, UNESCO, which has recently turned its attention to problems of educating children before they enter compulsory school. Another international, but nongovernmental, body in Paris fostering research on the same topic is the World Organization for Early Childhood Education (OMEP).

There is, in France, little formal evaluation that might be compared to the Coleman study in the United States or the Plowden Report in England. As already said, the *école maternelle* has not had education as one of its primary aims for more than a few years. Hence, there has been little research specific to this question. Nevertheless, the following examples of research being conducted in France on the general problems associated with educating young children have some bearing on the age group with which the present report is specifically concerned.

One study undertaken by *l'Institut National de Recherche et Documentation Pédagogique* under the leadership of Jean Vial (1967) aimed to create close coordination between preprimary schools and the first class in compulsory school and to evolve a pedagogical unity for the first three classes of primary school. The experiment was started in 1966-1967 with two experimental classes attached to five different schools. By 1967-1968, it had increased to 34 experimental classes, with only 25 children in each. The teaching of the three R's and other subjects was done in small groups with methods adapted as far as possible to each individual's learning capacity. The results of this study have not yet been published.

Soule, Peille, and Anfar (1971) found, in their study of 5- and 6-year-olds, that the repeating rate experienced by the children in primary school was primarily a function of the following four variables, ranked according to their importance:

1. Intellectual maturity.
2. Family life.
3. Behavior.
4. Instrumental factors.

In this study, two experimental designs were used. One involved having the teacher instruct the same group of students for 3 years, going with them from the *école maternelle* into the primary school. This group emphasized close contact with the preprimary and the primary schools as well as close contact with the family. The second design entailed a combination of preschool and primary school in which the children took courses appropriate to their abilities. If they were ready to take more advanced courses in the first or second grade, they were allowed to do so. If they were of age to be in first or second grade but still needed the relaxed atmosphere of the *école maternelle,* they were allowed to have that. There was a maximum of 25 pupils in each class, and the teaching was done to the whole class at the same time. There was little individualization of instruction. While the experiments were going on, seminars were held where the teachers and researchers could come together and discuss common problems. Where possible, the parents took part also.

The finding of this study was that the intellectual maturity of the child was the most important variable, and his home life came next. A follow-up study of children from broken homes, one-parent families, or working-class families indicated that these children experienced little success in the primary school. None of the instrumental factors, such as left-handedness, perceptual ability, or psychomotor difficulties, were particularly decisive for school success, but when the child was doing poorly, they tended to accentuate his difficulty.

Since 1967, the *école maternelle,* rue le Vau, Paris has been cooperating in a research project in which preprimary school teachers continue on with their children into the first years of primary school. The experimental classes have 25 children enrolled in them as compared to 45 in the central groups. The data suggest that the experimental groups do better, but there are no hard data in the study that would clearly indicate this fact. The teachers and the headmistress felt that the children in the experimental classes were making many gains in the affective and the emotional domain that children in larger classes were not making.

In an experiment directed by Claud Saint Marc (1971) on individualized instruction in the *école maternelle,* particular attention was given to children who were commonly thought to have learning difficulties or were predicted to have learning difficulties when they reached primary school. These children were gathered together in small groups twice a week and received structured language exercises that would help them in a wide variety of ways. This resulted in a considerable reduction in the number of repeaters. Out of 115 children no more than 6% (as against 33% in the other schools) were retained in first grade.

A study by Leory-Boussion (1971) led to the conclusion that there is only very limited value in attempting to teach children to read before the age of 5.

In recent years, there has been a growing interest in France in teaching young children a foreign language. "Teaching Foreign Languages at the pre-school stage" (Delaunay, 1971), describes a historical, psychological, and physiological study of two methods of learning a language: the natural (direct) method and the school (indirect) method. It enunciates the principles and the structures necessary for the initiation of teaching a foreign language in nursery schools. Teaching foreign languages to young children has officially been sanctioned in

France under the Peyrefille-Goppel agreement, which provides for exchange of teachers between Germany and France over a period of 2 or 3 months. This was started in 1971 and has grown to involve approximately 300 French and German nursery schools. No results have yet been published of this experiment.

From this brief review of research, four points in particular stand out:

1. That intelligence levels in children generally vary according to socioeconomic class. To help children from a lower socioeconomic class achieve their potential in school, it is essential to involve the entire environment of the child in the learning process.

2. The rate of failure (repeating) in primary school is a function of, in order of importance: intellectual maturity, family life, behavior, and instrumental factors (for example, perceptual or psychomotor difficulties).

3. Where children have received regular structural language exercises in small groups, the rate of failure has declined dramatically.

4. The French have instituted research into many of the problems of pre-primary education, but, except for those noted above, the findings have generally been inconclusive.

ACKNOWLEDGMENTS

The author wishes to express his gratitude for the cooperation of the many people who made this study possible, in particular Prof. G. Mialaret, World President of the *Organization Mondiale pour l'Education Préscolaire*; Mme. N. Masse, *Directeur des Enseignements du Centre International de l'Enfance;* M. M. Reuchlin, of the *Institut National d'Etude du Travail et d'Orientation Professionnelle*; Mme. M. Stambac, of the *Centre de Recherche de l'Education Specialisée et de l'Adaptation Scolaire*; and to Mesdames M. Abbadie, S. Parlant, S. Herbinière-Lebert (now retired), and J. Terney of the *Inspection Générale*.

BIBLIOGRAPHY

Austin, G. R. *A report on pre-school and elementary education efforts in six European countries*, OECD, 1971. (Stencil)
Berry, M. F. *La liaison entre facteurs du milieu familial et nouveau intellectual des enfants en début de scolarité*. Educational Research European Survey, 1970.
Blackstone, T. *Pre-school education in Europe*. Strasbourg: Council of Europe, 1970.
Blot, D. Les redoublements dans l'enseignement primaire en France de 1960 à 1966. *Population,* 1969, *4*, 685-709.
Delaunay, A. L'Acquisition précoce des langues vivantes par la méthode naturelle. *Revue Française de Pédagogie*, 1971, *14*, 5.
Graffar, M. L'Influence des facteurs sociaux sur la croissance et le développement de l'enfant. *Les Carnets de l'enfance*, UNICEF, Juillet-Septembre, 1971, 15.
Herbinière-Lebert S. *L'Education des parents d'enfants d'âge préscolaire par la coopération entre la famille et les éducatrices des jeunes enfants*. OMEP, 1970.

Leory-Boussion, A. Maturité mentale et apprentissage de la lecture–Etude longitudinale entre 5 et 8 ans. *Enfance*, 1971, *3*, 154-208.

Mignon, P., Mergny, R. Le jeune enfant dans un nouveau milieu: l'école. *L'Ecole maternelle française*, 1970, *1*. 11-12.

Prost, A. *L'Enseignement en France 1800-1967*. Librairie Armande Colin. 1968.

Reuchlin, M. *Les facteurs socio-economiques du développement cognitif.* Stencil. 1971.

Saint Marc, C. *Travaux de Centre de Recherche de l'education specialisee et de l'adaptation scolaire* (CRESAS). Numero Special, 1971.

Soulé, M., Peille, F., & Anfar, L. Le passage à la grande école *l'Education,* 10 juin 1971, *107.*

Trouillet, B. *Die Vorschulerziehung in neun europäischen Ländern.* Weinheim: Beltz Verlag, 1967.

Vial, J. *Institut Pédagogique National, Departement de la Recherche, Pédagogique, Programme de Recherches, Experimentation d'un cycle élémentaire "desenclave."* Stencil, 1968.

Council of Europe. *Committee for general and technical education, pre-school education in France.* Stencil. July, 1971.

Council of Europe. *Research into pre-school education jyväskylä symposium.* 1971, 46. Strasbourg, 1972.

Council of Europe. *Newsletter,* No. 1, 1972, p. 46.

Groupe d'etude pour la defense et la renovation permanente de l'ecole maternelle (GEDREM). January 28, 1970.

Institut Pédagogique National. *Les Enseignements pre-élémentaire et élémentaire.* Cahiers de documentation, série générale, 1970.

Ministère de l'éducation nationale. *L'Éducation préscolaire en France. situation-recherche pédagogique.* Stencil. Paris, 1971.

VIe Plan de développement économique et social. Annexes: Programmes d'actions détaillées. 1971-1975. (France)

Ministère de l'education nationale. *Direction de la pédagogie des renseignements scolaires et de l'orientation, service des renseignements généraux, sous-direction de l'adaptation et de l'éducation specialisée.* Circulaire No. IV 70-83, 9 février, 1970.

Ministère de l'éducation nationale. *Direction chargée des affaires budgétaires et financières.* DAF/No. 37/4.

OECD. *Economic surveys: France.* 1973.

OECD. *Reviews of national policies for education: France.* October 1969, STP(69)1.

OECD. *Classification de l'enseignement: Paris.* 1972.

OECD. *Reviews of national policies for education: France.* Paris, 1971.

OECD. *Labour force statistics 1959-1970.* Paris, 1972.

OECD. *La politique et la planification de l'enseignement.* Paris, 1971.

Rapport de la commission de l'éducation du 6ème plan (1971-1975). France, Chapitre III, Objectifs et effectifs par niveau d'enseignement.

Brogan, P. Bilingual schools on trial. *The Times Educational Supplement,* May 26, 1972.

Pre-school education in Europe: French pack them all in. *The Times,* March 3, 1972.

Programme de recherche, travaux du centre de recherche de l'éducation spécialisée et de l'adaption scolaire (CRESAS). Numero Special, 1972.

UNESCO. *La formation et la situation professionnelle des enseignants préscolaire.* Décembre 1965.

UNESCO. *World survey of Education II, Primary Education.* 1958.

United Nations demographic yearbook. 1970.

United Nations. *Analyses and projections of households and families.* 1971.

VIe Conférence des Ministres Européens de l'Education, Versailles, 20-22 mai 1969 *l'Education pour tous.* CME/VI/(69)8

Documents et échanges pour la défense et la rénovation des collectivités éducatives destinées aux jeunes enfants. *Petite Enfance,* No. 1, Septembre-Octobre 1972.

L'éducation. No. 158 (14 décembre 1972).

8

Early Childhood Education in Italy

INTRODUCTION

Preschool education in Italy can be traced to a Catholic priest, Abate Ferrante Aporti, who established an infant school at Cremona in 1828. Dissatisfied with the progress being made by the children, he investigated the conditions under which their preschool years had been spent. As a result of his work, he drew up the *Manual of Education and Teaching for Infant Schools* in 1833. This stressed moral habits, intellectual stimulation, and physical activities as necessary ingredients in infant education.

In 1894, the Agazzi sisters opened a home for preschool children where the accent was on training in sense perception and play activities based on concern for the individual needs. Other important preschool educators in Italy were Jean Bosco (1815-1888), Aristide Gabelli (1830-1891), Giuseppina Pizzigoni (1870-1947), and Maria Montessori (1870-1952).

Maria Montessori, the first woman physician in Italy, is one of the most famous of early childhood educators, and the "Montessori method" is still widely used in many countries. Its success in teaching retarded children prompted Montessori to question the effectiveness of standard public school practices with normal children. Around 1907, she accepted responsibility for the education of slum children in Rome, and this position provided for her the opportunity to experiment further with her methods in the now famous *Casa dei Bambini* (House of Children). Her first book, *The Method of Scientific Teaching,* describing her work with children ages 3 to 6 in the slum quarters of Rome, was published in 1909. In 1922, Montessori was appointed government inspector of schools in Italy, and this enabled her to test her theories on larger groups of preschool children.

The Fascist period from 1922-1943 saw two important pieces of educational legislation: The Gentile reform and the 1939 Bottai Act or *Carta della Scuola* (school charter), but most of the changes they introduced were swept away after World War II. The system then adopted follows the English pattern, where 5 years of compulsory primary education are offered to all children, followed by 3 years in a middle, vocational, art, or general postprimary school.

So far as concerns preprimary education, a state system was not established until 1968 (Act No. 444). Until then it had been almost entirely in the hands of the private sector—totally Roman Catholic organizations. However, there were a few *giardini d'infanzia* (kindergarten) attached to teacher training colleges that could be said to belong to the state system. For the record, it should be mentioned also that as early as 1962 a law was passed to provide for publicly maintained preprimary schools; Parliament, however, never voted any money to implement it.

The 1968 Act was a direct outcome of the work of the 1962 Commission of Inquiry, which had been appointed to study the state of public education in Italy. Its report, published in 1963-1964, recommended state sponsorship of early childhood education, not only because of its importance in the whole system but also because it provided a means for bringing about equality of opportunity.

ENROLLMENTS, PRESCHOOL EDUCATION (1960-1970)

Preprimary education (*scuole del grado preparatorio*) in Italy is defined in the OECD "Classification of Educational Systems" (1972) as follows:

> Length of Study: Up to three years.
> Entrance requirements: To be three years old.
> This type of education is not compulsory and is provided in nursery schools (scuole materne), kindergartens (gardini d'infanzia), and children's homes (case dei bambini). These are private schools. A recent decision to introduce State nursery schools has been made [p. 70].

The numbers of children in *scuole materne* (preferred name) for the years 1960-1961 to 1970-1971 are shown in Table 8.1. It should be explained here that in this report the term "public" refers to state schools only; "private" refers to those under other types of sponsorship—including communal. For all practical

TABLE 8.1
Enrollments in Scuola Materna in Italy from 1960-61 to 1970-71

| | | | (in 000's) |
Year	Private	Public	Total
1960-61	1,154	–	1,154
1965-66	1,335	–	1,335
1966-67	1,365	–	1,365
1967-68	1,409	–	1,409
1968-69	1,435	68	1,503
1969-70	1,471	100	1,571
1970-71	1,496	134	1,630
% of increase from 1960-61 to 1970-71	29.6	97.1	41.2

Source: Pre-primary School Services, Ministry of Public Education,
Rome.

purposes, there was no enrollment in the public sector until the passage of law No. 444 in 1968. The table indicates that there has been a 29.6% growth in enrollment in the private sector during the 10-year period. There was, of course, virtually no enrollment in the public preschools until they were established by law in 1968. During the first 3 years of their existence, however, their enrollments increased by 97.1%. This gives an overall increase (public and private) of 41.2% over the 10-year period. In 1968-1969, the first year for which there are comparative figures, it will be seen that 95 out of 100 children going to preschool were in fact attending a private one. By 1970, this had dropped to 93 out of 100.

Comparable figures for primary schools show that during the same 10-year period, 1960-1970, enrollments in the private sector grew by 14% and in the public sector by 13%, giving a total increase of 13%. The ratio of enrollments in private schools to the total enrollment figure indicates that 7 out of 100 children went to private schools in 1960-1961 and in 1970-1971. Enrollments in primary schools, therefore, favor the public sector; in preschools (as we have seen) the opposite is true.

The potential for growth in the primary school, however, is greater than the statistics reflect. According to the OECD's "Reviews of National Policies for Education—Italy" (1969), in 1964-1965 there were 3,979,422 primary school places available, while the number of children eligible for them was 4,427,018. There was, therefore, an actual shortage of physical space for 447,596 children. This was a little better than in 1961-1962, when the shortage was 575,365 places; but there is no doubt that the primary school enrollment situation in Italy is still extremely serious. In many instances, it is not a question of providing better education for some children, but of providing some education for all of them. The *International Herald Tribune* (Nov. 4, 1972) describes the position in these words:

> Although education is compulsory until the age of 14 here, young Italians who do go to school are not all necessarily getting educated. For one thing, nearly one in three has no place to sit: The nationwide shortage of classrooms is close to three million for a student body of over 10 million. Many if not most schools run on two shifts, and some on three. Classrooms are often improvised in rented quarters: garages, hallways, ramshackle buildings, whose doorways and staircases must be propped up for safety [p. 8].

Table 8.2 presents population attendance rates in preschools for the 10-year period 1960-1961 to 1970-1971. It will be seen that, in 1960-1961, 46.2% of the children between the ages of 3 and 5 were attending.

By 1970-1971, this had climbed to 58.3%. As shown in Table 8.1, over the 10-year period there had been a 41.2% increase in the children attending the preschool. During the same time, the Italian infant population between 3 and 5 had increased by 12%. Overall, then, there was a 26.2% increase in places available for children in preschool.

In 1970-1971, the percentage of children by single year of age and by age group enrolled in preschools in Italy was as follows:

Age	1970-1971	Age	1970-1971
6	95%	5-6	90%
5	85	4-6	80
4	60	3-6	65
3	20	2-6	52
2	1		

That the increases in the age grouping may be a thing of the past is suggested by recent statistics on population trends in Italy.[1] In 1966, there were 18.9 live births per thousand; in 1970, they had declined to 16.8—a 2.1% drop over the 4-year period. Population growth in Italy, therefore, appears to be slowing down.

The only information available on enrollments in different types of preschools is, unfortunately, for as long ago as 1954-1955. The figures then were:

Preschools conducted by		Pupils
(a) Communes		313,659
(b) Religious bodies		350,133
(c) Private bodies		388,258
	Total	1,052,050

[1] United Nations demographic yearbook. 1970.

TABLE 8.2
Population Attendance Rates in Scuola Materna in Italy from 1960-61
to 1970-71

			(in 000's)
	1960-61	1970-71	% of Change
Total age group 3 - 5 years in Scuola Materna	1,154	1,630	41.2
Infant population 3 - 5 years	2,498	2,798	12.0
% of age group enrolled	46.2	58.3	26.2

Source: United Nations Demographic Yearbook, 1970.

This shows that 18 years ago there was an almost equal balance between the different groups conducting preschools.[2] As already observed, all these groups are termed "private," for the purposes of this review, to distinguish them from the state preschools established since 1968. In fact, in many cases, a commune gives a subsidy to a private (usually Roman Catholic) organization to help in the operation of its preschool.

In some countries, the relative participation of women in the labor force has a bearing on the demand for places in preschools. For purposes of comparison with other reports in this series, relevant statistics are given for Italy in Table 8.3. They show that for both males and females the labor force participation rates have declined over the 10-year period 1960-1970. The participation rate for females, however, has declined less than the rate for males.

ISSUES OF DEBATE

Preschool education's importance in Italy must be seen within the broader context of education at the primary school level. According to the OECD "Reviews of National Policies for Education—Italy" (1969):

> During the last 60 years, the "population explosion" in Italy has caused an increase of some 17 million over ten years old. As a result of this expansion, Italy has constantly had to adjust its educational system. The changes made have been of great importance for the historical events which have repeatedly altered the normal course of the country's political, cultural, social and economic life [p. 31].

Table 8.4 indicates this general trend. It can be seen that the population's standard of education has been improving both in absolute and relative terms.

[2] UNESCO. *World survey of education* (Vol. 5). 1971.

TABLE 8.3
Labor Force Participation Rates - Italy

	1960 %	1970 %
$\dfrac{\text{Total Labor Force}}{\text{Total Population}} \times 100$		
(a) Total	43.3	37.0
(b) Males	62.7	55.5
(c) Females	24.9	19.3
$\dfrac{\text{Total Labor Force}}{\substack{\text{Population from} \\ \text{15 to 64 years}}} \times 100$		
(a) Total	64.1	55.7
(b) Males	93.3	83.6
(c) Females	36.7	29.1

Source: Labor Force Statistics, 1959-70, O.E.C.D., Paris, 1972.

Commenting on Italian censuses for 1951 and 1961, which covered persons over 6 years of age, the OECD document points out that the number of illiterates declined, with the proportion falling from 12.9% to 8.4% of the population. Those holding no school certificate, but able to read and write, fell from 17.9% to 15.7%. Practically all members of the new generation attend

TABLE 8.4
Trend in Educational Level

				(in 000's)
Year	Number of people holding at least a primary school certificate		Number of people with no school certificate	
1901	10	41%	14	58%
1911	14	51%	13	48%
1921	18	61%	12	38%
1931	21	66%	11	33%
1936	23	68%	11	31%
1951	29	74%	10	25%
1961	34	81%	8	18%

school. Also noted in the census figures was the percentage of the population holding a primary school certificate. This showed only a small increase from 58.9% to 60.8% during the 10-year period. A slight decline of those holding this certificate alone in the north (where there was an expansion in higher education) counterbalanced a rise in the number of such people in central and southern Italy, hence the relatively small increase.

The general educational situation in Italy continues to show imbalances in less favored areas such as Sardinia, Campania, Sicily, Basilicata, Molise, and Puglia, where the percentage of illiteracy is still quite high. The average individual years of study for Italians over 10 years old in all Italy in 1961 was 4.85 years; in the northwest, 5.45 years; and in southern Italy and the islands, 4.18 years.

A 1971 report by the Minister of Public Education, in discussing the second 5-year plan of 1971-1975, identifies six special projects of particular concern to the Italian government. One of these includes a series of experiments on interventions in early childhood education that may prevent some of the handicaps that children from disadvantaged homes bring with them to school. A second part of this project is an extensive study of the possibility of lowering the compulsory age of school attendance in Italy to 5 years. In both cases, the ultimate aim is to provide early programs that will improve the children's chances of succeeding when they get to school, particularly in the matter of literacy.

Following on the act of 1968, which provided for state nursery schools in Italy, the Ministry of Public Education made it clear in *The Educational Movement* (1969-1970 and 1970-1971 issues) that state intervention was intended progressively to offset the preexisting situation, where only 47% of preschool age children attended private-sector nursery schools. As at that time, there were no state nursery schools, and only 47% of the children, therefore, attended any preschool at all. The state schools envisaged (which will include special ones for handicapped children) will be supplied with yearly programs based on the requirements of the municipalities and an evaluation of local needs.

The general aim is to develop a preschool service where both state and nonstate nursery schools will be available to all children whose parents desire them to go there. The service will educate and develop the child's personality, prepare him for the compulsory school, and supplement the work of the family. Registration at any of the preschools will be optional and attendance, free.

Under review are the regulations that will enforce the law and create councils to direct the schools and represent the teachers. The act also authorizes monetary grants to private as well as public preschools.

These observations in the ministry reports identify four important issues of debate in preschool education: the provision of compensatory education; the relationship between public and private schools; parental and teacher involvement; and successful transition for the child from home to the preprimary school, and, hence, to the primary school. It is clear that the planners had it in mind that local communities should consider children most in need of pre-primary education before offering it to the whole population.

Another standing difficulty the 1968 law attempts to deal with is the marked environmental and demographic differences between regions. These will be taken into account in the allocation of the resources. The largest investments will be made, for example, in the south where the illiteracy rate is quite high and the population widely dispersed, and in the north where there is the largest growth in urbanization, caused by sizable internal migration from the south.

The problem of internal immigration is a serious one. From 1915 to 1918, rural workers represented about 60% of the active population, as against about 26% in 1965. During this time, Italy experienced a vast movement of people from the southern parts of the country to the northern, more industrialized, regions. This has created particularly difficult problems because the people from the south did not bring with them the same social values as those held in northern Italy, and they were totally lacking in a high regard for education. Speaking to this point, Gozzer (1971), of the Ministry of Education, has declared that the 5-year plan for 1971-1975 must make adequate provision for those southerners' children whom he described as being from an underprivileged social class, which, for the first time in Italian history, is being represented in preschools and primary school in increasingly large numbers.

Traditionally, the Italian parent from the lowest social class has valued education least and has been far less prone to send his children to school than his more comfortably placed compatriots. This now seems to be changing, but as Gozzer (1971) points out, these children are still coming to school much disadvantaged by their social backgrounds. This is one of the reasons why he considers early childhood education of such particular importance for, in his opinion, it can indeed forestall some of the later consequences of being raised in a socioeconomically deprived family.

In the matter of parents' freedom to choose the school and the kind of education for their children, the 1968 law adopted a compromise. At the same time as creating a state-run preprimary system, it provided also for financial aid to the established schools in the private sector. As shown in Table 8.1, the new public preschools are growing much more rapidly in terms of enrollment than the private ones. It may well be that, where parents have a choice, they are going for the very limited number of places that the state preschools offer.

Hitherto, private preschools have been attended almost exclusively by children from middle-class or upper-class homes. Indeed, it has often been difficult for lower class parents even to send their children to compulsory school, let alone preschool.

Parental involvement in the education of their children is positively encouraged by the new law, which envisages the establishment of parents' councils for each of the state preschools. Behind this is the thought that, both emotionally and educationally, parents need to feel that they can influence what is hapening to their children, and the child needs to feel that his parents are interested in his schooling. Similarly, the teachers are encouraged to form representative councils so that they can effectively put forward ideas about how the preschools should be run. These two elements, parental and teacher involvement, are of great potential importance in the development of the new preschool system.

A smooth transfer for the child from his home to the preschool, and then to the primary school, is another matter to which the Italians attach importance. Many of the children who come from disadvantaged homes find great difficulty in succeeding at the primary school; as the *International Herald Tribune* said (November 4, 1972), "It is hardly surprising . . . that one out of seven Italian children—and four out of five peasant children—flunk out before the fifth grade, and only one in four makes it as far as a high school diploma [p. 8]." As already observed, part of the motivation for the new system has been a desire for the preschools to make good these children's deficiencies before they have to compete in compulsory education.

One of the most telling drawbacks of these disadvantaged children is poor facility with the language. There is a very high correlation between this and failure at school. Borghi (1970), in examining this whole matter, concludes that nursery school education that gives special attention to language facility would be of inestimable value in helping these children to master not only their school work but the national tongue. He draws attention to the many dialects still being spoken in the country and then points out that it is only the Italian spoken by the middle class that is accepted in most schools. Thus, the first thing many children have to do on reaching school is to learn a second language.

Teacher training and its quality is another issue not yet resolved in Italy. The training is judged by many to be quite inadequate and, as might be expected, the most able teachers prefer to go to the more populous and developed localities. There appears no way, at present , of persuading teachers to go to the more difficult schools and/or the more remote or isolated parts of the country.

Commenting on the teachers' strike in November 1972, the *International Herald Tribune* said, "Struggling under these daunting conditions are teachers generally lacking in the most elementary professional training. Italy has no teachers' training colleges, and a new after-school program to 'teach teachers how to teach' has proved such a waste of time that its drastic overhaul is one of the strikers' main demands [p. 8]."

Borghi (1970) considers many of these issues, and his concluding words are: "Advocation of a state nursery school adopting methods attuned to advanced psychological and educational thought, and creation of a new two-year preprimary school inspired by the English infant school, are important features of the debate going on in Italy today on the reorganization of the structure of primary education [p. 1/99]."

The principal elements in this debate on early childhood education at the present time may, therefore, be summarized in the following form:

1. A greater equality of opportunity for all children, with special concern for those who are disadvantaged by social, economic, or geographical circumstances.
2. A growing awareness in all classes of society of the general value of education, particularly as it concerns facility in the national language at an early age.
3. Preschool education as an aid to the family in adapting itself to the demands of present day society, and as an easy bridge for the child between his home and the primary school he will enter when he is 6.
4. The provision of a state preprimary school system additional to the network of private (primarily Roman Catholic) schools which was all that existed up to 1968.

THE AIMS AND OBJECTIVES OF EARLY CHILDHOOD EDUCATION

For a view, first, of the national policy for education as a whole, La Morgia (1970) has a useful summary:

> The aims of Italy's educational system are not laid down in the Constitution. They are shown in the laws, syllabuses and ministerial circulars relating to the various stages of education, and are therefore reflected in the various types of school. Nevertheless, a few basic principles relating to schools are set out in articles 9, 33 and 34 of the Constitution.
>
> In article 9 the Republic encourages the provision of educational facilities in the same way as it encourages facilities for scientific or technical research. Article 3 states that the arts and sciences are unfettered and are to be studied and taught accordingly. The Republic is responsible for laying down general guiding principles regarding teaching and for providing schools to teach all subjects to all age groups. Moreover, corporate bodies and private individuals have the right to open schools or educational institutions, provided that no expense results to the state therefrom. The rights and duties of private schools are laid down by law. They are guaranteed complete freedom and their pupils are assured of an education equivalent to that offered in state schools.
>
> Article 34 of the Constitution states that anyone capable and worthy of profiting from it shall be entitled to reach the highest stages of education irrespective of financial status. The Republic effects this by means of grants, family allowances and other measures. A minimum of eight years' schooling is compulsory and free [p. 89].

The OECD's "Reviews of National Policies for Education—Italy" (1969) says, more briefly, that the traditional aim of education in Italy has been to provide the masses with elementary schooling, by teaching them reading, writing, and arithmetic, and to form an elite, mostly from the upper middle classes, who would attain a higher cultural level as exemplified by a university degree.

Within this general policy, the specific aims of the preprimary schools, as stated in the law of 1968, are the development of the child's personality, preparing him for compulsory school attendance and supplementing his upbringing in the family. The Presidential Decree No. 647 (September 10, 1969) entitled *"Orientamenti dell'attivita educativa nelle scuole materne statali"* expands on these principles governing the new state preschools, particularly in the following respects.

1. Their basic purpose is not only educative, but is concerned with the entire development of the child, hopefully maximizing his "real" capacities.
2. The general orientation of the schools and their operation are to foster the democratic principles under which the Italian republic operates.
3. The schools are to be concerned with fostering good parent-community relations. They are not to act as a substitute for the family, but to augment it.
4. Particular attention is to be given to the development of the child's personality. A situation is to be provided where he can develop this to the maximum of his potential.
5. The basic responsibility of the teacher is to foster a positive self-concept on the part of the child.
6. The teacher is to see that any assistant teachers employed in the school system also accept the concept of fostering positive self-concepts for all children.
7. The curriculum of the preschool is to reflect the development of the individual and the promotion of group activities more than any desire on the part of professional educators to set a rigid curriculum.

The National Didactic Center for the Preschools in a report with the same title lists nine areas of educational activity: religious instruction; emotional, affective, and social education; play and constructive activities; intellectual and cognitive activities; language education; graphics and arts; music education; physical education; and health education. Its concluding paragraph says that education in all instances is to be designed as far as possible on an individualized, not on a large group basis.

The preschool's position as intermediate between the home and the compulsory school presupposes active parental participation in the new preschools and, as we have seen, the 1968 Act envisages the establishment of parents' councils for each of the *scuola materna*. In fact, this recommendation applies to all public schools in Italy, clearly indicating the continuation of a policy that education at all levels should be receptive and responsive to the wishes of parents. This goes back at least to 1953 when the Italian government began to create centers for parent, home, and school orientation. One of a series of 10 centers initiated to work on special problems is the National Didactic Center for Preschool Education, to which reference has already been made.

Writing for the Council of Europe meeting on education in preschools, Professor Laenge of the University of Rome (1971) stresses this double function of the preschool: one, as an extension of the home; and two, preparing the child for primary school. This he sees as a natural linkage, and one that does not have to be developed artificially. The teacher should understand that she is sharing the responsibilities of the parents, and she must work to engender mutual trust and a cooperative attitude between them and the school. This is particularly important in preschools catering to children who come from disadvantaged homes and whose parents traditionally view schools as something outside their own existence. Professor Laeng regards such cooperation as one of the ways to educate children successfully for the society of tomorrow.

ORGANIZATION AND CONTROL

In Italy, the Ministry of Education is responsible for education at all levels in the public sector, and also for some administrative aspects of private schools that receive money from the state. There are three, or sometimes four, levels of school organization: The central (state), regional and/or provincial, and local.

The minister of education is assisted by a number of groups including the undersecretaries of state, who are appointed by the Council of Ministers. The other groups are the Higher Council of Public Education (the highest technical consultant body for education, elected by the teaching profession and representative of teaching staffs in schools of all types) and the Administrative Council, consisting of directors-general and heads of central services, and two representatives of the ministry personnel who advise on the coordination of the work within the department.

In the last few years, the government has made a strenuous effort to decentralize the organization of the ministry, particularly at the regional level where there is a superintendent (*provveditori agli studi*) who is responsible for the administration of all preprimary, primary, and secondary education. He is one of the most important officers in the organization and sees to the enforcement of the regulations applicable to educational establishments, whether state or private. Under him are a number of inspectors. Countrywide there are some 600 such inspectors responsible for both preprimary and primary education in the 94 provinces.

At the local level there are two senior officials concerned with preprimary and primary education—the primary school inspector (*ispettori scholastici*) and the director of methods (*direttori didattici*). All major decisions at the local level have to be passed through them.

General supervision of the Italian school system is the responsibility of the inspection service. For each 50 to 70 preprimary or primary teachers there is one director of education. For each 10 to 12 directors, there is one state inspector. The new preprimary school law stipulated that the preprimary schools were to have their own inspectors and directors, but until some preprimary teachers have met the qualifications for these posts they will have to be taken by ex-primary school teachers.

The World Survey of Education, Volume 5, UNESCO (1971) defines the functions of the Italian inspectorate as follows:

> The inspection service of the central authorities is staffed by inspectors who form part of the administration. Each directorate-general or central service has its own corps of inspectors: central and general inspectors, chief inspectors and auditors.
>
> The central inspectors are responsible for the inspection and professional guidance of the teaching staff. The country is divided into inspection zones in order to maintain continuity of inspection work in the areas concerned. Inspectors meet together at least once every three months in order to examine the results of their work and to propose lines of study and research in regard to educational and teaching methods, and to suggest ways and means of improving the functioning of educational institutions. The central inspectors are also responsible for in-service training and guidance on technical and educational matters, particularly in regard to the application of curricula and proposals for modifying or bringing them up to date.
>
> The central and chief inspectors supervise the smooth administrative running of all offices and institutions which come under the ministry. They make urgent on-the-spot decisions, report on the results of their inspection work, and propose any measures they deem necessary.
>
> The auditors see that the necessary accounting work is carried out in offices and schools [p. 654].

The education system itself consists of four stages catering for progressive age-groups: (*1*) preparatory or nursery (*istruzione delgrade preparatorio*); (*2*) primary (*istruzione primaria*); (*3*) secondary (*istruzione secondaria*); (*4*) university or education at colleges of advanced technology (*istruzione universitaria o superiore*).

The organization of preschools at preparatory level has been described in *School Systems: A Guide,* published by the Council for Cultural Cooperation of the Council of Europe (1970):

> These schools are not seen as part of the school system proper: their object is to educate and cultivate the children's personalities, and to help prepare them for

primary school, by reinforcing the influence and effort of the family. Attendance is optional and free.

State nursery schools are usually divided into three sections, corresponding to the age of the children. There may never be more than nine such sections, but one section may contain children of different ages, and in small towns a school may have only one section. Under the Act No. 444 . . . *kindergartens,* previously attached to primary teacher training schools, and nursery schools, formerly attached to the training schools for nursery school mistresses, have now become state nursery schools. . . .

State nursery schools are open at least seven hours daily, although exceptions may be made where local circumstances have been shown to warrant them. It is permissible to attend one session only, morning or afternoon. The schools are open at least ten months of the year. There is no real curriculum but educational guidelines have been laid down [p. 145].

The Ministry of Public Education's "The Educational Movement" (1968) states that the maximum and minimum enrollment in each section is 30 and 15 children, respectively. Special sections or special nursery schools are envisaged for children from 3 to 6 years of age suffering from intellectual or behavioural disorders, or physically or sensorially handicapped. These ad hoc sections shall not accommodate more than 12 children. The report adds that free transportation services operated for primary schools may be used for nursery schools also, if this will promote attendance. Nursery school children will benefit from the same forms of assistance (including insurance and medical attendance) envisaged for primary school children.

For sociological and pedagogical reasons, the staff of state nursery schools are all female. Their salaries and judicial status are the same as those of their counterparts in primary schools. The teaching staff have to hold the certified diploma issued by the ad hoc schools which qualify nursery school teachers, or by teacher training institutes; members of the inspectorate must be graduates in pedagogy, while management personnel must hold a diploma in superintendence or a degree in pedagogy.

As we have seen, 90% of Italian children who attend preprimary school do so in a nonstate school and the constitution allows corporate bodies or private individuals to set up private schools so long as this is not initially at the expense of the state. The basic organizational pattern of a nonstate, preprimary school, however, tends to conform quite closely with the pattern laid down in the law of 1968, since there are provisions in that law for subsidies to be paid to private agencies or local municipalities who have created preschool programs previous to its enactment. One of the major differences, however, as noted previously, is in the number of pupils assigned to any one teacher, which is considerably higher in the nonstate than in the state preschools.

In the autonomous regions—Sicily, Sardinia, Trentino—Alto Adige, Friuli-Veneziaguilla, and Valle d'Aosta—the administration of the new preschool state program is delegated to the office of the regional superintendent, but the organizational pattern is similar to that in the rest of Italy.

PHYSICAL SETTING: A VISIT TO A *SCUOLA MATERNA* IN ROME

This *scuola materna* was in a wing of a recently constructed concrete building that also housed a primary school. There were lawns on three sides and a playground, shared between the two schools, on the fourth. The preschool wing was on two floors, with ramps instead of stairs, this being considered safer for younger children. It had nine classrooms approximately 6 X 8 meters. A gymnasium was shared with the primary school. It was owned and run by the city of Rome and was, therefore, a public sector school.

The time of the visit was late December, and the classroom visited was decorated for Christmas and had a nativity scene built by the children. On a table nearby were presents the children had made to take home to their parents. On one wall were pictures of objects such as a moon, with the identifying word written below each one. These were used in the course of language lessons. Against another wall were a number of large brown boxes filled with toys. Boxes containing games were on the tables. The passages also had Christmas decorations either bought or made by the teacher. There was little representation of the children's work here or in the classrooms.

In this classroom, there were 26 children ranging in age from 3 to 6. In the *scuole materne,* children are not divided into age groups, since it is believed that it is beneficial for the older ones to help the younger. Each of the children in the class wore a smock tied with a bow under his chin. The room gave the impression of being quite full with these 26 children, two teachers, and all the materials for play and work.

At 9:00 the children were met at the door by the teachers and lined up to go to their classrooms, where an opening exercise lasted until about 9:30. During this the children talked with the teacher, put away their lunch boxes, donned their smocks, sang some songs, had a brief religious exercise, and did some physical exercises. From 9:30 to 10:30 they worked on Christmas cards for their parents, helped by the teachers. The cards seemed very similar to one another and did not reflect a great deal of originality. The teacher explained that the main reason for this was lack of supplies, which forced them to plan economically. At 10:30, the children had a 15-minute break to eat their snacks and to move around.

The class was settled down and working again by 11:00 o'clock, with the children writing in their notebooks. After looking at the various commercially prepared pictures on the walls, the children were asked to copy the captions many times, the teachers walking around and helping them. From 11:30 to 12:00 the children were allowed to play with the toys, and most of them chose building blocks. Again the teachers worked with the children individually as they proceeded on their various projects. At 12:00 there was a 90-minute lunch period, when they ate the cold food they had brought and then played in the classroom. They were not taken outside although it was a very pleasant day. From 1:30 to 2:30, the children worked again with their writing books on language skills. This consisted primarily of copying out new words and of talking to the teacher about what they meant, what the separate letters meant, and how they could be put together. From 2:30 to 3:00 they prepared to go home.

The general impression given by this classroom was that it was a good, safe place for children to spend a day, but the atmosphere was scarcely stimulating. There was paucity of materials for the children to work with (no paints or brushes, for example) or any other facilities to help the children develop their own creativity.

Apparently there was no particular curriculum for the teachers to follow. They planned the week's program about 1 week in advance and did not seem to set any specific objectives for the children to accomplish. This lack of objectives and the paucity of materials were encountered in other preschools visited in Rome. This suggests that the Italian government's first concern has been to provide the children with a physical facility and a teacher, there being insufficient money to do much beyond that at the moment. Each teacher interviewed wished the government could provide more money for more and varied types of activity for the children.

The teachers at this preschool, as in others visited in Rome, did not give the impression of having been adequately trained to deal with the problems of young children's education. Perhaps this is because, in Italy, a teacher chooses her profession at 14, and the training she gets is not of a particularly high quality. What appeared to be missing was creativity on her part to fill out a limited materials budget with her own ideas, such as inexpensive plants and other growing things, old magazines, assorted old clothing for "dressing-up," interesting pieces of wood or plastic, or small boxes either to build with or simply to decorate. This is surprising in a country where the teaching of the Agazzi sisters, who built most of their (museum) classroom curricula around the contents of the children's pockets, is so highly regarded.

TEACHERS AND THEIR TRAINING

The state preprimary teachers must hold the diploma awarded by a teachers' training college or an institute or must meet the teaching requirements laid down by the 1923 Royal Decree No. 1054. The average age of applicants for teachers' training colleges is fourteen. Nine years of compulsory education must have been completed beforehand.

In the "Classification of Educational Systems," OECD (1972), the following is said about preschool teacher training:

> (1) *Teacher training courses*
> Name of Institution: *Scuola magistrale* (teacher trainer colleges for pre-primary schools).
> Length of Studies: Three years.
> Entrance Requirements: *Licenza media*–(1st cycle certificate) or entrance examination.
> Certificates: *Diploma di abilitazione all' insegnamento nelle scuole preparatorio* (pre-primary teaching proficiency certificate). Full time. These courses include both theoretical and practical training. Practical training is provided in a pre-primary school attached to the training college [p. 71].
> Type of education: Secondary. (teacher training)
> Years of study: 9-11
> (2) *Teacher training:*
> Name of Institution: *Scuole del grado preparatorio* (Pre-primary schools).
> Place of training: Scuola magistrale (primary teacher training college for teachers in pre-primary schools) . . .
> Length of study: Three years.
> To have access to the "scuola magistrale", students must hold the 1st cycle leaving certificate (licenza media) or sit an entrance examination. The course includes theoretical and practical training. Students obtain the proficiency certificate in pre-primary teaching. For higher posts students are required to sit a provincial competitive examination (previous qualifications are taken into account). Pre-primary posts are open to women only [p. 81].

"Education in Europe–School Systems: A Guide," prepared by the Council for Cultural Cooperation of the Council of Europe (1970), offers the following information on preschool teacher training in Italy, particularly as it concerns the course work involved in this preparation:

> Curricula have never been formally laid down, so the course follows the examination syllabus for the following subjects: Italian, method of education, history, civics and geography, mathematics, bookkeeping and natural sciences, hygiene and child care, music and group singing, domestic science and needlework, plastic arts and drawing, teaching practice (with a written report), religion [p. 148].

Law No. 444, to which we already referred frequently, lays down the following requirements for preprimary teachers:

> Inspectresses must hold a degree in pedagogics. Principals must hold a supervisor's diploma or a degree in pedagogics.
> Inspectresses perform organizational and supervisory functions in State pre-primary schools and have the powers conferred on them by the laws and regulations.
> Inspectresses are drawn from the principals' register and are appointed by means of a competitive examination–taking account of qualifications and examinations–for which they are eligible after at least four years' service in the grade . . .
> Principals superintend the operation and activities of the State pre-primary schools

in the respective district. Principals are appointed by a national competitive examination—taking account of qualifications and examinations—which may be taken by State pre-primary school teachers holding the certificates prescribed in the first paragraph of Article 9 and with at least three years of service in the grade of "ordinario." The examination may also be taken by State pre-primary school teachers who do not hold the required certificates but have at least 10 years' service in the grade of "ordinario." . . .

State pre-primary school teachers must hold a diploma awarded by the Teacher Training Colleges or Institutes. A special qualification is prescribed, which is obtained by the competitive examination. Teachers have educational responsibility for the section assigned to them.

State pre-primary school teachers are entered on the register after provincial competitive examinations, taking account of qualifications and examinations.

State pre-primary school assistants must hold the certificate awarded on completing a first-level secondary course, or an equivalent certificate, together with an attestation that they have duly attended appropriate courses organized by the Ministry of Education.

Assistants help teachers in supervising and assisting the children. They are registered by means of provincial competitive examinations, taking account of qualifications and examinations [p. 5].

At the confrontation meeting that followed the completion of the OECD's "Reviews of National Policies for Education—Italy" (1969), an important question was asked about the training of primary school teachers. Since the same question is pertinent to training of preprimary school teachers, it is quoted here with the answer given:

(Q) A four-year training course is now provided for primary school teachers in the *instituti magistrali* which it is shortly proposed to extend to 5 years, thus bringing the *instituti magistrali* into line with the classical and scientific lycées and with the technical institutes.

Presumably this indicates that the general education acquired during these 5 years is the kind considered desirable for primary teachers belonging to a society whose general standards of education have already risen and continue to rise. Yet is it really believed that a pupil is capable of deciding at the age of 14 whether he wants to become a primary-school teacher or not? Or that pupils at this age can assimilate the relevant pedagogical training? [p. 205].

(A) The Italian representatives were compelled to admit that nothing had yet been decided with regard to the content of this training. The reform proposals now being discussed in Parliament contain no indication as to the new distribution of subject courses, nor as to the background or qualifications of the people who will be called upon to teach in these new schools. There is thus a danger that the basic principles on which teacher training policy should rest will be disregarded. The proposed plan can in fact be criticized on several points, since, although an improvement on the present situation, it fails to answer the essential problems.

The first criticism concerns the age at which students should choose their future career. The examiners do not think that a 14-year-old leaving middle school can yet be certain that his calling will be to teach in a primary school—an opinion which the Italian Delegation moreover appears to share. In the proposed *liceo magistrale* courses can no doubt be divided into two cycles, just as other upper secondary courses of similar length. The first two-year cycle, i.e. the *biennio* referred to in previous chapters, would be of a fairly general nature and would probably not include any specific vocational training, so that students could go back on their original decisions and be free to choose a different stream. This would postpone the age of final decision to 16 years [p. 231].

Italy trains about 10 times the number of teachers it can employ; the competition for jobs, therefore, is extreme. This naturally causes great job insecurity. The OECD report just quoted comments that, in Italy, a graduate teacher becomes a permanent staff member between the ages of 35 and 40 rather than 25 and 30, and that pay increases and security of employment only occur after his permanent appointment. What may have been sufficient in the way of teacher training in an earlier period, it continues, is no longer adequate. Many teachers in Italy still tend to view education as a selection process for the creation of an elite rather than as an attempt to foster equality of educational opportunity.

Table 8.5 shows the number of teachers involved in preschool education in both the public and the private sectors for the years 1960-1961 to 1970-1971, and shows a 23.7% increase in teachers in the private sector, an 85.3% increase in the public sector, and a total increase of 41.3% in the whole preprimary area. This 41.3% is considerably larger than the 27.2% increase in enrollments during the same period of time.

TABLE 8.5

Scuola Materna Teachers in Italy from 1960-61 to 1970-71

Year	Private	Public	Total
1960-61	31,441	n.a.[a]	31,441
1965-66	39,820	n.a.	39,820
1966-67	42,512	n.a.	42,512
1967-68	43,939	n.a.	43,939
1968-69	46,158	2,978	49,136
1969-70	39,888	3,381	43,269
1970-71	38,895	5,518	44,413
% of increase from 1960-61 to 1970-71	23.7	85.3	41.3

Source: Pre-primary School Services, Ministry of Public Education, Rome.

[a]Not available.

Figures for the pupil-teacher ratios in the preschools in Italy for the years 1960-1961 to 1970-1971 are given in Table 8.6. It will be seen at once that there are very important differences between the private and public sectors. The private sector in 1969-1970 had an average of 38 children for each teacher while the newly created public sector had only 24 children per teacher. Over the whole field, however, the pupil-teacher ratio remained the same during these 10 years.

Perhaps it is the much lower pupil-teacher ratio in the public sector that has begun to attract children away from private kindergartens (see Table 8.1—enrollments). A similar situation exists at the primary school level where, in 1960-1961, in the private sector, the pupil-teacher ratio was 29:1, and in 1970-1971 it was 27:1. In the public sector, in 1960-1961, however, it was 24:1, and in 1970-1971 it had dropped to 21:1.

FINANCING EARLY CHILDHOOD EDUCATION

Before discussing the financing of early childhood education in Italy, it is necessary to recall that the state system has only existed for 3 years, and that the vast majority of children, in excess of 90 out of every 100 attending, go to preprimary schools sponsored by the private sector.

The financing of education in general is described in Volume 5 of UNESCO's World Survey of Education (1971). It is there stated that approximately 80% of public education in Italy is financed by the state from budgetary income. This income derives from various sources, but no revenue is earmarked for specific purposes, all receipts being combined in accordance with the principle of indivisibility that governs budgetary procedures. Local authorities also make a significant contribution (approximately 20%), particularly by providing school premises and equipment. For certain types of schools (the *liceo* and teacher training schools), they also bear the cost of certain nonteaching staff. The education estimates form part of the national budget prepared annually by the treasury.

The proportion of expenditure for education in relation to national revenue is

TABLE 8.6
Pupil:Teacher Ratio in Scuola Materna from 1960-61 to 1970-71

Year	Private	Public	Total
1960-61	37:1	n.a.[a]	37:1
1965-66	34:1	n.a.	34:1
1969-70	38:1	24:1	37:1

[a]Not available.

approximately 5.6% and, in relation to total state expenditure, has recently exceeded 20%. Capital items represent about 17-18% of the education expenditure. Expenses for educational and scientific equipment are classified under recurring costs. The Italian per capita gross national product in 1968 was $1700. The 1968 per child expenditure was $5.80.[3]

This is the situation for all state-financed education in Italy, and it applies also to the newly created preprimary system. Attendance at these schools is free, as it is for all state schools.

Law No. 444 of 1968, establishing the new system, provides for its finance as follows:

> The expenditure consequent on the initial application of this law shall be charged to the funds provided for the establishment and management of state pre-primary schools under Article 31 of the law of 24th July, 1962, No. 1073, and Article 2 of the law of 13th July, 1965, No. 874, and for kindergartens, to the appropriations in the budget of the Ministry of Education.
>
> For the establishment of new state pre-primary school sections, the appropriations for this purpose in the 1966 expenditure budget of the Ministry of Education shall be increased by the following sums for the years 1966 to 1970:

1966	lire 1370 million
1967	lire 4300 million
1968	lire 5900 million
1969	lire 7640 million
1970	lire 9300 million

> A sum equal to 12% of the annual appropriations shall be made available to the scholastic foundations as a grant for assistance to needy pupils.
>
> The distribution of the sums indicated in the second paragraph among the provinces shall be effected annually by decree of the Minister of Education, having regard to the number of pupils attending the state pre-primary school and the socioeconomic conditions of the particular provinces.
>
> The annual appropriation established in the second paragraph of Article 31 of the law of 24th July, 1962, No. 1073, for grants, subsidies, etc. to nonState pre-primary schools, which, in the conditions provided therein, receive economically disadvantaged pupils, shall be increased by the following sums for the years 1966 to 1970:

1966	lire 1500 million
1967	lire 5300 million
1968	lire 7300 million
1969	lire 9370 million
1970	lire 11400 million

> Preprimary schools managed by independent territorial agencies and communal assistance agencies shall be allotted the following sums from the total annual appropriations resulting from the provisions of the preceding paragraph:[3]

[3] OECD. *Economic survey.* 1972.

1966	lire 900 million
1967	lire 1850 million
1968	lire 2250 million
1969	lire 2750 million
1970	lire 3250 million

The reader should recall an earlier statement that as early as 1962, a law was passed to provide for publicly maintained preprimary schools; Parliament, however, never voted any money to implement it. The sums of money referred to in the preceding quotation were reimbursements to town governments or to the private sector for money spent earlier on preschool programs.

These provisions clearly indicate that those children and regions that need financial help most shall receive the largest proportion of the new funds. The act, however, also offers assistance to the less needy and to preschools in the private sector.

As Table 8.7 shows, in 1965-1966 the first state appropriations were made to preschool education in the amount of 4 billion, 295 million lire. By 1970-1971, this had grown to 27 billion, 824 million lire. It is important to note, however, that from 1965-1966 to 1967-1968 the money appropriated was not spent on state preschools because they did not exist. It was given instead to support communal and private schools. In 1968-1969, the appropriations rose very rapidly and more money was given to the private than the public sector. For this year, the figures in the table are estimates. The increase in spending on the public sector over the years 1965-1966 to 1970-1971 was 224%, against a total percentage of expenditures increase of 548%.

Data on per pupil costs for both public and private preschools in Italy are presented in Table 8.8. There are no reliable figures for the year 1965-1966. For 1970-1971, in the public sector, the average cost of educating a child in preschool was $168. In the private sector, we have *estimated* that the cost was $90. This estimate was made on the basis of the private schools having approximately 54% higher enrollments than the public ones. The $90, therefore, represents 54% of $168. The assumption may be made that the basic current expenditures in the private preschools were very similar to those in the public sector; but whether this is true is unknown. If $90 is a correct figure, the total current expenditures in 1970-1971 in the private sector would be approximately $135 million, but, for the reasons given, this can only be a tentative figure.

The comparable cost for state-organized primary education in Italy in 1970-1971 was $203 per pupil. This compares with the $168 per pupil cost that this report has suggested it takes to operate a state preschool. There is great local variation in preschool cost data; however, in Brescia, it costs about $265 a year to run a state preschool. A private Montessori *"casa dei bambini,"* run by the Bank of Italy, costs $166 a month per child. It is stressed, therefore, that the

TABLE 8.7

Scuola Materna Expenditure in Italy from 1965–66 to 1970–71
(State contribution only)

Year	Private		Public		L'000,000 Current Total	$'000 Current Total
	Capital	Current	Capital	Current		
1965–66	n.a.[a]	n.a.	n.a.	4,295	4,295	6,878[b]
1966–67	n.a.	n.a.	n.a.	4,295	4,295	6,878
1967–68	n.a.	n.a.	n.a.	4,295	4,295	6,878
1968–69	n.a.	11,305(E)	n.a.	11,000(E)	21,305	34,177
1969–70	n.a.	13,900	n.a.	11,095	24,995	39,840
1970–71	n.a.	13,900	n.a.	13,924	27,824	44,413
% of increase from 1965–66 to 1970–71				224	548	546

Source: Republic of Italy, Ministry of Public Instruction – Report of the Educational
Movement 1965–66, 1967–68, 1969–70, and 1970–71.

[a] Not available.

[b] Official exchange rates, O.E.C.D.
(E) Estimated.

TABLE 8.8
Scuola Materna Per-Pupil Costs in U.S. Dollars from 1965–66 to 1970–71

	Private								
Year	Current Expend. '000	No. of Children '000	Per Pupil Cost	Current Expend. '000	No. of Children '000	Per Pupil Cost	Current Expend. '000	No. of Children '000	Per Pupil Cost
1965–66		1,365						1,365	
1970–71	134,640 (E)	1,496	90(E)	22,225	134	168	168,875 (E)	1,630	104(E)

(E) Estimated.

generalized figures given here for both the state (public) and the private sectors should be regarded with great caution.

INSTRUCTIONAL METHODS

There was no single method of instruction used in Italian preschools before 1968. As La Morgia (1970) has pointed out, the name taken by a preschool often indicates the methods it employs.

> The name of the school varies according to its guiding principles: children's homes (*asili infantili*), kindergarten (*giardini d'infantini*), creches (*case dei bambini*), and nursery schools (*scuole materne*). The name also changes according to methods of teaching. There are for example Ferranti Aporti Schools, Froebel Schools, Montessori Schools, and schools named after the Sisters Rosa and Carolina Agazzi. Whatever the name, however, to obtain state recognition as "schools of preparatory status,"[4] they must conform to the following requirements: Their teaching staff must be qualified and must be appointed with the approval of the "*provveditore agli studi*"; they must teach in accordance with the "General Principles of Preparatory Education"; rooms and equipment must conform to current regulations from the point of view both of teaching and hygiene [p. 92].

This well illustrates the wide variety of the preschools and the variation between their instructional methods. As already made clear, until 1968 all preschools were organized by either municipalities or private bodies, and the state had very little influence over their instructional methods. Act No. 444 of 1968, however, states unequivocally that one of the major purposes of the new preschools is to prepare children for the compulsory primary schools. This would seem immediately to bring the state into the area of instructional methodology, particularly in view of the concern felt about illiteracy.

The Agazzi method of instruction (named after the sisters Rosa and Carolina Agazzi, who evolved it under the guidance of Pietro Pasquali) was applied experimentally in Mompiano in the province of Brescia from 1896-1900. By 1902, it had gained official recognition and became the "Italian method" for preschool education, spreading gradually to all such schools. The method originated in the need—keenly felt—to reform the Aporti and Froebel kindergartens, which had become too oriented toward primary schools. It purported, therefore, to offer a correct interpretation of Aporti's and Froebel's ideas. Thus, the Agazzi preschools were based on the conception of spontaneous activity and the child's personality being allowed to develop, not by listening to the teacher's lessons and repeating them, but by his being able to see and discover for himself the world around him, to reason, to control his instincts and impulses, to move

---

[4] With Act No. 444, all Italian infant institutions became "*scuole materne*" and all have been required to apply the "guidelines."

freely in his social environment and in a spirit of collaboration. In this, "playing" and "doing" are inseparable. The essential starting-point is the family.

To achieve all this, the Agazzi method looks for objects of the natural environment, which need not be perfect and prearranged, but must belong to and reflect the practicalities of everyday life. Contact with reality should lead the child to think about and comprehend the structure and rationality of things and gradually understand their meaning and value. This involves providing him with a stimulating situation in which his sense perception starts with things and only afterwards extends gradually to qualities and forms. In this environment, the child must move freely, but freedom is understood as the discovery of his own dignity and awareness and the value of his own personality and that of others. The aim is therefore integral education, making the child healthy, good, thoughtful, industrious, well behaved, useful to himself and to others.

A constant preoccupation of the Agazzi method is order. As a means of ensuring this, "countersigns" are introduced. All the child's personal objects are identified by an image of his own choice, which will become for him a topic of conversation and learning. In addition to the countersigns, the "didactic museum" provides the child with material for investigation. This is a museum of the poor, a museum of humble things, composed of the objects that children treasure (and that come out of their pockets), things that a child can look at, touch, recognize, distinguish, and enumerate. These humble things can be used for all exercises in sensory development; distinguishing qualities, colors, contrasts; recognizing forms, material, size, and graduation. This will lead on, with the spoken language, to the whole linguistic aesthetic education. This concept of harmony and order includes musical education—singing or rhythmics—which receives a great deal of attention in the method, as does "doing"—or working—though it should always be remembered that the exercises are not ends in themselves, but merely serve to promote abilities and prepare for life. The background of all activity is moral and social education. So, in a poor school and with scant resources, a clever teacher can find ways to provide a very adequate educational experience for the young child.

About 86% of the preschool teachers in Italy presently follow the Agazzi method and only 6% the methods of Maria Montessori. This is because the Agazzi method is based upon studies of average children, not special ones, and it does not require the detailed preparation necessary in the Montessori system.

Nevertheless, Maria Montessori, the first woman physician in Italy, is their best known educator of young children. Her interest in the subject was first aroused by the lack of progress made by mentally retarded children who were brought to the clinic where she worked: Clearly a more adequate technique was required for teaching them. After studying the work of Sequin, who had been concerned with teaching basic discrimination skills to retarded children, she began to develop methods of her own, as a result of which retarded children were seen to make progress that no one hitherto had believed possible. As a result of this work, Montessori was given responsibility for directing the education of slum children in Rome. Here she set up her now famous House of Children (*Case dei Bambini*) where she continued her research and began to write extensively on instructional methodology for very young children.

The Montessori method has by now been so widely recommended that no more than a very brief review of it appears necessary in this report.

According to Montessori herself (1964), her "method has for its base the liberty of the child, and liberty is activity." She, therefore, devised activities for the child that would be self-selected and self-directed, using a "prepared environment," scaled physically and conceptually for maximum relevance to his world. In this, the child is free to move and to choose spontaneously what he will do, so long as he does not infringe on the rights of others. He can work at his own rate, sometimes concentrating on tasks for considerable lengths of time. The didactic materials have build-in "steps" and feedback mechanisms to enable the child to correct his own errors and hence learn to develop his skills by himself.

These early activities are planned to perform three stages of education: motor, sensory, and linguistic. The approach is that the acquisition of knowledge begins with the development and refinement of motor perceptual skills, the execution of common motor activities (for example, sweeping, washing, watering plants, buttoning, lacing, using scissors) providing an important part of the sensorimotor base necessary for the development of more complex learning. They educate themselves through the use of elaborate didactic materials designed to develop sensory discrimination skills and concepts of form, size, color, weight, temperature, and texture. Language education is based on auditory discrimination acquired during sensory education. It passes through three phases (naming, recognition, and pronunciation), and teaches the child to respond to sets of cues.

The motor, sensory, and language exercises are preparatory to academic learning, where a multisensory approach, similar to that advocated for the education of children with learning disabilities, is used. In reading, for example, the child begins by tracing sandpaper letters and sounding them and then progresses to the construction of words with large letters from a movable alphabet.

The Montessori method is designed to foster the development of certain desirable traits. Self-confidence results from the sense of competence acquired through mastery over error. Spontaneity is developed by the free choice of learning activities and by liberty within limits. Built into the didactic activities themselves are habits of work and order, persistence and discipline. Exercises are designed to teach the child to help himself promote self-reliance and independence. The direct feedback methods built into the didactic materials permit the development of the "whole child," the ultimate aim of Montessori.

But the Montessori method has had many critics. Miezitis (1971), for example, lists four of its commonly judged weaknesses. These are failures to provide: (*1*) opportunities for the expression of fantasy in representational and motor play—

viewed by some as necessary vehicles for emotional development; (2) small-group interaction and cooperative activities to promote social awareness; (3) work with unstructured, open-ended play materials to promote freedom of self-expression, which is regarded as a prerequisite for the development of creative problem-solving abilities; (4) verbal interaction with peers and teachers to promote language development.

The fourth of those failures is particularly germane in Italy where we have seen that the upgrading of literacy is a matter of high priority. In this matter of language facility, Karnes (1969) has shown that disadvantaged children in the United States instructed by the Montessori method made less progress than some other experimental groups and, in fact, regressed in the first year of the program. This, she believes, was caused by the children spending a great deal of time on manipulative skills and in working with things but very little talking with the teacher or with other children. There was, therefore, no real means by which they could improve their facility with language. This is an important finding, and one that has possibly been taken into account in Italy, in terms of the low pupil-teacher ratio in the new state nursery schools compared with the pre-schools in the private sector.

RESEARCH ON EARLY CHILDHOOD EDUCATION

The focus for early childhood education in Italy is the *Centro Didattico Nazionale per la Scuola Materna,* founded in Brescia in 1950. It is headed by Professor Aldo Agazzi and directed by Professor Franco Tadini. Its original charter assigned to it seven specific tasks:

1. To initiate pedagogical studies in preschool education.
2. To promote and guide experimental research that will help preschools prepare children for entry to the primary schools.
3. To study the present state of the art of preschool education in Italy, and to make recommendations to the ministry for its improvement.
4. To keep parents, teachers, and educational administrators aware of the importance of preschool education.
5. To organize a center concerned primarily with preschool education, and, through this, to provide courses for teachers and administrators to assist them in perfecting the methods they use; these should include visits to experimental schools.
6. To promote meetings between parents and preschool teachers to facilitate understanding of the child's problems on transition from home to school, and of the objectives of the preschool itself.
7. To create an understanding of the particular role of the preschool by publishing material relevant to teachers and to parents about the education of young children, both in Italy and elsewhere.

In 1970, the National Center published a book entitled *1950-1970—Venti Anni di Attivita* (20 years of activities), which documents the evolution of the National Center under the direction of Professors Agazzi and Tadini. They have developed a fine research institution producing a number of journals that abstract research findings for teachers and administrators. The center is also used to organize meetings of people responsible for the administration of preschool education in Italy. Together with these preschool administrators, the center has identified problem areas which need further research. These studies are then published as books and distributed throughout Italy.

A representative sample of the types of project on which the National Center has worked is the following:

From the preschool to the elementary school
The functions and directions of the preschool
Building and constructing preschools
The preschool and the community
Musical education in preschool
The problems of administering a preschool
Personality development in young children
The place of play in the preschools
Intellectual education in the preschools
Pedagogical methods for preschool education
Individualization of education in the preschools
The aims and objectives of preschool education (a study done in preparation for the new state preschools)

Educational research other than that carried out by the National Center is done almost exclusively in university departments of education and psychology.

Parisi (1969), studying "the sociocultural influences on language abilities at the beginning of school education," identified some aspects of language deficiencies of Italian children who are about to enter first grade. Three substudies were undertaken.

The first of these concerned syntactic comprehension as it develops in 3- to 6-year-olds as a function of sex and socioeconomic level. The comprehension of the syntactic structure of sentences was evaluated by using a test developed by Parisi and Pizzimiglio (1969), administered in three kindergarten schools. In the first school, parents belonged to the clerical, teaching, or professional class; the second school was in a working class district; and the third was at an intermediate level between these two. The results showed that syntactic comprehension increases regularly throughout the age range studied. Sex is not an important factor in determining differences in this ability. Parents' occupation has a clear influence on the child's ability to understand the syntactic structures of sentences; however, when entering preschool at the age of 3, children from different socioeconomic settings possess this particular ability more or less equally. Between 4 and 6 years of age, the effects of the socioeconomic variables begin to be seen. Thus, the authors conclude that when entering preschool the disadvantaged child has linguistic potential not revealed in his speech, and this is doomed to atrophy if not adequately developed.

In the second substudy, a test of syntactic comprehension was administered to two groups of children of high and low socioeconomic level attending the same preschool in the same class. The effect of environment was controlled. The results showed that the syntactic comprehension deficiencies of children who are socially disadvantaged and who attend socially homogeneous schools can be attributed partly to their family background and partly to the quality of the educational experiences to which they are exposed (that is, the teaching in the preschool). Language deficiencies could be partially eliminated, therefore, by acting on both of these factors.

In the third substudy, two groups of 5-year-old children were examined for differences in language production. They had attended socially homogeneous preschools but were of high and low socioeconomic level. A sample of spoken language was recorded for each of these children and 10 variables were considered. Evaluation of this material indicated that the socially disadvantaged children were deficient in comparison with those from better backgrounds. The most obvious differences in the use of language appeared in direct and indirect speech, in the choice of words, in different contexts, and in the use of subordinate clauses. In summarizing, the finding of this study was that socially disadvantaged children begin elementary school with serious deficiences in many aspects of their language ability, but that preschool experience can be of real help in making up for them.

Andreani and Cavallini (1970) are conducting a 4-year study (1968-1972) into (1) causes of underachievement of disadvantaged children of ages 6 and 7, and (2) pedagogical intervention to overcome such causes. Their areas of enquiry include:

1. Study of the environmental factors (family, status) that affect the intelligence.
2. Study of environmental factors that have an influence on the formation of personality traits and the socialization process.
3. The relationship between social class and language skill.
4. The typical profile of the underachievers compared with the normal and overachievers.
5. A definition of techniques of intervention to rehabilitate the underachievers.
6. Experimentation with such techniques.

Among the results of the first phase of this research program are that scores on intelligence tests rise with social class (mean score of the low social level: 95; on the higher level: 109), and that the difference increases on tests of scholastic progress (from 89 to 112). Consequently, the underachievers prevail in the lower classes, and the overachievers in the higher classes.

Linguistic skill correlates with social class more in writing than in speech. Social class also had an effect on reading skills, in particular speed and comprehension. Strong anxiety, expressed by aggressiveness toward teachers, parents, and schoolmates, and by a sense of guilt, is experienced by boys as a result of too rigid and selective a method of teaching. In this respect, overachievers and normal achievers are more agressive toward teachers and other adults, while underachievers are more agressive toward schoolmates and more anxious about what their parents will think.

Overachievement, the study found, is linked to status values and creates neurotic tensions. Underachievement is provoked by cultural disadvantage in the lower class, where it creates emotional disturbance; in the middle and upper classes, it is often the result of pre-existing emotional factors. Judgement by the teachers on the basis of social class increases scholastic difficulties for pupils already at a disadvantage. Other findings include the influence of parents on the child's emotional maturity, and the influences of the father's cultural level, size of the family, and order of birth on intelligence and ability to improve.

In the light of the results of phase one, this research study has been modified and continues. It will follow those children who are now 7 and in second grade, who were in first grade during phase one, and will concentrate on teaching methods and didactic aids.

In the Institute of Psychology, University of Pavia, research has been carried out to identify the factors that influence school achievement and maladjustment, with the view of trying out intervention methods to prevent the effects of cultural deprivation in early childhood. The program developed in a series of sequential phases, using a sample of 2565 primary school children. The research has dealt particularly with the relationship between social and intellectual abilities of pupils and the relationship between social class and personality traits.

The results obtained confirm those of other similar investigations. They document the important influences of social and family conditions on the development of abilities and personality traits that underlie achievement at school. On the basis of these findings the authors suggest that underachievers are characterized by an actual maladjustment and overachievers by a potential one. They point out that educators must realize that when they focus attention on achievement (as usually occurs in schools) there is the risk of increasing the emotional troubles that characterize both groups of children. If, however, the acquisition and the development of the basic skills are disregarded, there is the risk that the children will drop out or fall into greater difficulties when they move into higher school levels. This is what usually happens with underachievers. The solution suggested for this dilemma is an intervention by the teacher to foster intellectual curiosity in children who suffer from cultural deprivation.

The Institute of Education in the University of Florence has planned a research project on the study of foreign languages by children from 4 to 8 years old. The preliminary work has involved identifying hypotheses to be tested from both linguistic and psychopedagogical points of view.

Other research includes a study being conducted by Rumi and Gualco (1970) concerned with the smooth transfer of young children from home to school. This is concerned particularly with the community environment, the role of the parents, and the personality of the teacher. No results are yet available.

From this brief review of research four points in particular stand out:

1. Preschool is clearly seen as a preparation for primary school entrance; therefore, research should be directed at providing optimal preparation.
2. The development of language competence is highly correlated with socio-cultural background. Carefully planned preschool programs can help over-come some language deficiencies.
3. Children who come from economically disadvantaged homes are often prejudged by teachers to be less intellectually competent than their more affluent peers. Because the teachers then proceed to treat these children as if what they thought to be true was true, it becomes a self-fulfilling prophecy.
4. The early involvement of the parents in the child's education is very important, and schools should do all they can to encourage it.

ACKNOWLEDGMENTS

The author wishes to acknowledge the valuable help received from: Dr. F. Tadini, Director, *Centro Didattico Nazionale per la Scuola Materna*; Prof. A. Visalberghi, *Facolta di Lettere,* University of Rome; G. Losavio, Ministry of Education (*Scuola Materna*); D. Carusi, Provveditorata, Rome; M. Jervolino, President, Italian Section, *Organization Mondiale pour l'Education Prescolaire,* and Director, Maria Montessori Teacher Training Institute; M. Palocci, teacher, Maria Montessori Teacher Training Institute.

BIBLIOGRAPHY

Andreani & Cavallini. *Summary of the research and experimentation carried out in the primary school.* Associazone per la ricerca sperimentale sui problemi dei giovani. Milan, 1970.

Austin, G. *A report on preschool and elementary education efforts in six European countries.* Stencil—unpublished. OECD, 1972.

Borghi, L. (Ed.). *Primary education in Europe in the year 2000.* European Cultural Foundation, 1970. SC/1(71)16.

Evans, E. D. *Contemporary influences in early childhood education.* New York: Holt, Rinehart & Winston, 1971.

Gozzer, G., Ministero della Pubblica Istruzione. Personal communication, 1971.

Karnes, M. *Research and development project on preschool disadvantaged children.* US Office of Education, Washington, D.C., 1969.

Laeng, M. Symposium sur "l'education prescolaire-objectifs, methodes et problemes." Venise 11-16 octobre 1971, Conseil de l'Europe, DESC/EGT (71) (106).

La Morgia, V. In Schultze (Ed.), *Schools in Europe.* Weinheim: J. Beltz Verlag, 1970.

Miezitis, S. The Montessori Method: Some Recent Research. *Interchange, 2*(2). The Ontario Institute for Studies in Education. 1971.

Montessori, M. *The Montessori Method.* New York: Bentley, 1964.

Orlando, D. *Pedagogia dell'infanzia e scuola materna Brescia.* Ed. La Scuola, 1970. (Collana "Infanzia e Educazione").

Parisi, D. *Sociocultural influences on language abilities at the beginning of school education.* Estratto da: Giornate Internazionali di Sociolinguistica, Roma 15-17 Settembre 1969.

Parisi, D., & Pizzamiglio, L. *Svilupp della comprensione sintattica dai 3 ai 6 anni in funzione del livello socioeconomico.* Istituto di psicologia del CNR, 1969.

Rumi, M, & Gualco, S. *Il banbino e la scuola materna–Torino.* SEI, 1970.

Schultze, W. *Schools in Europe* (Vol. 3). Weinheim: J. Beltz Verlag, 1968.

Trouillet, B. *Die Vorschulerziehung in neun Europäischen Ländern.* Weinheim: J. Beltz Verlag, 1968.

Centro Didattico Nazionale per La Scuola Materna. *Venti anni di attivita: 1950-1970.* Brescia, 1970.

Annuario Statistico dell'instruzione Italiana, 1970.

Centro Didattico Nazionale per la Scuola Materna. *Orientamenti dell'attivita educativa nelle scuole materne statali.* DPR 10 Settembre 1969, no. 647.

Comitato Italiano OMEP. *Educazione prescolastica e regione, Legga.* 6 Dicembre 1971, no. 1044.

Council of Europe: September 30, 1971. Stencil.

Council of Europe: September 1, 1971. Stencil.

Council of Cultural Cooperation: Council of Europe. *Education in Europe–School Systems, A Guide.* Strasbourg, 1970.

International Federation of Teachers' Associations (IFTA) 38th Congress of Helsinki, Preschool Education, 1969.

Young Italians who go to school are not all necessarily getting educated. *International Herald Tribune,* November 4-5, 1972.

Law of March 18, 1968, No. 444: on the organization of preprimary schools.

Newsletter, Council of Europe, Documentation Center for Education in Europe. May, 1971, and June, 1971.

Ministry of Public Education. *The educational movement in 1967-68.* Submitted to the XXXIth International Conference on Public Education, Geneva. July, 1968.

Ministry of Public Education. *The educational movement in 1969-1970.* Submitted to the XXXIInd International Conference on Education, Geneva. July, 1970.

Ministry of Public Education. *The educational movement in 1970-71.* Submitted to the XXXIIIrd International Conference on Education, Geneva. September, 1971.

OECD. *Classification of educational systems.* Paris, 1972.

OECD. *Labor force statistics, 1959-1970.* Paris, 1972.

OECD. *Reviews of national policies for education: Italy.* Paris, 1969.

OECD. *The Mediterranean regional project, country reports, Italy.* Paris, 1965.

UNESCO. *La formation et la condition professionnelle du personnel enseignant prescolaire.* Decembre 1965.

UNESCO. *World survey of education II, primary education.* 1958.

UNESCO. *World Survey of Education, educational policy, legislation and administration* (Vol. 5). 1971.

United Nations demographic yearbook. 1970.

Early Childhood Education in Belgium

INTRODUCTION

In 1832, 2 years after Belgium's declaration of independence, Minister Lesbroussart invited local authorities to start *garderies* for small children. Since 1825, there had been some such institutions (that is, *salles d'asiles*) in the country, but these were privately run. Lesbroussart's appeal had little result, however, and by 1845 only 17 out of a total of 394 *garderies* in Belgium were publicly managed.

By about 1850, when notice was being taken of Froebel's teaching, the idea began to gain acceptance that *garderies* should not only be places where small children were looked after but also where they should receive their first instruction. This idea received official acceptance in 1879, when a law was passed empowering the state to require a community to annex a preprimary section to an existing primary school.

The first general directives for early childhood education were given in a circular issued in September, 1880. In 1884, new school rules established that preschool education was the responsibility of the local authorities. At this point, initiative on the part of central government ceased.

In 1921, a royal decree established preschools at Bruges, Laken, Brussels, and

Liège. At first, the children attended for 2 years. In 1926, the preschool was expanded to 3 years of education. During this time, a profound development was taking place based on research in psychology and pedagogy. The methods and ideas of Froebel were replaced by the teaching of Maria Montessori. This led, through a ministerial *arrêté* of June, 1927, to the creation of a new program replacing the general directives of August, 1890.

The structure and methods employed over the last 20 years in Belgian preschools (*écoles gardiennes* or *kleuterschool,* according to the language preferred) derive most largely from the work of the eminent educationalist, Ovide Decroly. Dr. Decroly's work is the basis for most of the organization and instructional methods used in the Belgian preschools. An organization was created in 1965 to further his ideas. In 1970, a commission on preschool reform was appointed, and expected to report in 1973.

ENROLLMENTS, PRESCHOOL EDUCATION (1960-1970)

The Belgian population consists of French-speaking and Dutch-speaking communities. This distinction is recognized in the provision of early childhood education. Of the children who attend preprimary school, 61% go to the *kleuterscholen* (Dutch), and 38% to the *ecoles maternelles* (French).

Early childhood education in Belguim takes the form of instruction given in preschools or in classes attached to primary schools. These preschools admit children from 2.5 years of age on September 1, up to the beginning of primary education. This results in a study period of normally 3 years, which may occasionally extend to 4.

Table 9.1 presents public and private preprimary enrollments for the 10 years 1960-1961 to 1970-1971. The percentage of increase over this period shows that schools classified as public have grown much more rapidly than those classified as private. Over the 10 years there has been a 13.1% increase in total enrollments. Points of interest are: first, that in the private sector there was the beginning of a decline in the number of children attending in 1968 (a similar decline in the total population became apparent in 1969); second, in 1960, as in 1970, the majority of children attended private schools; third, the ratio of attendance is changing (in 1960, 65 of every 100 children went to a private school; in 1970 this ratio had dropped to 59 to 100), and fourth, the 13.1% increase in enrollments in preschool may be compared with the 11% increase in primary school enrollments over the same period of time.

Table 9.2 presents population attendance rates in the preschools for the 10-year period 1960-1961 to 1970-1971. It shows that in 1960-1961, 90.1% of the children in the age group 3-5 were attending. In 1970-1971, this had risen to 103.9%. This percentage exceeds 100, because children of age 2.5 years may in fact be enrolled, whereas the population statistics do not take into account any

TABLE 9.1

Enrollments in Pre-Schools in Belgium from 1960-61 to 1970-71

			(in 000's)
Year	Private	Public	Total
1960-61	265	140	405
1965-66	278	166	444
1966-67	280	174	‚454
1967-68	280	180	460
1968-69	n.a.[a]	n.a.	n.a.
1969-70	278	187	465
1970-71	270	188	458
% of increase from 1960-61 to 1970-71	01.9	34.3	13.1

Source: Belgian Ministry of Education and French Culture, Central
Administration, Programming and Information, Brussels.

[a] Not available.

children under the age of 3. It will be noticed that there was a slight decline (1.3%) in the infant population between 3 and 5 years of age over the 10-year period. This is reflected in the decreasing number of children enrolled in the preschool previously mentioned. This decline in the population, together with the increase in the number of children attending preschool, gives a 15.3% overall increase in the age group enrolled in the preschools during the 10-year period.

TABLE 9.2

Population Attendance Rates in Pre-Schools in Belgium from 1960-61 to 1970-71

			(in 000's)
	1960-61	1970-71	% of Change
Total age group 3 - 5 years in pre-school	405	458	13.1
Infant population 3 - 5 years	447	441	-01.3
% of age group enrolled	90.1	103.9	15.3

Source: United Nations Demographic Yearbook, 1970.

According to the *"Evolution de la population scolaire"* (1968), the percentage of attendance by age group for the 10-year period 1960-1970 is as follows:

Age	1960	1965	1970
5	99%	99%	100%
4	93	95	95
3	81	86	90

In 1971-1972, the Belgian ministries of education provided more extensive information on the percentage of pupils in attendance by single year and by age group:

Age		Age	
6	99%	5-6	99%
5	99	4-6	99
4	94	3-6	96
3	90	2-6	80
2	15		

As already estimated, these figures confirm that nearly 100% of the children between 3 and 5 were enrolled in Belgian preschools in the year 1970. The exact figure is 95.6%.

As in other countries, there seems to be a correlation in Belgium between the increased use of preschools and a decrease in family size and gross reproduction rate. According to "Projections of Households and Family Size," prepared by the United Nations Secretariat (1971), the average household size in Belgium in 1846 was 4.87; in 1961 it had decreased to 3, a drop of 1.87 over the 115-year period. The gross reproduction rate in 1900 was 1.9 per thousand. In 1961 it had declined to 1.3, a decrease of 6 per thousand, or 31.6%. According to the United Nations Demographic Yearbook (1970), there were 1.2 fewer live births per 1000 population in 1970 than in 1966. This indicates that the downward trend is continuing.

Trouillet (1967) suggests that the high enrollments in preschools in Belguim are the result of certain aspects of the national life, particularly the relative number of women who go out to work and the large number of schools available. Table 9.3 presents OECD's "Labor Force Statistics" (1972), which confirm that, over the last 10 years, participation of women in the labor force has increased, whereas the male participation has declined.

ISSUES OF DEBATE

The parents' freedom of choice in selecting a school for his child has long been an important issue of debate in Belgium. The problem, hopefully, was solved

TABLE 9.3
Labor Force Participation Rates – Belgium

	1960 %	1970 %
Total Labor Force / Total Population × 100		
(a) Total	40.1	40.5
(b) Males	57.7	56.0
(c) Females	23.2	25.6
Total Labor Force / Population from 15 to 64 years × 100		
(a) Total	62.2	63.6
(b) Males	88.5	87.0
(c) Females	36.4	40.3

Source: Labor Force Statistics, 1959-70, O.E.C.D., Paris, 1972.

when the School Pact of November 20, 1958, was signed by the three principal political parties. This promised a 12-year truce over the parents' rights and prerogatives, and the possibility of their exercising such selection. The major aim of the pact was to bring about a balance between the different school systems.

M. Coulon (1966) criticizes the structure of the three-parties commission supervising the pact by observing that:

> What is needed in the commission is qualified teachers to widen the horizons of the problems to be met . . . what is missing in national education is an operational, permanent advisory body (or a staff) of the ministry, capable of suggesting a fundamental, coherent educational strategy which would be acceptable to the various political parties [p. 27].

Vanbergen (1970), considering the happinesses and unhappinesses of pluralism, concludes that the discussion would be a better one if it were concerned with building on the strengths of pluralism rather than its divisiveness. The task, as he sees it, is to build toward "the society in which we wish to live tomorrow [p. 3]."

There is no dispute in Belgium over the amount of preschool education provided, except for children aged 2. Considerable pressure is now being placed on the Belgian educational school system to provide places for 2-year-olds. There are two opposing views about the desirability of this. A number of mothers and fathers want it, for a variety of reasons; others, however, question what kind of care may be provided for children of this age, and what may be the psychological consequences of their being in school for a relatively large part of the day. Attention to this aspect of the matter has been drawn recently by Berthoud (1972) in an article about Belgium in *The Times,* appropriately titled "A Place to Dump Kids All Day Long." In Belgium, he observed a growing tendency for parents to leave small children at school for practically the whole day (from before 8:00 in the morning to 6:00 or 7:00 in the evening is not uncommon). The schools, for their part, appear to feel a moral obligation to look after them once they have been left there. The problem is most acute in heavily industrialized areas where, for economic reasons, a high proportion of mothers go out to work. Among the remedies under consideration is the provision of facilities in or near the factory or the main housing areas. This would enable the mothers to spend at least some part of the day with their younger children.

Libotte-Loffet and Thirion (1971) are of the opinion that provision of the preschool to children under 3 is an irreversible tendency in Belgium. The important thing is not to deplore this tendency, but to take advantage of it and discover the optimal conditions for the young child's development.

In the matter of quality preschool education, De Landsheere (1967) points out its close dependence on teacher training and the need for this to be improved. He mentions that, in practice, preschool education is so difficult that it requires the highest level of training that can be provided. The training of teachers for preschools (as well as others) must, therefore, become the responsibility of universities and the institutes of education connected with them.

Writing in the same context, Libotte-Loffet (1972), President of the Belgian International Organization for Preschool Education, observes that the crucial step in teacher training is the selection of candidates for teacher training, which she believes to be procedurally weak. Other requirements to which she draws attention are: first, the need for greatly expanded in-service postgraduation training; second, improvement in the definition, the objectives, and methods of preschool education; and third, a change in attitude of preschool teachers from merely dispensing information to fostering the growth of education in young children. They can do this most effectively by using observational techniques followed by specific remedies for weaknesses thereby identified.

Mme. Libotte-Loffet goes on to raise a number of other issues of fundamental importance. The education of children between the ages of 18 months and 6 years she sees, not as a purely pedagogic matter, but something much wider in scope. To this end she advocates the development of preschools into what she calls child centers. These centers would serve both parents and children of the community and would provide such services as family planning, prenatal and postnatal physical examinations, and neighborhood libraries containing toys and games as well as books for children to borrow. These centers should be planned for and included in the building of modern apartment house complexes. The child's place in such a center would be, not a passive recipient of information, but someone actively interacting with his environment. The teacher's role would be to observe that interaction, to provide stimulation to the child that would ensure his maximal growth, to create a feeling of security, and to foster the concept of self-worth. This concept is now realized in some preschools in Belgium, and Mme. Libotte-Loffet further proposes that a commission should be formed to study the needs of the child and the family on a national scale, and in all relevant aspects, so that allowance may be made for them in the children's centers that are in the process of being created.

Two concepts in particular lie behind the development of education in Belgium: first, that it should have high priority in the national life; second, that it is important as a means for democratization. Derivière (1969), writing about young children, makes clear the national conviction that education develops the entire personality, helping to form the individual regardless of the social class from which he comes. A prerequisite for this is promotion of the intellectual potential of young people. In this approach, preschool education provides an important input that enables a smooth transition between the home and the formal schooling that will follow later.

There is, however, the further question of smooth transfer between the preprimary and the primary school. Most Belgian preschools are attached to primary schools, and it would seem reasonable to expect that this would provide for an easy transfer from one to the other. This assumption, however, is not confirmed by the facts. Statistics for 1968 show that 32.7% of the children in the French-speaking primary schools repeated at least the first year, as did 13.9% of the children in the Dutch-speaking schools.

In summary, the principal issues of debate in the matter of preschool education in Belgium at the present time appear to be the following:

1. Free choice of a child's school by his parents; costs to be paid by central, provincial, or local government.
2. Provision of education for children of 2 years of age, to meet the demand of parents.
3. Upgrading of preschool teacher training, both preservice and in-service.
4. Improving the quality of preschool education through more careful definition of its aims and methods.
5. Ensuring an effective transition between preprimary and primary schools.

THE AIMS AND OBJECTIVES OF EARLY CHILDHOOD EDUCATION

There are three guiding principles behind all education in Belgium (including preprimary). They are:

1. Complete freedom in the establishment of educational institutions. This was guaranteed by the law of 1831 and reaffirmed in the School Pact of 1958. Such freedom extends not only to the opening and conduct of schools, but to all pedagogical, psychological, and instructional matters as well.

2. Neutrality in education. This was prescribed by the law of 1959, based on the School Pact, which demands perfect objectivity in the presentation of facts and ideas and absolute respect for the different religious and philosophical convictions of pupils. The pupils may attend any school of their parents' choice.

3. Equality of culture. This is assumed by the Language of Instruction Act of July, 1963. In principle, teaching is done in the language of the region: French in the southern area, Dutch in the northern provinces, and German in the east. In the district of Brussels, which is officially bi-lingual, parents choose the language in which their children will be educated. There are no mixed classes.

Libotte-Loffet and Thirion (1971) indicate that since its creation the first objective of the preschool has apparently been to provide a functional education that would be an integral part of the child's early development. It should offer an easy introduction to school life for the child fresh from home and, later, facilitate his transfer to the primary school.

In more precise terms, the objectives and methods of the Belgian preschools were usefully summarized as follows for a meeting of the International Federation of Teachers' Associations, at Helsinki in 1969.

(1) Preschool education has as its final objective the physical, intellectual, emotional and social maturing of the child to permit him to enter the primary school with every possibility of success in an atmosphere of freedom and confidence.

(2) In order to carry out adequately their social task, nursery schools ought to be able to call upon a team of psychologists and medical and social help. This however, is not available.

(3.1) All the lessons in the nursery school have regard for the child's personality and seek to develop it to the maximum by encouraging creative effort by the child in every sphere: the intellectual (puppetry, dramatization, music), the physical (dances, games), the emotional (make-believe games) and the social (working in teams, rounds).

(3.2) The nursery school teacher takes note of the deficiencies and failings which she observed in the child's behaviour. She speaks about these to the mother when she brings her child to school and tries to induce her to collaborate with the school in setting right and correcting the faults that have been noticed.

At the end of the year in some nursery schools INIZAN aptitude tests are given to the children. The parents are then invited to a meeting at which the teacher explains the shortcomings revealed by the tests and ways to overcome them at home: language handicaps (dumbness of the child whose mother does not trouble to speak to him), babyish behaviour of the only child or of the last in a large family (emotionally disturbed children for whose sake the source of the disturbance must be traced).

(3.3) Pre-school education allocates an important place to education in language, to creative effort, orally or in writing, to correct and easy speech, and to the correction of errors by means of the study of picture books, oral composition, stories of walks, scenes made up by the children in the course of their puppetry and dramatisation lessons, the composition of little songs and poems.

Similar situations prevail in the natural sciences where the introduction to the subject is based on continued observation of plants and animals, followed by exercises in synthesis.

Writing is now introduced by means of rhythmic shapes, in addition to the usual manual exercises designed to make supple the hands [p. 61].

In 1958, and again in 1967, the International Organization for Preschool Education met in Belgium. Comparison of the topics discussed at those two seminars reveals a distinct change in emphasis over the 10-year period. In 1958, most of the topics discussed related to the traditional care-giving functions of preschool education, such as social, motor, and emotional development. The emphasis was on the preschool as an extension of the home and, hence, on good care-giving. The 1967 meeting, while it was still concerned with most of the things discussed in 1958, showed a distinct interest in the educational possibilities of preschools. What lay behind this was a growing conviction in Belgium that preschools, as well as providing an easy introduction to the world outside the home, should also prepare the child for entry into primary school. The 1958 meeting also gave a great deal more attention to the training of teachers and their special role in the preschool.

The Plan of Educational Activities in Preschool (1951) and the Plan des Écoles Libres Catholiques emphasize the importance of the maturational process.

Preschool is a maturation school. Its principal role consists of stimulating the development of the child's personality by giving him the possibility to explore his needs, to move, and to show an interest in other individuals and things around him. Thanks to an adequate school organization and an elaboration of a rich environment, preschool education is well adapted to the needs and interests of a child of 3 to 6 years of age. The teachers animate this environment and help the child to a better understanding of what he discovers and favors in his social adaptation. It is the task of the teacher to structure this environment in a functional way, enrich it regularly and exploit all the resources. The educational value of the school milieu is dependent on the imagination, the tact, and the professional ability of the teachers. The preschool provides happiness and security for the child. It is educative and makes the child acquire good habits, individual and social. It initiates his ability to cooperate and take responsibility. It teaches the child his language, to observe, and to use different techniques creatively and expressively. It develops his attention, memory, and skills, as well as his objective thinking, his understanding of numbers, place, time, and cause. It allows small children to live fully and intensively and at the same time gives them the possibility of reaching the maturity level for primary school education [p. 17].

Preschool education in Belgium should, therefore, be seen as education in its proper sense and not merely as a transition "care" period between home and primary school.

Parental involvement in preschools in Belgium is greatly encouraged since, particularly for the younger children, the preschools are seen more as an outward extension of home than a downward extension of "real" school. The International Federation of Teachers' Associations meeting (1969) suggests the following five ways by which cooperation is secured between the family and preschool:

(1) The quarter-hour's talk, morning and afternoon, with any mother who wishes it;

(2) Invitations to parents to take part in the activities of the school societies;

(3) Children's entertainments arranged by the friends of the school, distribution of presents as a welcome on enrollment to the school, as well as on St. Nicholas Day (for the Dutch-speaking) and at Christmas (for the French-speaking children). Easter eggs, children's dances, mothers' festivals, etc.

(4) By "Nursery school weeks" when educational subjects are discussed; e.g., introduction to arithmetic, to counting, to writing, the aims of the school society, the duties of the nursery school; and

(5) By monthly conferences "The Parents' School," where an educational topic e.g., the left-handed child—the child with speech defects—the only child—is dealt with by a specialist whose address is followed by a discussion [p. 62].

In 1970, a commission was appointed to study the problems of educating young children in the preschool. This is part of a much larger study embracing the entire preprimary, primary, and secondary educational systems in Belgium. This commission has produced a large number of documents dealing with different aspects of the subject. To illustrate its approach, one example may perhaps suffice. For mathematics, as treated in the document "Preschool Education, Mathematics Activities, Provisional Programs, 1972," the following objectives are proposed:

(1) to help the child organize his milieu, and contribute to the elaboration of his ideas of space, number, relationships, structure, time, and form . . . ;

(2) to help the child understand the existence, precision, economy, and beauty of a new method of expression: mathematical language in its graphic form;

(3) to awaken his curiosity and his taste for research by the practice of mathematical methods. This will be done by appealing to his curiosity and stimulating his own initiative to study mathematics further [p. 1].

Another instance of the seriousness with which Belgium is developing the preschool curriculum is a recent circular, No. 7/176, "Plans of Activities in the Pre-schools" (1951) issued by the Ministry of Education and Culture. Here, the recommended activities are developed in great detail for children of 3, 4, and 5 years of age. The circular discusses the educational milieu and how it should be set up, the importance of teachers' attitudes and the significance of games in the development of young children. The principal educational activities are listed with their objectives as follows: social and moral education; road safety education; education based on psychomotor development; health education and education through thought and language.

ORGANIZATION AND CONTROL

Schools in Belgium may be state-controlled, administered by the provincial or communal authorities, or run by private individuals. The great majority of private schools are Catholic, but there are also Protestant and Jewish institutions, and schools that are either nonreligious or uncommitted. The state subsidizes schools run by the provincial or communal authorities and by private individuals under the terms and procedures set forth in the Act of May 29, 1959. One of the terms of the act is that schools shall adopt the structure and syllabuses enforced in state schools or approved by the ministry (Vanbergen, 1972).

Therefore, education in Belgium is organized on a national basis. There are two ministries of education, one representing the Dutch part of Belgium, the other representing the French. There is a dual representation of each high administrative position. The ministries are separate but work together closely. They have similar but not identical structures. It is the private sector (primarily Roman Catholic), however, that administers the largest number of schools in Belgium. For this, it has a relatively complex and comprehensive administrative structure that can be thought of as a third "ministry of education."

In addition to these three administrations at national level, there are educational authorities at provincial and communal levels. Hence, there are four principal types of schools in Belgium: state, provincial, communal, and private. This same division of sponsorship applies to preschools, and the proportion of children who have been attending each type in the recent past is shown here:

Type of school	1960-61	1965-66	Percentage of change
State	6%	9%	3%
Provincial	0%	1%	1%
Communal	29%	25%	-4%
Private	65%	63%	-2%

As yet, no comparable data are available for 1970, but it appears that there is a mild decline in the number of children attending preschools in the private sector and an equivalent increase in the number attending those run by the state. These facts are borne out by the enrollment figures given in Table 9.1. It is important to note, however, that in 1965 as well as in 1970, the statistics indicate that a large majority (59%) of children are attending preschools privately sponsored (mainly Roman Catholic).

In line with the Decrees of May 15, 1928, July 18, 1946 and June 18, 1948, the Primary School Inspectorate was created. In each of the ministries of education, there is one inspector general for primary and preprimary schools, under whom are 25 chief inspectors and 166 cantonal (district) inspectors, who hitherto have also served for both preprimary and primary schools. In 1972, a change was made that will provide up to 14 cantonal inspectors who will be concerned solely with the preprimary level. For each part of the country, five cantonal inspectors inspect only preprimary schools. The cantonal inspector visits every school in his district at least twice a year. Once or twice a month he sends the reports on the classes he has visited to his chief inspector. The chief inspector visits every school under his authority at least once every second year. Every 3 years he submits a report on the state of the preprimary and primary schools to the inspector general. At least three times a year, he calls a meeting of his cantonal inspectors to insure unity of views and teaching procedures. Private educational sponsors have their own inspectors, while in certain large urban areas there are municipal inspectorates for all levels of school.

It was originally a matter for concern that cantonal inspectors were recruited from primary school teachers. It was felt that they were insufficiently sensitive to the issues and problems that face teachers attempting to educate children from 2.5 to 6 years old. The later creation of posts solely for the inspection of preprimary schools, however, may well relieve this uneasiness.

PHYSICAL SETTING: A VISIT TO AN ANGLEUR[1] KINDERGARTEN

The preschool visited was built in 1967 and was located in a high-rise apartment complex on the outskirts of the commune Angleur. It was designed, not only as a school but as a community center, by a group consisting of architects, teachers, and community representatives. The building itself was one story high and took the form of a ladder. One of the "legs" contained four classrooms: two for primary classes and two for preprimary. There were three cross-over passages, rungs as it were, to the other leg of the building, which contained a large gymnasium, the office of the principal, and several other rooms. The open spaces between the passages were used as a play area and contained a shallow pool and a number of devices where the children could climb, swing, or otherwise amuse themselves. The basement of the building housed the community medical consultant service.

The classrooms were approximately 25 feet by 25 feet. The one observed for most of the morning had 24 children registered. It contained four large tables, a large doll-playing area, easels, a sand table, many books and plants, three bird cages, and a number of tools, playthings, and modelling clay. The walls were

[1] Angleur is a town located near Liège, Belgium.

covered with examples of the children's work. The other preprimary room was equally well equipped.

The gymnasium was approximately 30 feet wide and 50 feet long and contained walking-beams, sand-filled bottles, blocks of a variety of sizes and shapes, and a large number of small mats on which the children might work or play.

The school opened at 9:00 o'clock in the morning. The time from 9:00 to 9:30 was permissive, and on the day of the visit was being used for greeting the children, talking about home and school, and then cutting out small cardboard coins to be used later in an instructional period. At 9:35, all of the children stood up and sang a few songs with the teacher, while some played simple musical instruments such as pipes and rhythm instruments. From 9:45 to 10:15, the class gathered around the large table with the teacher and started working on the week's project, which happened to be the need for roads in Ceylon. The children's paintings, made the previous day, depicted people in Ceylon building a road to an isolated mountain village. After examination, the discussion centered on the difficulty of doing this kind of work with only hand tools as opposed to the modern road-building equipment that is used in Belgium. At the sand-table some of the children were making their versions of the mountain road using models of trucks, heavy equipment, and working men. Discussion of the building of a road led the teacher easily to the subject of money. She first showed the children real Belgian coins and then used their milk money for counting. She then pursued the concept of 10 and the several different ways this could be arrived at with the coins they had. The children then handled the money themselves, being shown how to sort it in groups by size and value and how to count it properly. From 10:15 to 10:45, there was a break for milk and biscuits, either brought from home or purchased at the school. Afterwards came a visit to the gymnasium. The children played marching games, walked along the balancing beam, and ran around sand-filled bottles that had been set as an obstacle course. At 10:45, they went back to their classroom where they continued counting coins and examining their sizes and shapes.

Curriculum

A preschool teacher has many options he can exercise with the curriculum for his class. The host for this visit believed strongly in the project method, and all through the year she probably has three different continuing projects, some lasting a month, some a week, and others just a couple of days. She followed the ideas of Decroly closely. She provided the children with a wide variety of things to observe, touch, feel, and count; then, in her lessons, she associated them with whatever the children were presently doing, as exemplified by the monetary discussion. Later the children were encouraged to talk about the subject to show that they had understood it.

At this preschool considerable importance was attached to parental participation. During the first half hour of the morning and in the afternoon, parents were encouraged to talk with the teacher about problems they might be having with their children. They might stay if they wished, for a short time, to watch the children at play. There was also good communication between this teacher and her colleague in the primary school. In fact, on the day of this visit, a preschool class joined a primary school class across the courtyard where a lesson on traffic safety was in progress. She felt certain this cooperation helped the children in their transfers to the primary school.

Daily Schedule in a Belgian Preschool

Class aged 5

8:45 A.M. Duty roster, allocation of tasks. The various duties are then carried out by the children responsible for them, working in groups of 2 to 4.

9:00 A.M. Weather observation and report (state of the trees and the playground and reading of the outdoor temperature); introduction to arithmetic and to the concept of time (the calendar); illustrating the weather report and graphic representation of the temperature. At the end of the month: analysis of the previous 4 weeks.

9:30 A.M. Library—free exercises, followed by study of picture books, introduction to oral composition (books, pictures, slides, films).

10:00 A.M. Snack and recreation.

10:30 A.M. Improvised recitation: explanation of texts and memorisation.

10:45 A.M. Puppetry or dramatisation, revision of vocabulary learned in the verbal expression exercises at 9:30 A.M.

11:30 A.M. Routine chores, preparation for going home and for luncheon for those who are staying.

1:30 P.M. Practical activities—sewing, weaving of common articles for girls. Odd jobs of own choice for boys (joiner's workshop). In the summer when the weather is suitable, planting, looking after flower beds and kitchen garden, rearing small animals: rabbits, guineapigs.

2:30 P.M. Recreation.

3:00 P.M. Story hour or conversation about familiar topics.

3:20 P.M. Daily chores, tidying up, and preparations for going home.

TEACHERS AND THEIR TRAINING

As early as 1880, attention was being given to the training of teachers for Belgium. The first colleges to undertake this were in Brussels, Liège, Ghent, and Mons. Their courses were based on the teachings of Froebel and lasted 1 month, after which a teacher's certificate was granted. Provincial and private institutes were also allowed to give these certificates provided they were in accordance with state regulations. It was not until 1919, however, that specific preprimary certification became obligatory for teachers concerned at this level.

De Landsheere (1967), in an article on "The Necessity of Reform," makes these points in principle about teacher training:

(1) The nuclear civilization requires a new leap forward for education, the most important since it became obligatory;

(2) Reform of preschool teacher training is closely connected with general educational reform, as well as with the training of master teachers at all levels;

(3) The preschool teachers' tasks present such a degree of difficulty that we must not retreat from the equally difficult problems that arise in the course of their recruitment and training [p. 5].

In Professor De Landsheere's view, the way to provide this better kind of training is to make the training of all teachers (including preschool) the responsibility of the universities and their institutes of education. The seriousness with which training is regarded in Belgium is borne out by the certification requirements for preschool teachers being changed in 1971 to conform with those of primary school teachers. De Landsheere's suggested shift in the location of such training, however, has not as yet been inaugurated. Belgian primary and preprimary school teachers are still being trained in teacher training institutes, not in the universities.

In the new program adopted in 1971, the training of preschool and primary school teachers is almost identical. It consists of two cycles. The first is somewhat generalized, including studies of the mother-tongue, two foreign languages, history, mathematics, biology, hygiene, music, art, and gymnastics. Any candidates who obtained diplomas on leaving school at 18 are exempt from this part of the course. During the second cycle, which lasts 2 years, the courses are mainly concentrated on child psychology, pedagogy, and sociology. Practice teaching experience is required only for those intending to be preprimary teachers.

Table 9.4 gives an estimate of the number of teachers in preschools in Belgium between 1960-1961 and 1970-1971. It is interesting to note the much more rapid growth in the public sector than in the private sector over this 10-year period, with the growth in total number over the 10-year period being 42.9%. Some caution should be exercised in using this table, particularly in the public sector, since the figures are estimates and not the result of an exact count of teachers.

Table 9.5 presents the pupil-teacher ratio in preschool for the years 1960-1961, 1965-1966, and 1969-1970. Over this 10-year period the teacher-pupil ratio has dropped in both the public and the private sectors by about seven students per teacher. This fact is accounted for by the rapid growth in the number of preschool teachers (Table 9.4) and a slow increase in the number of enrollments (Table 9.1). Again, it should be noted that in the public and total columns in Table 9.5, two of the three figures are based upon estimates.

TABLE 9.4
Pre-School Teachers in Belgium from 1960-61 to 1970-71

Year	Private	Public	Total
1960-61	7,648	4,242[a]	11,890[a]
1965-66	9,438	6,087	15,525
1966-67	9,683	6,438	16,121
1967-68	9,544	6,666[a]	16,210[a]
1968-69	9,652	6,796[a]	16,448[a]
1969-70	9,788	7,204[a]	16,992[a]
1970-71	n.a.	n.a.	n.a.
% of increase from 1960-61 to 1969-70	28.0	70.0[a]	42.9[a]

Source: Belgium Ministry of Education and French Culture, Central
Administration, Programming and Information, Brussels.

[a]Estimated from available data.

The Royal Decree of October 27, 1966, set class sizes for nursery schools as follows: average of 20-30 pupils, one class; average of 31-60 pupils, two classes; average of 61-90 pupils, three classes, and so on for each succeeding 30 pupils. The class size of the preschool must not exceed 30 children. The decline of 7 children per classroom (Table 9.4) is a direct result of this legislation.

The pupil-teacher ratio in the primary schools of Belgium is: private sector— approximately 22:1; public sector—approximately 20:1. This has been quite stable over the 10-year period studied, thereby indicating that the Belgians have been putting more of their resources into the reduction of teacher-pupil ratio or class size in the preschool than they have in the primary school.

FINANCING EARLY CHILDHOOD EDUCATION

The financing of education in Belgium has had a somewhat difficult history. In 1954-1955, the Socialist Liberal government undertook an educational reform, and the resulting act, passed without the support of the Social Christian deputies, established the following principles:

1. Primary schools were to be built and maintained by the local authorities. Free primary schools, mostly Roman Catholic, but including some Protestant and other private schools, were to be organized by private bodies. Some municipalities subsidized free primary schools with heating, school meals, transportation, and added 10% to the salaries paid by the state.

2. Secondary and vocational schools were to be built and maintained by the state, the provinces, and the municipalities, or by independent (mostly Roman

TABLE 9.5
Pupil:Teacher Ratio in Belgian Pre-Schools from 1960-61 to 1970-71

Year	Private	Public	Total
1960-61	35:1	33:1[a]	34:1[a]
1965-66	29:1	27:1	29:1
1969-70	28:1	26:1[a]	27:1[a]

[a]Estimated from available data.

Catholic) organizations. Free and vocational schools were subsidized to a limited amount (3,000,000 Belgian francs in 1955-1956).

3. Teachers must possess the appropriate certificates and would be paid by the state.

4. Schools must observe the language regulations so that teaching could be done in French, Flemish, or German, according to region.

5. In both the state primary and secondary schools, parents should choose the denomination of religious instruction (Roman Catholic, Protestant, or Jewish) for their children. In 80% of the cases, the Roman Catholic faith, taught by priests, was preferred.

Differences between Roman Catholics and Socialists over matters of education continued until November, 1958, when a joint national committe drew up a final agreement (ratified May, 1959) under which tuition fees in all primary and secondary schools were abolished, and the state undertook to pay all teachers' salaries. The principle that parents could choose between state and free schools was maintained. Thus, under Belgian law, parents have the right to choose the education for their children and to expect the state to provide adequate finance for the schools of their choice.

The 24th article of this law (May 1959)[2] sets out the conditions governing state subsidies for education. Those affecting preschools are the following:

(a) To benefit from state subsidies, all preschools must conform with the law as concerns physical premises, curriculum, and management. They must also be subject to state inspection. The schools must be located in convenient places, and their organizing agency must provide necessary materials and equipment. All teachers must be Belgian citizens with the appropriate teaching certificate. They must not have been deprived of any of their civil and political liberties. They must be in sufficiently good health so as not to endanger that of their pupils.

(b) The state subsidizes the municipal, provincial, and free (private) schools directly by monthly payments to the teachers, in accordance with the Royal Decree of August 24, 1963. For preschools with two classes, there must be an average attendance of 31 children. For those with three classes, there must be an average of

[2] *L'éducation préscolaire en Belgique.* September, 1971.

61; for four classes there must be 91, and so on for each additional 30 children. The number of children counted is the average number present for a half-day during the first 30 calendar days from the opening of the school year. Children who are 2.5 years old are included as part of this average in an existing class, but they may not be counted to justify the creation of a new class. A special set of rules for receiving State subsidies was set up for minority classes in the two linguistic regions. In the ministerial circular of September 15, 1965, a minimum of 10 pupils per one preschool class is required in areas with less than 1000 inhabitants [p. 3].

The third article of the law of May, 1959, empowers the state to construct schools when it regards this as necessary. Additionally, it may subsidize the construction of schools managed by provinces or local authorities, but not in excess of 60% of the cost. Provinces and communes now also receive aid from the state for the modernization or re-equipment of schools. Maintenance grants are also given on a yearly basis for such items as heating and lighting.

The Belgian per capita gross national product in 1968 was $2670. According to the OECD Economic Survey (January, 1973), the 1969 per child expenditure on education was $4.97. At the preschool level, the subsidy for each child is 750 Belgian francs in addition to the teacher's salary. Additionally, 70 francs per child are provided to cover the cost of materials and books.

There are a very small number of private preschools in Belgium. These charge fees, receive no subsidies, and are not, therefore, subject to state regulations. They are essentially for the children of well-to-do parents.

It is not easy to single out data on preschool expenditures in Belgium, chiefly because money is allocated en bloc for the expenses of both primary and preprimary schools. Table 9.6 gives estimated figures based on information from the Belgian Ministry of Education and the University of Liège. This refers only to current expenditures (public sector) for the years 1960-1970, during which period current expenditures of the Belgian preschools increased by 167%.

There was about a 100% increase in per-pupil cost over the 10 years. Comparable per pupil expenditures for the primary school, also based on estimates, are: 1960-1961, $112; and 1970-1971, $272. In United States dollars, the total current expenditure for educating children in both public and private preschools in 1960 is estimated to have been $42,930,000, and in 1970-1971 it would have been $97,096,000, approximately a 127% increase. Again, it should be noted that these figures *should be used with extreme caution,* since they are based upon estimates and not upon hard factual data.

INSTRUCTIONAL METHODS

The instructional methods used in the preschools in Belgium have gone through three distinct phases. It is easiest to present them in chronological order. From 1890 until the mid-1920s, the methodology of Froebel was generally

TABLE 9.6

Pre-School Expenditure in Belgium from 1960-61 to 1970-71

Year	Public Current Expenditure		Number of Children	Per Pupil Cost $
Year	Belgian Francs	U.S. dollars		
1960-61	740[a]	14,840[a, b]	140	106[a]
1965-66	1,310[a]	26,394[a]	166	159[a]
1970-71	1,978[a]	39,856[a]	188	212[a]
% of increase from 1960-61 to 1970-71	167			
Total increase				106[a]

Source: Henry G., University of Liege.   (Private sector expenditure
        figures not available.)

[a]Estimated.

[b]Official exchange rates, O.E.C.D.

accepted for the preschool instruction of young children. From about 1927 the ideas of Maria Montessori became increasingly popular, and Froebel's methods were modified to incorporate them. Then, in 1950, the teachings of Decroly became dominant and have continued until the present. But Montessori and Froebel have not been discarded; the Belgians have developed a somewhat eclectic policy, and they continue to use what they consider the best of Froebel and Montessori, adapting it to the newer methods of their countryman Decroly.

Decroly's teaching methods are reflected in the Plan of Educational Activities in Preprimary School (*Plan des activités à l'ecole maternelle*) (1951), which replaced the program of 1927. Some communes have created their own pre-school programs, but most of these are very similar to the national plan of 1950.

The best known of Decroly's educational principles is *L'enseignement pour la vie par la vie* (education for life by living). His three major postulates for pedagogical activity in the preschool are:

1. The school should, as far as possible, reflect life by living.
2. Each idea should be developed by passing from a generalized view to an analytical stage and then to a stage of synthesis.
3. The acquisition of that knowledge should be supported by general methods that combine, in time and space, observation, association, and expression in all of their forms. It is the major task of a teacher to facilitate this process by his methods of instruction.

Dr. Decroly might be compared very favorably with John Dewey in the United States. Decroly was a student of Dewey in the sense that he read a great deal of what Dewey wrote and endorsed a great many of his ideas. It is fair to say that Decroly was Europe's progressive John Dewey.

In Decroly's opinion, a preschool should be a place where children grow intellectually, emotionally, and socially, surrounded by complete security. It is the task of the teacher to provide an appropriate milieu for the child so that he may maximize his development. Decroly stresses four points: the child, the milieu, the activities, the teacher.

From the start, the child's needs, interests, and individual development are of greatest concern to the teacher. Hence, it is vital for him to spend a great deal of time observing the child. In Decroly's view, the teacher's assistance to the child should come mainly from creating a milieu and a set of activities that, from observations of the child, will foster his growth to the maximum. For the child, the milieu and activities interact with each other and are the source of progress in his physical, affective, intellectual, social, and moral development. The teacher should encourage the child to observe and experiment with the milieu, to associate facts in time and space, and to express them from his own point of view. This need for the child to express his own ideas explains the great importance given to language development in Belgian preschools.

As to the milieu and the activities of preschool, the teacher's job is to provide the necessary materials. These will include dolls, live animals, birds, plants, flowers, all of which the child can comment on, observe, touch, and feel. The role of the teacher in all of this is not to be a giver of information or purveyor of facts but to provide the child with an environment that is most favorable to his natural development and to observe his behavior closely.

One outgrowth of Decroly's writing has been the development of the idea that the preschool teacher should instruct children as a good mother does. Since the end of World War II, the inspectors have referred to this idea by using the term *Notion Mère* (mother concept). The term implies that the preschool teacher will teach her children those skills and facts necessary for success in primary school just as a good mother does at home.

Therefore, the instructional methodology uses what in the United States is called the project method, created by Kilpatrick, a student of John Dewey. Decroly modified this method and adapted it to the Belgian system. This method of instruction calls for the teacher to plan activities of either long or short duration that will facilitate four things: observation, association, synthesis, and, finally, expression of ideas.

RESEARCH ON EARLY CHILDHOOD EDUCATION

Since 1969, closer cooperation has been fostered between the Belgian Ministry of Education, school administrators, teachers, and research workers. The reasons and results of this have been given by Vandenberghe (1972). The aim of the policy has been to induce teachers to participate actively in the development of the reform and to give them wide responsibilities in putting decisions into effect. Contact between teachers and universities has been promoted by organizing activities in university research centers that would provide initiation into new techniques (programmed teaching, modern mathematics, language teaching laboratories, etc.), and by starting a series of research projects involving developmental or operational research.

Operational research, where it involves the active cooperation of a large number of teachers, has emerged as one of the most effective ways of stimulating innovation. It encourages teachers to think about their profession, take a more rational and even scientific approach to their problems, and be prepared to challenge their own methods. The interest shown is already great enough to justify consideration of "consultation bureaus" at university institutes engaged in educational research, where teachers can bring their problems and get professional assistance in solving them.

The main areas of interest in research as they concern preschool education in Belgium are:

1. The creation and evaluation of a nursery school program for children less than 3 years old.
2. Testing the school maturity of children at the end of preschool, and of those who, for various reasons, have stayed on in nursery school after the compulsory age for entry into primary school.
3. Further differentiation of early childhood education according to differences in the maturity process and cognitive development, and for children who are physically handicapped.
4. Methods for the education of disadvantaged children.
5. The skills and aptitudes necessary for educating 5-year-olds.

Research on preschool education is also fostered by the Administration of the Studies of the Ministry of National Education, which has organized commissions to work on the plan of educational activities for preschools in connection with the reform of fundamental teaching (the Ministerial Circular of June 21, 1971 gives guidance for this). These commissions come together regularly to discuss the extension and adaption of preschool programs to new research findings on the psychological development of the child, especially as concerns mathematics, language, music, and psychomotoric education. Several committees are studying the extension of preschool facilities, and the following outline has been suggested:

1. *Crèches* from 0 to 18 or 24 months.
2. One prenursery class for the 2- to 3-year-olds.
3. Two classes for the 3- to 5-year-olds.
4. Two classes of transition for the 5- to 7-year-olds.

The legal age for compulsory education would consequently be reduced by one year to become 5.

The prenursery classes could be organized both as a part of the *crèches* and in the preschools. In the *crèches,* there would be one preschool teacher and one caretaker for 15-20 children. In the prenursery classes, there would be two caretakers for each group of 20 children, and a preschool teacher on duty between 7:00 A.M. and 7:00 P.M. As already observed, the preschool is administratively bound to the primary school and is often in the same building. The high percentage of failure, particularly in the French-speaking part of the country, at the end of the first primary year, however, shows that this arrangement has not led to any real coordination between these two levels of education. The proposed change of structure would surely be an improvement. *Inter alia,* the first directives for the new program may call for more systematic preparation for the learning of reading, writing and mathematics in the last year of the preschool.

These changes are a consequence of the general effort to renovate the entire educational system. These efforts started a few years ago at the secondary level. The first directives about "fundamental education" are addresses to the primary schools, but certain of the recommendations apply also to the preschools. Among the most important are:

1. The basic idea of starting with the child and developing.
2. Less teaching for best teaching.
3. Formation more than information.
4. Intensive practice of language and mathematics.

Testing the maturity level of school beginners is now clearly seen as increasingly important in Belgium (Andrianne, 1965). The need for it stems from the high percentage of children (above all in the French-speaking part of the country) who repeat the first year in primary school—up to 25%, and increasing. (The percentage of repeaters at all levels in primary school is 32.7%.) The percentage of underage children in primary school is fairly constant, approximately 3%.

Solutions that have been discussed for this problem include a later school start, obligatory school readiness tests, and the creation of special schools for repeaters.

Van Assche (1967) studied 56 children of less than 6 years old in the first class in primary school and came to the following conclusions: The average intelligence level of the under 6s in the study was higher than that of the 6-year-olds (control group), both groups being in the first class in primary school. Fourteen of the under 6s had an I.Q. of 130 and more. No significant difference was found in the scholastic success of the two groups. Social adaption was more difficult for the under 6s, who mostly came from a better sociocultural background. They had been accepted at school on explicit request from their parents, who were convinced of their above-average talent. These under 6s usually had more varied interests, but they were less persistent than the control group.

An experimental mathematics program for preschool children was introduced in September, 1972, and is available to schools on request. The program gives a relatively detailed outline of how to teach mathematics. The intention is not to teach the subject systematically, but to provoke the child's curiosity and intellectual activity. It is presented in three chapters: exploration of space, measurement and quantity, and sets and relations. In the matter of reading difficulties in primary school, research results point to the use of pedagogic and didactic methods in preschool as a possible preventive.

New ideas about preschool institutions are being developed by the Belgian OMEP committee. They foresee the education of young children in a broader context and envisage "centers for the first childhood." These centers would group and coordinate different services already existing or soon to be created, such as family planning consultation, prenatal consultation, infant consultation, *mini-crèche* to receive children according to the parents' needs, and a nursery school with a center of leisure for young children. Parents would be associated with the management and organization of these centers.

An intensive training project for children of 5 to 6 years of age has recently been started by the Educational Department in Antwerp on an experimental basis. The emphasis is on activities that develop and train observational functions, verbal expression, psychomotor development, and behavior of children in a group. Three experimental classes in a disadvantaged area of the town and an observation class in a middle-class area have been selected for study. Results of this project were available in 1973. It is expected that they will throw further light on the problems of transition from preprimary to primary school and on the repeating rate, which is relatively high in the disadvantaged areas.

Since 1969, an interuniversity project (Brussels, Ghent, Liège, and Mons) funded by the Van Leer Foundation has been directed at compensations for sociocultural handicaps affecting children from birth to 7 years of age. Its stated objectives are: (*1*) to determine the origin of affective and cognitive handicaps imputable to socioeconomic and cultural conditions and to identify the prerequisites for primary school that are negated by these conditions—proposals for compensation to follow diagnosis; and (*2*) to define a theoretical basis and optimal forms of a preschool education that will prevent the development of handicaps.

In Brussels, the *service de psychologie génétique* in the Free University is doing fundamental work on the relationship between particular features in the environment and the degree of psychological development in children from birth to 7 years, according to the adapted scale of Brunet-Lézinne.

In Ghent, children from 4 to 6 living in disadvantaged areas are being studied in a structured program concerned with visual-motor education, the use of language, and concept formation. This is being done in the psychology faculty of the University of Ghent.

In Liège, diagnostic evaluation of sociocultural handicaps and action-research are being done at the *Laboratoire de Pédagogie Experimentale* in the university for children from 2 to 6 years old. The diagnosis is made within a general theory of development, using human ethnology methods. The action-research relates to curriculum building, summative and formative evaluation and, especially, teacher training.

In Mons, in the *Service des Sciences Psychopédagogiques,* three lines of inquiry are being pursued: the progressive development of activities for the improvement of cognitive functions; the improvement of material conditions and social relations at home and at school; and the adaptation of practical educational means for use by parents with their own children (diapositive, booklets at home).

From this research several important points emerge:

1. The need for good preprimary education is seen clearly in the high rate of failure in Belgian primary schools. Extensive research has been begun to identify causes and remedies.
2. One of the main areas of research interest is the level of maturity of children in the early primary grades. It is believed that many later school failures can be traced to immaturity, and tests are being developed that will help diagnose it earlier.
3. Another cause of failure has been socioeconomic and cultural factors. Their effect might be minimized by emphasizing parental involvement in the educational process.
4. Research also is being done on building a preschool curriculum that will meet the special needs of disadvantaged children.
5. The ministries of education are studying the effects of combining the preschools with the first two grades of the primary school and making it a single ungraded educational unit.

ACKNOWLEDGMENTS

The author wishes to acknowledge the valuable help received from: M. Vanbergen, *Directeur Général, Ministère de l'Education Nationale et de la Culture Française*; M. Coulon of the *Direction Générale de la Documentation et de la Programmation*; Madame Libott-Loffet, *Président de l'Organisation Mondiale pour l'Education Pré-Scolaire Belgique*; Messrs. Van den Hereweghe and Pollentier of the *Ministère de l'Education National Néerlandophone*; Messrs. Delot and Gilmant of the *Ministère de l'Education Nationale française*; and M. de Landsheere and Mlle. Thirion of the *Université de Liège.*

BIBLIOGRAPHY

Andrianne, L. In Trouillet B. (Eds.), *Vorschulerziehung in neun Europäishen Ländern.* Weinhem: Beltz Verlag, 1967.

de Coster, W. *Pilot project, early childhood education, Ghent, Belgium.* Bernard Van Leer Foundation, Seminar on Curriculum. Jerusalem, November 15-25, 1972.

Coulon, M. *La planification de l'enseignement en Belgique.* Université libre de Bruxelles, Institut de Sociologie, 1966.

De Landsheere, G. *Pour une nouvelle formation des maîtresses de jardins d'enfants. Nécessité d'une réforme.* Séminaire international, OMEP, Liége, September 1967.

Derivière, R. In Schultze (Ed.), *Schools in europe.* Weinheim: Beltz Verlag, 1969.

Libotte-Loffet, M. *Le jardin d'enfants, parents et enfants, essais de psychologie familiale.* Liège: OMEP, 1960.

Libotte-Loffet, M., & Thirion, A. M. Les stimulations, dans *Journée d'étude sur la prévention dan la première enfance* (1971) à paraître dans Acta Psychiatrica, Belgica.

Trouillet, B. *Die Vorschulerziehung in neun Europäishen Ländern.* Weinheim: Beltz Verlag, 1967.

van Assche, L. In Trouillet, B. (Ed.), *Die Vorschulerziehung in neun Europäishen Ländern.* Weinheim: Beltz Verlag, 1967.

Vanbergen, P. *Où en est la question scolaire?* Editions Labor, Bruxelles D/1970/258/22.

Vanbergen, P. *Creativity of the school* OECD CERI/CS/72.08: Paris, August 7, 1972.

Vandenberghe, R. *Professional support to the school.* OECD CERI/CS/72.06: Paris, November 2, 1972.

Wall, W. D. *In l'enseignement gardien, textes et documents.* No. 225-226, juillet-août 1967. Ministère des affaires étrangers et du commerce extérieur, Bruxelles.

Annuaire statistique de l'enseignement. Année Scolaire 1966-67.

Council for cultural cooperation of the Council of Europe. *Education in Europe, school systems: a guide.* Strasbourg, 1970.

Council of Europe, Documentation Centre for Education in Europe. News Letter No. 5/71.

Council of Europe. News Letter No. 2/72.

Conseil de la Coopération Culturelle. *Guide des systèmes scolaires, l'education en Europe, 1970.* Strasbourg, 1965.

Conseil de l'Europe. *L'éducation préscolaire en Belgique.* Strasbourg, September 1971. Addendum au DECS/EGT(71)89. Also August 1971, DECS/EGT (71) 89.

l'education scolaire en Europe: Développements, problèmes et tendances. Rapport Présenté par la Belgique dans le cadre des directives contenues dans le document no. CCC/EGT(71)24.

L'Enseignement en Belgique: Information Belges. 15 December 1967.

Evolution de la population scolaire depuis la pacte scolaire-prognose. 1968.

International Federations of Teachers Associations (IFTA) Congress of Helsinki, 1969. *Pre-school Education.* EDC-2652/69.

Ministère de l'éducation nationale et de la culture. Documentation et programmation, *L'Enseignement Gardien,* 1963.

Ministère de l'éducation nationale et de la culture, *Hommage à Ouide, Decroly,* January 1964.

Ministère de l'éducation nationale; Direction générale de l'enseignement primaire et gardien. *Plan des activités à l'école maternelle.* 7/176, 1951.

Ministère de l'éducation nationale et de la culture francaise. *Administration des études, structures, programmes et méthodes.* Document no. 6, June 1, 1971.

Ministère de l'éducation nationale et de la culture française; administration des études; structures, programmes et méthodes. *Enseignement préscolaire, activités mathematiques* (programme provisoire), 1972.

Ministère des affaires étrangeres et du commerce extérieur. *Textes et Documents, l'enseignement gardien.* No. 225-226, juillet-août 1967.

OECD. *Classification of educational systems, Belgium, Denmark, United States.* Paris, 1972.

OECD. *Labour force statistics 1959-1970.* Paris, 1972.

Organisation Mondiale pour l'éducation préscolaire (OMEP). *L'Enfance nous appelle.* Comptes rendus de la 7e Assemblée mondiale, Bruxelles 2 au 11 août, 1958.

Organisation mondiale pour l'éducation préscolaire (OMEP). *La formation du personnel pour les institutions destinées aux enfants d'âge préscolaire.* comptes rendus du séminaire international organisé par le comité Belge de l'OMEP, Liége, 25-28 September 1967.

Berthoud, R. Pre-school education in Europe: 'A Place to dump the kids all day long.' *The Times,* March 2, 1972.

L'Ecole des Petits, Revue Pédagogique Mensuelle, 1971-1972, Mai–No 9. Juin–No. 10.

United Nations demographic yearbook, 1970.

United Nations. *Analyses and projections of households and families.* 1971.

10

Early Childhood Education in Germany

INTRODUCTION

Early childhood education in Germany can be traced to a letter written by Martin Luther in 1524 urging German municipalities to provide schools for young children and indicating to parents their duty to send their children to school. Luther's reasoning obviously was that to understand and to appreciate the Bible it was necessary to be able to read. Although Luther's efforts were lost in the Thirty Years' War (1618-1648), his pronouncement fostered belief in the value of education, especially for religious purposes, and parental acceptance of responsibility for a child's education, which led later to acceptance of compulsory school attendance.

By edicts in 1717 and 1736, Frederick William I ordered that children should be sent to school, where schools existed, and established schools in certain provinces. In 1763, the *Landschulregelment* of Frederick the Great, asserting the principle of compulsory school attendance, laid down the broad lines by which the Prussian state proceeded.

Between 1800 and 1820 *Klein-Kinderbewahranstalten* (day care centers) were established to provide care and protection for children of working women. These

were founded and maintained primarily by religious societies and private philanthropists, including women's societies.

Thirty institutions called *Bewahranstalten,* run by the mill owners, were
created in Berlin between 1830 and 1842. The untrained teachers conducted
these schools were generally women with strong religious beliefs and firm
convictions about disciplinary action to maintain order among children.

In reaction to the conditions prevalent in these institutions, Froebel opened
his first kindergarten at Blankenburg in Thuringen in 1837. Froebel's *Bildung*
(education) emphasized the importance of play. Through play, Froebel believed,
most of a young child's learning occurs. His methods were a supplement to the
home and an extension of the family's role. They did not replace the responsibility of home or family. His basic methods stressed "natural" education.

The kindergarten movement in the mid-1800s was adopted by the middle
class, and the children of the poor for whom it had been designed were ignored.
In 1851, the Prussian government proscribed kindergartens because of "their
radical teachings," leaning toward democracy. Kindergartens after 1860 were
organized and operated by private (religious) groups. Preschool education in
Germany remained essentially denominational (Catholic and Protestant) until
1920 and, to a large extent, remains so today.

The first planning committee concerned with preschool, *"Deutscher Ausschuss
für das Erziehungs and Bildungswesen,"* was set up in 1953 to study the
situation of kindergarten in Germany. It issued a report in 1957 emphasizing the
importance of early childhood education and urging rapid improvement of the
existing situation. Progress was slow because of other demands on the German
educational system during its recovery from the war. The committee,
"Deutscher Bildungsrat," in 1965 again recommended expansion of preschool
facilities and again the response has been less than desired.

A document entitled "Report of the Federal Government on Education
1970," recommending the importance of expanding pre-school education in
Germany, was issued in 1970. Its recommendations, which offered detailed
outlines and guidance for accomplishment by 1985, are still being discussed.

ENROLLMENTS, PRESCHOOL EDUCATION (1960-1970)

Preprimary education in West Germany, according to the "Classification of
Educational Systems" (OECD 1972), has the following characteristics:

1. *Kindergarten*
   (Pre-primary Schools).
   Length of study: 1 to 3 years.
   For children of preschool age (3 to 6 years). Majority of these institutions are
   private and are not (yet) part of the educational system.

2. *Schulkindergarten*
   (Pre-primary classes for children of school age).
   Length of Study: 1 (2) years.
   Entrance Requirements: 6 years.
   Full-time. For children of school age who are physically and mentally retarded. Most
   of these classes are state-run and are part of the educational system [p. 46].

Table 10.1 presents information on the number of children enrolled in public and private kindergartens in the Federal Republic from 1960-1961 to 1970-1971. It can be seen that both the public and private sectors grew at approximately the same rate, 41.8% for the private, 42.2% for the public, over these 10 years. During the same period, primary school enrollments grew by 13.1%, indicating that growth in the kindergarten sector was much more rapid than in the primary. The ratio of children attending private preschools to those attending public preschools does not show a statistically significant change over the 10-year period.

Table 10.2 presents population attendance rates in kindergartens for the 10-year period 1960-1961 to 1970-1971 and shows that in 1960, 33.4% of 3- to 5-year-olds eligible were attending kindergarten. By 1970-1971, this had grown to 39.3%. During the same period, that segment of the population had grown by 20.9%. As shown in Table 10.1, the total enrollments had increased by 41.9%, leaving, therefore, a 17.7% overall increase in attendance rates for the 10-year period.

These statistics do not include enrollments for the *Schulkindergarten (Vorklassen)*, which are not available for the entire time sequence presented; nor are

TABLE 10.1
Enrollments in Kindergartens in Germany (F.R.) from 1960–61 to 1970–71

Year	Private	Public	Total (in 000's)
1960–61	652	165	818
1965–66	762	190	953
1966–67	789	195	983
1967–68	824	203	1,027
1968–69	842	209	1,051
1969–70	884	220	1,104
1970–71	927	234	1,161
% of increase from 1960–61 to 1970–71	41.8	42.2	41.9

Source: Statistisches Bundesamt, Wiesbaden.

they fully proper to this study, being part of the compulsory school system. Nevertheless, it is important to note that in 1964 there were 10,107 children in *Schulkindergarten,* and by 1970 this had grown to 33,262—a percentage of increase of 228.1%. This is a much more rapid growth rate than in the kindergartens. The reason for this is that it began with a much smaller base, therefore multiplying itself more rapidly. There is also increasing concern in the country for a transitional year or a year in a waiting class for children who are immature and not ready to enter the normal first grade.

The number of children attending some form of early childhood education in 1970-1971 by single-year and multiple-year age groupings was:

Age	Percentage	Age	Percentage
6	99%	5-6	84.5%
5	70%	4-6	68.0%
4	35%	3-6	53.3%
3	10%	2-6	43.0%
2	1%		

The possibility of attending a kindergarten in the Federal Republic is largely dependent on where the child lives. For children between the ages of 3 and 6 in Baden-württenberg and Berlin, the chances are 1 in 3. In Bremen, they are 1 in 4. In Saarland, they are 1 in 6, in Hamburg 1 in 10, and in Schleswig-Holstein 1 in 20.

As may be seen in Table 10.3, however, the number of kindergarten places in each *Land* had increased markedly during the period 1960-1969. For example, in Bremen, 769 places existed in 1960; by 1969 there were 7714—an increase of

TABLE 10.2
Population Attendance Rates in Kindergartens in Germany (F.R.) from 1960-61 to 1970-71

			(in 000's)
	1960-61	1970-71	% of Change
Total age group 3 - 5 years in kindergartens	818	1,161	41.9
Infant population 3 - 5 years	2,446	2,951	20.9
% of age group enrolled	33.4	39.3	17.7

Source: United Nations Demographic Yearbook, 1970.

TABLE 10.3
Kindergarten Places by Land (in 000's)

	1960	1969	Increase	% of Increase
Baden-Wurttemberg	222	294	72	32.8
Bayern	149	180	31	20.8
Berlin	13	19	6	53.5
Bremen	1	8	7	600.0
Hamburg	14	24	10	68.0
Hessen	68	95	27	39.4
Niedersachsen	44	63	19	43.7
Nordrhein-Westfalen	212	284	72	34.1
Rheinland-Pfalz	71	85	14	20.4
Saarland	16	29	13	81.5
Schleswig-Holstein	10	16	6	62.2
Total	818	1,097	279	34.0

Source: Ministry of Labor and Welfare, Nordrhein-Westfalen.

1003.1%. Also showing a dramatic increase over the same period was Saarland, with 81.5%.

First priority for available preschool space is given to those identified as most needing the experience: children from large families, children with working parents, or children from economically deprived areas. Stating that talent and ability to learn are based much more than realized on environment and its interaction with a child, the "Report of the Federal Government on Education 1970" stressed the need for the state to compensate for poor social conditions with education. Social need then becomes the criterion for assigning kindergarten space.

The following statistics appear to offer further reasons for the rising demand for early childhood education in West Germany. In 1967, the live birth rate per 1000 population in Germany was 17.8%. In 1970, it had fallen to 13.3%—a 4.5% drop in four years (United Nations Yearbook, 1970). With this has gone a decrease in family size. In 1871, the average household size in Germany was 4.63; in 1900 it was 4.49; in 1950, 2.99; and in 1967, 2.69. Over this 96-year period it has, therefore, declined steadily by a total of 1.94 persons. In 1950, the gross reproduction rate in the Federal Republic was 1 while in 1967 it was 1.1, indicating a .1 percentage increase over that 17-year period ("Analyses and Projections of Households and Families," Population Division, Department of Economics and Social Affairs, United Nations Secretariat). It is still, however, a very low gross reproduction rate. Lower birth rates may account for the increased demand in early childhood education as smaller families seem to encourage mothers to put their children in preschools.

Table 10.4 shows participation rates for West Germany.

These statistics illustrate the fact that, while the participation rates for both men and women have declined slightly over the 10-year period, in the case of married women there has been a four percent increase. This appears to support the view held in a number of countries that increasing participation of married women in the labor force increases the demand for public preschool care for very young children.

ISSUES OF DEBATE

The reform of preschool education in West Germany has recently developed into a keenly discussed problem (Schultze, 1970). A campaign to promote preschool education and early reading unique to the Federal Republic occurred when it became apparent that, compared with the situation abroad, an "education emergency" existed in the kindergartens. A widespread change in the concept of talent and a growing realization that preschool age is the most receptive period for a child also had impact on the debate.

TABLE 10.4
Labor Force Participation Rates – Germany (F.R.)

	1960 %	1970 %
$\dfrac{\text{Total Labor Force}}{\text{Total Population}} \times 100$		
(a) Total	47.8	45.1
(b) Males	64.0	61.1
(c) Females	33.6	30.6
$\dfrac{\text{Total Labor Force}}{\substack{\text{Population from} \\ \text{15 to 64 years}}} \times 100$		
(a) Total	70.5	70.9
(b) Males	94.9	94.9
(c) Females	49.3	48.6

Source: Labor Force Statistics, 1959-70, O.E.C.D., Paris, 1972

In the Republic there is still a divergence of opinion as to the proper objectives of preschool education. Westphal (1972) lists four instances of changed insights that are gaining ground:

1. In conflict situations the rights of the child must gain importance in relation to parental rights;
2. More democratic, freer forms of relationships between parents and children are developing and have their positive effects on the education of children;
3. The authorities do not reject experiments in parent-children associations but retain the right to ensure compliance with official guidelines concerning personnel, space, pedagogical, and hygienic standards;
4. The strengthening of parental educational capability—materially and pedagogically—is the explicit policy of the federal government [p. 6].

The right, prerogative, and privilege of parents to raise their children as they choose is a matter of fundamental concern in present-day Germany. Many parents are not willing to give up the care and education of their young children to either private (primarily religious) or state-run early childhood education organizations, even though they are aware of the "acknowledged benefits" of their children's having this experience. The reasons behind such resistance are beyond the scope of this paper; they are complex and numerous. In the last 10 years, however, as Tables 10.1 and 10.2 indicate, the pattern is changing.

Another problem of growing concern is posed by the children of foreign workers (*Gastarbeiter*). In 1971, there were approximately 2.6 million foreign workers, or about 5.1% of the total population of 51 million. The number rises to 3.5 million, or 6.8% of the population, if one counts the wives and children. The total number of these children is 800,000. In 1972, in Frankfurt, two out of every five children born had foreign parents. Baden-Württemburg predicts that by 1978 one out of every five pupils at school will be coming from a foreign home. These children clearly need kindergarten experience, especially to help them master the German language. In some cases, the foreign parents resist sending their children to kindergarten simply because they are unaware of its benefits, yet many wish to remain in Germany. How to provide equality of opportunity for such children is a very serious problem, and it is one that must be faced if their parents are to be retained as an important element in the labor force.

Some of the reasons for emerging public interest and criticism of early childhood education in Germany have been given by Stahl (1972).

Educators (parents as well as educationalists) are rendered insecure by the growing complexity of life and the manifold and often contradictory recommendations made by education experts.

The discrepancy existing between research undertaken into the minutest details in order to preserve life and promote it, and the thoughtless development of means and methods conducive to harming it.

The isolation of technological and administrative perfectionism from real human needs.

The finance policy which neglects our present-day educational tasks [p. 22].

Nowhere, Stahl continues, is this confusion and complexity of life better exemplified than in the present discussion of issues about kindergartens. She points to two conflicting sets of issues in particular that confuse parents as they attempt to understand what they should do for their young children: (1) freedom versus authority in the child socialization debate and (2) work versus play in the early education debate. There is no doubt that these two matters, the question of authority and the question of play, are important issues for the German people at the present time.

Wolf (1971) suggests that individualized compensatory education begun in the kindergarten can make an impact upon the deficits that some children from poorer homes bring with them to the classroom. Accepting the traditional functions of school, he believes that kindergarten should prepare the children more successfully for school entrance.

Another point of view is given by Robinson of the *Deutsches Jugendinstitute*. He is much more concerned with creating programs that are "rational," systematic, and individualized to meet the growing complexities of today's society. His methods, he hopes, may lead to new forms of kindergarten whose main emphasis will not be on the transmission of traditional knowledge but on maximizing the creative talents of each individual child.

The forms of kindergartens in Germany as identified by Zimmer (1972) are: (1) traditional Froebelian play-oriented; (2) cognition-oriented (compensatory education), based on the teaching of Piaget; (3) subject-oriented, stressing motivation, the new mathematics, and the link between preschool and primary school; (4) communist, new left-oriented kindergarten, stressing societal reform along party lines; and (5) a worker's kindergarten, which Zimmer himself favors, hopefully blending the best in the other four types.

Widely discussed is the number of physical places needed to meet the growing demand for kindergartens in the Federal Republic. Some of the *Länder* and city states that have been constantly criticized for their lack of kindergarten facilities reply that their ability to provide education is limited and, therefore, Germany should consider consolidating educational facilities in the *Länder*.

Another matter for concern in Germany is the lack of regulations governing the physical aspects of kindergartens. At present there is great diversity across the country. Differences in the availability of space and facilities, in particular, are more marked in the rural than the urban areas. Indeed, most urban communities make much more adequate provision for kindergartens than is the case in isolated rural areas where the need is sometimes greater.

Teacher training is also an important issue. Opinions on this subject vary from "there is no formal teacher training" to "there is teacher training, but it is oriented more toward welfare and social concepts than toward education." According to reports published in 1969 by the *Arbeitsgemeinschaft Deutscher Lehrerverbände,* the best solution to the problem would be to combine the strengths of the welfare, social, and educational training institutions into a single unit that would attempt to maximize the benefits it could give to German children by better preparation for future kindergarten teachers.

The question of pupil-teacher ratio is also giving cause for concern. There are marked differences between rural and urban settings. In some of the poorer (principally rural) *Länder,* the ratio is 40 or 50 to 1, as compared with 15:1 in some of the larger cities.

The relationship of the kindergarten to the primary school is another topic of contention. Many people believe that the kindergarten should be oriented more toward preparing children for the first year at primary school. Others side with the view that the kindergarten has its own unique and special function that has almost nothing to do with such preparation. Again, there is no immediate answer to the question, but a sizeable research effort is being made to obtain pertinent information on this issue and possibly a solution may emerge from this. Associated closely with this search for the true purpose of the kindergarten is the question of early reading, and a good deal of work is being done here to discover more adequate ways of teaching young children to read.

Concerning organization, control, and financing of preschool, educational views differ as to whether this should be public or private and whether the first year of regular school should be designated as kindergarten or as a preschool year. The latter point will be clarified when it is decided if preschool education should be assigned to the educational ministries or to the social ministries.

In summary, the outstanding issues are these:

1. Equality of educational opportunity.
2. Rights and privileges of parents in choosing the kinds of education they desire for their children.
3. Adequacy of training of kindergarten teachers.
4. Disparities across *Länder* and city states in the provision of economic resources for education.
5. The assignment of control and finance of preprimary education to the education or social ministries.

THE AIMS AND OBJECTIVES OF EARLY CHILDHOOD EDUCATION

Federal Chancellor Willy Brandt, in the forward to the 1970 report of the Federal Government on education, stressed that education and science must have priority in the country's development as these were areas in which it no longer enjoyed its former international stature. The report that follows looks at the entire structure of education in Germany and recommends reforms to meet a number of important objectives. Two of its seven "general aims for education" have policy implications for the kindergarten level. These are:

Open Educational System
    The prime aim is a democratic, efficient and flexible educational system which is open to every citizen from pre-school education to further education for his personal, professional, and political education.
Equality of Opportunity and Self-Determination
    The constitutional principle of equality of opportunity must be realized through an intensive and individual promotion of those being taught at all levels of the educational system.
    Education should help people to shape their own lives. The younger generation must experience the possibilities of greater flexibility and freedom, so that they can learn to choose usefully for themselves. Education should create a permanent basis for liberal co-existence through learning and experiencing democratic values and through an understanding of social development and its changes. Education should awaken joy in independent, creative work [p. 11].

So far as concerns early childhood specifically, the report calls for an expansion of preschool education; for here should be the starting point for dismantling class barriers. Preschool education should give the child a feeling that learning is a pleasure, and its goals should be to stimulate independence, consideration for others, and an ability to recognize simple problems and their possible solutions.

Calling for doubling the number of kindergarten places, the report suggests improvement in training and salaries as an inducement to the number of teachers being doubled. All children of 3 and 4, whose parents so desire, should be able to attend a preschool at this level.

Since kindergartens traditionally have been outside the education establishment and have had more of a social welfare than an educational orientation, this is about as close as we can get to an official statement of what their broad objectives should be. Their methodology (which implies certain aims and now seems to have gained fairly general acceptance), however, can be traced to Froebel, who believed that children should be brought up in harmony with themselves, God, and nature and that the best medium for education in those early years was the child's own innate desire to play. As Froebel, in Blackstone (1971) epitomizes it "The plays of children are the germinal leaves of all later life, for the whole man is shown and developed in these. . . . Play is not trivial, it is highly serious and of deep significance [p. 13] ."

Play being the natural way of teaching children, the principal aim of the Froebelian kindergarten was to watch the child grow and to provide him with a milieu that would encourage and maximize his development. Indeed, the word "kindergarten," which Froebel coined, means a place where children grow, and that is how he perceived it. Since the child was innately good and free from original sin, it was only necessary to provide a rich, varied, and stimulating environment in which he could choose what to learn. A structured curriculum was the negation of this. The materials and concepts developed by Froebel for this environment include:

1. Use of a ball to teach the unity of mankind with God.
2. Sitting in a circle for purposes of identification both as a member of the group and as an individual, the ultimate aim being appreciation of the unity of mankind.
3. Respect for the individual and the need to individualize education.
4. Encouragement of self-direction and self-control, based on a concept of self-worth and democracy.
5. Importance of group activities in learning about social relationships which would be important later in adult life.
6. Concern for the child at the center of all decisions taken in school, and the creation of a child-centered curriculum.

In most parts of the Federal Republic, Froebel's methods are still employed. Recent directives issued in Lower Saxony, for example, reiterate that the aim of the kindergarten is mainly play activities, and that through play the child learns to concentrate, to exercise his imagination, to acquire the means of self-expression suitable to his stage of development, to gain skills in the use of simple tools, to learn cleanliness and order, and to become accustomed to being with other children. Elsewhere, however, discussion (stimulated by work done in the United States) is turning away from Froebel in the direction of structured kindergartens, particularly for children from disadvantaged homes. To this end, the German government, through its universities and research institutions, has launched a number of projects to create appropriately structured programs for use in these circumstances.

Here, then, is evidence of kindergarten education beginning to be used, not only for promoting individual talent, but for overcoming class barriers imposed by social conditions. This must be seen in relation to the policy for primary schools which too commonly in the past, many Germans believe, has been overselective and class-conscious. The call now is for a reconsideration of the objectives of kindergartens and the first one or two years of primary school. Some have suggested lowering the entrance age to 5 and having a school that would be concerned with 5-, 6-, and 7-year-olds to facilitate the transfer from preprimary to primary school.

In summary, until recently most West German kindergartens have employed Froebelian concepts. Their aim has been for the child to develop his physical, moral, and mental attributes through play. Now, however, the need to expand kindergarten facilities, combined with a call on kindergartens to cater more specifically to disadvantaged children, has promoted research and a national debate on the proper policies for preschool education. It seems fair to say that this whole matter is apparently in a state of transition.

ORGANIZATION AND CONTROL

Education in West Germany is organized at three levels: the Federal, the *Länder,* and the local. There is a close working relationship between all three. "Reviews of National Policies for Education: Germany" (OECD, 1971) says that the federative structure inherent in the 1949 Basic Law constituting the republic is the determining factor in responsibility for educational policy and planning. In calling for a "democratic and social federal state," the Basic Law adopted the constitutional tradition of the Deutsches Reich and the Weimar Republic.

To coordinate education throughout Germany, the *Länder* have, according to the 1972 OECD publication, acknowledged the need to maintain a minimum degree of coordination and uniformity in policy. To do so, they set up the "Permanent Conference of Ministers of Culture" (*Kultusministerkonferenz*) in 1949 for voluntary coordination and exchange of information. It has concluded more than 300 skeleton agreements since it was founded.

Highlights of the 1972 OECD report mentioned above included the statement that education in Germany is not exclusively a public or a private concern; the family, church, industry, and social institutions all play a part in supplementing the state and local authorities. Also, under the Basic Law, the care and upbringing of the child is the right and duty of the parent, with the state watching to insure they fulfill this obligation. Parallel to this, the constitution provides the right of private schools, subject to the consent of the state, to serve as alternatives to the public schools that come under the jurisdiction of the *Länder.* Broadly uniform, and under the aegis of the state, the school system shows differences among *Länder*, although these are becoming fewer.

Obligatory schooling, the report adds, lasts 12 years, 9 of them full-time. This comprises the common *Grundschule* from the first to the fourth or sixth grades, not including preschool, followed by either the *Hauptschule* (fifth to tenth grade) or the *Gymnasium* (fifth to thirteenth grade). Additionally, in Hessen and Berlin, there are comprehensive schools for the tenth to thirteenth grades.

Kindergarten classes are usually in buildings separate from the primary schools, and they normally operate on a double-session basis with one group of children in the morning and another in the afternoon. Very few children attend all day.

Preschool education for children 3 to 6 years old, the report states, involves kindergartens not supervised by the school authority that have a welfare, social, and educational character and are sponsored mainly (75%) by welfare organizations (*Arbeiterwohlfahrt, Caritasverband, Innere Mission*), towns, churches, or other private societies. Also included are *Schulkindergarten* and *Vorklassen*, classes for children of compulsory school age who need additional maturity, and testing facilities where 5-year-olds are prepared for *Grundschule* attendance with instruction tailored to their age group.

Reform plans announced in the same report call for the expansion of the kindergartens into the first phase in the educational system, as the years 3 to 6 are decisive for the development of learning, speaking, and creative abilities. The first two years (3- and 4-year-olds) would provide grounding for the third year, which would provide for easy transition to the reformed *Grundschule*. Although attendance would be voluntary, it is estimated that most children would go to these improved kindergartens, doubling the number of places and increasing the financial requirements more than 100%. Close cooperation between these and the primary schools would be essential; and "social pedagogues" should be employed to avoid too early emphasis on pure education.

Subsequent to this OECD report, there was a confrontation meeting between the examiners of the system, representatives of the German Ministry of Education and all administrative groups concerned. At that meeting, the following suggestions were made as a means for modernizing the Kindergartens:

1. Extend enrollments of 3- and 4-year-olds from 20% of age group in 1970 to 70% in 1980 or 1985. Kindergarten groups average 30 children at present; by 1985 this is planned to fall to 20-23. Staffing provisions are also planned to improve by 25% in the 15-year period.

2. Add a third year of preschooling (for 5-year-olds): This would be administered and provided by the school authorities, and hence could mean lowering the age of beginning compulsory schooling by 1 year, and might mean ending *Grundschule* 1 year earlier. It is planned that by 1985 *all* 5-year-olds will be in school, rather than just over half, as at present.

3. Develop special curricula for these age-groups: Improve the training of personnel; provide public money to cover expenditures at present met by nonpublic bodies; review scales of parental contributions.

These suggestions are currently under discussion in the ministry and, where possible, they will be implemented in the near future.

Each *Land* has created its own pattern for organization, construction, financing, and staffing of its schools but, as previously stated, there is cooperation among *Länder* through the *Kultusministerkonferenz*. Although the kindergartens are not part of the formal education structure, they are subject to some of the regulations that apply there, including inspection by the Ministry of Education. *Schulkindergarten*, however, are part of the educational system and therefore are subject to all of its organizational constraints. The *Länder* have had to increase the number of these because of the number of young children having difficulties in their first years at primary school. In 1969, 27.9% of the 6-year-olds in Germany were in *Schulkindergarten* instead of the first grade. This situation has increased interest in the proper role of the kindergartens, and many people believe there should be a greater element of continuity between them and the primary schools.

PHYSICAL SETTING: A VISIT TO A HESSEN KINDERGARTEN

It is important to note that the kindergarten visited in Hessen was a model one and therefore more representative of future hopes than of the current norm in Germany. It was a parish kindergarten, consisting of a two-story, reconstructed, church-owned building and a small new one, situated in a quiet by-street, just beside the church.

In the old building, there were two groups, each with two rooms. Every corner of the old building was used. A kitchen for the children, where they sometimes cooked for themselves, was below the staircase.

The new building housed three groups which had two rooms for each. It also contained personnel rooms, wash rooms, a tea-kitchen, and the leader's office. An open lobby had been remodelled for gymnastics. One corner of the hall was used as a breakfast-room for the children, and tea and milk were available there.

The rooms were well lighted with many windows. Some of the rooms had exits to the playground and others exited to the next room. Each child had 2 square meters for his use, and desks, chairs, and partitions were supplied for the needs of every group. The play materials were prepared and unlocked on the shelves.

The old and new buildings had individual playgrounds with sand piles, play-things, and walls for painting. The yard of the old building was partly shadowed by old trees—an advantage on hot summer days, and their leaves provided an autumn amusement for the children.

As the governesses arrived, there were already some children and their mothers present.

The class visited was in the old building where there were more staircases, angles, and corners for the children. During the next half hour the group grew to its normal size of 23 children. The two governesses—one fully trained, the other a probationer—welcomed the children and talked with their mothers. The 14 boys and 9 girls, including 3 children of foreign workers, went to their room and took their favorite toys from the shelves: boxes of bricks, colors, dolls, and picture books. Most of them then joined small groups; only a few played alone.

The day included:

an unstructured play period until about 9:30 A.M. (free breakfast from 9:00 to 10:00 A.M.).

a part of the curriculum unit on "residence," first with the whole group, then with small groups.

a period for gymnastics from 11:00 A.M.

On this particular morning, two interested mothers had asked to join the children. One had done this before. She took a box of plastic bricks from the shelf, sat down at the table and began to build. Some children came to her asking "What are you doing here?" She replied "I want to build a crane. Do you know how it should be made?" She then discussed possible constructions and experimented with the children.

The other mother, visiting the group for the first time, was very uncertain. The governess helped her with a group of children who had pulled out a box of old clothes and begun to dress up. The governess and the mother wanted to develop role-playing with the children, for some of the children were unable to freely enact different parts. They tried to provide playing-proposals to the theme (based on a television play viewed previously). With these proposals they hoped to structure the play.

At about 9:00 A.M., tea and milk for the children and coffee for the governesses and the mothers were brought from the new building. One of the children hurried to put cups on the table while others took their breakfast from their pockets and sat down to eat.

The governesses then prepared material for the curriculum-unit "residence." Two days before the children had made an excursion to the old part of the town where they saw framework houses. Then they were taken to a new quarter to visit the skyscraper flat of the governess. They had taken the lift and viewed the street from the balcony. They also dropped an orange to see what would happen if something were to fall from that height.

This excursion incorporated various themes that the governesses wanted to explore. First they suggested that the children express the excursion in pictures. With these pictures they wished to illustrate the differences between the old and the new forms of the houses and the reasons behind the different forms of constructions.

The mothers had brought some items which they wanted to look at with the children. This exercise had been discussed at the last parents' meeting.

In the meantime, Stefan, a small boy, arrived very late and very excited. On his way to school he had seen a traffic accident and an ambulance coming for the injured. More and more children came to Stefan, who was standing in the middle of the group talking very excitedly. Again and again Stefan tried to explain as imaginatively as possible the intensity of the crash and how they pulled the blood-covered man from the car. His young listeners were enthusiastic and began to transfer the story into a play. Boris, who was the son of a foreign worker and spoke only a few words of German, wanted to make himself indispensable as the rushing ambulance driver.

In the meantime, one of the governesses gathered some children around the tables where painting material had been prepared. One of the mothers was rather uncertain and tried to give her ideas and pictures to the governesses; but they suggested that the mothers themselves should explain the material to the children. One of them looked around to see who would pay attention to her. She called her own daughter, but she was occupied with Stefan's story and did not want to come. Then the governesses supported the parents and tried to gather the group of children to the curriculum unit. It was obvious their interest in the planned occupation was not large and only those with a special achievement-motivation agreed to the request of the governess. As time passed, the play around Stefan became so interesting that the group around the adults grew smaller and smaller. Uncertainly, the mothers asked the governesses if they should intervene. The governesses reminded them of the discussion during the evening sessions with the parents when one asked, "What is more important? The interest of the children in a new theme or our interest to carry on a prepared theme? We should support the interest of the children." The governess replied: "The interest of the children appears clearly in the situations that they describe and play by themselves. Our task is to take up these situations, to explore them with role playing and puppet shows, with discussions, by painting and building, by excursions, and so on. By using this method we can be surer of doing what the children like and exploring with the children what they like to explore. What they like doing, they learn best. By using this method we can be more confident that the children will learn the skills they will eventually need to master the situations in which they have to live." Meanwhile, the theme of "accident and wounded" is played in different variations by nearly all the children. Some took colors and painted an accident and police. Others built streets of bricks and reenacted the scene with cars. Another group recreated the scene using chairs to represent the crushed cars. The wounded were transported. The governess asked, "Where?" A child answered, "To the hospital."

A hospital was then built of bricks.

"What happens to the wounded in the hospital?" Nobody knew exactly. A girl who was once hurt roller-skating told how she was treated by the doctor. The children then brought blankets and first-aid to treat the wounded.

The second governess watched the scenes and pointed out to the mothers the children's need for information. "What happens with the wounded in the hospital?" She took from her cupboard a curriculum-unit entitled "A Child Comes into the Hospital." She turned the pages to find ideas so she could take the initiative in the children's play.

By about 11:00 o'clock the children had become increasingly restless. They had explored this subject long enough and there was no further value in pursuing it. So, the class went to the gymnastics room.

TEACHERS AND THEIR TRAINING

Teacher training in the Federal Republic is the responsibility of each *Land* and, as a result, varies considerably in location and mode. "Reviews of National Policies for Education: Germany" (OECD, 1972) states that the self-governing and *Länder*-financed *Pädagogische Hochschulen,* which do research on theory and methods of teaching, also train teachers in a 3-year course for the *Grund-*

schulen and *Hauptschulen* (elementary and middle schools) and sometimes for the *Realschulen*. In some *Länder*, teachers are trained in special departments and institutes of the universities.

Recent trends detailed in the OECD review include the special courses (under the 1969 general regulations of the Conference of Ministers of Education and the West German Rectors' Conference) that lead to a diploma in education. Also, the *Pädagogische Hochschulen* have progressively adopted a university approach to improve the technical quality of teacher training.

Today the *Hochschulen* are either academic institutions, university departments, or university affiliates. An increase in *Hochschulen* from 1386 in 1960 to 3502 in 1969 was stimulated by a 1963 call for more teacher training from the Conference of Ministers. During 1960-1969, the number of students rose from 33,100 to 68,800. Also increasing were new positions to cover new fields of teacher training and research activities.

The "Report of the Federal Government on Education" (1970) states that "up to the present day, there has never been . . . a specific training course or even a special qualification for the pre-school sector [p. 108]" within the framework of teacher training. Numerous other sources, however, indicate that there are courses and programs for training kindergarten teachers. This apparent contradiction may arise from the fact that the term "kindergarten teacher" is more often replaced now by "child care officer."

The OECD's "Classification of Educational Systems" (1972) gives the following information about the training of kindergarten teachers in the Republic where the average age of entry in a course is 16 years.

Kindergarten (Pre-primary school):
Place of training: Fachschulen für Kindergärtnerinnen und Hortnerinnen oder für Sozialpädagogik (Specialized secondary technical schools for Kindergarten teachers).
Length of Study: 2 years
   Students must have *Realschule* leaving certificate or equivalent. Instruction is theoretical (psychology, children's literature, hygiene, pedagogics, etc.) as well as practical (drawing, music, gymnastics, modeling, etc.)
   The final examination is divided into two parts and students are required to sit the 2nd part after a further year (3rd year), teaching.
Schulkindergarten (Pre-primary classes for children of school age).
Place of Training: Höhere Fachschule für Jugendleiterinnen oder fur Sozialpädagogik (Advanced technical schools for social pedagogy).
Length of Study: 3 years
   Students must have *Realschule* leaving certificate or equivalent and at least two years of practical experience.
   The final examination is divided into two parts and students are required to sit the 2nd part after a further year (4th year), teaching [p. 59].

Kindergarten teachers are responsible to the *Lander* youth offices rather than to the education ministries. Preschool teachers are considered more as child care personnel than educators.

According to Stahl (1972), in a 1967 reorganization of training for kindergarten teachers and youth leaders by the Conference of Ministers of Education of the Federal *Länder,* the term "kindergarten teacher" became "child care officer" and "youth leader" became "social pedagogue." Under this reorganization, child care officers were to be trained at specialized schools, admitting young men and women who could furnish proof of successfully completing 10 years of formal education and 1 year of practical placement. Their training over 3 years comprises four semesters of studies at the specialized school itself, passing a final examination and two semesters of practical work. After this, state recognition can be obtained.

Social pedagogues, however, are trained at colleges or academies. To be admitted, a candidate must have completed 12 years of formal education and possess the *Fachhochschulreife.* Training extends over 4 years, six semesters of which are spent at a training establishment and two on a professional practical placement. This leads to state recognition as a social pedagogue.

According to Stahl, to date, not all of the *Länder* have been able to follow this set of recommendations in all respects. The reasons for this are a continuing shortage of qualified preschool teachers, the lack of opportunities for practical training under qualified supervision, and the competition from outside the preprimary sector for people who are trained in these skills.

For a long time in Germany, specialized vocational education has been available for the training of nursery assistants. This is based upon the assumption of the completion of 9 years of formal schooling and takes 2 years to complete. The trainee is then qualified to assist in the care of small children in a variety of institutions. Such assistants receive about 90% of the salary of a kindergarten teacher.

The Conference of the International Federation of Teachers' Associations, meeting in Helsinki in 1969, discussed the problem of the shortage of preschool teachers in Germany and suggested that it might be ameliorated by providing better training, opening the profession to men, paying higher salaries, improving objective information about the profession to attract suitable recruits, and by making efforts to improve the social prestige of teachers.

TABLE 10.5
Estimated Kindergarten Teachers in Germany (F.R.) from 1960–61 to 1970–71

Year	Private	Public	Total
1960–61	7,000	28,000	35,000
1965–66	8,200	32,800	41,000
1970–71	10,000	40,000	50,000

In 1970, there were 5079 places in 64 kindergarten training institutions; in 1971, there were 6650 places in 83 institutions; in 1972, there were 7000 places in 100 institutions; by 1974, it is estimated that the kindergarten training colleges will be graduating 3500 qualified teachers. If, as has been estimated, there are approximately 50,000 kindergarten teachers working in Germany at the moment, and if we assume at least a replacement rate of 10% being necessary to maintain the present level, the certification of 3500 new teachers per year obviously will not meet the demand, let alone supply the need created by new kindergartens being opened.

Stahl (1972) estimates the total staff in German sociopedagogical (preprimary) institutions is about 50,000, subdivided as follows:

Youth leaders, social pedagogues, kindergarten teachers, child care officers	52%
Nursery assistants	25%
Persons with a short-term training or trainees working on a practical placement as part of their overall training [p. 20].	23%

This is the most recent available estimate of the number of kindergarten teachers in Germany. Using it and the enrollment figures given in Table 10.1, Tables 10.5 and 10.6 have been prepared. All figures are estimated, but they are judged by Dr. Zimmer of the *Deutsche Jugendinstitut* to be reasonable. The pupil-teacher ratio proves to be the same as in the model kindergarten visited in Hessen. In "Reviews of National Policies for Education" (OECD, 1972) it is stated that "Kindergarten groups average 30 children at present." The "Report of the Federal Government on Education, 1970" states that in the Federal area in 1961 the number of pupils per teacher across all levels of education was 20.1. In 1967, it was 17.0. The number of pupils per class for the same years is 20.1 and 17.9 respectively, which makes our estimated pupil-teacher ratio for kindergartens (23:1) appear reasonable.

Dr. Stahl (1974), in a private communication, suggests the actual pupil-teacher ratio was 45:1 since the ratio of 23:1 refers not only to the kindergarten teachers but also includes all related professionals, such as nursery assistants and student teachers.

TABLE 10.6
Estimated Pupil:Teacher Ratio In Kindergarten From 1960-61 to 1970-71

Year	Private	Public	Total
1960-61	23:1	23:1	23:1
1965-66	23:1	23:1	23:1
1970-71	23:1	23:1	23:1

FINANCING EARLY CHILDHOOD EDUCATION

Free education in Germany begins at the compulsory school level. Its cost is shared between the federal government, the *Lander,* and the local municipalities. In the OECD's "Reviews of National Policies for Education: Germany" (1972), it is stated that the shared financing by state and municipal sponsors funds the state, paying teachers (civil servants). The municipality carries the material costs. In some *Länder,* however, both state and municipality contribute to personnel and material costs. Percentages of costs shared by the federal government, *Länder,* and municipal governments are given as follows in the UNESCO publication's "Federal Republic of Germany" (1971) for 1962 and 1967:

	1962-1963	1967-1968
Federal Government	8.6%	11.7%
Lander	61.0	63.5
Communities	30.4	25.0

It is clear from these data that the *Länder* pay by far the largest share of the cost of education, with this share increasing over the 3 year period. Amounts vary between *Länder,* of course, because some are wealthier than others.

Financial support of preschool education in the Federal Republic comes from several sources: (*1*) from the voluntary youth services (most of which are maintained by the two major Christian churches or other parishes); (*2*) from local child service authorities under the auspices of various political groups; (*3*) from *Land* youth offices or their branches, in the form of subsidies to all kindergartens other than those run on a commercial basis. In 1970, the *Länder* contributions to the cost of kindergartens were as follows:

	DM (in thousands)
Total	198,745
Schleswig-Holstein	4,806
Hamburg	44,674
Neidersachsen	11,772
Bremen	8,133
Nordrhein-Westphalia	24,177
Hessen	23,492
Rheinland-Pfalz	6,021
Baden-Wurttemberg	15,208
Bayern	22,228
Saarland	207
Berlin (West)	38,628

In the same year, contributions from the nongovernmental (primarily Church or welfare) organizations to kindergarten education were:

	DM (in thousands)
Total	120,065
Schleswig-Holstein	1,988
Hamburg	N.A.
Niedersachsen	11,385
Bremen	1,182
Nordrhein-Westphalia	52,850
Hessen	5,995
Rheinland-Pfalz	5,974
Baden-Wurttemberg	18,563
Bayern	9,648
Saarland	1,004
Berlin (West)	11,476

The combined total expenditure, governmental and private for 1970, amounts to approximately 319 million DM. The average per pupil expenditure per annum is $3.08, as compared with a per capita gross national product (1969) of $3,040.

In the Federal Republic, kindergartens are not, however, entirely free; most parents must make contributions. What they pay varies from *Land* to *Land*, from school to school (depending on the sponsor), and in accordance with their own income and the number of children they have. Thus the fees may be as low as 25% of the cost or as high as 50%. Taking an average across the whole of the republic, it would be fair to say, therefore, that the parents, the state, and the other sponsoring organization each pay about one-third of the cost of the country's kindergartens.

Table 10.7 presents expenditure data for both public and private kindergartens for the years 1965-1966 to 1970-1971. It is important to note that they represent disbursements from public (*Länder*) funds only and do not portray the entire cost of kindergarten education. Over this 5-year period, expenditures in the private and public sector have risen by almost exactly the same amounts, giving a total increase of 63.7%.

Per pupil costs for public and private kindergartens for the years 1965-1966 to 1969-1970 are given in Table 10.8. These also refer only to the *Lander* contributions and again do not represent the total cost. If we assume that these account for approximately one-third of the cost of educating a kindergarten child, the other two-thirds being paid by parents and private sponsors, the actual cost per child in 1970 was approximately $162 a year. This figure appears to be a reasonable estimate, for it is similar to the per pupil yearly costs identified in the reports on several other countries in this series. The only actual data on current operating costs per child come from a model kindergarten in Hessen where it is $424 annually. The estimate of $168 is only 41% of that cost, but it would not be unusual for a model school to be more expensive to run than a normal one.

TABLE 10.7

Public Expenditure on Kindergartens in Germany (F.R.) from 1965–66 to 1969–70
(Contribution from Länder only)

Year	Private		Public		DM '000 Total Capital Current	$ '000 Total Capital Current
	Capital	Current	Capital	Current		
1965–66	n.a.	49,573	56,003	111,384	216,960+	54,327+[a]
1966–67	n.a.	49,814	56,775	123,774	230,363+	
1967–68	n.a.	54,901	38,418	133,590	226,909+	
1968–69	n.a.	63,760	55,267	146,682	265,709+	
1969–70	n.a.	76,139	108,278	170,716	355,133+	90,573+
% of increase from 1965–66 to 1969–70		53.6	93.3	53.3	63.7	66.7

Source: Ministry of Labor and Welfare, Nordrhein, Westfalen.

[a] Official Exchange rates

TABLE 10.8

Kindergarten Per Pupil Costs in United States Dollars (from 1965–66 to 1969–70)
(Contribution from Länder only)

Year	Private			Public			Total		
	Current Expend. '000	No. of Children '000	Per Pupil Cost	Current Expend. '000	No. of Children '000	Per Pupil Cost	Current Expend. '000	No. of Children '000	Per Pupil Cost
1965–66	12,413	165	75	27,891	652	43	40,304	818	49
1969–70	19,418	234	83	43,529	427	47	62,958	1,161	54
Total Increase			8			3			5

Source: Ministry of Labor and Welfare, Nordrhein, Westfalen.

(Total per pupil cost (excluding parents', private sponsors', and states' contributions) in 1969–70 is estimated at $162.)

INSTRUCTIONAL METHODS

Kindergarten education in Germany does not lend itself to easy description in terms of instructional methods. West Berlin and each of the 10 *Länder* organizes it in its own way. The one common factor is the predominance of the use of the child-centered play orientation developed and popularized by Froebel.

The child-centered play orientation approach cultivates the young child's natural talents and gives him time to play with materials especially designed for him. It is clearly an extension of the home, rather than an attempt to supplant the home. The home and school work closely together. The kindergarten emphasizes the total life experience of the child and attempts to give him as many experiences as possible from which to derive benefit.

According to Lazerson (1972), the kindergartens operate on the principle that, since all education begins with the child, instructional methodology employs materials which draw upon his inner needs. Since all children are naturally active, the educational environment should offer outlets for physical exercise. Teachers must be trained in the child's special needs and possess the qualities of warmth and tenderness necessary in a mother-supplement.

The kindergarten teacher's method is like that of a good gardener. She does all she can to nourish health tendencies in children and weed out destructive ones. The child's gardener provides for the young human plant the proper conditions for growth and harmonious development, suitable climate, soil and exposure, careful nurture, and happy occupations for activities of soul, mind, and body.

According to this methodology, one of the most crucial phases in learning is the development of the senses. The child is, therefore, freed to see, hear, feel, taste, and smell all kinds of things. Materials are provided to meet these needs.

The instructional method evolved from Froebel's earlier concept of using "gifts"—wool balls, wooden geometric objects, and metal rings—which symbolically taught the young the nature of the universe. Stress was laid on group activities—marching, dancing, singing—which allowed the child to express himself while helping him learn to work with his peers.

Stahl (1972) sees German kindergarten as organized to help a child live a natural life suited to his needs. Free play, she states, is emphasized more than directed play or incentives for systematic learning and working. As a result, technical equipment is not considered very important. Nevertheless, parental involvement and cooperation are stressed.

At the age of five, the child enters the *Vermittlungsgruppen,* a transitional stage which prepares him for primary school. Thus, according to Stahl, the purposes of preprimary education have been completed.

RESEARCH ON EARLY CHILDHOOD EDUCATION

With its strong scientific tradition, the Federal Republic of Germany clearly recognizes the potential value of research in the solving of many of its educational problems. As the Report of the Federal Government on Education (1970) says:

> Causes of the current deficiencies in the educational system and the effects of new structures and content can only be analysed and made evident by scientific research. Thus educational research is a basic prerequisite for educational reform [p. 208].

The document "Educational Organization and Development in the Federal Republic of Germany 1970-1971" also emphasizes the need for a broadly based scientific research program embracing a large number of experiments. One of the things it recommends for investigation is the possibility of attaching elementary education to primary education. In fact, research institutes have been at work since the 1960s on topice relevant to the teaching and learning processes and the relationships between education and society. The initiative for such research projects has come variously—from the research establishments themselves, universities, educational authorities, foundations, the Federal Education Council, and from the Science Council.

In the 1970 report, the following should perhaps be given specific notice. Among the establishments:

The German Institute for International Educational Research, Frankfurt: This has a staff of some 50 scientists. Its interests have included: a project of international comparisons of attainment; investigations of the sociology of the teacher; economic analyses of educational installations; analyses of the reasons for selecting certain secondary-school educational installations and for pupils' failures in certain courses of study. It has also worked on the development and trying out of curricula.

The Institute for Educational Research in the Max Planck Society in Berlin: (about 160 staff members including 60 scientists) which is engaged in particular in basic research. This includes: an investigation of factors that influence pupil performance; analyses of the relations between education and behavior in the vocational world; and investigations of social processes in early childhood. In addition the Institute has carried out a considerable number of special surveys and documentations.

In the University of Constance (60 staff members including 20 full-time scientists) seven groups are investigating various problems of educational planning, the effects of the educational processes and influences on teaching.

The Education Center in Berlin (about 160 staff members, including 40 scientists) is integrated within the Berlin school administration. Its primary assignment is curriculum development and to provide academic advice for school experiments in science.

Also affiliated to the Land Educational Administration is *the State Institute for Educational Research and Planning in Munich* (some 15 staff members, including 10 scientists). Among its responsibilities are the provision of academic advice for developments in the Bavarian school system and the compilation of data for regional educational planning.

Rommel (1972), commenting on the need for planing and experimentation in education, had the following to say to a special Working Group for Innovation Models (WG-IM) set up to define areas of special interest for experimentation. He said definition of the areas was based on the so-called "Interim Report on the Development Plan for Education" of the BLK, which discusses aims for preschool education, particularly expansion of preschool for the 5-year-olds. This report left open, however, many questions including whether the preschool for the 5-year-old was to be part of a new introductory stage of primary school.

A conference on preschool, organized by the Working Group on Preschool Education and held in Hannover in September, 1970, considered, among other things, results of various experimental programs serving as pilot projects for reform at this level of education. The conference reached no general consensus on what new preschool education should be. Agreeing on only one point—that more preschool education is needed—it concluded that these results were controversial and because the experiments were confined to limited sets of circumstances, they were not in a form to be applied generally. The conference felt it was time that an objective evaluation should be made of the manifold audio-visual material now being offered to the preschools.

In North Rhine-Westphalia, a 5-year project begun in 1971 is questioning whether the reform plan to lower the age of entrance in primary schools from 6 to 5 years by 1980 has pedagogic value and if it will lead to optional success in developing the talents and promoting the education of small children. It is comparing the performance of 50 preschool classes attached to primary schools with classes for the same age-group in 50 autonomous kindergartens, with a view to discovering which of the two environments is the better for educating 5-year olds. The results of this work will be an important factor when it is decided if early childhood education should be given in preschool classes attached to primary schools or in the kindergartens.

Experiments have also been made in Hessen on the incorporation of preschool classes into the primary school. These, however, for children of 5 and 6 years old, are distinct from the 5-year-olds only in the North Rhine-Westphalia experiment.

Another North Rhine-Westphalia research project is concerned with the organizational and educational recommendations in the reform plan, particularly the overall aim of equality of educational opportunities and the importance of early childhood education in its sociological context. Ten different operationally-defined objectives concerned with the cognitive, emotional, and social development of the child are included in the plan. The cognitive part includes linguistic programs and basic structures in mathematics, geometrics, and logic. The emotional part consists of music modeling, and movement. The social development part takes in social and habit training.

Long-term educational plans for Hamburg and Berlin envisage the lowering of the compulsory school age by 1 year in 10 to 15 years time. In 1969, Hamburg started experimental preschool classes with different populations (that is, social groups) for 5-year-olds. These classes will be in the charge of trained teachers and of educational sociologists and are to gradually replace the school kindergarten classes. Roughly 1000 of these were planned for Hamburg in 1969, the capital cost being estimated at 140 million DM. Running costs for staffing and teaching materials would be about 21 million DM per year.

In Berlin, some preschool classes for 5-year-olds have been using programs based on American models adapted to local conditions. Emphasis is given to progressive training in learning and to creative games. The experience gained with these preschool classes is commented on and evaluated by Hoenisch, Niggemeyer, and Zimmer (1969).

In Freiburg, experimental preschool classes (*Modellkindergarten*) were started in September, 1969, to identify and test improved methods of work in the kindergartens. The first results are due for publication in 1973.

Other German research results include those reported by Wildauer, (1968) on the possibility of enriching preschool education by introducing children to the techniques of analyzing and synthesizing concepts in ways appropriate to their age. These show positive advantages from such a program in comparison with traditional methods used in kindergartens. Also discussing the need of enrichment programs for children from 3 years old is Hillebrand's paper "The Contribution of Preschool Educational Problems" (1970).

Other researchers investigating early childhood education include Hagenbusch (1968), Schultze (1970), and Schurrmann (1971). Hagenbusch and Schultze report that research on cognitive development in preschool shows that a one-sided emphasis on intellectual training hinders the natural development of the child.

Schurrmann, reporting the results of a study of the concept of "more" and "less" in children from 2 years and 8 months, to 5 years of age, states there were no significant differences by age in the "more" section of the experiment, although there were significant differences across ages in the ability to verbalize the concept. These disappeared by age 5.

Since 1968, preschool programs in Hannover have been carried out with socially disadvantaged children to enable them to start school more equally prepared. These center on group solution of problems. A number of recommendations are given for the training of preschool teachers for such programs (Harde, Sierslebel, and Wogatzki, 1969).

Tausch (1968) published a study on the attitude of kindergarten teachers showing that the climate in kindergarten is authoritarian with teachers initiating most of the activities. This was particularly true during verbal classroom interaction.

A number of pilot programs testing various school experiments and reform concepts have been launched cooperatively by the Federal Government's Ministry of Education and Science, and the *Länder* Ministries of Education. Attracting particular attention is the project "Kindergärten in Rural Districts" since few rural children have nursery and preschool facilities, which are too difficult to maintain in sparsely populated areas. Six villages in Saxony, therefore, are testing a mobile form of kindergarten in which play groups meet for a day twice each week with a visiting nursery school teacher. On the other days mothers, trained by the nursery teacher, lead the groups.

Other current studies on preschools include one of visual comprehension of Nickel (1969), whose results indicate that successful training in visual perception depends more on age and socioeconomic status than on intelligence.

"Sesame Street," a well-known American program for preschool-age children, produced by the "Children's Television Workshop" in the United States, was purchased by German television and will be translated and adapted to German rules and norms. Some 200 of the half-hour programs were scheduled to be broadcast beginning in January 1973.

Areas of substantial research in Western Germany today, as listed by Stahl (1972), include the planning of scientific test projects, the creation of model institutions for study, the creation of documentation centers for didactic play, the development of teaching and learning programs for preschool institutions, and the expansion of training centers for teachers.

In general, the results of research on early childhood education in West Germany are as follows:

1. Education for 5-year-olds is generally considered desirable by the Germans. The inclusion of the age group in the primary school is under consideration.
2. Among the most important uses of preprimary education is the elimination of socioeconomic differences in children. This is possible with increased emphasis on socioeconomically disadvantaged children.
3. In rural areas, experiments are being conducted in the use of travelling preprimary teachers and part-time schools.
4. Techniques of analysis and synthesis of concept have shown favorable results compared to traditional methods.

5. Methods emphasizing the natural, overall development of the child appear better than those limited to the intellectual domain.
6. In nearly all areas, research into problems of preprimary education in West Germany has been institution so recently that findings are, at best, only tentative.

ACKNOWLEDGMENTS

The author wishes to acknowledge the valuable help received from Dr. Jurgen Zimmer, *Deutsches Jugendinstitut,* Munich; Prof. O. Schmalohr, *Pädagogische Hochschule Rheinland,* Aachen; Mr. M. Walter, *Kultusministerium Nordrhein-Westfalen,* Düsseldorf; Dr. Freund, *Statistiches Bundesamt,* Wiesbaden; Dr. Oevermann, Max Planck *Institut für Bildungsforschung,* Berlin; M. Tumbraegel, *Sozialministerium,* Mainz; and Dr. A. D. Buss, President, German section, World Organization for Early Childhood Education, Berlin.

BIBLIOGRAPHY

Blackstone, T. *A Fair Start—The provision of pre-school education.* London: Allen Lane The Penguin Press, 1971.

Figgen, W. *Vorläufiger Rahmenplan für die Erziehungsund Bildungsarbeit im Kindergarten.*

Fittkau, B. *Notwendigkeit und Möglichkeit von Erzieher-Training zur Forderung freiheitlich-demokratisch-sozialer Haltungen und Verhaltungsweisen.*

Hagenbusch, A. M. Einige Gedanken zur derzeitigen Kindergarten-arbeit. *Welt des Kindes,* Deutschland 1968, *46*(2), 55-9.

Harde, O., Siersleben, W., & Wogatzki, R. *Lernen im Vorschulalter.* Dortmund: Schroedel Verlag, 1969.

Hilldebrand, M. J. Zum Problem der Vorschulterziehung. *Westermanns Pädagogische Beiträge,* 22e annee cahier 7, Juli 1970, 341-351.

Hoenisch, N., Niggemeyer, E., & Zimmer, J. *Vorschulkinder.* Stuttgart: Klett Verlag, 1969.

Lazerson, M. Historical antecendents of early childhood education. In *Policy Research in Education* (reprint series), the Center for Educational Policy Research, Harvard Graduate School of Education, Cambridge, Mass., 1972.

Nickel, H. Die Bedeutung planmässiger Übung für die Entwicklung einer differenzierend visuellen Auffassung im Vorschulalter. *Zeitschrift für Entwicklungspsychologie und Pëdagogische Psychologie* 1969. 1.

Oerter, R. Vorschulerziehung oder Was nun in Wissenschaft und Praxis. *Bayerische Schule,* Feb. 11 and 25, 1972.

Pichottka, J. *Intelligenz-Zuwachs durch Frühlesen.* Article from Deutsches Jugendinstitut (undated).

Robinsohn, S. B. *Zur gegenwärtigen Curriculum—Diskussion—eine Einführung.* Stencil from Deutsches Jugendinstitut (undated).

Rommel, L. *Comments on Working Group for Innovation Models* (WG-IN). Stencil from Deutsches Jugendinstitit, 1972.

Rost, D., Standte, A., & Vietzke, E. Über Probleme des Vorschulischen Lesenlernens—eine vergleichende Darstellung deutscher Untersuchungen (III). *Deutsche Schule,* 11/1971.

Nugent, J. Doesn't Anyone Speak German Anymore? *International Herald Tribune,* March 27, 1973.

Schultze, W. Vorschulerziehung in der Diskussion. *International Review of Education,* 1970, *16*(1), 23-45.

296 10 EARLY CHILDHOOD EDUCATION IN GERMANY

Schultze, W. *Schools in Europe* (Vol. 1, Part A). Weinheim: J. Belz Verlag, 1968.
Schultze, W. Vorschulerziehung in der Diskussion. *International Review of Education,* UNESCO Institute for Education, Hamburg, Special number, XVI/1970/1.
Schurrmann, U. Kognitive Fähigkeiten junger Kinder. *Psychologische Beiträge,* April 1971, 609-617.
Stahl, M. Pre-school education in the Federal Republic of Germany. *OMEP International Journal of Early Childhood,* XIII World Assembly of OMEP, Irish University Press, 1972.
Stahl, M. Personal communication, October, 1974.
Tausch, W. *Study on attitudes of kindergarten teachers.* Stencil from Deutsches Jugendinstitut (1968).
Thiersch, R. *Zur Situation der Vorschulerziehung, Gutachten.* Deutsches Jungendinstitut (undated).
Thomas, H. *Innovation in education* (E1/71.03). Germany, CERI Technical Report.
Westphal, H. In *International Journal of Early Childhood,* Supplement 1, XIII World Assembly of OMEP, 1972.
Wildauer, G. *Zur Entwicklung der geistigen Tätigkeit in Vorschulalter.* Volk und Wissen. East Berlin: Volkseigener Verlag, 1968.
Wolff, R. Kann Vorschulerziehung gesellschaftliche Ungleichheit kompensieren? Selbstbetrug oder Rattenfängerei? *Die Grundschule,* 3 fg. H, Okt. 1971.
Zimmer, J. Comments from a personal interview at Deutsches Jugendinstitut, 1972.
United Nations Secretariat, Population Division, Department of Economic and Social Affairs. *Analyses and projections of households and families* (ESA/P/WP.28/Rev 1). August 1971.
Conference on Pre-school Education, papers and reports. Organized by the Working Group on Pre-school education at Hannover. September 16-20, 1970. Friedrich-Verlag, Velberb. Hannover.
Council for cultural co-operation of the Council of Europe. *Education in Europe, school systems: A guide.* Strasbourg: 1970.
Council of Europe. News Letter No. 2/72.
Der Minister für Arbeit, Gesundheit und Soziales des Landes Nordrhein-Westfalen, IV B 2−6272/1971. Tageseinrichtungen für Kinder in der Bundesrepublik Deutschland. 1960 bis 1969. Stand 31.12. 1969.
Deutscher Bildungsrat Empfehlungen der Bildungskommission Strukturplan für das Bildungswesen. Stuttgart: Klett, E., 1970, 398.
Der Bundesminister fur Arbeit und Sozialordnung: Sozialpolitische Informationen, Jahrgang VI/15, 27 mai 1972.
Deutscher Bundestag, Wissenschaftliche Dienste, Materialen Nr. 27, Vorschulische Erziehung, Probleme und Initiativen, November, 1971.
Deutsche Press-Agentur, dpa, Hintergrund Archiv und Informationsmaterial, Kindergarten und Vorschulerziehung in der Bundesrepublik, Hamburg 9, September, 1971, Teil I and Teil II.
Institut voor Onderwijskunde: Preprimary education European Cultural Foundation, Study Project Europe 2000, Project 1, Subject III, Study 9D.
International Review of Education XVI/1970/1 Special number UNESCO Institute for Education, Hamburg.
International Federation of Teachers' Associations (IFTA) Congress of Helsinki, 1969, Pre-school Education.
Modell Kindergarten im Nordrhein-Westfalen: Landeskonferenz Uber die Arbeit in Modell Kindergarten am Sept. 1970 in Dusseldorf. Bonifacius Druckerei Paderborn.

OECD. *Classification of educational systems.* Paris, 1972.

OECD. *Economic surveys.* 1972.

OECD. *Labor force statistics, 1959-1970.* Paris, 1972.

OCED. *Reviews of national policies for education–Germany.* Paris, 1972, ED (71)3.

OMEP. *International Journal of Early Childhood,* Supplement 1, 1972, Irish University Press.

Reports of the Federal Government on Education, 1970, Bildungsbericht, 1970. Der Bundesminister für Bildung und Wissenschaft.

Sozialpolitische Informationen: Grundsätze zur Eingliederung ausländerischer Arbeitnehmer und ihrer Familien vom April 1972 Der Bundesminister für Arbeit und Sozialordnung, 24 mai 1972.

Statistisches Bundesamt Wiesbaden, June 14, 1972.

UNESCO. *Educational Organization and Development in the Federal Republic of Germany in 1970/71.* Bonn. August 2, 1971.

UNESCO. *World survey of education II, primary education.* 1958.

Vorschulerziehung: FU–Pressedienst Wissenschaft, Berlin, Febuary, 1972.

United Nations yearbook. 1970.

Early Childhood Education
in The Netherlands

INTRODUCTION

Freedom, a fundamental concept in early childhood education in The Netherlands, is embodied in the parents' right, guaranteed in the 1885 constitution, to choose both the type of school and the type of instruction for their children.

The desire for early schools for 3- and 4-year-olds in the Netherlands arose partly from the need of the poor for child care during working hours and partly from the conviction of the religious sector that education in a particular faith was best begun early in the child's life. Thus the first preschools were the secular "minding schools" (*bewaarschool*) and the religious "keeping schools" (Roman Catholic *bequineschools* and Protestant *matressenschools*) designed around 1800 initially to provide care for children of working-class parents. All three provided psychohygienic care and, in fact, were used extensively by rich and poor alike. For the poor, they were free, but middle and upper class families were charged about 10 guilders a week.

Officially, these early schools were intended to be supervised by the staff of the elementary schools; in reality, however, there was no such supervision. Those in charge generally were untrained elderly women or shopkeepers. Under them, conditions so deteriorated that by the late 1800s local physicians sounded an alarm that gave the impetus for corrective legislation.

Froebel, in the early nineteenth century, and Maria Montessori, early in this century, were important influences on the development of early childhood education in the Netherlands. A less structured and more modern design of Froebel's *"spielgaben"* provided the basis for the educational programs until some 50 years ago, when the Montessori method started to come into favor. The Dutch Montessori Society was founded in 1917 and started teacher training the following year. A further contemporary influence was Langeveld, whose view that the family is the fundamental unit on which later education should be based has had a strong impact on early childhood education in the Netherlands.

In 1860, about 50,000 4- and 5-year-old children in a country of 3.3 million people went to preschool. In 1890, the total Dutch population had risen to 5 million, and the preschool population to 117,000 children attending over a thousand infant schools. Today, in a population of 13 million, 500,000 4- and 5-year-old children go to 6600 preschools. In this 112-year period, the preschool population has risen by a factor of 10 while the total population has only risen by a factor of 4.

Compulsory education in The Netherlands was established by law in 1900 for children from 7 to 12 years of age. This was extended to 15 years by acts passed in 1920 and 1969. In 1955, a Preprimary Education Act established preschools for 4- to 7-year-olds. These schools have both a play and a work program.

Blending Froebel, Montessori, and Langeveld, the prevailing purpose of kindergartens in the Netherlands today is to provide a program that insures optimum freedom for the child while an adult is responsible for his education.

ENROLLMENTS, PRESCHOOL EDUCATION (1960-1970)

For present purposes, the characteristics of early childhood education in The Netherlands will be taken as defined in the OECD "Classification of Educational Systems" (1972), namely:

> Length of study in years equals 2 or 3 years.
> Entrance requirement is to be 4 years old.
> Preschool is provided for children from 4 to 6 or 7 years of age.
> Both public and private kindergartens are fully financed from state funds [p. 10].

Table 11.1 shows the number of children in public and private kindergartens in the Netherlands from 1960-1961 to 1970-1971. During this 10-year period, enrollments in the private sector grew by 17.5% and in the public sector by 46.4%. The overall increase was 23.6%. It is important to note the number of children attending private as opposed to public kindergartens. In 1960, 79% were in private ones. In 1970, the figure had dropped to 75%. It should be further realized that the large increase of 46.4% in the public school enrollments is due more to the fact that there was a very small base to start with than to a

TABLE 11.1

Enrollments in Kindergarten in the Netherlands from 1960-61 to 1970-71

			(in 000's)
Year	Private	Public	Total
1960-61	314	84	398
1965-66	354	103	457
1966-67	361	108	469
1967-68	369	112	481
1968-69	371	118	489
1969-70	371	122	493
1970-71	369	123	492
% of increase from 1960-61 to 1970-71	17.5	46.4	23.6

Source: Central Bureau of Statistics, the Netherlands.

particularly rapid growth in its total enrollments. In the primary schools over these 10 years, there was a 3% increase in enrollments, and the rate of private-public attendance had changed only slightly. In 1960, 73% went to private primary schools; in 1970, it was 72%. It is plain to see, therefore, that almost 75% of Dutch children attend a private kindergarten as well as a private primary school.

The educational system of The Netherlands reflects the three major groups within its population: Roman Catholics, Protestants, and nondenominational. OECD's "Educational Policy and Planning—the Netherlands" (1967) shows how this is expressed in pupil distribution and school sponsorship at the primary level:

	Population	Pupils	Schools
	%	%	%
Roman Catholic	40	45	38
Protestant	38	27	29
Nondenominational and other denominational groups	22	28	33
Total	100	100	100

These figures deserve close study. They indicate that for the Catholic population, the number of pupils who attend their schools and the number of schools they manage are very closely related to their proportion of the population. For the Protestants, this is not the case. They provide 38% of the population, yet only 27% of the pupils and 29% of the schools are controlled by them. The explanation is that an increasing number of Protestants are sending their children

TABLE 11.2
Population Attendance Rates in Kindergarten in the Netherlands from
1960-61 to 1970-71

	1960-61	1970-71	(in 000's) % of Change
Total age group 4 - 5 years in kindergarten	348	428	23.0
Infant Population 4 - 5 years	449	476	6.0
% of age group enrolled	77.5	90.0	16.1

Source: Central Bureau of Statistics, the Netherlands.

to nondenominational schools of one type or another. This trend is also seen at the preprimary level. Table 11.1 showed that it was in the public sector that the most rapid growth was taking place. We can hypothesize, then, that this growth will continue because of the choice by many Dutch people, both Catholics and Protestants, to send their children to nondemoninational schools. This appears to demonstrate a growing lack of confidence in religiously sponsored education.

Table 11.2 gives attendance rates in kindergartens from 1960-1961 to 1970-1971. In 1960, 77.5% of the children aged 4 and 5 were enrolled; by 1970-1971 this had increased to 90%. Over the 10-year period, there has been a 6% growth in the infant population of ages 4 and 5; but, as the table shows, there has been an overall increase of 16.1% in the number of children enrolled in kindergartens. It should be explained here that the totals presented in Tables 11.1 and 11.2 are not in agreement because Table 11.1 includes many 6-year-old children while Table 11.2 does not. Children who reach 6 years of age after October 1 must remain in kindergarten until August of the next year. This represents about 60,000 children.

The number of children aged 4 and 5 in The Netherlands who attended kindergarten between 1961 and 1970 was:

Children	1961	1965	1970
4-year-olds	160,000 70%	183,000 76%	205,000 82%
5-year-olds	198,000 88%	215,000 92%	243,000 95%

The percentage of pupils in attendance by single year of age and by age group during 1971-1972 was as follows:

Age	Percentage	Age	Percentage
6	99%	5-6	97%
5	95%	4-6	91%
4	80%	3-6	70%
3	5%	2-6	56%
2	1%		

As to future demand for places in kindergarten, the most important factor is birthrate. In 1966, the number of live births per thousand was 19.2. By 1970 this had declined to 18.4, a drop of .8% per thousand, or 4.2% (United Nations Demographic Yearbook, 1970).

Kohnstamm (1973) states:

> A new problem in our preschool system is the adaptation to this new situation. Classes and schools have to be closed. . . . The fight between the several school-systems for souls (children) becomes sharper because of the scarcity (personal correspondence from Kohnstamm).

That this recent decline is part of a long-term pattern is confirmed by the following information provided by the United Nations Population Division (1971). In 1899, the average size of household in The Netherlands was 5.51 persons. By 1930 this had dropped to 4, and by 1960 to 3.5. The gross reproduction rate over the same period fell from 2.3 to 1.5. Hence, the average size of household has decreased by one child over the 60-year period and the reproduction rate by .8, or 34.8%, both very significant drops. These factors are contributing to the increasing demand for early childhood education as a means for enlarging the social contacts of young children. The increased participation of women in the labor force is also offered as a reason for a greater demand for places in preschools. Table 11.3 shows how this has risen over the 10-year period 1960-1970.

ISSUES OF DEBATE

One of the basic concepts behind the Dutch educational system is freedom for parents to choose an education for their children in accordance with their principles and beliefs. This is safeguarded by the constitution.

Hence, while nothing may be done educationally that will stand in the way of this freedom, The Netherlands Ministry of Education and, indeed, the population itself are faced with a considerable problem of coordination to insure that the national system is fully efficient. The main task of the policy makers,

TABLE 11.3
Labor Force Participation Rates - The Netherlands

		1960 %	1970 %
$\dfrac{\text{Total Labor Force}}{\text{Total Population}} \times 100$			
(a)	Total	36.4	36.9
(b)	Males	77.7	74.7
(c)	Females	22.3	25.3
$\dfrac{\text{Total Labor Force}}{\substack{\text{Population from} \\ \text{15 to 64 years}}} \times 100$			
(a)	Total	60.3	58.0
(b)	Males	91.0	85.5
(c)	Females	25.6	30.0

Source: Labor Force Statistics, 1959-1970, O.E.C.D., Paris, 1972.

therefore, is to assess what the public wants from its schools and to see that it gets it.

In the last 50 years, more than one attempt has been made to reorganize the educational system, but without notable results.[1] One of the stumbling blocks has been the small number of children from lower-class homes who go on to higher education, and, in the last few years, a considerable effort has been made to encourage their continuing school.

In economic (though not necessarily social) terms, the Dutch population ranges over three groups: an upper class (4.4% in the year 1960), a middle class (42.8%), and a lower class (52.8%).[2] Within this latter group, there is a relatively small proportion (about 1%) of people living in slums, caravans, or the remote rural areas whose children start life at a considerable disadvantage and tend to do badly when they get to school. These children are a matter of growing concern in The Netherlands.

One way of insuring their improvement in school is to plan carefully for it, and this includes arranging for the children to attend preschool. This, however, raises

[1] OECD *Educational policy and planning—The Netherlands* (1967).

[2] CBS 13e Algemene Volkstelling 1960. D1 10. Beroepsbevolking. A. Algemene inleiding, p. 31.

problems. From 1900-1940, Dutch kindergartens were relatively structured, and activities there were carefully worked out. In the last 30 years, they have become intentionally much more freely organized, thus, it is not surprising that those who now propose a return to structural programs for these disadvantaged children run into difficulty with the people presently responsible for the kindergartens. De Vries (1972) has written about this issue:

> It might be too simple to classify the normal Dutch kindergarten as "unstructured" as there is enough structure to be found in the schools, but as to the stimulation of emotional, social, and cognitive development of children, little systematic planning is to be found. The philosophy behind this lack of systematic stimulation is that the pre-school period should be a time in which the child is free to develop through play and spontaneous activities. One may question the reliability of this philosophy. As there was and is in general little knowledge on the value and results of systematic stimulation, the philosophy of a free and spontaneous development could have served as a sop.
>
> By lack of a system in which one knows what to do first, what to elaborate and what to do next, another structure for the kindergarten could flourish, namely a system in which activities were chosen because they were nice to do, or were thought to be of some use from a psychohygienic point of view or as a preparation for scholastic achievement in the elementary school [p. 4].

In the same context, a research project is already under way at the University of Utrecht under Dr. de Vries' direction to study the benefits of a more structured program and to devise something that will compensate for the disadvantaged environments in which these Dutch children are reared. At the Research Institute for Applied Psychology, University of Amsterdam, another group under the leadership of Dr. van Calcar is working on a preschool curriculum that has much broader aims than the one being considered in Utrecht. It is also working to arrange visits to the parents of kindergarten children and encourage their involvement in their children's education. Of the other groups that are working on the creation of new preschool programs, we should in particular mention the work done at the Kohnstamm Institute for Educational Research in Amsterdam, and in the Free University of Amsterdam under Dr. Groenendaal. The latter is adapting a program designed by Marion Blank, which uses Frostig materials.

There are, then, three different attitudes about this matter in the Netherlands. The traditional one is that of the teachers who presently run most of the kindergartens. Another is exemplified by the group in Utrecht, who still take a school-oriented point of view but are concerned with upgrading curriculum to compensate for disadvantaged family background. A third attitude is seen in Amsterdam, where it is doubted that the curriculum alone can compensate for differences in upbringing, and means are being sought for improvement outside the strict confines of the school.

Teunissen (1972) disappointedly reports the results to date of increasingly structured preprimary educational programs in The Netherlands. Educational projects, he observes, have demonstrated small gains in reading and little or no gain in the area of IQ. The differences in reading generally vanish within a few months of entrance into first grade. He expressed the hope, however, that concentration on academic skills in preprimary schools would not be rejected merely because it is difficult to prove in research situations that there are real benefits from early cognition.

Teunissen also touches on the concern that primary school teachers often feel when preschool teachers begin to introduce their children to reading, writing, and arithmetic. In the opinion of the primary teachers, this is unquestionably their prerogative. It is Teunissen's view that this area of friction would be removed if a reform now being advocated to integrate the preprimary and the primary school systems were generally adopted. This idea is being tested already in several experimental schools where the children range from 4 to 12 years old. One of the major aims of this experiment is to make the transition between the preprimary and primary levels as flexible and smooth as possible. Results are being watched carefully by the government, with a view to legislation that might bring primary and preprimary education (to be compulsory at the age of 5) together in the same building. The enactment of such a law would also clearly have implications for the training of preprimary and primary teachers.

Associated with lowering the compulsory school age to 5 and combining preschool and lower primary is the possibility of even younger children entering the system. By August, 1974, the entrance age in any case was lowered from 4 to 3.9. The Dutch National Foundation for Educational Research (SVO) has commissioned a study of the effect of allowing even 3-year-olds to enter kindergarten. One side effect of this lowered entrance age is preschool teachers' concern for their status. Many of them fear that if they have to look after younger children, their prestige and level of pay will fall, or at least fail to keep up with those of the primary school teachers.

In brief, the principal issues of debate concerning early childhood education in The Netherlands are these:

1. Reconciling freedom of choice by parents as to their children's school with the provision of a good overall educational system by the state.
2. Easing the child's transition from preprimary to primary school.
3. Special provision for disadvantaged children.
4. Reconciling three conceptions of what preschool education should be.
   a. a somewhat heterogeneous nursery school
   b. an introduction to learning
   c. a process in which parents and the local community are essentially involved

5. Lowering the age of entrance to kindergarten to 3.9 years in 1974 and possibly to 3 sometime later.

THE AIMS AND OBJECTIVES OF EARLY CHILDHOOD EDUCATION

The basic aim of kindergarten education in The Netherlands is to foster the social, emotional, and cognitive development of young children. The schools are expected to offer an environment favorable to this by providing opportunities for children to learn to play and interact within their own age group. There are various views in The Netherlands on the kindergarten's responsibility to teach moral and ethical principles, but all would agree that they should at least teach the rudiments of good manners.

Unofficially, most educators would agree that the following are included in a typical preprimary program:

1. Motor skills (climbing, running, jumping, balancing).
2. Manipulatory skills (using scissors, crayons, paste, paints, clay; building with blocks, working with puzzles, bead tying, buttoning).
3. Control and restraint (listening to stories, sitting still, reacting to music).
4. Appropriate behavior (independence-dependence in adult-child relations; coping with fears, angry feelings, guilt, developing happy qualities, fun, humour, healthy optimism).
5. Psychosexual developments (identification, learning sex roles, formation of conscience).
6. Language development and intellectual development (cognitive learning, concept formation, self-understanding and self-esteem, creativity, academic subject matter).

There is no "official" set of objectives for kindergartens in The Netherlands: This would threaten the national concept of freedom in education. But it is possible to recognize at least six that appear to be generally accepted for education as a whole and several of these apply at the preprimary level.[3] The six are:

1. To develop positive moral and civic values and cultural attitudes among all the people and to provide them with the skills necessary for self-fulfilment, so that they may appreciate and contribute to the cultural experience of society....
2. To maintain the freedom of religious, social and other groups to pursue and intensify their own development....

[3] OECD *Educational policy and planning, The Netherlands.* 1967.

3. To provide adequate education for all individuals and groups to the highest levels that they demand.

The formal policy of The Netherlands government is not to tolerate any restrictions upon, or limitations of, this principle. Prerequisites for entrance to any school cannot include availability of school places. If a sufficiently qualified citizen stands at the door of any type of school he must be admitted, and it is the responsibility of the appropriate government authorities to anticipate his requests so that school capacity will be adequate to accommodate him.

4. To provide society and the economy with the trained manpower resources required for optimum functioning. . . .

5. To develop a large and increasing capacity in people to adjust themselves to the career and work changes demanded by modern technology. . . .

6. To promote the free development of science, providing support for scientific training and research activities whose results are available for innovation in society in general and in the economic sector in particular [p. 26-28] .

Of these objectives, the third is especially important for kindergarten education. It has promoted a good deal of discussion in recent years, particularly in the context of equal educational opportunity being provided for all children from all social groups. This is not to suggest that there are problems of equality of opportunity so far as entry is concerned. The question is the extent to which improved performance by the kindergartens can ultimately ameliorate the meager participation rates of young people from low income families in higher education. According to the 1960 census, about 50% of the Dutch professional population is formed by unskilled workmen. In the same year, only 23% of the boys who attended secondary school were from working-class homes, a percentage that had not changed since 1946.[4] So, about 77% of the boys in the first form of secondary school have been coming from higher occupational or middle-class homes.

Research is now under way to develop new kindergarten programs specifically to help children from low income families succeed in their early years at school and make them wish to stay on longer. A good example of what is being done is The Utrecht Language and Thought Program (de Vries, 1972). This aims to give verbally handicapped children from poor homes a better start in elementary school by enabling them to understand the teacher when she tells a story, explains something, or gives an instruction. In addition, children are encouraged to answer questions in a comprehensible language. In short, the earliest opportunity is offered them to learn to communicate effectively in a schoolroom setting.

---

[4] *Ide ontwikkeling van het Onderwijs in Nederland,* Dutch Central Institute for Statistics (CBS), 1966.

ORGANIZATION AND CONTROL

As might be expected from the Dutch belief in "freedom of education," a number of different bodies play a decisive part in its organizational structure. As a first break-down, distinction should be made between governmental and nongovernmental schools, kindergartens, primary and secondary. In the case of nongovernmental preprimary schools, parents generally have two options: either to send their children to a denominational kindergarten (Roman Catholic or Protestant) or to one that uses teaching methods they especially favor (for example, Pestalozzi, Froebel, or Montessori).

Legislation for kindergarten education is provided in the Infant Education Act, which became effective January 1, 1956. This law is concerned with the organization and financing of teacher training and the development of early childhood education programs. Kindergarten education is not seen as part of the school system proper, nevertheless, its pedagogical and social functions are fully recognized. The law prescribes autonomy for preprimary and primary education, but it obliges the government to finance a school as soon as a specified number of parents request one. In municipalities with a population over 100,000, the necessary number of parents is 90; for populations between 50,000 and 100,000, the number is 60; for smaller municipal areas, no more than 30 need apply. In special cases the number can be reduced even further, but never below 20. Applications for state grants can be made also by the municipalities or religious organizations. They are made on the condition that the children in attendance will be between 4 and 5.5 years of age when school opens and will live within a radius of 3 kilometres. In 1972, 22.6% of the country's preschools had been organized by local authorities and 77.4% by private institutions.

Public kindergartens are placed under the inspection of the municipal and national government. There are two head inspectors, assisted by 28 inspectrices and inspectors. Their task is to see that state laws are enforced and to act as pedagogical leaders to teachers. Only on legal matters would they have any authority in the private sector.

The administration of public infant schools is the responsibility of the appropriate burgomaster and the *wethouders* (law keepers), who, *inter alia,* discuss and appoint teachers in consultation with the school inspectors. Every kindergarten has a head teacher. An additional teacher is appointed as soon as the number reaches 38, and for every additional 37 another teacher is supplied. The privately sponsored kindergartens are organized along similar lines, and the same regulations apply. When they are set up, the cooperation of the municipal council is sought. This may be given in the form of financial assistance for building, or the provision of existing accommodations provided the requirements of the Infant School Act have been met.

Every parent is at liberty to decide whether he sends his child to an infant school. The age of admission is 4 years. In accordance with the Education Act, the child has to leave when he is 7 years old. If a written medical statement confirms that a child is not yet suited for general primary education, he may remain at the kindergarten until his eighth year.

For every public kindergarten, there is a parents' committee that is entitled to address itself to the municipal corporation in matters of interest to the school. In municipalities with more than one parents' committee, a parents' council may be set up. At least twice a year (in most kindergartens more often) there is a meeting of parents and teachers organized by the parents' committee in collaboration with the headmistress.

Since about 1870, there have been day nurseries in the Netherlands, mainly in the larger cities. Originally most of the children were of unwed mothers. Since about 1955, an increasing number of working mothers (not necessarily unmarried) have been asking for places, although the percentage of working mothers in the country is still relatively small.

About 10 years ago, a totally new development started with the establishment of play-groups, led by both professional staffs and parents. The initiative for opening a play-group or child center has mostly come from a number of middle-class mothers, often with financial support from the local authority. The child centers are open to all children, irrespective of religion. This is the first time in recent history that an educational institution in Holland has not developed along religious lines. In most cases only 2- and 3-year-olds are admitted for two or more mornings a week.

Most of the child centers are now embraced by a national organization, the *"Werkgemeenschap Kindercentra,"* which has its office in Oosterbeek, close to Arnhem. It now has over a thousand members, and for a large part of its budget is financially dependent on the Ministry of Social Work. Child centers are never directly subsidized by the state. A start is being made with specific in-service training for the professional workers in those child centers, most of whom have only a minimum of specialized schooling. Although things may change a little if the entrance age for kindergartens is lowered from 4 to 3.5 or 3 years, considerable growth is still to be expected in the number of those centers.

There exist also some preschool provisions for children between 2 and 4 years old. These were created in 1968 as an experiment by an association of university women (*Nederlandse Vereniging van Vrouwen met Academische Opleiding*) and are open three mornings a week.

Some social associations have opened playrooms for small children, which are subsidized by the Ministry of Cultural Affairs. Finally, there are a few *garderies* in the big cities for children of working mothers. They are open between 8:00 A.M. and 6:00 P.M. from Monday to Saturday.

Since World War II, a limited number of special nursery schools have been created for children from 1 to 4 years old from very poor families. These day care centers, often financed by the community, have psychohygienic aims. One staff member is provided per eight children. Children are accepted here, not because their mothers go out to work, but because their parents are not judged to be good educators. The day at these centers usually lasts from 9:00 A.M. to 12:00 A.M. and 2:00 P.M. to 4:00 P.M. with Wednesday afternoons free, though a few are open in the morning only. Nearly all the children attend full-time.

PHYSICAL SETTING: A VISIT TO A UTRECHT KINDERGARTEN

The school visited in The Netherlands, a Protestant kindergarten, was situated to the south of the city-center of Utrecht, in one of the older quarters of the town. When one enters the street on which the school is located, one is immediately struck by the newness of the school-building. Inside it consisted of three spacious classrooms and a hall with a row of pegs. Two of the classrooms were on the ground level; the third was on the first floor. On the street-side, the classrooms had windows low enough for the children to see what happened in the street. At the back of the school, there was a small kitchen and a room for the teachers and visitors. Since the school was surrounded by houses on all sides, there was only a small playground, which got sunshine in summer only. It had a sand pit where the children could play, as well as a swing, a see-saw, a scooter, balls, a skipping-rope, and a shed with toys.

The children were divided into three groups by age, the newcomers always being placed in the lowest group. When the group with the youngest children becomes too large, the older children move up from this group and, correspondingly, from the group above. This usually takes place after Christmas. The children's parents ranged from unskilled laborers to office clerks to shopkeepers. There were no children from higher occupational class homes in this preschool.

The following observations relate to the oldest group of children, who are looked after by the headmistress herself.

About 9:00 o'clock the children arrived, many of them being brought by their mothers. At the request of the teacher, many children had brought autumn leaves and wild plants gathered over the weekend, and these (a theme for discussion later) were put on a big table in front of the class. The children were then told to bring their chairs and sit around the table in a semicircle. The first 20 minutes were spent on religious instruction. Then the teacher turned to the things the children had brought, and their interest visibly increased. Those who had brought a bag were encouraged to come in front of the class and to show some thing out of it. Each time the teacher asked a question, such as, "Who knows what this is?" or, "What is the name of this leaf?" After some of the bags had been dealt with in this way the interest began to flag because they all contained much the same things. At this point the teacher stopped asking questions and asked for all the remaining bags to be turned upside down on a big table. Then the children started working, the teacher having given them the following options:

1. Pasting the same number of paper toad stools as there were circles on a work sheet.
2. Painting autumn leaves with an adhesive and pressing the wet side on to a piece of black paper.
3. Drawing something about autumn on paper.
4. Shaping something characteristic of autumn in clay.
5. Drawing on the blackboard (two children only).
6. Making a composition from the leaves and the things brought in that morning (three children, assisted by a student-teacher).

The children were allowed to choose for themselves what they would do. After some squabbles, the teacher helped them with their choices and then gave them the job of passing out sheets, getting paste, putting on aprons, and so on. After that, she explained the particular task again to each group.

At 10:00 o'clock (the children had been at work for about half an hour) everyone stopped to drink milk, eat an apple, or whatever else he had brought from home. After this, each child continued his task. In the meantime, the teacher walked from one group to another and showed great interest in what the children were doing. After another 30 minutes everything that was finished was hung on a line which was stretched across the classroom. The clay models were placed on top of a cupboard.

At 10:45 everybody who was finished had to sit with arms folded, while those who were not had to complete their work as quickly as possible and clear away their things. The children were very busy and noisy, and at one point there was such chaos that the teacher became angry, and a child who had been warned several times already was sent out of class (2 minutes later he was allowed to come in again). When everybody was silent at last (about 10 minutes later), a student-teacher, a third-year student at a teachers' seminary, gave a gym lesson. All chairs and tables were put aside, and the children took off their upper clothes and shoes. The lesson consisted first of some rhythmical movement exercises such as walking slowly or quickly to the beat of a tambourine, then the performance of material tasks (for example, shoving small bags filled with pips to each other), and finally a game played in a circle, drop the handkerchief.

At the end of this lesson, the children had to dress themselves again. Most of them succeeded in this, but there was difficulty in tying shoelaces, something to be taught later in the year. When the classroom was tidied up, it was still not time to go home, so the teacher read a story until 12:00 o'clock.

The afternoon (1:30 until 3:30) of this visit was spent in the other two classrooms. The teacher of the intermediate level split her class in small groups according to age and stage of development. She liked to work with one group at a time when she had something new to teach. While she was teaching one group, the others played by themselves with blocks, dolls, or in a little kitchen.

On this particular afternoon, the teacher was giving a lesson in geometrical forms to a group of six children sitting around a table. Each child was given a box containing colored wooden shapes such as triangles, squares, and rectangles. The teacher (25 years old) knew exactly what she was going to do and gave a strongly programed lesson. She wanted to teach the children to name the different shapes: square, half-square, rectangle, half-rectangle, and so on. At the same time, she wanted to make them appreciate that these shapes have different areas. The following dialogue ensued:

Teacher: Take a piece like this out of the box (showing a square). What shape is this?

Child: A square.

Teacher: Is this a square too? (showing a triangle)

Child: No, it isn't.

Teacher: Place this shape on the square. What do you see?

Child: There is room for another piece.

Teacher: We call such a shape a half-square. Put it back in the box.

The rectangle was dealt with in the same way, but the children could not answer the questions, and the teacher had to prompt them. Probably this new subject was too difficult for the children at the time it was introduced to them. The next task the children were given was making a neat row on the edge of the table.

Teacher: Put your square on the table. Take two half-squares. Place the two half-squares against the square. You must not have a piece left.

None of the children understood what the teacher meant. A demonstration was necessary, and they had to repeat the exercise several times. After that, they were allowed to choose whatever pieces they liked, provided they fitted together and made a symmetrical shape. Even then the teacher had to help and correct mistakes.

The final visit of the day was to the youngest group. Most of the children in this group were playing by themselves, it being a rule to reserve the afternoon for free play. The teacher was looking after a group of children who had newly arrived and had to learn a few basic things to keep up with the rest of the class. They had, for example, to practice handling paste and paste-brushes, washing the paste-brush, coloring, cutting, clearing things away, and kindred elementary activities. All newcomers began by making a little book in which they practiced cutting, pasting, and coloring.

During lunch-time, the following points were discussed with the head of the school:

Play and work scheme: In this scheme all the activities that take place in the kindergarten are described in a general way. A work schedule helps in allocating the daily tasks and occupations to the staff.

Contact with the parents: Once a year the teachers make a house-to-house call on parents. Besides this, one morning in the year is "open" for the parents to come and watch their children in class and many of them take advantage of this opportunity to see the school. Once a week, on a fixed day, there is a consulting hour when parents can talk with the teachers, but this is also possible any day before or after school hours. When a child has his birthday, his father or mother may come to the school from 9:00 to 9:30 to join in the customary celebration.

Primary school: When leaving this kindergarten most children go on to the nearest Protestant primary school (though there are others in this quarter of Utrecht). After Christmas, those transferring the following summer are prepared by exercises in preparatory arithmetic and writing. The practice of these skills occupies about 30 minutes per day.

TEACHERS AND THEIR TRAINING

The first teacher-training schools for preschool children were established in the second half of the nineteenth century. In 1900, only 40% of the teachers held diplomas; the rest were helpers. By 1930, this had risen to 68%, and today only trained personnel staff the schools.

The OECD "Classification of Educational Systems" (1972) gives the following information about the training of nursery school teachers in The Netherlands:

> Entrance requirements: to be between 16 and 20 years of age and to have completed at least 3 years of a senior secondary school or a junior secondary school certificate (m.a.v.o.)
> Certificate: Section A: nursery school teacher's certificate. Section B: nursery school headmistress' certificate
> Time requirements: Section A: full-time. Section B: part-time.
> Other information: Section A: Pupils holding the 2nd cycle secondary school-certificate or the primary teacher's certificate are admitted to the 2nd year. Section B: Holders of the nursery school teacher's diploma can prepare a nursery school headmistress' certificate in 1 year of part-time studies in section B [p. 22].

Nursery school teachers in The Netherlands cannot teach in primary schools nor can primary school teachers teach in nursery schools. Nursery school teachers can be appointed as teachers in special schools (special infant education) and in schools educating mentally handicapped children so long as the children are not at compulsory school attendance age.

In 1972, there were 43 kindergarten training colleges. This number seems very high for a small country, and it reflects the demand of each of the three major groups to train its own teachers. During the 10-year period between 1960 and

1970 the number of teachers in preprimary schools in the Netherlands had increased from 11,800 to approximately 16,000, an increase of 4200. If that increase were averaged over the 10-year period, it would appear that the preprimary schools needed an additional 320 teachers per year. The total production from the 43 kindergarten teacher training colleges was about 2000, or 50 teachers per institution. In the last few years, this has created a surplus of teachers, who are now accepting employment in the United States and Germany. This surplus of trained teachers is a factor in the government's consideration of lowering the entrance age for kindergartens. It has also led to resistance on the part of certified preschool teachers to the use of kindergarten assistants who are not fully trained. They advocate the reduction of class size in order to employ more certified teachers.

The aim of kindergarten teacher training in The Netherlands is to prepare the trainees to teach children between the ages of 4 and 6. The main subjects of study are literature, general psychology, music (both oral and instrumental), history, personal hygiene, religion, and art. The basic theoretical courses are child psychology, child development, history of education, personality psychology, child care, and cooperation between family and school. The methodologies taught are based principally on Froebel and Montessori.[5]

De Vries (1972) draws attention to the lack of integration of psychological and pedagogical methodologies and rather low entrance requirements for students training as kindergarten teachers. An influential journal for teachers says that to be called a good kindergarten teacher, one should:

1. Try to study each child who enters kindergarten and his home environment.
2. Appreciate the fact that you (the teacher) may make mistakes.
3. Plan the daily activities carefully.
4. Give special exercises and individual tasks.
5. Know the goals and means to attain them when one gives exercises and tasks.
6. Keep an eye on every child.
7. Be interested in the way the child is doing his work.
8. Spend much time on working with materials that stimulate the development of the senses and cognition.
9. Spend little time on choosing tasks (let the child choose them).
10. Be open to the ideas of all publications, college and professional.
11. Work with all available materials in the course of the year.
12. Be able to work with children who need extra help and watch others in the meantime.
13. Be on constant search for new stories to tell the children.

[5] *The training and professional situation of pre-school teachers.* UNESCO, 1965.

It would be difficult to disagree with any of these precepts, but it may not be easy for the teacher constantly to live up to all of them.

Van Calcar (1972), in describing the development of a compensatory early childhood education program in Amsterdam, has the following to say about in-service teacher training:

> We have to start from the principle that teachers will change their methods and techniques only if emotional support and guidance are provided from the very start. In the beginning, the suggestions for innovation will be given with elaborate indications, attuned to the less imaginative or less capable teacher. However, as soon as the required approach and methods are understood, too precise instructions start to impede some teachers' inventiveness and creativity. In order to make the new teaching model suitable to large groups, there must therefore be propagated greater flexibility in its use. Some teachers will continue to need detailed advice, whilst others will need only a broad guide. . . .
>
> Another problem is that outsiders often consider teachers' difficulties as professional shortcomings. To counter this, a campaign should be launched to educate the inspectorate, the local authorities, teacher-training establishments, colleges of higher education, universities, teachers' unions, parent associations, and community associations, through specialist journals and the mass media.
>
> Genuine educational reform will be possible only when there exists in the whole community a movement in which solidarity forms a central theme . . . [p. 4].

It has too often been forgotten that changes in educational techniques mean renunciation of traditions strongly rooted in people's way of life. The result is emotional tension that hampers the adoption of even the simplest changes in attitude. This is why even the simplest educational improvements are often not put into practice.

Van Calcar straightforwardly states an essential and difficult truth—that the reform of education at any level, not just the preprimary school level, depends primarily upon changes in teachers' attitudes. As he suggests, it is only in a very warm and supportive environment that they will take the risk involved in changing their methods.

Table 11.4 gives statistics for kindergarten teachers in The Netherlands from 1960-1961 to 1970-1971. In the private sector, the percentage of growth has been 31% and in the public sector 65.8%, again reflecting the different increases in enrollments in the two sectors. The public sector is much the smaller, and, therefore, it is much easier to see dramatic gains in enrollments. The total percentage of increase in the number of teachers over the 10 years is 38.3%. When compared with a 23.6% total increase in enrollments, this indicates a decline in pupil-teacher ratios.

Table 11.5 presents the pupil-teacher ratios for kindergartens in The Netherlands for the years 1960-1961 to 1970-1971. In the private sector, the number of pupils per teacher has been reduced by three and in the public sector by four. For comparison, the pupil-teacher ratios in primary schools for these same years

TABLE 11.4
Kindergarten Teachers in the Netherlands From 1960-61 to 1970-71

Year	Private	Public	Total
1960-61	9,114	2,421	11,535
1965-66	10,478	3,079	13,557
1966-67	10,680	3,204	13,884
1967-68	10,957	3,335	14,290
1968-69	11,129	3,546	14,675
1969-70	11,510	3,791	15,301
1970-71	11,941	4,013	15,954
% of increase from 1960-61 to 1970-71	31.0	65.8	38.3

Source: Central Bureau of Statistics, The Netherlands.

were: 1960, 34:1; 1965, 32:1; and 1970, 31:1. According to Doornbos and
Geerars (1972), there were some 6400 nursery schools with about 500,000
children in The Netherlands in 1970 and approximately 16,000 teachers to staff
them. In round figures, this gives 75 children and 3 teachers per nursery school.

FINANCING EARLY CHILDHOOD EDUCATION

In 1951, the educational budget totaled 422 million guilders; by 1965, it had
risen to 3194 million. In 1951, expenditures for educational and cultural
purposes were 8.5% of the total figure; in 1965, they amounted to 25%.

More striking still is the fact that a growing share of the national income is
being directed to education and culture. In 1950, it was 2.6%; in 1965, it was
5.6%; by 1975, it was estimated that the percentage must rise to 8% if present or
imminent desiderata are to be met. In 1967, while the per capita gross national
product stood at $2400, the per capita expenditure on education alone was
$6.86.[6]

TABLE 11.5
Pupil:Teacher Ratio in Kindergarten

Year	Private	Public	Total
1960-61	34:1	35:1	35:1
1965-66	34:1	33:1	34:1
1970-71	31:1	31:1	31:1

[6] OECD *Economic surveys.* 1972.

With this increased spending on education in the Netherlands has come an increased concern for the deployment of the money and the planning and evaluation that should be associated with it. In reviewing the problems of accounting and future planning, the OECD report "Educational Policy and Planning: The Netherlands" (1967) observes:

> This has consequences for planning with respect to governmental schools (municipal) as well as for finance (the municipalities pay for the schools at the pre-primary and primary levels, and, within the limits of the law, control the grants for non-governmental schools). The equality of governmental and non-governmental schools, which in practice has led to a majority of non-governmental schools in most types of education, has resulted in a division into three (sometimes four) vertical sub-systems. This has meant still greater decentralisation.
>
> Many aspects of education cannot be regulated directly, but rather through the setting of conditions for receiving grants. Both of the above points make it clear that—within the limits set by laws—the system of finance is one of the instruments by which the Dutch education establishment is governed . . . [p. 36].
>
> The finance input is the key to controlling the real inputs into the educational system. Therefore, the basis on which decisions are made on the level of financing for various parts of the system must be sufficiently rational to result in a deployment of real resources which reflects the objectives they are to serve. . . .
>
> The conditions for state financing of non-governmental schools are the same as the regulations which are enforced for governmental schools. However, for governmental schools, they are in the nature of binding regulations, whilst for non-governmental schools they should be regarded as the terms on which a grant is made. They concern requirements regarding teachers' qualifications and the curriculum and regulations for state inspection [p. 42].

This pattern of financing of education in The Netherlands includes, of course, the preprimary. Preprimary and primary education are responsibilities of the local municipalities, which may set up and maintain schools themselves, but the main source of funds for both public and private schools is the central government. If an application is made for money to start a new kindergarten and the legal conditions are met, the result will be a 100% subsidy, regardless of the applicant. These conditions are laid down in the Infant Education Act (1956) and relate to the minimum age for entrance, the number of hours per day, the play and activity plan, teacher education, pupil-teacher ratio, and the hygienic state of the building. The subsidies for private schools in the municipality are reckoned from the average expenditures in public schools of the same type.

The salaries of teachers in public and private kindergartens are fixed by the state. No municipality is allowed to pay more or less. The salaries depend primarily upon the type of certificate held, the number of years spent in teaching, and the specific functions performed (for example, administrative on top of teaching duties will call for additional remuneration). Salaries for nursery school teachers are generally about 75% of the average salary of their colleagues in primary schools.

A fixed sum per annum is given to both private and municipal preprimary schools for construction, modernization, equipment, and renting additional space, with due consideration given to the rising costs of construction and modernization of buildings. A further amount is fixed annually by the Minister of Education to cover the costs of maintenance, lighting, heating, and general small repairs. A small charge is set by law for all preprimary schools (48 DF a year, 1972), which most parents must pay. Parents may make additional contributions on a voluntary basis. Those with very low incomes, however, are exempt from any fees. Reductions may be granted when two or more children of the same family are attending school.

Table 11.6 presents information on expenditures in kidnergartens in The Netherlands from 1965-1966 to 1968-1969. Both the capital and current expenditures in the public sector reflect the enrollment picture shown in Table 11.1. As already observed, enrollments in the past 10 years have risen much more rapidly in the public than the private sector. Correspondingly, the increase in both capital and current expenditures has been almost twice as rapid here. It should, however, be kept in mind that the public kindergartens still have a much smaller proportion of preschool population than the private ones. During the period 1965-1966 to 1968-1969 for which figures are available in Table 11.6, the total capital and current expenditures rose by 39.8%. Some projections are made on current expenditures from 1960-1975. There is reasonably close agreement between these figures and those officially projected in 1967, which forecast that current expenditures for preprimary schools would be 80 million guilders in 1960, 145 million in 1965, 200 million in 1970, and 305 million in 1975.[7] The recurring costs over this 15-year period will increase approximately 3.5 times. The enrollments in preprimary education during the same 15-year period have grown about 15%. It is clear to see, therefore, that costs are rising much more rapidly than enrollments.

Table 11.7 shows per pupil expenditures for both private and public kindergartens in The Netherlands from 1965-1966 to 1968-1969. Over this period, the public sector consistently spent more per child than the private, but the amount of increase was almost identical. One of the reasons for the larger expense in the public sector may well be that the schools are smaller and, therefore, cost more to run. There certainly does not seem to be another easy explanation for the $28 difference at both the beginning and the end of this period between the two sectors. The average expenditure per pupil, both public and private, was $125 a year in 1965-1966; in 1968-1969, it had grown to $144.

---

[7] *Educational policy planning, The Netherlands*. 1967.

TABLE 11.6
Kindergarten Expenditure in the Netherlands from 1965-66 to 1970-71

Year	Private		Public		DG 000's Total Capital Current	$ 000's Total Capital Current
	Capital	Current	Capital	Current		
1965-66	45,612	134,788	17,391	44,541	242,332	67,308
1966-67	47,180	158,757	19,503	54,244	280,287	
1967-68	47,995	172,694	19,877	61,886	302,452	
1968-69	58,579	184,173	25,454	70,783	338,989	93,642
1969-70	n.a.[a]	n.a.	n.a.	n.a.	n.a.	n.a.
1970-71	n.a.	n.a.	n.a.	n.a.	n.a.	n.a.
% of increase from 1965-66 to 1968-69	28.4	36.6	46.3	58.9	39.8	39.1

Source: Central Bureau of Statistics, The Netherlands.
[a] Not available.

TABLE 11.7
Kindergarten Per-Pupil Costs in The Netherlands in U.S. Dollars from 1965-66 to 1968-69

Year	Private			Public			Total		
	Current Expend. 000's	No. of Children 000's	Per Pu- pil Cost	Current Expend. 000's	No. of Children 000's	Per Pu- pil Cost	Current Expend. 000's	No. of Children 000's	Per Pu- pil Cost
1965-66	37,437	317	119	12,371	84	147	49,809	398	125
1968-69	50,876	371	137	19,553	118	166	70,429	489	144
Total Increase			18			19			19

INSTRUCTIONAL METHODS

Traditionally, kindergartens in The Netherlands have had great freedom in the choice of instructional methodology, as there is still no single one that is used consistently; nor, indeed, is there any national policy that suggests one set of methods might be better than another. Exercise of this freedom is closely connected with the fact that almost anyone can organize a kindergarten and then use any instructional method he wishes so long as he can get the required number of parents to patronize the school. This has encouraged a great diversity of approach to methodology in order to meet the wide variety of parental wishes as to how their children should be educated.

In practice, however, both private and public kindergarten must indicate in their general curriculum plan the instructional methodologies to be used in implementing it. This plan is drawn up by the preschool teachers and then discussed with the local inspector, the burgomaster and the aldermen. It is usually reviewed also by the inspectors from central government.

Until Dr. Maria Montessori came to influence the Dutch preschool system in the early 1920s, most kindergartens had based their educational programs on the works and *Spielgaben* of Friedrich Froebel, often in the modernized, less structured, and more individualized way promoted by the influential director of the teacher-training school in Leiden, Wybrandus Haanstra.

In 1917, the Dutch Montessori Society was established, and a year later the first Montessori course for teachers of preprimary and primary schools started in The Hague. The director was Mrs. C. Philippi, who became a very strong proponent of Montessori's ideas and methods, but who also had much contact with other leaders in the field, such as Decroly, Piaget, and Buhlers. Notwithstanding the founder's original intentions, the Montessori schools in The Netherlands remained a middle-class affair, with a few (public) exceptions in the big cities. In 1940, 5% of the preschools were following the Montessori system, and 84% called themselves *Froebelschool* or *Montessorischool.* The original name, *bewaarschool* (keeping school), for all preschools was, therefore, gradually replaced by *Froebelschool* or *Montessorischool.* Today the general name for all 6600 preschools is *kleuterschool* (the word *kleuter* meaning a child between 4 and 6). Recently, the percentage of Montessori preschools has dropped to less than 4 because of the immense increase in new *kleuterschools.* Most of the *kleuterschools* followed a mixed curriculum influenced by a postwar anticognitive wave of "creativity" and "free expression" on top of the heritage of Froebel, Montessori, and their Dutch "reformers." Other important influences come from a group of leading women in the field and, to a considerable degree, from publishers specializing in preschool materials.

After World War II, the planning and running of the *kleuterschools* was almost exclusively a female affair, Professor Bladergreen and Mrs. Nijkamp being particularly influential. During the last 10 years, however, some male newcomers from the universities have taken interest in them, mainly for reasons derived from the hypothesis that at preschool age more can be done to compensate for environmental handicaps. As already observed, these men have suggested curriculum reforms and have developed specific programs for fostering language and cognitive development as well as curricula for stimulating general motivation to learn among disadvantaged children and their parents. These proposals entail reform of the predominantly middle-class curriculum into one more sensitive to environment and the needs and values of the disadvantaged groups in Dutch society.

In summary, it may be said that changes in the instructional methodology in the Dutch kindergartens will come primarily from the pedagogical centers working in close cooperation with the teachers. As the OECD report entitled Educational Policy and Planning in The Netherlands (1967) says:

> Improvements can be effected only through the free acceptance of new methods and the voluntary co-operation of the teachers and school governing bodies. It is obvious that in order to achieve optimal pedagogical results, provision must be made for wide distribution of information. The role of the pedagogical centres must therefore be regarded as very important ... [p. 37].
>
> As a consequence of the principle of freedom (resulting in the fact that the majority of Dutch schools are run by private institutions), both pedagogical research and the introduction of its results are not considered to be primarily the responsibility of the Government, but rather of these private institutions. As a matter of fact, however, the Government does not stand aside with regard to these activities. The most important role in this field is played by the pedagogical centres [In 1972 there were three national and some 30 regional ones (Doornbos and Geerars, 1972)] and by the universities. . . .
>
> The pedagogical centres founded by the national associations of governing bodies of non-governmental schools and the national teachers association (for governmental education, also by the municipalities and the State together with non-denominational private organisations), came into being after World War II.
>
> Roughly speaking their activities can be divided into four aspects: (1) Studying existing pedagogical problems; (2) Experimenting with new methods; (3) Introducing the results of their experiments into the schools; (4) Generally introducing the idea of renewal among the teachers, for example, "classical" teaching methods versus the individual approach to students [p. 129].

Specific research topics mentioned earlier in this chapter and described in the last provide examples of such work carried out since this report was published 9 years ago.

One final note may be of interest to the reader. The original Montessori-made materials are produced in Holland and sent all over the world. The international Montessori Society is headed by Maria Montessori's grandson in Amsterdam. This gives some idea of how deeply rooted the Montessori tradition is in the Dutch preschool system.

RESEARCH ON EARLY CHILDHOOD EDUCATION

De Vries (1971), speaking at an educational research symposium in Finland on the research problems of preschool education, discussed the research currently being done in The Netherlands. This is summarized below:

Until recently all psychological studies on children of nursery school and kindergarten age in Holland have been descriptive, hypothetical, and done with the so-called phenomenological method. Recent studies are still descriptive but try to develop instruments for systematic observation.

Work in Progress

(1) A longitudinal study on the influence of nursery school education on toddlers; this is a project of the Department of Culture and Social Work, directed by Dr. G. A. Kohnstamm.

(2) The activities of the Pedagogical Institute of the Free University of Amsterdam. Dr. Groenendaal is working on a translation, formulation and evaluation of the theories and the enrichment program of Marion Blank. Dr. Hamel is studying cognitive development of children in kindergarten and elementary school.

(3) Studies on social behavior in the Department of Developmental Psychology in Nijmegen. Professor Monks is directing a research project in which the development of three age-groups of 150 children are being studied, ages 4, 9, and 14 years. This is an interdisciplinary investigation of the social, medical, motorical, cognitive, and emotional development of children. The research project has just started. From the same Institute in Nijmegen a study of Dr. Ahammer will appear in 1972 on types of frustration appearing in toddlers 1½ years old when their toys are taken away.

Dr. van Lieshout is studying social development of children in kindergarten. His report is called "Stability in Social Interaction between Pre-school Children."

(4) A group of clinical psychologists has adopted the behavioristic and learning-theoretical therapeutic approach. Training centres are to be found in Greningen, Utrecht, and Amsterdam. We may soon expect a series of studies on systematic modification of problem behavior from this group. Behavior therapy with children is one of their topics.

(5) Finally three enrichment programs have to be mentioned. Two of them are focused on the kindergarten, the project of Dr. Gerstel in Haarlem and the project of the Institute for Pedagogic Studies in Utrecht; the third is focused on the first form of elementary education. This project of the Pedagogic Center in Enschede is mentioned because of its well-considered research design.

Holland has no tradition yet in empirical studies. Many research studies have been of inferior methodological quality. Much time is spent now on the development of instruments which may improve the quality of research in the future. Besides, the necessity of control groups in experimental studies becomes more and more clear, so an improvement may soon be expected [p. 3].

De Vries' observations provide interesting commentary on a situation that had already been outlined as follows in OECD's report, "Educational Policy and Planning in the Netherlands" (1967).

In recent years complaints have been heard, both in educational circles and in Parliament, about the insufficiency of educational research and the lack of coordination in this field. To improve the situation in both of these respects, the Minister of Education and Science in 1963 appointed a study group (professors of education and higher civil servants), which suggested creation of a body responsible for the promotion and co-ordination of education research.

According to this advice the Minister for Education and Science installed in December 1965 the Foundation for Educational Research. To this foundation the planning, co-ordination and stimulation of research is delegated. The foundation has funds available to promote research projects. It does not carry out such projects itself. As members of the governing board are appointed [by the Minister] experts from the circles of the pedagogical centres and the national educational organisations of the different denominations, and professors of pedagogy, psychology and sociology. The head of the Research and Planning Department of the Ministry represents the Minister in the board.

It may be noted, moreover, that in 1963 a "Register of current social science research" was begun which also aims at greater co-ordination in the field of research. It gives information on projects being carried out so as to avoid duplication of effort. As has been already mentioned, research is carried out mostly by the university institutes and institutes related in some way to universities. Smaller projects are often carried out under the auspices of the pedagogical centres [p. 130-131].

The Foundation for Educational Research fosters three different kinds of research. It alone is responsible for work which could be classified as basic or applied research, while action research may be stimulated by both the Ministry of Education and the foundation.

A good example of the kind of research that is funded by the Foundation for Educational Research is the University of Utrecht's work to help kindergarten children from lower class homes. Three kinds of help were seen to be necessary: first, to the child; second, to the family; and third, to the whole school population. Accordingly, three distinct programs were conceived, one for each of these groups, but all had the same aim: to give the children of unskilled workers the best possible start in elementary school.

The first program, directed toward the individual child, was called the Language and Thought program. Its object was to show how the correct use of language for the organization and transmission of information could be taught to children so that they could answer questions about things in relation to space and time. It was based on a highly structured discussion between teachers and small groups of six or seven children for 20-minute periods during the day.

The second (family) program was based on the assumption that one of the best ways to prevent intellectual retardation is to create and maintain an interest on the part of the lower-class parents in the cognitive development of their children. Home visitors taught them how to observe their children, read to them, play games, and take a lively interest in the schools they attended.

The third program, called school readiness, began with the supposition that existing kindergarten activities have to be changed if lower-class children are to be prepared for the tasks in elementary school, especially for reading and arithmetic. The children in this study were between 4.5 and 6 years of age, and they were assigned randomly from a common population to the experimental and control groups. In 1968-1969, before the start of the experiment, the whole population of a series of kindergartens was tested on entry to elementary with the same battery of tests as would be used on the experimental group that was to follow them. These children were followed through 1970, 1971, and 1972 as a control group.

The results of the three different approaches in this compensatory program at Utrecht are somewhat varied. The family program showed hardly any effect on intelligence or language test results at school. The children involved in the school readiness and the language and thought programs, however, both showed gains in IQ tests and in language and arithmetic. The overall results of the experiment show that improvement can be expected only in those areas of cognition or skill development that are specifically taught. This conclusion is very similar to that noted in the United States in Head Start programs.

Another enrichment program was introduced by Dr. van Calcar in a number of elementary schools serving the working-class population in Enschede. He chose the first grades of 34 schools for this project and 6 schools to provide the controls. The criteria with which he was concerned were socioeconomic background, average IQ, average reading score and average arithmetic score. He trained the teachers in the experimental classes to use remedial reading programs and to persuade the parents to help by taking a particular interest in the projects in which their children were involved.

At the end of the first grade, a comparison was made between the experimental and control schools. The results showed that 33 out of 34 experimental schools obtained better average scores on a technical reading test than did the children in the control schools. On the comprehensive reading test, 29 experimental schools obtained better average scores than the control schools. It can be concluded, therefore, that this enrichment program was successful.

A nursery school started by Dr. Kohnstamm in 1970 was designed so that the development of the children there can be followed subsequently through kindergarten and primary school. For every child in the nursery schools, a matched control child has been found who does not attend nursery school but stays at home. The children are being tested with a variety of instruments, among them the Bayley infant scale, the Stutsman IQ test, and a vocabulary test specifically developed and standardized for this project. When they leave the nursery school, the children are again to be tested with the Stutsman vocabulary test as well as the Terman-Merrill intelligence test and the Utrecht language level test. The major aim of this experiment is to try to identify the benefits of nursery school education.

In the northern part of The Netherlands, the province of Friesland, two languages are spoken, Frisian and Dutch. The advantages and disadvantages of bilingual education have been, of course, much discussed, and an inquiry known as "Project Friesland" has recently been inaugurated to discover to what extent and in what domains children with a Frisian language background are handicapped by this if they go to monolingual Dutch schools. The project is also concerned with the degree to which handicaps can be overcome.

In the first phase of the project, four groups of Frisian speaking children were to be followed from the end of the last kindergarten year (Spring, 1972) up to and including grade 3 (1975) in primary school. The control group was to consist of children from a rural Dutch-speaking area near Utrecht. The cluster of criterion variables was to be "school success." Every year several achievement tests (general ability and language proficiency) were to be administered (readiness tests are used in the kindergarten year) and the scores analysed.

If, after a year's follow-up, language handicaps were located, the second phase was to be an experimental one. By means of an interview schedule, information about the home situation would be gathered, and kindergarten teachers would be requested to fill out a personality rating scale for each child. Different teaching strategies would be tested in order to overcome the problems identified. This was to start in 1974. A third phase would be the introduction of those programs that were proven successful in the Frisian schools.

A project in the University of Amsterdam for the development of compensatory early childhood education, under the leadership of van Calcar, is concerned in a broad sense with how an intervention program should be set up. Four specific aspects of intervention are being investigated. The first is educational help, that is, in-service upgrading of the teacher's competence. The second, links between school and family, is based on the proposition that any reform in education will fail if the family is left out. The home is the child's first school. Even when he goes to school proper, he spends a lot of time at home and each day learns both there and at school. Everything learned at home should be related to what is learned at school and further developed. The third aspect is the link between the school and the community, and the fourth relates to emotional guidance. In short, this project is taking a very broad social approach toward changes in education.

This brief look at current research illustrates once again the observation that there are real divisions of opinion in The Netherlands as to how young children should be educated.

In general, then, four conclusions can be drawn from current research in the Netherlands on preprimary education:

1. Home environment is a critical factor in the school readiness of children. Significant improvement resulted from programs that included home enrichment; however, playgrounds which dealt only with home enrichment, with no cognitive reinforcement in school, failed to produce discernible improvement in children's subsequent school performance.

2 Experimental programs, involving intense teacher-pupil discussion, experimental activities, and remedial reading, have been shown to be highly successful in improving students' performance.

3. One of the major areas of research is the effect of bilingualism (Dutch-Frisian) on children in Friesland. Results are not yet conclusive.

4. A significant amount of research is currently in progress throughout The Netherlands on many aspects of preschool education, including its general benefits for the student later. Because of the absence of a Dutch tradition of empirical methodology, much time is now spent in the development of research tools. Therefore, results from this research are as yet only embryonic.

ACKNOWLEDGMENTS

The author wishes to acknowledge the valuable help received from: Dr. A. Kohnstamm of Proefkreche '70 in Amsterdam and Dr. A. de Vries, University of Utrecht; Dr. F. Teunissen, formerly of the Foundation for Educational Research; Dr. A. Wood, van Leer Foundation; Dr. H. Veldkamp, Head of Research and Planning, and Mr. A. Kastelyn, his associate, of the Dutch Ministry of Education.

BIBLIOGRAPHY

Austin, G., & Antonsen, K. *A review of pre-school educational efforts in five countries* (Mimeographed). OECD, 1971.

Blackstone, T. *Pre-school education in Europe, Studies on permanent education* (N 13/1970). Council of Europe, Strasbourg.

van Calcar, C. *Development of compensatory early childhood education.* Amsterdam seminar on curriculum in compensatory early childhood education, Bernard van Leer Foundation, CurSem/PR/12, The Hague, 3 November, 1972.

Doornbos, D., & Geerars, C. M. *Creativity of the school* (OECD, CERI/CS/72.15). Paris, Nov. 1972.

van Heek, F. The hidden talent, milieu, secondary school selection and educational performance. In *Pedagogica Europea* (Vol. 4). Amsterdam: 1968, 19-41.

van Hulst, van der Velde, & Verhaak (Eds.), *Vernieuwingsstreven binnen het Nederlandse enderwijs in de periode 1900-1940.* Welters-Noordhoff, Greningen, 1970.

Kastelyn, A. In a report on a visit to The Netherlands by Dr. G. Austin, OECD, 1972.

Kohnstamm, G. A. Project Compensation Programme, Department of Education, University of Utrecht, December 12, 1968.

Kohnstamm, G. A. Early Childhood Education in the Netherlands. Paris: OECD, Sept. 24, 1973. Mimeographed.

Kohnstamm, G. A. *On the development of educational goals for an experimental day care center in The Netherlands.* Amsterdam: Mimeographed. January 1970.

Kohnstamm, G. A. *Teaching children to solve a Piagetian problem in class.* Den Haag, 1967. Mimeographed.

Schultze, W. *Schools in Europe* (Vol. 2). Weinheim: Beltz Verlag, 1968.

Teunissen, F. In a report on a visit to the Netherlands by Dr. G. Austin, OECD, 1972.

Trouillet, B. *Die Vorschulerziehung in neun europaischen Landern,* Weinheim: Beltz Verlag, 1968.

de Vries, A. K. *Pre-school education and development, psychology research into the age group 2-7 years in The Netherlands.* Council for Cultural Co-operation, Council of Europe, Educational Research Symposium in Finland on research into pre-school education, Jyvaskyla, 10.12.1971.

de Vries, A. K. *Early childhood education in the Netherlands* (stencil). 1972.

de Vries, A. K. The Utrecht Language and Thought Programme. SVO Project 083, Dept. of Ped. Studies, State University of Utrecht, 1972.

Wijnstra, J. M. Project Friesland, A short description of the project and the population under study, State University of Utrecht, Pedagogical Institute, Department of Research on Teaching. 1967.

Wilson, H., & Herbert, G. *Notes on a visit to experimental day care center '70* (stencil). Amsterdam, Dec. 1970.

Ide ontwikkeling van het Onderwijs in Nederland' Dutch Central Institute for Statistics (CBS), 1966.

Council of Europe: *Research into pre-school education.* Jyvaskyla symposium, 1971, Strasbourg, 1972.

Council of Europe: *Comite de l'enseignement general et technique.* Symposium sur l'education pre-scolaire, objectifs, methodes et problems, DECS/EGT (71) 86, 18 aout 1971.

Council for cultural co-operation of the Council of Europe. Education in Europe. *School systems, a guide.* Strasbourg, 1970.

Central Bureau of Statistics, 13th Algemene Volkstelling 1960. D1. 10. Beroepsbevolking. A. Algemene inleiding.

International Federation of Teachers' Associations Congress of Helsinki, 1969, Pre-school education.

Ministry of Education, Arts and Science. *Dutch school System.* 1960.

OECD. *Classification of educational systems.* Paris, 1972.

OECD. *Economic surveys—The Netherlands.* 1972.

OECD. *Educational policy and planning: Netherlands.* Paris, 1967.

OECD. *Reviews of national policies for education: The Netherlands.* 1970.

OECD. *Educational Programs for socially disadvantaged populations, Project Compensation Program* (CERI/DP/68.04, Mimeographed). Paris, Dec. 30, 1968.

OECD/CERI. *Some notes on the evaluation of compensation programmes* (Mimeographed). Paris, October 1, 1969.

UNESCO. *World survey of education, II primary education.* 1958.

UNESCO. *La formation et la situation professionnelle des enseignants pre-scolaires.* Decembre 1965.

United Nations. *Analyses and projections of households and families.* Prepared by Population Division, Department of Economic and Social Affairs of the United Nations Secretariat, ESA/P/WP.28, 1971.

United Nations demographic yearbook. 1970.

12

Implications for American Early Childhood Education

The preceding chapters have presented an overview of the development, growth, and current status of early childhood education in seven countries in Europe, and in Canada. In this overview, the following issues of debate were identified. In some cases, the issue is germane to a country alone, but in most cases, they span countries and are found in the United States as well.

(*1*) In all countries the issue of equality is important. This includes concern for equality of educational opportunity, economic equality, and equality of men, women, and children.

(*2*) In all countries, there is special concern about young children who come to preschool or primary school with special needs, because of their poor home background, economic and cultural constraints, or handicaps (physical, emotional, or intellectual).

(*3*) The importance of education as it contributes to the social and economic well-being of the nation itself.

(*4*) Parental freedom of choice in a preschool. This freedom can be broken down into two major issues: (*i*) religious as opposed to secular (private versus public); and (*ii*) the freedom of parents to raise their children as they wish, even if at variance with what the state wishes.

331

(5) The child's problems associated with transition between the home and the preschool and the preschool and the primary school.

(6) The orientation of preschool programs—whether they are to be concerned with the social, emotional, and intellectual development of the whole child or more oriented toward any one of these issues (as is commonly found in compensatory preschool programs).

(7) The lowering of compulsory attendance age.

(8) Pupil-teacher ratios and pupil-adult ratios.

(9) The integration of handicapped children into preschool (this includes physically, emotionally, and intellectually handicapped children).

(10) The roles of both men and women in society in terms of their desire for personal freedom and equality on the one hand and their responsibility as parents on the other.

(11) The weakening of the family structure and the demise of the extended family.

(12) The isolation of children from small families who live either in high-rise urban flats or rural isolation.

(13) The lack of play space in urban settings.

(14) The inadequacies of training for preschool and primary school teachers concerning the transition from home to preschool to primary school.

(15) The disparity of financial ability to pay for education across countries, states, or regions.

(16) The struggle over who shall control the preschool program and receive the money—the health, welfare, or educational agencies. Coupled with this issue is the question of who shall pay and how much—the government (federal, state, or local) or the parents.

(17) The clarification of preschool aims and objectives.

(18) The integration of the efforts of health, welfare, and educational agencies in small centers readily available to parents and children.

In studying the current development and growth of ECE programs in these countries, the issues just identified fall into two general categories—sociological changes and changes in the role of preschool education. Sociological events include changes in demographic features, such as household size, birth rates, and women's participation in the labor market. Changes in the demand for and role of preschool education are marked, for example, by increases in enrollment of children at younger ages, an increase in the number of students training to be preschool teachers, lower pupil-teacher and pupil-adult ratios, increased emphasis on cognition in ECE curriculum development projects, and the statement of instructional objectives in behavioral terms.

This chapter will provide some elaboration of these findings and an effort will be made to draw from them some general implications for early childhood education in the United States. Most of the trends identified in the earlier chapters have a parallel development in the United States.

BACKGROUND

The first evidence of this parallel development and growth is seen in the historical background. Concepts of early childhood education in the Western world did not begin in a vacuum. They appear to be linked with social thought about freedom and humanitarian principles of living. Interest in the status of children's rights and children's development as a historical theme are coupled with periods of social revolution and reform which began over 200 years ago. These periods appear to cycle, rising and falling with changes in sociological phenomena.

For instance, in Europe, Rousseau's writings during the tumultuous times preceding the French Revolution indicated that new thoughts about the meaning of childhood and the rights of children were part of a total reassessment of the people's concept of their own rights. While Rousseau elaborated on childhood as a unique time of life, this may have been a reaction to the new status given adults. The freeing of serfs gave a new dimension to adulthood, thus differentiating it from childhood. One could hypothesize that as people are allowed to take more responsibility for their own lives, they in turn take more responsibility for the lives of their children.

This concept of sociological change being linked to changes in how childhood is viewed was further developed by Froebel's contribution to early childhood education. Froebel's writings first appeared in a period of industrial revolution preceding the 1848 wars in Europe. This period was identified by increasing political liberalism and a growing interest in personal freedom. Froebel's philosophy embodied this drive for freedom to such a degree that kindergartens were closed in Prussia in 1851 because of their democratic teaching. Froebel advocated releasing the child from work so he might develop and grow through various forms of play. At this time, play was first recognized as a crucial factor in childhood learning.

Concurrently, the United States was experiencing a similar change. During the American transcendental social renaissance of the 1830s, Horace Mann stressed the importance of education for the growing child. Although the moral character-building tone of this education appears to be very rigid, Mann recognized the importance of education for children which demonstrated two purposes during a period of sociological change. First, it taught the virtues of honesty and hard work, values thought to be necessary in building a new country; and second, it served to socialize a burgeoning population of immigrants.

Mann's educational philosophy influenced educational curriculum development until the writings of John Dewey appeared during the late nineteenth and early twentieth century. Dewey's writings advocated the advantages of a child-centered curriculum and the necessity for children to be free to discover and learn. Much of the progressive education movement in the United States was based on Dewey ideas.

Societal interest in child development and psychology was beginning to occur in the late nineteenth and early twentieth centuries in both Europe and the United States. In the US, one of the leading advocates of the study of children was Stanley Hall, who initiated the child study movement. In 1893, the creation of the National Association for the Study of Children gave added force to the child study movement. In England, James Sully founded the British Association for Child Study in 1895. In France, the Free Society for Child Study, presided over by A. Binet, was created in 1900. At the same time (1900) a Swedish woman, Ellen Key, published a book called *The Century of the Child*. This, too, had a great influence. In Italy, Maria Montessori began to preach "the crusade for childhood," at the same time opening the first *"case dei bambini"* in the working-class areas of Rome. Finally, in Switzerland in 1903, Claparede introduced a course in child psychology at the University of Geneva, and in 1909 the first International Congress of Child Psychology was held in France. In the United States, on April 9, 1912 President William Howard Taft signed the bill that created the US Children's Bureau—the culmination of a process that began with the first White House Conference on Children in 1909. This ended a period of social reform which preceded the first World War.

The 40-year period of time from 1870-1910 seemed to culminate in a broad and increasing awareness of the importance of early childhood education. Four other periods marked by social changes and reform legislation in the United States had important implications for young children. These periods were World War I, the Great Depression of the 1930s, the Second World War, and the War on Poverty during the 1960s. In all four instances, the federal, state, or local governments made the decision whether or not to provide for the care of young children based on societal and economic needs, not on the needs of the child. It is clear that interest in children and their development and education tends to be linked with other major changes in society.

Lazerson (1972) identifies three themes which have dominated the history of ECE: (*1*) the expectation that schooling of young children will lead to social reform; (*2*) the importance of the early years in terms of later development; (*3*) the impact of early childhood education on later schooling.

The societal factors and incidents that stimulated changes in how childhood and early childhood education were viewed varied with the different historical periods. But through it all, the rationale for the provision was basically the same. That is, a class of people were seen as struggling for more personal freedom and control over their lives through the acquisition of education. This concept holds for the people of Rousseau's time, who wanted to bring up their children in an atmosphere free from political oppression, as well as it holds for those people of the mid-1960s in the United States, who wanted to free children from the limitations of economic oppression.

It is interesting to note that most of the history of social changes in thinking about children is rooted in the concept of political and sociocultural deprivation. Social legislation has been focused on classes of oppressed people for the past 200 years. Initial society-provided child care in both Europe and the United States focused on protecting the child's welfare and health. Under common law, children were considered the almost exclusive property of their parents, and children were valued property as long as their labor was needed. Thus, intervention into the parent-child relationship was done hesitantly and was viewed at best as a necessary evil. The earliest child welfare services were orphanages and foster care agencies established during the nineteenth century to provide for children of paupers or orphans. These early child care programs were motivated by a peculiar combination of religious charity and community self-interest groups. They sought to give dependent children the care and instruction needed to become self-supporting adults. Few could argue that the family was undermined if substitute care was offered when parents died or disappeared. In these situations, early child care centers focused on the welfare and health needs of the child when the parent was absent.

This kind of "child-saving" early intervention was prevalent in the United States as well as in Europe. In the United States, much of this early reform took place in the urban slums, where first and second generation immigrants lived. Writers like Jacob Riis and Robert Hunter wrote about how the poor lived. Social and welfare workers like Jane Addams and Robert Wood opened their houses to help the poor. The needs of the children were of great importance to these social reformers, and, being practical people, they started to aid the child where his need was greatest, that is, in the areas of welfare and health. When a beginning had been made in those areas, then education became the important next step. It is important to note that these early attempts at helping poor children almost always started as private efforts that only much later were taken on as responsibilities of the local, state, or federal government. The step from child protection to child education represents an evolving differentiation between the function of health and welfare agencies and their services, and the private preschools and their educational curriculum and child development concerns. In the United States, the person most easily identified with education and young children is G. Stanley Hall. He could easily be called the father of child development in the United States. Hall and his students, Gesell and Terman, made the study of the child an important part of psychology. The whole child study movement grew out of his pioneering efforts. By the end of the nineteenth century the preschool or kindergarten was firmly established in the United States. It was, however, almost entirely run and supported by the private sector and was, for the most part, offered to the children of the middle class. A small but important number of preschools were run for the children of the poor.

The development of preschools was not rapid between 1900 and 1960. There was some greater provision during the two World Wars, but this declined when the wars ended. The greatest growth took place in the provision in middle-class communities of half-day kindergarten for 5-year-olds.

This brief historical background traces relatively parallel developments in early childhood education in both Europe and the United States. It indicates that social policy as it concerned children in all countries studied has evolved quite slowly. Where there have been periods of rapid growth, the demand for child care was usually based on what the parents or society needed at that moment, not on the child's needs.

SOCIOLOGICAL CHANGES

Having looked briefly at the historical development of early childhood education, let us now examine the first of the two major trends behind recent (since 1960) increased demand for ECE.

Similar to the data presented for the eight countries, decreases in household size, reproduction rates, and increases in women's participation in the labor force have had an overall effect on the demand for early child care in the United States. In 1790, the average household size in the United States was 5.79. Between 1890 and 1910 it was 5; between 1920 and 1950 it was 4; in 1960 it was 3, and in 1974, 2.97. In that 189-year period, the average household size in the United States declined by 2.82 persons.

This data clearly indicates that, in the United States in 1975, the extended family was a thing of the past. It indicates that the most common family consists of the parents and a child. It also reflects the increase in single parent families. One of the reasons behind the demand for preschool is the need to provide adults and other children for young children to interact with.

Gross reproduction rates in the eight countries studied declined over the 76-year period from 1900 to the present. The United States data reflect the same trend, its gross reproduction rate declining from 1.8 in 1910 to 1.4 in 1965. The major exception to this downward trend came during the post-World War II baby boom of the late 1940s and 1950s. In the United States, the baby boom peaked in 1957. Since that time, the decline in gross reproduction rates has continued.

In 1966, the rate of births per 1000 women was 18.4. In 1970, it was 18.2. In 1973, it was 15, the lowest in the country's history.

In 1974, the total fertility rate (an indicator which shows how many children a woman would have if she continued bearing children at that rate throughout her childbearing years) for the United States dropped to 1.9 per 1000 women, or less than 2 children per woman. The previous low was 2.2 in 1935-1939. The high came in 1957 when the rate was 3.8, or exactly twice what it was in 1974. Approximately 2.1 children per 1000 women is the fertility rate needed to maintain the present population. The United States dropped below this rate in 1971-1972. If this trend continues, we reach zero population growth by approximately the year 2000, if no allowance is made for immigration.

The prime factor behind the decline in birth rates has been education about planned parenthood and the medical advances, like the pill, associated with this education. There are many methods of birth control now legally available and many courses in school and out about how to plan for wanted, not unwanted, children.

Another factor contributing to the reduced fertility rate has been the legalization of abortion. These laws were first passed in 1967 in California, Colorado, and North Carolina. By 1970, 15 states had adopted similar laws. Sklar and Berkov (1974) concluded that legalized abortion has had a marked impact on illegitimate fertility in the United States. Illegitimate births for all women declined from 1970-1971. The teenage illegitimate fertility rate rose more sharply between 1965 and 1970 than other age groups, and tended to decline the least between 1970 and 1971. It was also noted that while in 1971 legitimate and illegitimate fertility declined equally, it was not apparent that legal abortion had played a key role in the decreased number of legitimate births. Sklar and Berkov (1974) indicate that in 1971 the birth rate decline in nonabortion states was 5% while in abortion states it was 8%. This is a much smaller decline than for illegitimate birth rates, which, in abortion states, declined 12% compared to a 2% decline in nonabortion states.

The more interesting aspect of planned parenthood for our purpose is to stress the fact that it gives women more control over their own lives. In line with a concept mentioned earlier, an increased sense of freedom actually has the effect of giving a greater sense of responsibility for one's life. This appears to provide for having greater responsibility for the children one chooses to bear. Another interesting aspect of the abortion legislation was its timing. The first abortion legislation changes came during a period when preschool programs were coming to fruition around the United States. The decrease in birth rates was coupled with an increased demand for early education, probably reflecting a greater awareness of this value of education on the part of parents.

A second component of this social change is that, in considering more fully the rights of children, the rights of women were reconsidered. The concept of Head Start has always been to supplement the parents, not supplant them. Women's roles today include actively participating in the rearing of their children in cooperation with preschool educators as well as developing their own resources and capabilities outside the child-parent dyad.

The effects of lower birth rates on the demand for preschool care are interesting to consider. It might have been expected that with fewer children per family, the demand for early care would be reduced because the mother or father would want to keep the child home to enjoy raising him or her. However, the data do not support that. As families have grown smaller, the demand for earlier and more extensive preschool provision has risen. It seems that when a family has only one or two children, parents can easily see that by seeking care for these children outside the home they (the parents) will be freer to seek to live their own lives more fully. Coupled with this parental concern for greater personal freedom is the practical need of the child from a small family to be provided with the opportunity to learn how to play with other children his or her own age. This is particularly true for children who live in highrise apartments or in rural isolation. It is also a particularly pressing problem for children of one-parent families. In recent years, preschool has also become important for children who come from homes that do not provide the readiness skills that middle-class children commonly bring to school. This last factor is the prime reason some educators offer for the creation of Head Start and Follow Through. A more careful look at these programs will indicate that education is only one important component in a Head Start program. From its beginnings, Head Start has been a comprehensively oriented program stressing welfare, health, and education needs of children.

Historically, women's role has been a constantly changing one. Society's concern regarding the status of women has typically paralleled changes in economics, industrialization, and education needs. The first movement for women's suffrage came in 1830, under President Andrew Jackson. This period was the same era in which Horace Mann pressed the advantages of primary education for all children. Full women's suffrage was granted in the United States in 1920, a period when progressive educators were moving to change educational practices in the country. More recently, there has been an increased demand for more equality in employment and legal status for women. It has paralleled an increased demand for equality of opportunities for children. Since the beginning of World War II, in 1941, the number of women in the labor force has risen rapidly.

Labor force participation rates for women in the eight countries studied rose from 1960 to 1970, while the rates for males remained stable or declined. The United States has followed a similar pattern. In 1960, its total labor force was 66.8% (males, 91.7%; females, 42.6%) of its population between 15 and 64 years of age. In 1970, the total participation rate had risen to 67.8% (87.2% for males and 48.9% for females). These figures indicate male participation rates declined by 4.5%, while female rates rose almost exactly the same amount (4.3%). In 1974, the total labor force was approximately 91 million—61.2% of the population. The male participation rate was 78.8%; the female rate was 45.6%. During this 4-year period, both male and female participation rates declined, 8.4% and 3.3% respectively. It is important to note that over the 14-year period 1960-1974, the male participation rate dropped 12.9%, while the participation rate for women, despite a deep recession in the last few years, grew over the period by 3%. This increased participation rate of women in the labor force reflects an important and, at the moment, poorly understood change in our society, which has many implications, particularly concerning the care of young children. It is important to note that the role of woman in modern society has increased in complexity, not decreased. She has *not* given up any of her household duties (although modern labor-saving devices make them easier to accomplish). She has, because of social and economic pressures as well as her own desire, entered more fully into a life outside her home. She must now contend with all these problems and at the same time be a wife and mother to her husband and children, a complex task indeed.

No one variable can singly represent why an increased demand for early education has occurred. Another factor behind this demand is the higher levels of education achieved by women. Higher levels of education contribute to the reduced birth rate as well as an increased demand for preschool centers. Glick (1975), in a Bureau of the Census report, states that:

> Elementary school dropouts average one or two more children than college graduates. . . . The differences arise from many causes, such as variations in proportions marrying, age at marriage, number of children wanted, and degree of efficiency of family limitation practices. . . . Negro women 35 to 44 years old in 1974 with 8 or fewer years of elementary school had borne an average of about 5,089 children per 1,000 women as compared with only 2,408 for Negro women of the same age who had completed one or more years of college. That is a much wider range than the one of 4,029 to 2,426 . . . for the two extreme educational groups of white women [p. 3].

The level of education has changed for both blacks and whites in the 100 years from 1870 to 1970. In 1870, 79.9% of the nonwhite population was illiterate, compared to 11.5% of the white population. The illiteracy rates in 1970 were 3.6% for nonwhites and .7% for whites. In 1870, only 2 out of 100 persons were graduated from high school. In 1970, the figure was 76 out of 100.

These data suggest that there is a strong correlation between level of education and the number of children a couple have. It seems clear that one of the results of education is that more educated women know how and choose to control their reproductive function much more than do less educated women.

Another societal change associated with education and employment that affects the demand for the care of young children is the rising divorce rate, increasing the number of single parent families. Lower marriage rates and later marriage also produce fewer children, thereby leading parents to look for earlier child care for their smaller families. It is safe to conclude that any policy analysis about provision of early childhood education must take into account these societal changes.

The demographic and societal changes noted here have had some observable effects on the lives of young children and have had major impact on the demand for early childhood education. In 1964, 10% of 3- and 4-year-old children were enrolled in preschool. By 1970, this figure had risen to 21%, and in 1974 enrollments had increased to 29% of all three 3- and 4-year-old children. During the same period, the percentage of 5-year-olds attending kindergarten rose from 58% in 1964 to 79% in 1974. Clearly these large increases reflect the social changes discussed above.

THE CHANGING ROLE OF PRESCHOOL

The historical section of this book traces the development of preschools through welfare, health, and educational concerns. This educational concern, at least in the United States, was brought to prominence by a variety of authors writing about the importance of education during the early years of a child's life. Two well-known works are *Intelligence and Experience* (Hunt, 1961) and *Stability and Change in Human Characteristics* (Bloom, 1964). These authors believed that a great deal more could be done to foster cognitive, social, and emotional growth on the part of young children than had been done previously through the use of preschools. They felt it was particularly important for children who had special needs. These children they commonly identified as "disadvantaged."

This belief in the ability of early childhood education to make an important difference in the lives of young children resulted ultimately in the creation of the Head Start program as part of the War on Poverty in 1964 and 1965. It was hoped by the original authors of that legislation that important changes in the ability of poor children to succeed in primary schools would take place as a result of early preschool intervention.

The review earlier in this book of the different issues of debate concerning early childhood education and its benefits or potential benefits discussed at length, for a variety of countries, the aims and objectives of preschool, its organization and control, the training of its teachers, its instructional methods, its cost, and the results of research. When one looks at these same issues in the American context of preschool programs such as kindergartens, prekindergartens, Head Start Programs, Follow Through Programs, or ESEA Title I early childhood education programs, one finds both important similarities and differences. The differences tend to fall under such categories as the number of children per teacher, the age at which preschool starts, and such organizationally related matters. In the area of philosophy and pedagogy, preschool programs in the eight countries studied, and the United States, tend to be similar. It is probably, therefore, safe to say that preschools in these countries and in the United States are more alike than they are different. This book has documented that many of the basic principles of preschool education are variations of Froebel's basic idea that it is through play that young children learn. This one fact in itself makes most preschools quite similar. In addition, many preschools are organized in agreement with Rousseau's basic idea that childhood is a time of unfolding and flowering. Childhood is seen, in this context, as a period of rapid growth that is internally controlled, and it is a task of society (preschool) to provide the rich environment to foster the maximum growth but not to direct that growth.

The preschools that were in existence before 1965 in the United States were for the most part provided for children of the middle class and were oriented toward fostering growth and development in the social and emotional domains. Little emphasis was put on school learning or readiness skills, for middle-class children normally did quite well in school, and the emphasis was unnecessary. Those preschools which were run and organized for the poor were oriented toward child care and protection and not toward school readiness. It was commonly believed that the children of the poor had little ability to benefit from education; therefore, not much emphasis was put on its importance in these preschools.

In the 10 years from 1965 onward, there has been a substantial and important growth in enrollment, as was documented earlier, in the area of kindergarten and prekindergarten education in the United States.

A large proportion of this growth was for children with special needs. What was new and different about these early childhood education programs, such as Head Start, was that from the very beginning they were comprehensive programs. These early programs included components concerned with social services, health, nutrition, and education, and they stressed parental involvement. The great insight of the planners of these programs for the poor was that hungry, unhappy, or sick children don't learn easily and well. The planners of the early intervention programs benefitted from a few model early childhood education programs for the poor organized in California and New York. It is strange that so little research has been done on what must be the obvious benefits of Head Start programs on young children's welfare and health. Almost all of the research has been concerned with the educational aspects of this program, rather than with careful documentation of benefits which the original authors of the legislation viewed as equally important in the welfare and health sector.

The early attempts at creating Head Start programs were provided under the leadership of educators who had been planning early childhood education programs for middle class children. In some ways, early versions of programs such as Head Start and ESEA Title I early childhood education programs were not significantly different from conventional preschool programs run by either the private or public sector in the United States. It must be kept in mind that the creation of Head Start was done on a crash basis; the first monies appropriated in the spring of 1965 were spent on 6-week summer intensive intervention programs. It must also be remembered that the only available source of manpower for conducting those programs was the teachers of preschools who had time and interest in attempting to provide a program for these young children in need. These teachers were drawn mainly from middle class kindergartens.

The creation of an educational component in these preschool programs has proven a far more difficult task than many early advocates of Head Start believed. This is due to two factors: One, there was little educational theory available on how to educate children with special needs. What was available was based on the theory of people like Decroly in Belgium, Montessori in Italy, Piaget in Switzerland, Gesell, Hunt, and Bloom in the United States. All of these writers indicated that the early years were important. Few of them, however, went the next step of offering practical suggestions as to how one could create a program that would make an impact on the intellectual development of young children. Therefore, one of the earliest and most difficult tasks, and a continuing one, has been to devise early childhood education programs that could translate theory into practice and document the fact that practice made a difference in the intellectual and academic achievements of the young.

The second factor in the difficulty of this task is that few early childhood educators appreciated the quantum jump from the provision of welfare and health care for young children with special needs to the provision of a comprehensive program which was concerned with all three components. The historical evolution of preschool education in the eight countries reviewed, plus the United States, indicates it was a significant jump from welfare concern to health concern. It has taken many years to provide good health care for young children. But if that is a difficult step—and it is—it is many more times difficult to add to those first two basic components of welfare and health a third component of education. Clearly, education of disadvantaged children is much more difficult to plan, provide, and put in place than is the provision of welfare or health services. It is not surprising that with only 10 years of reasonably intensive work on the provision of education for the poor that we have not made any massive or surprising breakthroughs, although we have learned a good deal.

In the years since 1965, we have learned some important facts about the provision of preschool care of young children, particularly concerning the aims and objectives, organization and control, and teacher training in instructional methods for young children with special needs. It is interesting to note, for instance, that when one refers to children with special needs, it is not their educational needs that are used as criteria for identifying them, but their economic needs. The research done on programs such as Head Start in the United States suggests that, in areas of aims and objectives, it is crucially important for any program which wishes to experience a degree of success in the social, emotional, or cognitive domains, as it affects young children's learning, to include the following components: The aims and objectives of the program must be documented carefully and set forth in objective terms; the teachers need to be trained to teach to those objectives and their success and/or failure must be constantly evaluated and revisions made in the program based on what those evaluations say. It seems clear in terms of preschool or early childhood education programs that just to send a child to school earlier is not the way to bring about greater equality of opportunity. It is much more important to ask what is done with the time, rather than just to provide the time. The time itself does not seem to be a crucial variable. Careful planning, teaching toward the attainment of objectives, and constant evaluation followed by revision based upon what the success or failure of the attainment of the objective seems to be, are crucial variables.

One way of thinking about the success or failure of a preschool program is to judge it in terms of the attainment or lack of attainment of its specified objectives. Another way of saying this is: Does the program demonstrate any specificity of effect? This is an important issue on which early childhood education in a variety of countries including the United States has been able to shed some light. Work in England and Wales on cognitive learning and work in Sweden in the affective domain both indicate that preschool programs can produce a specificity of effect. The evaluations of preschool programs done in the United States (both Head Start planned variations and Follow Through planned variations) indicate the same specificity of effect. In research done on Head Start and Follow Through programs, it has been documented that academically oriented preschool programs produce gains in the academic area; the discovery-oriented preschool programs foster growth in the affective area. Recently presented findings from the planned variation Follow Through study make this point. The Follow Through planned variations looked at a wide range of programs. The extremes of those programs were classified as the Englemann-Becker direct instruction approach and the Bank Street child discovery approach. Looking at the growth in the cognitive area and at locus of control or self-pacing, the growth curves in Figure 12.1 are apparent. These graphs show that these two approaches get to about the same point at the same time, but by quite different routes. They indicate that whatever the specific orientation the preschool takes, it is in this area that the most rapid and pronounced growth will take place. This is an important finding since there are very different opinions on what should be the orientation and emphasis in preschool programs. It appears that those who wish to start off in the affective or social domain can create

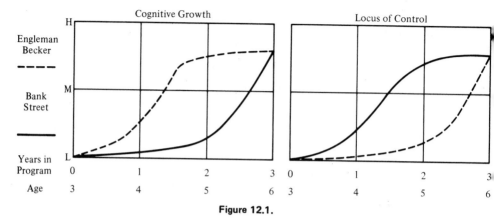

Figure 12.1.

programs which will have those specific effects and those who wish to start off in a cognitive intellectual domain can do so and can design programs that will have the same specificity of effect.

This identification of specificity of effect as a result of school programs has also been identified in terms of the effect of the home. In two studies (Coleman, 1975; Austin and Postlethwaite, 1974), the fact was documented that there are important differences in terms of specificity of effect in the areas of reading, mathematics, science, and language. Both the Coleman and the Austin-Postlethwaite study indicate that home variables seem to have a very specific effect upon reading ability, while school has a much more specific effect in the areas of mathematics and science. The Austin-Postlethwaite review was a secondary analysis of work done by the International Association for the Evaluation of Educational Achievement. It concerns mathematics, reading comprehension, and science. The objective was to look for a relationship between age of entry into school and achievement as measured at ages 10, 13, and 14. Principal findings suggest a specificity of effect between early entrance into school and greater achievement in mathematics, but not in reading comprehension or science. The authors suggest that gain in achievement based on early education may be due to the sensorimotor experiences which are so commonly part of early childhood education programs. It is further suggested that the carefully planned and sequenced curriculum approach to teaching mathematics may have an effect here. Tables 12.1-12.3 and Figures 12.2-12.5 present the data for national mean scores for 13-year-olds for mathematics (populations 1a and 1b), 10-year-olds and 14-year-olds for reading comprehension and 10-year-olds for science, and their relationships to official-effective ages of entry (effective age of entry—the year in which 75% or more of an age group enter formal school).

It seems fair to state the following general conclusions about the different aims and objectives of early childhood programs as they are represented by the results of the Head Start planned variation study.

TABLE 12.1
Official and Effective Age of Entry, Mean Scores, and Standard
Deviations in Mathematics - Age 13

	OAE	EAE	Population 1A		Population 1B	
			Mean	S.D.	Mean	S.D.
Australia	6 years	5 years	20.2	14.0	18.9	12.3
Belgium	6	3	27.7	15.0	30.4	13.7
England	5	5	19.3	17.0	23.8	18.5
Finland	7	7	15.4	10.8	16.1	11.6
France	6	4	18.3	12.4	21.0	13.2
Germany (FR)	6	6			25.5	11.7
Israel	6	4			32.2	14.7
Japan	6	6	31.2	16.9	31.2	16.9
Netherlands	6	4	23.9	15.9	21.4	12.1
Scotland	5	5	19.1	14.6	22.3	15.7
Sweden	7	7	15.7	10.8	15.3	10.8
United States	6	5	16.2	13.3	17.8	13.3

OAE - Official Age of Entry
EAE - Effective Age of Entry

1. In terms of a wide variety of cognitive skills, Head Start is effective in accelerating the growth rate of disadvantaged preschoolers.
2. Relative to the condition of no preschool programs, the effects of Head Start are quite homogeneous, with no systematic difference between sponsored and nonsponsored programs.
3. Head Start programs are quite homogeneous in their ability to promote general cognitive development.
4. No Head Start program is above average in its effectiveness on all of our measures (Weisberg, 1974).
5. The gains promoted by the Head Start experience tend to disappear after a year or two unless a follow-up effort is made.

In terms of the question of organization and control, a number of important things have been learned in the last 10-year period since the creation of early childhood education programs sponsored by the federal government. We have learned that, unless there is continuity between the preschools and the primary schools that accept the children from the preschools, much of what has been gained or much of the head start that has been achieved in the preschool will be

TABLE 12.2
Official and Effective Age of Entry, Mean Scores, Standard Deviations
in Reading Comprehension and Science – Age 10

	OAE	EAE	Reading Comprehension Mean	S.D.	Science Mean	S.D.
Belgium (FL)	6	3	17.5	9.2	17.9	7.2
Belgium (FR)	6	3	17.9	9.3	13.9	7.1
England	5	5	18.5	11.6	15.7	8.5
Finland	7	7	19.4	10.8	17.5	8.2
Germany (FR)	6	6			14.9	7.4
Hungary	6	5	14.0	9.8	16.7	8.0
Israel	6	4	13.9	11.0		
Italy	6	5	21.6	9.6	17.5	9.1
Japan	6	6			21.7	7.6
Netherlands	6	4	17.7	9.5	15.3	7.6
Scotland	5	5	18.4	11.1	14.0	8.3
Sweden	7	7	21.5	10.5	18.3	7.3
United States	6	5	16.8	11.6	17.7	9.3

OAO – Official Age of Entry
EAE – Effective Age of Entry

lost. We have learned that it is not enough just to create a preschool. One must be concerned with following through in those areas where initial success has been experienced.

This experience led to the creation of the program "Follow Through," which attempts to do exactly that; that is, to maintain or follow through on preschool attainments: some of the findings from research studies on Follow Through have led to the creation by the Office of Child Development of a new program called "Developmental Continuity." Concern for this concept of developmental continuity led former Secretary Caspar Weinberger of HEW, in 1974, to make the following comments about this new effort:

> In the past there has been a tendency to divide those (preschool) experiences into isolated segments. . . . One approach to the problem is called Pre-School-School Linkages. In this approach, parents and teaching staff in both Head Start and early primary grades agree to a compatible educational approach and a coordinated curriculum. Regularly scheduled conferences and workshops for Head Start and primary teachers assure continuity. An alternate approach has also been developed, called the Early Childhood Schools. In this one, Head Start and primary elementary children will be in the same building [p. 2].

TABLE 12.3
Official and Effective Age of Entry, Mean Scores, Standard Deviations
in Reading Comprehension – Age 14

	OAE	EAE	Reading Comprehension	
			Mean	S.D.
Belgium (FL)	6	3	24.6	9.6
Belgium (FR)	6	3	27.2	8.7
England	5	5	25.3	11.9
Finland	7	7	27.1	10.9
Germany (FR)	6	6		
Hungary	6	5	25.5	9.8
Israel	6	4	22.6	12.8
Italy	6	5	24.0	9.2
Japan	6	6		
Netherlands	6	4	25.2	10.1
Scotland	5	5	27.0	11.5
Sweden	7	7	25.6	10.8
United States	6	5	27.3	11.6

OAE – Official Age of Entry
EAE – Effective Age of Entry

One can conclude that one of the important points which has come out of the intensive investigations of preschools in the last 10 years is the idea of developmental continuity as it concerns the transition from preschool to the primary school. In the future, educators at both these levels are going to have to work more effectively and closely together for the ultimate benefit of the children.

Preschools in the United States and Europe have traditionally encouraged more parental involvement than have the primary schools. One of the outgrowths of Head Start, Follow Through, and Title I early childhood education programs in the United States has been an escalating demand on the part of the parents that they be more actively involved in the decision-making process for the education of their children than has been true in the past. The American Head Start program is a good example of how these changing social and demographic forces resulted in a new concept of early childhood education. The original interest in health and welfare needs of the child was combined with social clamor to provide a sound educational base for preschool children. While this program was created to provide educational equality for poor children, the motivation was not to supplant the home, but to use it as a resource for educating the child.

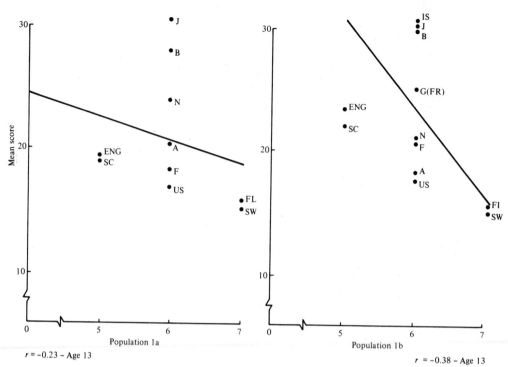

Official age of entry

Figure 12.2. Mathematics performance at official age of entry.

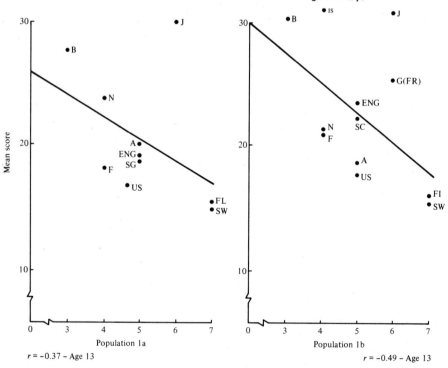

Effective age of entry

Figure 12.3 Mathematics performance at effective age of entry.

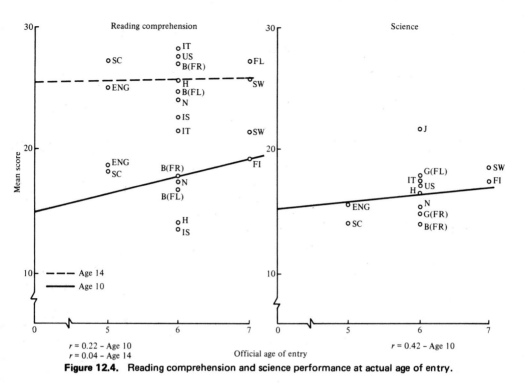

Figure 12.4. Reading comprehension and science performance at actual age of entry.

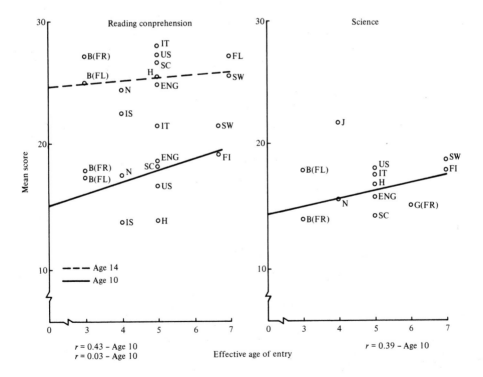

Figure 12.5. Reading comprehension and science performance at effective age of entry.

Head Start programs tried to involve parents in two ways: first was the attempt to integrate the home and the school in the total education of the child. Even though the program was a social response to free the children from economic oppression and the limiting nature of their environment, it recognized the importance of building on the primary relationship between the family and child. It sought a role of supplementing, not supplanting, the parent. This attempt represents a new synthesis of the two societal institutions, the school, and family. Second, the gains made by preschools are difficult to sustain on a long-term basis into the primary school. Attempts to remedy this with Follow Through programs have had mixed results. The alternative, then, might be that in the future society should spend more money providing adult education to parents particularly during the first 4 years of the child's life. This education could take place through a variety of media as well as in a number of places. The education of the parents about child care should stress welfare and health as well as intellectual growth. These broad educational concerns lead to the recommendation that people concerned with welfare, health and education of young children work cooperatively to supplement what the parents are doing, since the parent in all the countries studied is seen as the prime educator. This concept is the basis on which the program called "Home Start" was initiated. The intent of that program was and is to aid the parent at home in providing a more adequate environment for the child, and one that will aid his or her growth.

The training of teachers in the United States does not reflect much of what we have learned in the first 10 years of intensive study about how to educate disadvantaged children. This is probably primarily due to the fact that the professors in the schools of education concerned with training preschool teachers were themselves trained 20 or 30 years ago and still believe primarily in the emphasis on social and emotional growth of young children and not the commitment that many of the Head Start and Follow Through programs have to stimulate cognitive and readiness growth in preparation for primary school. This will change, given time, and there are beginning indications in the schools of education that, as new people come into the profession, this orientation will be more adequately represented.

As the earlier paragraphs in this chapter have indicated, a great many changes have taken place, at least in the federally sponsored preschool programs over the last 10 years. Nowhere is this more apparent than in the struggle over the proper instructional methods to use for young children. There is a wide divergence of opinion represented here, the extreme positions being taken by Englemann and his direct instructional approach, and at the other extreme, the Bank Street College child discovery approach. In the Englemann approach, it is taken for granted that the instructional method will be dominated by the teacher. The teacher will, in fact, plan and prioritize the areas in which the learning is to take place, create behaviorally stated objectives, teach constantly towards those objectives, evaluate constantly for their attainment, and revise the program in light of successes or failures.

The discovery approach being implemented by Bank Street College, on the other hand, says that the child's needs should be the prime determinant of the method of instruction used and that the teacher should be present only as a resource and a guide once the child has indicated where his curiosity and his interest take him. At this time, there does not seem to be any clear evidence that over a long period of time one of these methods is more effective than the other. Only time and a great deal of additional research will afford further insights into the problem. The ultimate answer is probably that different children need different kinds of instructional methods, and no one method is suitable for all children.

In the area of financing preschool education in the United States, the following figures are presented. These are estimates, since there is little hard data on the actual cost of running preschool programs in this country. In 1965, the average cost for running a public kindergarten attached to a primary school was about $400 per child per year. In 1970, that increased to about $700, and by 1974, to $1050. These estimates are based on the average per pupil cost in a primary school, grades K-8. For comparison purposes, in 1968 it cost $1050 per child to run a full year Head Start program. In 1973, it cost an average of $1249 for a full year program. The costs in that year ranged from $778 to a high of $1918. In 1974, the total cost was about $1693; the range was from $1049 to $2430. In 1974, it cost, on the average, 60% more to run a comprehensive Head Start program than it did a public preschool.

Over the 5-year period 1965-1970, the cost of public kindergarten increased by 75%. For the 5-year period 1968-1973, a Head Start program increased by 19% in its average cost. The $700 average cost for a US kindergarten in 1970 is higher than for any of the eight countries reported. Their expenditures for preschool ranged, in 1970, from a high of $621 in Sweden to a low of $110 in France.

CONCLUSIONS

This review of international preschool education arrives at the following conclusions that a policy maker in preschool education should consider:

1. The creation of a comprehensive preschool program (including components concerned with welfare, health, and education) is not an easy task, particularly if the population of children it chooses to serve has special needs in any or all of the areas named.

2. Early childhood comprehensive education programs are not the solution for all of society's ills. When carefully planned, executed, and evaluated, they can make an impact in the cognitive, social, and emotional domains. But they

cannot, by themselves, do much about reducing racism, poverty, or other social ills.

Manipulation of single variables like age of entry, pupil-teacher or pupil-adult ratio, level of financing, methods of instruction, and organization and administration will not make great differences by themselves. The variable of time is a good example. English children start school at age 5, the French at 6, and the Swedish at 7. It is an observable fact that, by age 10, it is impossible to say that the English children read more or less well than the Swedish children, yet they have been in the school 2 years longer. The real question is not time, but how the time is used and to what purpose.

3. This study supports the findings of Davie *et al.* in England, who concluded that preschool is helpful for middle-class children and crucial for disadvantaged children. It goes further, however, to agree with findings of the Coleman Report of the United States and the Plowden Report in England on primary school. The author believes these findings apply equally well to preschool. They are: first, comparing the effects of preschool to no preschool, the effects of preschool are significant for 1 or 2 years after the experience; second, that differences in outcome between preschool *A* and preschool *B* are difficult to document with present day testing procedures. The home background variables, even in preschool children, have a powerful effect on their achievement levels.

4. The role of the family, the child's place in that family, and the role of women in society has changed. There is a need to offer additional assistance to families by providing care for young children. This is motivated by the social needs of children raised in the urban and rural isolation in small families to have experiences with children of their own age. The problem is also intensified by the fact that small families do not have the support system of the extended family that has been available in the past.

The desire of parents to be free both to work and to see to the care of their children may lead in the future to a greater use of part-time employment, shorter work days, and more flexible hours for parents of very young children. The whole area is one that needs more study and more understanding of the parent's need to be involved in the total care of the child and yet free to pursue an active and independent life. This issue is at least as important a factor behind the demand for preschool education as is a strong parental belief in the benefits of early education.

5. The issue of equality of opportunity for all people has brought an increased demand for preschool. This demand has led to a need for a smoother transition from home to preschool or day care centers and the entrance into primary school. This concern for early education has led to increasing discussion of unifying the preschool and early primary school experience along the lines of Follow Through or the new developmental continuity schools, which encompass ages 3-9. There is increasing agreement that the period of time from conception

to age 9 or 12 should be looked at as a single unit with relation to the provision of health, welfare, and educational care for young children.

6. Welfare, health, and educational activities as they concern young children should be brought together. Welfare and health agencies now work more closely with each other than either does with education. Head Start and Follow Through are good models of what can be done cooperatively when the three agencies work together to create comprehensive programs. The research on these programs suggests that early identification, diagnosis, and correction of problems are important. One recalls that some of the best known early childhood educators were medical people—Decroly of Belgium; Montessori, Italy; and Gesell, the United States.

Each agency has much to learn from the others. Welfare agencies, for instance, learned long ago that aid to dependent children, for instance, was not something that could be given for a few years and then stopped, but that needed to be continued so long as the need was there. Educators must begin to take the same position concerning children who do not experience continued, or even occasional, success in school. Head Start or Follow Through are good beginnings, but they do not go far enough.

7. The issue of parental involvement with welfare, health, and education agencies in the period of time from conception to age 9 or 12 is one of increasing importance. Research suggests that involvement of the parents may be as important a factor as the help from the agencies themselves. Parents are, after all, the child's first and most important source of education. Any social policy that ignores this fact will not be as successful as it could otherwise be.

BIBLIOGRAPHY

Austin, G., & Postlethwaite, T. N., Cognitive results based on different ages of entry to school: a comparative study. *Journal of Educational Psychology,* 1974, *66*(6), 857-863.

Bloom, B. S. *Stability and Change in Human Characteristics.* New York: John Wiley & Sons, Inc. 1964.

Coleman, J. Methods and results in the IEA studies of effects of school on learning. *Review of Educational Research,* Summer, 1975, *45*(3).

Glick, P. (Ed.). U.S. Bureau of the Census, *Current population reports* (series P-20, No. 279). Population profile of the United States: 1974, Washington, D.C.: US Government Printing Office, 1975.

Hunt, J. McV. *Intelligence and Experience.* New York: Ronald Press. 1961.

Lazerson, M., The historical antecedents of early childhood education. *Early Childhood Education,* The seventy-first yearbook of the National Society for the Study of Education, Part II, 1972.

Sklar, J. / Berkov, B., Abortion, illegitimacy, and the American birth rate. *Science,* Sept. 13, 1974, *185*(4155).

Weinberger, C. Office of Child Development, *Project developmental continuity.* April 29, 1974.

Weisberg, H. *Short term cognitive effects of Head Start programs: a report on the third year of planned variation*—1971-1972. Cambridge: Huron Institute, June 1974.

Index

A 6
B 7
C 8
D 9
E 0
F 1
G 2
H 3
I 4
J 5